Courtly Love Undressed

THE MIDDLE AGES SERIES

Ruth Mazo Karras, Series Editor
Edward Peters, Founding Editor

A complete list of books in the series
is available from the publisher.

Courtly Love Undressed

Reading Through Clothes in
Medieval French Culture

E. Jane Burns

PENN

University of Pennsylvania Press
Philadelphia

Copyright © 2002 University of Pennsylvania Press
All rights reserved
Printed in the United States of America on acid-free paper

10 9 8 7 6 5 4 3 2 1

Published by
University of Pennsylvania Press
Philadelphia, Pennsylvania 19104-4011

Library of Congress Cataloging-in-Publication Data

Burns, E. Jane, 1948–
   Courtly love undressed : reading through clothes in medieval French culture / E. Jane Burns.
     p. cm. — (The Middle Ages series)
   Includes bibliographical references and index.
   ISBN 0-8122-3671-8 (cloth : alk. paper)
   1. French literature—To 1500—History and criticism. 2. Costume in literature 3. Courtly love in literature. I. Title. II. Series.

PQ155.C7 B87 2002
840.9′355—dc21   2002024395

This book is dedicated to my grandmother who always wore fancy hats and sparkling jewelry, to my aunt Alice who could transform a scarf into a turban with a few swift strokes, to my mother who taught me to love shoes, and to my aunt Zabelle who sewed elaborate Flamenco costumes on a portable sewing machine and then danced in them. It is also dedicated to my dad who was a natty dresser, to my uncle Marty who wore red suede shoes every Christmas, and to Fred whose preferred outfit is still a t-shirt and jeans.

I wrote this book in the spirit of all those women who, as girls, played with dolls because of the clothes.

Contents

Introduction   The Damsel's Sleeve: Reading Through Clothes in Courtly Love   1

Part I   Clothing Courtly Bodies   17
1   Fortune's Gown: Material Extravagance and the Opulence of Love   19

Part II   Reconfiguring Desire: The Poetics of Touch   57
2   Amorous Attire: Dressing Up for Love   59
3   Love's Stitches Undone: Women's Work in the *chanson de toile*   88

Part III   Denaturalizing Sex: Womenen and Men on a Gendered Sartorial Continuum   119
4   Robes, Armor, and Skin   121
5   From Woman's Nature to Nature's Dress   149

Part IV   Expanding Courtly Space Through Eastern Riches   179
6   Saracen Silk: Dolls, Idols, and Courtly Ladies   181
7   Golden Spurs: Love in the Eastern World of *Floire et Blancheflor*   211

Coda: Marie de Champagne and the *Matière* of Courtly Love   231

Notes   237

Bibliography   295

Index   319

Acknowledgments   325

Introduction
The Damsel's Sleeve: Reading Through Clothes in Courtly Love

This book offers a reassessment of courtly love through the lens of the elaborate garments that typify court life in literary accounts of the French High Middle Ages. It argues, in brief, that many of our most basic assumptions about courtly love are called into question when we consider them in relation to the varied functions of sumptuous clothes that provide social definition for key players in love scenarios. Indeed, our perceptions of courtly desire, of the range of gendered subject positions in love, of the negotiability of class status through the practice of love and even the symbolic location of the western court itself, begin to shift substantially when we consider them through the lens of the luxury goods and other bodily adornments that so often define courtliness. We will examine in particular the lavish silks used to fashion elite garments, which are decorated in turn with gold and silk embroidery or with silver, gold, and jeweled ornament, and the equally ornate silks used to make bed coverlets, bed curtains, banners, and tents that festoon the courtly milieu. We will look at the standard unisex outfit of *chemise*, tunic, and mantle displayed on men and women alike, along with the more highly gendered male armor and female skin, as garments of another sort. Elite costumes wrought from natural elements such as garlands of flowers and leaves, whether used materially or metaphorically to mark partners in love, will also come under consideration as key icons of courtly dress.

What follows, then, is a study of material culture as it is represented in select lyric and romance texts, didactic literature, vernacular sermons, and sumptuary laws that imagine and construct various functions for luxury clothes and elite attire in the French Middle Ages. What historical individuals actually wore in twelfth- and thirteenth-century France, how those material objects were produced, consumed, traded, and displayed, is a different, though related, matter—one that has been amply researched by costume historians, art historians, archaeologists, anthropologists, and economic and cultural historians.[1] We know, for example, that medieval clothing, in addition to indicating class differences, was used to mark religious, military, and chivalric orders in the later Middle Ages and to single out pilgrims, Jews, Muslims, heretics, lepers, prostitutes, the insane, and individuals condemned to death.[2] Studies of heraldry underline the importance of color and iconography in recording family lineage.[3] Some sources suggest that pious women may have used religious garb as a covert form of resistance against their husbands.[4] And yet, the extent to which historical individuals in French courts displayed on their person garments that resemble those described in literary accounts of courtly love remains more difficult to determine.[5] Manuscript illuminations provide little help in this regard since the visual images that accompany Old French love stories from the twelfth and thirteenth centuries typically do not render courtly dress in the elaborate detail that narrative accounts provide.

Scholars have most often understood the ostentatious display of luxury dress in courtly literature as a means of self-definition for members of the ruling elite. Following the lead of historians, we have rightly taken literary representations of courtly attire as a visible show of wealth and a public record of status.[6] Literary scholars have further assessed the complex functions of cloth and clothing in courtly settings as indices of guilt or innocence in adultery, as subtle means of redefining political and personal identity through cross-dressing, as a code for gendering an otherwise unsexed amorous body, and as an incipient attempt to enforce social order between status groups.[7] Conduct books reveal moral concerns about the production and consumption of fashionable clothes while also indicating that women's management of clothing and linens provided new opportunities for self-definition.[8] Embroidery and clothwork have been examined as a rich trope for the intersection of history and gender, while descriptions of cloth linings have been read as metaphors of literary representation.[9] Underwear provides a cultural icon of gendered social status in a range of medieval French texts.[10] Clothing, furnishings, and personal objects bearing mottos enact a mystifying performance of aristocratic identity in the later Middle Ages.[11]

My interest here lies in exploring how the garments displayed on members of the ruling elite in courtly literary accounts were invoked and marshaled in a range of cultural discourses as potential—if not actual—regulators of gender, courtly desire, and the symbolic space of court life. In specific instances, such as sumptuary legislation, vernacular sermons, or didactic literature, we can see how medieval discussions of clothing convey cultural anxieties, expressing concern that individual items of dress have failed to perform an appointed or desired regulatory function. While French medieval sumptuary laws record the monarchy's wish to enforce class distinctions through the regulation of luxury dress, vernacular exempla and sermons often document a clerical concern with making gender visible in clothes.

At times, courtly literary texts reiterate and reinforce these cultural paradigms, using opulent garments to display noble wealth and signal elite status or to distinguish clearly gendered knights in armor from ladies in lavish gowns. But key scenes in lyric and romance texts also deploy clothing in more pointedly disruptive ways, as they narrate the trials and triumphs of protagonists in love. In these instances, lavish garments often subvert indications of class and rank they are designed to enforce, and luxury dress transgresses the gender boundaries it is presumed to uphold. Indeed, reading courtly love stories through the clothes of their protagonists will help us see that gender in courtly love scenarios is often configured along a sartorial continuum, rather than in terms of naturally derived categories of woman and man. A closer look at courtly garments will show further that fictive amorous encounters do not only enable and privilege the rise of men's status through the practice of love, as we have often thought, but that the deployment of rich clothes can also enable, symbolically, an increase in the social status of women in love. In addition, the expression of female desire, so often effaced in courtly lyric and romance, can be registered in various ways through fabric and clothes. And finally, consideration of the geographic provenance of costly silks as imported goods will help revise our general presumption of court life as distinctively western, revealing instead a crucial easternness within the lush fabric and adornment of courtly protagonists in love.

We might begin by considering the tale of the demoisele d'Escalot, a love story that uses luxury dress to trouble courtly conventions in a number of unexpected ways. This brief tale demonstrates vividly what a simple piece of cloth can do.

The Damsel's Sleeve

The anonymous closing volume of the thirteenth-century Lancelot-Grail Cycle, *La Mort le roi Artu*, stages the passionate and problematic love affair between Lancelot and Guenevere in relation to an equally rash and feverish "fole amor" exhibited by the demoisele d'Escalot for Arthur's best knight.[12] Consigned generally to the ranks of countless unnamed and unspecified "damsels" who appear sporadically but consistently throughout Old French romance narratives to guide and test questing knights on their adventures, the demoisele d'Escalot has drawn remarkably little scholarly attention. And yet, her story provides a particularly cogent example of the complex positioning of courtly couples within the highly gendered codes of courtly love. It does so specifically through the use of clothes, and more precisely in terms of a single silk sleeve. This unassuming *demoisele* boldly initiates a courtship with the incomparable Lancelot, ordering him unequivocally to announce her desire publicly by displaying on his helmet an item of her own courtly dress: "Vos m'avez otroié que vos porteroiz a ce tornoiement ma manche destre en leu de panoncel desus vostre hiaume et feroiz d'armes por l'amor de moi" (10; You have agreed that you will wear my right sleeve at the tournament in place of the banner on your helmet and fight for love of me).[13] The gesture is both familiar and surprising.

That a courtly lady's sleeve might function as a love token attached to the helmet of the knight willing to defend and protect her forms part of a well-known constellation of courtly traditions involving the exchange of love tokens and the concomitant exchange of women as valuable beauties to be won in combat.[14] Within the standard paradigm, the lady's sleeve serves as a surrogate for her inspiring presence, propelling the knight who loves her to accomplish feats of extraordinary prowess that bring honor and credit to his name. In one Old French *chanson de toile*, for example, the heroine Bele Ydoine "offers her sleeve as a love token to her suitor" who, upon receiving it, immediately enters the fray of the tournament where he performs magnificently because "the beautiful lady's love motivates him and increases his strength."[15]

Typically, knights have everything to gain from wearing a beloved lady's sleeve. But Lancelot does not. First of all, he is not in love with the demoisele d'Escalot; he consents against his will to display her sleeve at the tournament only because of a prior binding oath (*don contraignant*) he cannot escape.[16] And just as the sleeve misrepresents his desire, it also obscures his very identity, causing the glory of his stellar performance in combat to accrue to a champion known only as "the knight who wears a lady's sleeve on his helmet." As Gauvain reports to King Arthur, "Certes, sire, je ne sei qui cil chevaliers est qui porte cele manche desus son hiaume; mes je diroie par droit qu'il a ce tornoiement veincu et qu'il en doit avoir le pris et le los"

(17; To be sure, sir, I don't know the identity of the knight who wears that sleeve on his helmet, but I will say truthfully that he has won the tournament and should be praised and lauded for it).[17] Lancelot's public identity as a prized and proven chivalric champion rests, in this instance, not on his own name or family identity but on a piece of clothing belonging to a lady.[18] Foregrounded in this scene, as the knight's identity recedes, is the visible, memorable icon of the lady's partial dress. Onlookers at the tournament can only name Lancelot's prowess by referring to the *demoisele*'s sleeve. Insisting that he wear what she wears, this lady has fashioned her beloved to a degree as a knight in women's clothes. While, on the one hand, this item of women's clothing reinforces normative gender assignments in which knights fight for ladies, it also significantly undermines the viewer's ability to define the masculinity associated with chivalric identity apart from women's dress.

Indeed the sleeve episode impels other knights to want to cross the gender line more overtly, if only metaphorically, and take up the position typically reserved for ladies. When Gauvain tells the demoisele d'Escalot of Lancelot's extraordinary feats at the Winchester tournament, he asserts, "et tant vos di ge bien veraiement que, si ge estoie damoisele, je voudroie que la manche fust moie, par si que cil m'amast par amors qui la manche portoit, car ge ne vi onques a nul jor de ma vie manche mieuz emploiee que ceste n'a esté" (23; I tell you in truth that if I were a damsel, I would want that sleeve to be mine and the man wearing the sleeve to be in love with me, because I have never in my life seen a sleeve put to better use). This sleeve "put to good use" initially in expressing female desire also provides, in this instance, a point of border crossing between the highly regulated categories of knight and lady in the courtly world. In the case of Lancelot's helmet, a classic marker of courtly masculinity fuses with the "manche a dame ou a demoisele" (31; a lady or young woman's sleeve), creating a hybrid, cross-gendered costume. The gesture thus reconfigures his assigned subject position as well as hers. Similarly, if we can imagine Gauvain as a lady, wearing a dress and giving his sleeve to a knight in combat, the established meaning of knights "fighting well" in the courtly context changes valence significantly. For whom are they fighting, really? For ladies or for other knights?"

In Lancelot's case, the sleeve facilitates border crossings of both gender and class. As the demoisele d'Escalot dresses him up in a fragment of her attire, she also clothes a noble with the dress of a lower-ranking vavasor's daughter. In response to conjecture that the "knight with the sleeve" might be Lancelot, King Arthur expresses disbelief that Lancelot would actually court a woman of the *demoisele*'s rank: "ge ne porroie pas croire que il meïst son cuer en dame ne en damoisele, se ele n'estoit de trop haut afere" (36; I can't believe that he would give his heart to a lady or young lady, if she wasn't of sufficiently high rank).[19] And in fact Lancelot has not courted this lady but followed a more standard feudal model of courtship, positioning himself as a supplicant lover to an all-empowered aristocratic lady as overlord: in this instance, the queen, Guenevere. The demoisele d'Escalot herself signals the discrepancy between her social standing and that of Arthur's knights generally when rebuffing Gauvain's lovesuit in an earlier scene on the grounds that she is a "povre demoisele" too lowly for the attentions of a "trop riches hom" and a "trop hauz hom" (24; a man too wealthy or too highborn). The courtly lady's sleeve, typically employed to signal the knight's desire and guarantee his prowess, here threatens symbolically to falsely announce Lancelot's sentiments, to obscure his heroic achievements, to complicate his gender assignment and potentially to endanger his social status. But it does more.

Indeed, this simple piece of cloth holds the potential of significantly transforming the standard commodification and exchange of women as objects of desire in the courtly landscape. Typically, conferral of the sleeve indicates the courtly lady's acceptance of a knight's prior lovesuit, as in the case of Bele Ydoine above. When the sleeve is given, so too is the lady transferred.[20] At times, the culturally charged sleeve becomes fetishized as a material substitute for the lady herself, as when the hero in *Galeran de Bretagne* begins kissing the sleeve his beloved Fresne has given him, treating the self-portrait she has embroidered on the cloth as a physical body: "Ycy est Fresne la plaisant, / C'est cy son nez, ... / Cy son ci oeil dont ill esgarde, / C'est cy son front, c'est cy sa face, / C'est cy sa gorge qui me lace" (vv. 3236–40; Here is the delightful Fresne. Here is her nose, ... here are the eyes with which she sees. Here is her forehead, here her face. Here is her chest that entraps me).[21] The besotted lover then folds the sleeve into a silk case and stores it next to his heart (v. 3276), much as the lovesick Lancelot in the *Chevalier de la charrete* swoons over the hairs lodged in Guenevere's comb before placing them inside his *chemise*.[22] Such fetishism does not characteize the demoisele d'Escalot's story, because the love in question is hers alone.

Indeed, what is recorded in the public display of her courtly sleeve, what is *seen* by viewers at the Winchester tournament, is not in fact Lancelot's love for this damsel but the inordinate influence she has wielded over him.[23] If the sleeve Lancelot wears says little about his own desire, it loudly and publicly proclaims the wish and will of a woman to take a renowned knight as a lover, to court him and attempt to win him through the public imposition of an item of courtly dress. To be sure, this heroine's passion and pleasure are brutally displaced from the courtly scene later in the tale when she is made to die literally of love sickness. Rebuffed by Lancelot, who wishes to remain faithful to Guenevere, the demoisele d'Escalot lies down on a bed and dies, Ophelia-like, without apparent effect on the further development of the tale: "Lors se parti la damoisele de devant lui et s'en vint a son lit et se cocha a tel eür que onques puis n'en leva se morte non" (68; The damsel walked away from him, went to her bed and lay down, never to get up again, except dead). Nineteenth-century English painters of the pre-Raphaelite school tended to focus on the tragic demise of this lovestruck medieval heroine, representing her with flowing red hair and an ample white dress, adrift in a boat—the "Lady of Shalott" murdered by love.[24] Certain passages in the Old French account corroborate this reading. When the demoisele d'Escalot confronts Lancelot after the tournament in which he has only reluctantly worn her sleeve, the lady asserts that she will die without his love. Her portrait at this moment constitutes a graphically literal rendering of the hopeless plight suffered by unrequited troubadours in the Occitan tradition or by male lovers who die only metaphorically of lovesickness in Andreas Capellanus's *De Amore*. As the *demoisele* explains to Lancelot, "Je vueill bien que vos sachiez veraiement que ge sui a la mort venue, se je n'en sui par vous ostee.... Si tost com ge vos vi, ge vos amai outre ce que cuers de fame peüst home amer, car onques puis ne poi ne boivre, ne mengier, ne dormir ne reposer, einçois ai puis traveillié jusques ci en pensee et toute dolour et toute mesaventure soufferte de nuit et de jour" (67; I want you to know in truth that I have come to the brink of death unless you save me.... From the moment I saw you, I felt a stronger love for you than any woman's heart can feel for a man. Since that moment, I have not been able to eat or drink, sleep or rest, but have been wrought up with thoughts of you, suffering pain and misfortune both day and night). Lancelot dismisses this lady as a casualty of "fole amor": "Ce fu folie, fet Lancelos, de baer a moi en tel maniere" (67; "It was madness," Lancelot said, "to set your heart on me in this way"). And yet, even this encounter records yet another shift in gendered subjects, no less important than the gender crossings involving Lancelot and Gauvain discussed above. In this instance, the demoisele d'Escalot plays the traditional distraught and sleepless male lover to Lancelot's "dame sans merci." And all the while she is dressing him in her clothes.

More importantly, until this calamitous moment, it is not the "world's best knight" but the relatively unknown *demoisele* who has dictated the publicized terms of this couple's relationship.[25] Her gesture defies a longstanding courtly convention, articulated in both lyric and romance, that only men should initiate the lovesuit; women's assigned role is to concede. The lyric paradigm, established by troubadour poet Bernart de Ventadorn and reiterated tentatively by *trobairitz* Na Castelloza, occurs in the romance context when the heroine Soredamor explains in Chrétien de Troyes's *Cligés*, "Ce n'avint onques / Que fame tel forfet feïst / Que d'amors home requeïst, / Se plus d'autre ne fu desvee" (No woman has ever made the mistake of asking a man's love, unless she was out of her senses).[26] The narrator of the thirteenth-century *Roman de la poire* reiterates, "Li hom doit estre un poi plus baut: / la dame doit d'amors proier, / et cele li doit otroier" (The man should be more bold; he should ask the lady's love and she should grant it).[27] The countess Marie de Champagne, figured in Andreas Capellanus's twelfth-century treatise on the art of love, reinforces this view by citing sleeves specifically among other sartorial accoutrements as gifts that women might properly *accept* from their suitors: "A lover is permitted to receive from her partner these gifts: a napkin, hair bands, gold or silver tiara, brooch, mirror, belt, purse, tassel, comb, gauntlets [sleeves], gloves, ring, jewel-box, picture, bowl, vessels, plates, a pennant for remembrance."[28] This account, along with the expanded list of love tokens found in Drouart la Vache's thirteenth-century rewriting of Andreas's text, represents women principally as *recipients* rather than givers of love tokens.[29]

Courtly literary texts provide brief glimpses of an alternative scenario, especially within relationships of mutual affection and exchange. The lovers in Marie de France's *Eliduc* are said to have spent all their time in courting, talking, and exchanging gifts.[30] Indeed, this particular lovesuit is initiated by a woman who sends a ring and belt as tokens of her desire (vv. 510–14). We learn indirectly in *Erec et Enide* that Morgan had secretly fashioned an entire garment of gold and Almerian silk as a gift for her unsuspecting lover.[31] Fresne, the "pucelle franche" whose epithet rhymes with "manche" in *Galeran de Bretagne*, reminds her suitor that attentive lovers might receive from the ladylove both a "manche" and a "ganz d'amours" (vv. 3197–98; a sleeve and a glove signaling love).

In these examples, female protagonists, on whose bodies courtly ideology has traditionally been mapped, can use courtly garments and adornment to redraw the contours of that amorous map, positioning themselves as desiring subjects. It is significant, for example, that the image Fresne embroiders of herself on her sleeve, an image later so extravagantly fetishized by the swooning hero, does not in fact depict her as an object of desire but as a desiring subject, a love poet, with a harp around her neck: "Une seue manche bien faicte, / Ou elle a de fin or pourtraicte / S'ymage et sa harpe a son coul" (vv. 3159–61; One of her finely made sleeves, on which she had drawn in fine gold threads a portrait of herself with a harp hung from her shoulders). It is similarly when singing a song that the heroine Lienor in Jean Renart's *Le Roman de la Rose ou de Guillaume de Dole* turns the tables on the underhanded seneschal, accusing him of having stolen her belt, alms purse, and brooch (vv. 4778–87), items she had earlier sent him under the pretense that they were love tokens from a countess. Far from standing in for a desirable female body, these items of personal dress function to secure Lienor's status as an astute and independent subject.[32]

The tokens of belt, purse and brooch appear in the *Prose Lancelot* when Guenevere instructs Lancelot to display on his helmet her pennant and a band of red silk cloth, sending, along with them, items of female attire that stand in for her physical body: the brooch that lies at her neck, a comb full of her hair, the belt from around her waist, and her alms purse.[33] And yet, the articles most closely associated with the queen's body in this instance: her comb, belt, brooch, and alms purse, recede from our attention as emphasis falls on the way Guenevere dictates Lancelot's chivalric attire. In addition to commanding that her pennant and silk banner decorate her suitor's helmet, much as the demoisele d'Escalot commands Lancelot to wear her sleeve, Guenevere further requires that her knight's shield bear a diagonal white stripe.[34] Thus does this lady dress the knight/lover at her command, much as the female protagonist in the allegorical *Roman de la poire* refashions the chivalric costume of her beloved when conferring as love tokens both a *panon* (pennant) for his lance and her own *couvrechief* (headscarf) to be attached to his helmet.[35] This lover, now equipped to ensure victory for the "fins amanz" against rival "medisants" in the allegorical tournament, credits the lady with outfitting him: "Dame, vostre merci, bien m'avez atorné" (v. 193). But what does this mean?

To be sure, in bestowing their sartorial gifts, these ladies metaphorically give themselves as gifts to the knight in question while ensuring his success on the real or allegorical battlefield of love.[36] And yet, their individual gestures also constitute an important public expression of female desire, significantly different from a private exchange of love tokens, which must remain secret.[37] Conferral of the lady's sleeve, scarf, or silk banner provides a record of amorous attachment displayed openly in the chivalrous arena, allowing female protagonists to move visibly into the position of the desiring subject. Not only does this transfer of fabric alter the conventional paradigm of the heroic knight who desires, defends, rescues, and trades the often objectified ladylove, but giving the sleeve, scarf, or silk banner also recasts, most graphically, the standard description of female beauty in narrative portraits of courtly heroines.[38] Conventional accounts of the ideal beloved fragment the lady's body into isolated and desirable erotic parts under an admiring male gaze, moving from her forehead to her eyes, her nose, her lips, her hips. When a lady gives her sleeve or scarf, by contrast, she enacts a different kind of bodily fragmentation, aptly deploying a portion of her own dress to assert visibly *her* amorous desire through cloth. In this instance, the medieval heroine's body is no longer represented as seductive flesh covered, however thinly, by costly clothes. Rather, clothing is something she deploys to suggest the possibility of an alternative system of female passion, pleasure, and love service, signaling the lady's will, her command, her gift and contract. Instead of shaping her body, this key article of female attire marks the lady's potentially substantial influence in shaping the course of courtly love. It also raises a question about courtly space.

We have typically assumed that the love expressed between courtly partners takes place within the social context, however fictively it may be presented, of a seemingly western court. Whether in the castles and courts of Provence and Champagne, where troubadours deliver their love songs or the lady Marie pronounces her judgments in love cases staged by Andreas Capellanus, or in the prototypical castles where King Arthur holds court in the Lancelot stories, the site of amorous coupling in the courtly literary tradition remains not only elite and aristocratic but presumably also distinctively western. If we return for a moment to the demoisele d'Escalot's sleeve, however, that garment is said to be made of silk, a luxury fabric imported to France from the east from the time of the second crusade through the thirteenth century.

What does it mean, then, that the demoisele d'Escalot's powerful claim to status as a desiring female subject in the courtly world is made through fabric that is imported from so-called foreign lands lying vaguely across the sea, from named sites "d'outremer"? To be sure, wearing a silk gown or displaying a silk sleeve connotes a level of opulence available in the French Middle Ages only to elites. But we witness in this instance something more specific: the use of eastern luxury goods to express western female desire. Indeed, literary courtly ladies, whose pure white skin and delicate facial features are typically augmented by extravagant attire fashioned from foreign fabrics, stand firmly at the cultural crossroads between Christian France and the middle eastern cities that give their names to the cloth these ladies wear: Phrygia, Damascus, Constantinople. If we consider the material composition of the demoisele d'Escalot's silk sleeve, its provenance in eastern lands and its associations with Saracen cultures, we can begin to see how literary representations of luxury goods used in the courtly milieu to establish wealth and status, to mark gender and express desire, situate those key aspects of courtliness within a larger, eastern frame. Reading through the silk cloth of this lady's sleeve calls into question the very polarization of the terms east versus west, suggesting yet another border crossing facilitated by the practice of courtly love. In this sense, the lady's elegant sleeve helps us to see the extent to which courtly players are not simply westerners wearing eastern clothes but are clothed bodies for whom costly silks, gems, and precious metals imported from the east have become intrinsic markers of ostensibly western identities.

The demoisele d'Escalot's sleeve provides a material trace that can guide us on an unexpected journey through alternative readings of courtliness. It prompts us to question a number of conventions of amorous coupling that have become the trademark of courtly love in the medieval French literary tradition. That single, underread sleeve encourages us to ask, first of all, what luxury attire can tell us about female desire, which is so rarely recorded in medieval lyric or romance adventure stories, which tend instead to focus on men as desiring subjects. It pushes us to wonder whether courtly clothes could be deployed in other venues to restructure the highly codified gender hierarchies that typically govern amorous relations in the courtly world. It spurs us further to investigate how items of luxury dress might provide social mobility for women in a system of courtly encounter that we have understood formerly as facilitating social mobility for men. Finally, the sleeve episode helps us to rethink these key issues of courtly desire, gender identity, and class status in relation to the material fabric of the demoisele d'Escalot's costly dress, allowing us to see the extent to which our visual recognition of courtliness as a western phenomenon relies in fact on eastern opulence.

Reading Through Clothes

We have tended to *read through* these important features of courtliness without perceiving them fully because we have not paid enough attention to the wide-ranging functions of elite clothing in the courtly world. Following the lead suggested by the demoisele d'Escalot's sleeve, I want to advance here a strategy of *reading through clothes* in lyric and romance texts. That will mean taking the surface and texture of courtly attire into account as we attempt to understand how courtly ideologies and identities based on class, gender, and place are forged and reinforced while also being reshaped and subverted in literary representations of luxury dress.[39] My interest is in reading the clothed body figured in courtly narratives as a social body, in line with Elizabeth Grosz's formulation of the body as "the political, social, and cultural object par excellence, not a product of a raw, passive nature that is civilized, overlaid, polished by culture." The body, Grosz contends, is both "a cultural interweaving *and* a production of nature" and as such must be regarded as a site of social, political, cultural, and geographical inscriptions, production, or constitution.[40]

Rather than having the status of some matter or ground on which cultural constructions are built, the courtly body can be understood in this light as a set of clothes that make, mark, delimit, and define the body presumed to lie beneath. In fact, there is no body in any foundational sense prior to the garments placed upon it. As Judith Butler has explained for bodies more generally, "the mimetic or representational status of language, which claims that signs follow bodies as their necessary mirrors, is not mimetic at all. On the contrary, it is productive, constitutive, one might even argue *performative*, in as much as this signifying act delimits and contours the body that it then claims to find prior to any and all signification."[41] To avoid confusion with the more familiar paradigm of clothes covering a corporeal body beneath, I have chosen to call the social bodies forged from both fabric and flesh in courtly literary texts "sartorial bodies." These sartorial bodies are not tangible objects with an independent existence in literary texts. They emerge from a reading practice that conceives of clothes as an active force in generating social bodies.

Those who study the effects of clothing, along with other bodily adornments such as jewelry, makeup and hairstyles, have asked where the body stops and the social world begins.[42] To what extent can the range of material artifacts used in "dressing up" the body be considered a kind of social skin, resulting from the systematic modifying of the visible surface of the human body?[43] The collapse is particularly evident in various forms of transvestism where, as Marjorie Garber has shown, the body no longer functions as a ground for clothing laid upon it. Rather, the clothed body itself becomes the carrier of meaning.[44] But this is not only true of transvestite dressing up. In the pages to follow I will argue that in many ways the elite dress of courtly couples in medieval French literary texts generates corporeal bodies that are fabricated from clothes. To study sartorial bodies in this sense does not mean replacing the notion of a sex-based biological identity with a concept of clothes as generative of a false social identity. I do not wish to argue here that "clothes make the man" (or the woman, as the case may be) in courtly love scenarios in the sense that inappropriately lavish clothes or gender-crossed garments can mislead the uninformed viewer. On the contrary, *reading through clothes*, when clothes are seen as material objects balanced on the threshold between culture and nature, will mean reading for clothed bodies that so thoroughly combine both terms of the definition that they have no independent existence—such that neither *clothes* nor *body* could be understood or assessed separately. Reading for "sartorial bodies" in the sense that I employ the term here will mean reading for a range of bodies that are not naturally sexed or conventionally gendered, bodies that can move at times unpredictably across lines of social class, and bodies that might provide a crossing place between cultural currents of east and west. Reading through clothes will mean reading for bodies forged from what we might call a sartorial corporeality, courtly bodies generated by clothes that extend the flesh of literary protagonists symbolically and ideologically.

It is, paradoxically, the work of material cultural studies generally to investigate the very tangible material objects and artifacts of a given cultural moment while also examining the more abstract and often elusive cultural work they might perform in a specific historical context.[45] Clothing in particular functions as a physical, marketable commodity that also holds the power of defining social identities in ways that might disrupt prevailing economic and social systems. Anthropologist Jane Schneider has shown, for example, the relevance of cloth to shifting political and economic alliances, demonstrating how specific social units—whether dynasties, social classes, elites, ethnic groups, or women—have enhanced their social position while creating a distinctive cloth style.[46] Hildi Hendrickson has explained in a related vein how postcolonial Africans use western items of dress to reinforce their own African identities—reminding us that "the meaning of body or commodity is not inherent, but is in fact symbolically created and contested by both producers and consumers." She concludes that "the power of industrial systems to define those meanings—and of materialist analyses to account for them—is more limited than it may appear." This means that "dressing of the body can be empowering and creative, even if it does not become more deeply subversive."[47] Clothes can define their wearers socially both within and against established conventions and prevailing ideologies. Literary representations of clothes can do the same for fictive protagonists.

It is at this point that the ethnographer's study of the economic consequences of material fabric and the cultural anthropologist's interest in how clothing provides the body with a kind of social skin intersect with recent developments in feminist theory and reading practices. Feminist film critics have charted an important turn from a seventies feminist position that, following Simone de Beauvoir, saw clothing as frivolous adornment that restricted and enslaved women within a myth of femininity to more current efforts that have revealed how those very accouterments of femininity can produce a counterideology of resistance.[48] Elizabeth Wilson's *Adorned in Dreams* advocates the power of clothes as a site of female fantasy, expression, and daring play,[49] while Angela McRobbie shows how young working-class women in Britain use clothes, makeup, and their budding "femaleness" to disrupt the social order at school.[50] Social historians like Laurel Thatcher Ulrich have argued a similar case for early American culture, stating that "if textiles are in one sense an emblem of women's oppression, they have also been an almost universal medium of female expression."[51]

Once we begin to see how clothing, through its unique positioning between the body and society, can articulate a politics of gender and status that might trouble ruling paradigms, whether economic or ideological, we can ask how literary representations of courtly clothing too might be used for purposes beyond the ostentatious display of wealth.[52] We have seen here, for example, how the demoisele d'Escalot's sleeve, Guenevere's pennant, and the *couvrechief* belonging to the anonymous lady in the *Roman de la poire*, when viewed in their full materiality as cloth or as portions of female dress, can unsettle the amorous conventions that a simple or straightforward courtly love token would typically underwrite. Indeed, at key moments in courtly French literary texts, items of luxury dress can work against, while remaining within, established hierarchies of social status, enshrined paradigms of desire and gender difference, or polarizing divisions between the cultures of east and west. I will survey the complex and intricate relations between courtly love and sartorial riches in Chapter 1, "Fortune's Gown: Material Extravagance and the Opulence of Love," while also examining in detail how wearing courtly clothes can potentially leverage increased independence and social mobility for bourgeois women in amorous encounters. Chapters 2 and 3 ("Amorous Attire: Dressing Up for Love" and "Love's Stitches Undone") explain how courtly ladies can accede to the subject position typically reserved for male protagonists and express desire and pleasure through touch, in particular through their tactile connection with clothes and clothwork. Chapters 4 and 5 ("Robes, Armor, and Skin" and

"From Woman's Nature to Nature's Dress") show how knights and ladies in courtly romance, whether clad in unisex attire, armor, or lavish gowns, can be seen to function less as discrete, naturally sexed bodies than as spacings on a gendered sartorial continuum. Chapters 6 and 7 ("Saracen Silk: Dolls, Idols, and Courtly Ladies" and "Golden Spurs: Love in the Eastern World of *Floire et Blancheflor*") examine how the courtly lady herself, however much she may be formed in the tradition of Pygmalion's ivory statue, often emerges, through association with imported fabrics, as a hybrid creature providing an important contact zone between material cultures of east and west. These chapters investigate a range of sartorial bodies articulated in different ways across varied twelfth- and thirteenth-century courtly texts. Close readings of key passages from the *Roman de la Rose* by Guillaume de Lorris and Jean de Meun are featured throughout the book, along with analyses of select passages from medieval treatises on the art of love; Chrétien de Troyes's *Cligés, Erec et Enide, Le Chevalier de la charrete,* and *Perceval ou le conte du Graal*; Jean Renart's *Roman de la Rose ou de Guillaume de Dole*; and Gautier d'Arras's *Ille et Galeron*; among others. More extended readings of select Provençal *trobairitz* are found in Chapter 2, of the Old French *chanson de toile* in Chapter 3, and of Robert de Blois's *Floris et Lyriope* and the *Prose Lancelot* in Chapter 4. Chapter 5 offers a detailed analysis of Marie de France's *Lai de Lanval*, Chapter 6 features a key passage from the Arthurian Vulgate Cycle's *Estoire del Saint Graal*, and Chapter 7 provides a detailed reading of the Byzantine romance *Floire et Blancheflor*. The Coda applies the strategy of reading through clothes to the highly problematic prologue of Chrétien de Troyes's *Chevalier de la charrete*.

To read through clothes, in the manner I am proposing here, is to admit a relational dynamic between courtly garments and the literary protagonists who wear them, to grant to items of luxury dress the ability to affect and shape their wearer while the wearer also affects them. In this view, the material world of the courtly literary text is not simply a composite of tangible objects that are created, selected, and deployed by fictive protagonists as a backdrop to narrative action.[53] Rather, the view of material culture I have found most useful in "reading through clothes" in the French Middle Ages understands material objects as exerting a substantial effect on the cultural formations and literary paradigms in which they participate. As Peter Corrigan suggests, clothing, as well as being an object to which things happen, also "*provokes* things to happen" (435). We can thus understand clothing as an *active* force in social relations, a form of material culture that "far from merely *reflecting* society, ... can be seen to construct, maintain, control and transform social identities and relations," as Roberta Gilchrist has explained.[54] In this view, literary representations of luxury dress and the fictive protagonists wearing them exist in a dynamic relation much as Anthony Giddens has described for social structures generally. In his analysis, the structural properties of social systems (within which we could include clothes) are not wholly external to individuals but constitutive of them in ways that are both constraining and enabling.[55] The approach is especially useful for feminist analysis of material culture because it allows for the possibility of at least partial female agency while also acknowledging structural and ideological relations of gender.[56] Reading through clothes in courtly literary texts will open up new possibilities for reconfiguring the full range of those gendered relations. It will help us situate key issues of gendered desire and social mobility that are derived from the practice of love within an expansive courtly geography, stretching eastward to include, within the very definition of courtliness, cultural elements from sites far beyond the limits of medieval France.

It is the aim of this book to "undress" courtly love as we have known it and to provide a view of what heretofore has gone largely unseen: that courtly clothes forge complex sartorial identities, which allow us to rethink the traditional terms of amorous encounter. Reading through clothes in courtly literary texts will enable us to see beyond the dolled-up beauty as an object of desire and begin to envision dressed-up women as subjects who effectively deploy clothes as an important currency of courtly exchange. Examining the varied ways in which clothes convey gender differences in courtly love scenarios will reveal a spectrum of possibilities along a sartorial continuum that allows for a wide range of subject positions beyond male and female. And finally, considering where the silks, gems, and precious metals used to generate elite garments come from will enable us to see courtly, aristocratic bodies as cultural crossing places that challenge the presumed cultural hegemony of west over east.

The purpose of undressing courtly love in this manner is not to arrive at a naked body beneath those lavish clothes but to immerse ourselves in the textures, colors, and folds of fabric that constitute a significant cultural body of their own. Taking up the invitation posed by the demoisele d'Escalot's highly charged sleeve, we can enter more fully into medieval French literary representations of luxury attire and see what they have to tell us about courtly coupling in some of the most formative antecedents of the western romantic love story.

PART I

Clothing Courtly Bodies

Chapter 1
Fortune's Gown: Material Extravagance and the Opulence of Love

Jean de Meun's thirteenth-century version of the *Roman de la Rose* opens with a standard clerical condemnation of courtly love as a kind of incurable torment that enflames the hearts of fools and makes them suffer unrequited desire.[1] Jean's spokesperson, Lady Reason, further condemns the folly of this consuming love when it becomes a form of covetousness, when the love of bodily pleasures becomes confused with the insatiable love of riches.[2] Different from the reciprocal affection of Ciceronian friendship that Reason condones, the pursuit of physical pleasure and passion more often resembles the obsessive pursuit of tangible material gain, the "couvoitise de gaaing" that plagues all rich men and misers (vv. 4744, 4773–75). Not only are merchants, lawyers and doctors driven by this love for profit and terrestrial goods (vv. 5042–61), knights, kings and beggars (v. 5017) also fall under the purview of those who love "to amass treasure" (vv. 5089–92).

The image recalls the more tangible transactions of courtly lovers in Andreas Capellanus's twelfth-century Latin treatise, *The Art of Courtly Love*,[3] where the male suitor is said uncontrollably to amass as much wealth as possible, obsessively seeking a level of "material wealth which might nurture his love."[4] To "attain" the ladylove socially requires considerable material comfort, Andreas warns in Book 3, thus making courtly lovers avaricious for luxury goods and women alike.[5] Reason in Jean's *Rose* denounces courtly generosity specifically as a mere cover for these avaricious desires. Courtiers, she claims:

Ne veulent pas estre repris
de la grant ardure et dou vice
a la covoiteuse Avarice,
ainz en font les granz courtoisies
donc leur proeces sunt proisies
et celebree par le monde. vv. 5204–9

(Do not want to suffer reproach for possessing the burning passion and vice of covetous Avarice. Therefore they perform acts of great courtliness, which cause their good qualities to be applauded and celebrated throughout the world.)[6]

Most important, however, Reason develops her case against courtly lovers by invoking the excess and opulence of another lady, Fortune, conjuring before the besotted lover's eyes an image of extravagant female courtly dress. Among "walls of gold and silver," the entire roof "glowing with the clearest and most brilliant precious gems" (vv. 6063–73), Fortune "adorns and dresses her body, and clothes herself like a queen in a long dress that trails behind her, redolent with many different perfumes and displaying the exquisite colors of silks and woolens tinted from plants, grains, and many other ingredients used to color the luxury fabrics that rich people wear":

Lors pare son cors et atorne,
et se vest, conme une reïne,
de grant robe qui li treïne,
de toute diverses ouleurs,
de mout desguisees couleurs
qui sunt es saies et es laines
selonc les herbes et les graines
et selonc autres choses maintes
dunt les draperies sunt taintes
don toutes riches genz se vestent. vv. 6092–6101[7]

If Fortune emerges in this account as an image of avarice, she is presented more specifically as a courtly queen whose sartorial elegance scintillates and beguiles. It is an elaborately dressed *lady* named Fortune, Reason warns, that misguided lovers pursue, a version of wealth cast in elegant courtly clothes.

As the metaphors of obsessive love and avarice entwine in Reason's speech, wealth itself becomes allegorized in a courtly register as a "dame et raïne" (v. 5176) who effectively mimics the God of Love, piercing the hearts of her ardent lovers with three perilous blades that entrap and enslave them:

Li premiers est travaill d'aquerre;
li segonz, qui les queurs leur serre,
c'est poor qu'en nes toille ou emble
quant il les ont mises ensemble,
donc il s'esmaient sanz cessier;

le tierz est douleur du lessier.
Si con je t'ai dit ci devant,
malement s'en vont decevant. vv. 5167–74

(The first is the labor of acquisition. The second, which weighs on their hearts and worries them constantly, is the fear that someone might rob them and carry off their riches once they have acquired them. The third blade is the pain of leaving the riches behind. As I have told you before, they [these riches] cruelly deceive.)

Riches in this account make men "pine away" like courtly suitors bound helplessly and hopelessly in the "service" of a haughty courtly lady:

Et le torment et le domage
Qui languissent en son servage. vv. 5183–84 (my emphasis)

([Riches/she] tortures and harms them, making them pine away in her service/servitude.)[8]

That other lady, Fortune, is denounced more specifically for using ornate lavish attire to trick and deceive unwary lovers. As her wheel turns, we are told, Fortune moves into the opposite chamber of her house, "dirty, weak, cracked, and crumbling" (sale, foible, decrevee et crolant, vv. 6116–17), where she sheds her superficial luxury dress and falls into a debased state of nakedness:

Et quant iluec se voit cheüe,
sa chiere et son habit remue,
et si se desnue et desrobe
qu'el est orfeline de robe
et semble qu'el n'ait riens vaillant,
tant li vont tuit bien defaillant. vv. 6121–26

(When she sees where she has fallen, she changes her countenance and her attire; she disrobes and undresses until she is wholly without clothing and appears to have nothing of value, being utterly lacking in material goods.)

This impoverished creature who "goes to crouch in a whorehouse" (se vet au bordel cropir, v. 6129) is Fortune undisguised, according to Reason, a lady stripped of vain ornaments that have no lasting value or profit. If Fortune appears to distribute riches and honor, dignities and authority, glory and worldly prosperity, she will inevitably cast her followers from their high estate into the mire, with their luxury dress, like Fortune's own, finally in tatters (vv. 4823–66).

Chapter 1

I begin with this account of Fortune's ornate attire because it illustrates a tendency in twelfth- and thirteenth-century narratives generally to weave tales of courtly love within a web of material extravagance, focusing in particular on the luxurious dress of amorous players. The passage also records the disapproval often expressed by clerical writers who regard such opulence as superficial, fleeting, and fundamentally feminine. But Reason's depiction of Fortune's gown does much more. It provides a range of conceptual possibilities for understanding the complex relations between the gender and status of sumptuously clothed elite bodies in a wide array of courtly literary texts. Initially, the portrait of Fortune from Jean de Meun's *Roman de la Rose* reiterates misogynous paradigms of women as superficially overdressed or depraved in nakedness. Either Fortune appears in a bejeweled and golden palace, lavishly clad in costly silks and brocades, or she plummets to the muddy depths of poverty, stark naked. The choices suggest a clear separation between courtly bodies and the garments that might cover them, drawing a discrete distinction between Fortune's sartorial options. And yet this account of Lady Fortune as an icon for the fate of courtly lovers also provides a crucial option between the extremes of opulent clothing and unadorned skin. This alternative, which literary narratives of courtly love tend to cultivate and exploit, offers the oxymoronic image of a sartorial body: a body defined neither as clothed or naked, and one that also eludes conventional gender stereotypes.

When describing the rocky island on which Fortune's house stands, Jean de Meun characterizes the site of this allegorical lady's fluctuating movements as a water-washed rock constantly covered by pounding waves that it repeatedly sheds, as one would remove, the Old French suggests, an article of clothing:

Li flot *la* hurtent et debatent,
qui tourjorz a lui se conbatent,
et maintes foiz tant i cotissent
que toute en mer l'ensevelissent;
aucune foiz se redespuelle
de l'eve qui toute *la* muelle. vv. 5895–5900 (my emphasis)

(The waves strike it [the rock] and beat against it, assailing it repeatedly, many times hitting it so hard that they engulf it completely. Yet each time, it unclothes itself (*redespuelle*)[9] from the water that has drenched it.)

Although the term for rock (*roche*) is grammatically feminine in Old French and thus represented by the direct object pronoun "la," in lines 5895 and

5900 above, the metaphorical body that this pronoun represents does not carry the stereotype of gendered femininity attached to Fortune's excessively adorned self. This is not a naked female body clothed artificially with seductive feminine attire. Rather, the watery clothing of Fortune's abode remains tellingly indistinct from what appears to be a more rocky and ungendered substrate. Indeed, the liquid garments that clothe this site cling and slide away without the discrete separation that more opaque and tangible material might supply. Most importantly, the metaphorical clothing of Fortune's bedrock has a transformative effect, actually reshaping a body that it constitutes, composes, and recomposes:

Mes el ne retient nule forme,
ainceis se tresmue et reforme
et se desguise et se treschange;
tourjors se vest de forme estrange. vv. 5903–6

(It [the rock] does not retain any one shape. Rather, it constantly changes and recasts itself, taking on a new shape as it metamorphoses. Thus does it continually dress itself in a different and unexpected manner.)

To be always "dressed in a different manner" means more, in this instance, than simply donning and removing varied garments as the allegorical Lady Fortune does. Here, the rock "always changes and recasts itself," suggesting that this kind of aqueous clothing effects substantive alterations in the body being clothed. It is that transformative effect of lavish courtly attire, over and above its potential ability to deceive and disguise, that many courtly tales cultivate and that Reason finds especially objectionable. The house of Lady Fortune is to be avoided by courtly lovers, Reason states, not only because it is perilously undependable and fickle, casting the unwary visitor from the comfort of luxury clothes and adornment into the destitution of base nakedness (vv. 5317–22, 6085–88). Fortune's seductive power lies also in what Reason calls her "perverse" ability (v. 6135) to confuse the sartorial representations of social categories, impoverishing and dishonoring good people while rewarding the wicked with attributes heretofore belonging to the highly esteemed and richly endowed:

Et por ce qu'el est si perverse
que les bons en la boe verse
et les deshoneure et les grieve,
et les mauvés en haut eslieve
et leur done a granz habondances
dignetez, honeurs et puissances. vv. 6135–40

(She is so perverse that she throws good people into the mud, undresses and humiliates them, while raising up bad people and giving them dignities, honor, and power in great abundance.)

The combined threat of love and luxury attire in the courtly world is thus not only to feed avarice but also to effect substantive change in social ranks and gendered subjectivities by eroding the hierarchical divisions that structure each of them.

We learn, most significantly, from Fortune's example that clothing the courtly body can involve more than placing superficial, detachable garments on a stable frame of flesh and bones. To be sure, in many instances of opulent dress in courtly culture of the French Middle Ages, the function of lavish attire appears initially to follow Fortune's dichotomous pattern of rags or riches, nudity or luxury dress. Certainly, much early French sumptuary legislation attempts to regulate the social rank and status of the aristocratic classes in these terms, understanding luxury attire to be an ornate and costly cover for an otherwise naked body whose class status should accurately be encoded in surface adornment. Moralizing discourses throughout the twelfth and thirteenth centuries attempt to regulate gender by distinguishing the artificial cover of clothes from bodies presumed to be naturally sexed as male and female. However, the rhetorical insistence of both sumptuary legislation and numerous Latin and vernacular sermons attests in fact to the difficulty of maintaining such distinctions, as we will see. When bourgeois women are denounced for effectively dressing up in noble garb and courtly men are accused of wearing the "prideful costume" of women, the lines ostensibly marking categories of class and gender are shown to be repeatedly challenged and remade through the transformative effects of clothing and ornament.

The Sartorial Body

Indeed, the power of luxury dress to conflate surface and substance, in keeping with the second paradigm of Fortune's tale, opens especially rich possibilities for literary protagonists to move across established lines of both class and gender in courtly narrative. If we take Fortune's story as a point of departure, we can begin to interrogate courtly love as a site where clothes create and produce a range of sartorial bodies that challenge clerical tirades against gendered conspicuous consumption and material extravagance in court culture. It is in literary accounts of courtly love and their depiction of the lavish giving known as *largesse* that the concept of the sartorial body is expressly cultivated and most fully developed. In these instances, costly garments received initially as gifts become representative of the recipient who wears them, functioning less as a removable disguise or a visual trick to be shunned than as a new skin.

To understand this view of courtly dress will mean envisioning clothing in the courtly world, in line with Terence Turner's formulation, as a kind of "social skin" that combines corporeal features of the physical body with adornment that significantly transforms and alters that body.[10] From this perspective we can imagine not only how the material of courtly clothing might be deployed by its various users to different ends—to signal social rank or to convey gender differences, but also how those material garments themselves might construct, maintain, control, and transform social identities based on gender and class distinctions, and how they might do so in unregulated, unexpected, and disruptive ways.

Following the model of Fortune's watery dress, we might ask, then, how lavish courtly attire could be used to negotiate both status and gender in the courtly world. What happens to borders between social ranks when luxury clothes, displayed as a means of self-definition for the courtly elite, begin to circulate among men of different social classes in a cultural economy of *largesse*, the conspicuous giving so central to courtly life? Furthermore, what happens when women are the recipients of such costly garments, whether as a courtly lady, a bourgeois wife, or an enamored queen?

In contrast to the clerical critique of love's opulence found in Jean's *Roman de la Rose* and Andreas's Book 3, for example, the anonymous thirteenth-century *Art d'amours* stages an image of women skillfully trading costly garments as a form of currency in gaming. These "women in love" deploy clothing that has a function beyond being worn or shed, luxury garments and adornments that do more than mark male avarice or signal female self-indulgence. Adapted from Ovid's *Ars amatoria*, but containing a third book designed specifically to advise women in matters of love, this text claims, "Affiert aux damoiselles amoureuses savoir jouer a pluseurs jeux, comme aux tables, aux eschas, et cetera. Et doivent hardiement jouer pour une bourse de soye oui pour une ceinture, pour une plice" (It is befitting to amorous maidens to know how to play games, such as tables, chess, et cetera. They should play boldly for a silk purse, or a belt or for a fur-lined tunic).[11] Women wearing these items of costly dress would begin to resemble the opulently clad Fortune in Reason's critique, but without the negative consequences that Reason details.

What effect, then, does women's deployment and circulation of such ornate clothes have on the economy of sartorial exchange in courtly encounter more generally? If courtly clothes, when functioning in line with Fortune's watery attire, have the ability to generate ever-changing and noncorporeal bodies, bodies produced by a relatively seamless interaction between cloth and flesh, what are the ideological implications of such sartorial bodies in the context of courtly love?

In this chapter I will consider the regulatory functions ascribed to clothing in medieval French sumptuary law and in vernacular sermons with a view to understanding how the concepts of clothing operative in those discourses are undermined even as they are articulated, and how they are further challenged in vernacular love treatises and courtly love stories. In closing, I turn to the highly acerbic, antifeminist diatribe voiced by the Jealous Husband in Jean de Meun's *Roman de la Rose*. We will see how even this text's virulent attempts to regulate and patrol woman's femininity and social status through control of her clothes also document the ability of courtly attire to produce the opposite effect. But first a look at the material extravagance of love.

Material Extravagance and Court Culture

It is a commonplace of medieval French scholarship that the courtly world depends on material extravagance and opulence, reflecting a culture obsessed with self-display and ostentation as a form of self-definition among members of the ruling elite. Certainly material extravagance characterizes the court culture we see depicted in literary texts in the twelfth and thirteenth centuries where lords and kings, bound by a code of *largesse*, generously distribute their holdings in land, castles, arms, armor, food, clothing, and women to vassals who share in the impressive wealth.[12] Life at the Arthurian court in particular revolves around elaborate feasts and costly tournaments to which knights and ladies come suitably attired in silks and brocades, ermine and gold.[13] Heavily embroidered mantles, bed hangings and curtains, sumptuous bed coverlets, tapestries and jewel-encrusted goblets, amply decorate the courtly milieu. From the time of Geoffrey of Monmouth's pseudohistorical chronicle of the Kings of Britain (ca. 1136), King Arthur's court, modeled on the munificence of Alexander the Great, is described as "surpassing all other realms in the multitude of its riches, the luxuriousness of its décor, the nobility of its inhabitants" and in the "extravagant dress" of its courtiers ("le faste des habits," Bezzola, 545, 547). Even adjacent courtly venues such as the fairy Morgan's castle in *La Mort le roi Artu* exhibit a magnificence that rivals the king's own opulence.[14] The walls of Morgan's castle, draped in silk fabric, are more richly adorned than any church or nunnery, her elegant table more lavishly set with gold and silver implements and more abundantly provisioned with food than the extravagant tables of Camelot (58). Knights and ladies of this court "estoient tuit et toutes vestues si richement que onques a feste qu'il eüst tenue jour de sa vie n'avoit li rois Artus veüs gens si richement ascemés come il estoient communalement par la sale" (57; All those in the room were more richly attired than anyone King Arthur had ever seen at the festivities he himself hosted).[15] One of the most telling marks of the ruling, aristocratic class in courtly literary texts is its movable, detachable luxury goods, which can be traded independently as currency.

Garments in particular circulate widely as a form of monetary exchange among members of both courtly and uncourtly worlds. Romance narratives describe jongleurs whose participation in weddings and festivals is compensated in rich clothes, a practice denounced in sermons as taking payment in "robes precieuses de vair ou de gris."[16] The wedding scene in Chrétien de Troyes's *Erec et Enide* tells how minstrels were paid with luxury garments:

Ce jor furent jugleor lié,
Car tuit furent a gré paié:
Tot fu randu quanqu'il acrurent,
Et molt bel don doné lor furent:
Robes de veir et d'erminetes,
De conins et de violetes,
D'escarlate, grise ou de soie. vv. 2055–61

(That day the minstrels were pleased because they had been well paid. Everything owed to them was paid and they received many lovely gifts: clothes of fur and ermine, of rabbit and purple cloth, of dark gray wool or of silk.)[17]

Outside the courtly milieu, clothes can be seen to function as currency when a successful courtesan is described in one of Jacques de Vitry's exempla as having fleeced her lover of everything he could spend on her except his cloak. The lesson implies that this garment too might readily have served as payment, "totum spoliavi; sola capa illi remansit."[18] Even the pope's elegant and sacred robes revert to currency in an anecdote from Jacques de Vitry's private life, narrated in a letter that recounts how upon arriving in Rome to be consecrated in his new post of bishop, he discovered that the pope, Innocent III, had died two days before. The pope's body, not yet buried and abandoned by cardinals preoccupied with the election of a new pope, had been stripped of its rich garments by thieves who rightly assessed their material worth.[19] If these literary and didactic examples describe clothing in medieval French culture as a form of wealth, they also reveal how that form of material wealth could pass readily from one individual to the next across social strata, moving from lord to jongleur, from customer to courtesan, or from the pope to a common thief.

The courtly tradition of *largesse* itself requires that royalty and nobles demonstrate publicly their requisite generosity by distributing items of luxury dress to lower-ranking members of their retinue. At Erec's coronation in *Erec et Enide*, the "wealthy and generous" King Arthur gives elegant luxury clothing to each of the four hundred knights he has dubbed:

Chevax dona a chascun trois,
et robes a chascun trois peire,
Por ce que sa corz mialz apeire.
Molt fu li rois puissanz et larges:
Ne dona pas mantiax de sarges,
Ne de conins ne de brunetes,
Mes de samiz et d'erminetes,
De veir antier et de dïapres,
Listez d'orfrois roides et aspres. vv. 6603–10

(He gave three horses to each one and three suits of clothes so that his court would appear more impressive. The king was very powerful and generous. He did not give cloaks made of serge or rabbit fur or coarse wool, but of heavy silk (samite) and ermine, cloaks entirely of fur and silk brocade, bordered with heavy gold embroidery.)

King Arthur's prototypical *largesse* is further attested in Béroul's twelfth-century *Roman de Tristan*, when the luxury garments of elite spectators at Queen Iseut's adultery trial become alms for the adulterer himself. The courtly Tristan, disguised as a beleaguered leper, tauntingly beseeches King Arthur to share his riches by asking specifically for costly articles of clothing:

Tu es vestu de beaus grisens
De Renebors, si con je pens.
Desoz la toile rencïene
La toue char est blanche et plaine

Tes janbes voi de riche paile
Chaucies et o verte maile,
Et les sorchauz d'une escarlate.
...
Por Deu me donne ces sorchauz.[20]

(You are dressed in handsome gray cloth from Regensburg, I think, and beneath the linen from Rheims your skin is white and smooth. I see your legs covered with rich silk and green net and leggings of dark colored wool.... In God's name, give me your leggings!)

"The noble king took pity on him," we are told, much as the "regal and imposing" King Marc does shortly thereafter, giving the seemingly diseased man not money but his own royal, fur-trimmed hood (vv. 3731, 3742).

If courtly *largesse* is indeed a cover for avaricious consumption, as Reason contends in Jean de Meun's *Rose*, it poses an even greater threat to the maintenance of class distinction. As we shall see, the generous giving of luxury garments associated with *largesse* creates a material version of Fortune's wheel, constantly churning up social ranks through the donation of costly clothes between individuals of different social strata. As the foregoing examples attest, the conspicuous conferral of luxury attire as a necessary mark of courtly generosity mutually constructs the identities of both giver and receiver. Clothing passed from the nobility to jongleurs, knights, or paupers marks the ruling elite as generous while also making recipients of aristocratic dress visibly more courtly than their lineage or occupation would otherwise indicate. The problem is staged cogently in Jean Renart's thirteenth-century *Roman de la Rose ou de Guillaume de Dole* when the noble Guillaume lavishes luxury clothing on townspeople. He gives his host the innkeeper a newly made cloak and offers a "priceless" brooch to the innkeeper's wife. He confers a belt with a silver buckle on a female singer, and hands his own cloak made of ermine to the performer Jouglet (vv. 1825, 1834, 1842, 1830).[21] As the narrator explains, "Puis qu'il a tot mis a la mine, / je ne sai qu'il en feïst el" (vv. 1831–32; I don't know how he could do more, since he had given everything away). The stereotypically generous Guillaume also gives "a magnificent sleeveless tunic, lined with whole squirrel furs" to the chamberlain Boidin (v. 1816), who wears it on his return to court, where it both increases his own status and furthers Guillaume's reputation as a generous noble. On seeing the well-dressed chamberlain, the emperor Conrad realizes the garment should belong to an individual of higher rank and asks, "Qui vos dona / Tel sorcot?" (vv. 1871–72; Who gave you such a tunic?) Boidin replies:

> ...—Cil, fet il, qui n'a
> Talent de prester a usure.
> Onqes si gentil creature,
> Ce sachiez, ne fu ne si large.
> Puis que j'alai en cest voiage
> Ou ge ne voil demorer gaires,
> A il doné de robes vaires
> Et de joiaus, qui vaut .c. livres. vv. 1872–79

(Not a usurer. Never was anyone so noble and generous, in truth. In my brief visit he gave away furs and jewels worth a hundred pounds.)

From this the emperor concludes, "—Bien a le sorcot emploié.... si est rois qui puet doner rien" (vv. 1888, 1890; He's certainly made good use of that tunic.... To give is to be a king.)

Thus the very act of distributing items of luxury dress that distinguishes Guillaume from lesser nobles and townspeople, the generous donation of costly apparel that gives him, metaphorically, the distinctive social standing of a king, also risks closing the visual gap between himself and those of lower social standing. Indeed, as soon as lesser nobles or townspeople begin to wear the articles of clothing Guillaume has distributed, they will become visibly and financially more wealthy than before.[22]

If luxury attire is a marker of accrued wealth and social status in literary representations of medieval French culture, it also remains, by its very nature, precariously detached from its bearer. Precisely because it can circulate as currency, the lavish and costly dress that so effectively marks members of the ruling elite in courtly society can also produce a visual confusion among social ranks. Joinville's *Vie de Saint Louis* provides a particularly cogent example of this dilemma when Robert de Cerbon (Sorbonne) critiques Joinville himself for being "plus noblement vestu que le roy car vous vestez de vair et de vert, ce que li roys ne fait pas"[23] (More nobly dressed than the king, since you are wearing fur and costly green cloth, which the king does not). Joinville retorts that his clothes are from his parents and thus an appropriate and accurate indication of his family standing, in contrast to Robert de Sorbonne, who errs more seriously. Sorbonne, Joinville alleges, is a "filz de vilain et de vilainne" who has left the clothing of this rank behind to wear instead "un plus riche camelin que le roy" (a more costly camel hair wool than the king). A comparison of the *surcots* worn by both men follows, as Joinville attempts to argue that clothing should reflect one's lineage, rank, and status (18). His remarks demonstrate, however, how readily luxury clothes can in fact be used to contravene that very position, enabling a "filz de vilain" to usurp visually the place of a king. This is precisely the dilemma that medieval French sumptuary laws attempt to address.

Sumptuary Legislation and the Regulation of Status

Substantial anxiety about how social status might be determined and regulated through clothes is recorded in French sumptuary laws as early as 1229. These royal decrees document the high nobility's desire to establish visual proof of their elite status against increasing encroachments from non-nobles wearing courtly clothes.[24] During the rapid period of economic growth that characterized the thirteenth century, seigneurial classes in France were under increasing pressure to distinguish themselves visually from members of non-noble ranks, especially the rising merchant class and the upwardly mobile but non-noble, landholding knights.[25] One can see from the *Livre des métiers*, in which Etienne Boileau records the regulations governing various trades in mid-thirteenth-century Paris, that luxury trades flourished: those dealing with hats and dressmaker's supplies, luxury fabrics, ornaments for hair, gloves, belts, buckles, and decorative chains are mentioned in particular.[26] Large quantities of rich cloth were produced in Beauvais, Etampes, Louviers, Chartres, Tours, and Provins[27] and more readily available than ever to non-nobles wishing to affirm their rising fortunes through the display of costly dress.[28] Royalty for its part made use of lavish processions and ceremonies surrounding the consecration of the king to define royal power through visible extravagance. During these ceremonies, which became increasingly opulent from the reign of Louis IX on, the archbishop vested authority in the king by conferring upon him the insignia of sovereignty: the ring, crown, sword, and scepter, as well as specific items of royal dress such as the dalmatic and royal mantle.[29]

Here the king, literally dressed by the archbishop, is figuratively made by him as well, fashioned out of the visible vestments of his office. The process finds its most telling formulation in the words of Gilles d'Orléans, contemporary of Philip the Bold, who distinguishes between terrestrial kings and Christ in majesty: "the former are not born kings; they are born naked and impoverished even though they are the sons of monarchs or princes."[30] Whereas Christ's royalty exists in his very body, in his nakedness, a terrestrial king's biological heritage, transmitted through the flesh, is not enough to guarantee kingship. He must be *made* into a king through public receipt of the proper clothes.[31] Sumptuary laws in thirteenth-century France hold similarly that noble attire must be reserved for the nobility and appropriate knightly garb for varying levels of knighthood. The very need to insist on such a match attests to an understanding that nobles too, like the king described by Gilles d'Orléans, can be *made* through the public display of clothes. The garments under regulation here are understood not as cultural symbols that accurately reflect one's inherited rank but as traded goods, material objects that, despite bloodlines and biology, might actually produce and visibly guarantee one's social station.

Sumptuary laws flourished in Italy and southern France from the mid-thirteenth through the fifteenth century as urban legislation designed primarily to curb public display of finery among aristocrats, especially women.[32] The sumptuary regulations by royal decree that apply to northern France in the thirteenth century, however, address class boundaries more specifically. They attempt to regulate, along with other expenditures, the dress of non-noble men and the women of their rank who have been usurping the visual distinction previously reserved for members of the aristocracy.[33] In so doing, these royal decrees attest to the power of clothing to overwhelm biological heritage and effectively forge a social body from cloth.

We are told by one chronicler, for example, that after the royal victory against rebellious aristocrats at the Battle of Bouvines (1214) the celebrating populace of "knights, bourgeois, and peasants came out of their lodgings draped in scarlet ... even peasants, inebriated by the thought of seeing themselves dressed in the emperor's clothes, began thinking they were peers of the most powerful men. They have only to obtain a suit of clothes beyond their station to become convinced that their *being* has been transformed."[34] The knights mentioned here in the same category as bourgeois and peasants play at being noble by dressing in costly garb much as the servants who publicly transform their social status by wearing lavish garments during the investiture of Louis VIII in 1223. The *Journal of Nicholas de Braye* describes the opulent dress of those servants as follows: "It's a pleasure to see the golden brocades and red silk garments sparkle in public, on the streets and intersections. Male and female servants revel in the joy of flashy finery, forgetting their station as domestic workers as they gaze on the splendid fabrics displayed on their bodies. Those who did not possess garments suitable for such an occasion borrowed someone else's" (Baudrillart, 168; my translation). Thus do clothes generate social bodies outside economic status and station.

An early example of French sumptuary legislation responds to such sartorial crossing of class lines by setting maxima for the cost of cloth used to dress non-nobles and minima for garments of the aristocracy. The royal ordinance of 1229 draws the line between counts, barons, and distinguished or bannered knights on the one hand and lesser knights and squires on the other: "Counts and barons can provide no more than two sets of clothing to knights and other members of their retinue. Domestic squires cannot wear garments made of cloth that costs more than six or seven sous per yard. By contrast, sons of nobility—counts, barons and distinguished knights (*chevaliers bannerets*)—are prohibited from wearing cloth that costs less than sixteen sous per yard, whereas counts and barons can distribute to members of their entourage cloth costing more than eighteen sous per yard" (Baudrillart, 168; my translation).

When French dress codes begin in earnest in 1279 under King Philip III (Philip the Bold) the categorization of class by dress has become more refined: "It is decreed that nobody, no duke, count, prelate, baron or anybody else, whether cleric or layman, may own or have made more than four suits of fur clothes per year."[35] Here counts and barons are distinguished from a higher nobility that alone has the right to own five fur robes per year. The lesser lords are allowed only two or three such outfits, and burghers cannot possess fur robes at all unless their total wealth exceeds one thousand pounds (Duplès-Agier, 7). Wherever the crucial dividing lines are drawn—between nobles and non-nobles or between the baronial class, lesser nobles, and burghers—these examples of royal sumptuary legislation attempt to enforce class hierarchy by regulating men and women's costly dress. And yet they reveal in so doing how lavish attire can sculpt and fashion noble identities socially, generating sartorial bodies that have no "natural" status.

The royal ordinance of 1294, issued by Philip the Fair, provides the most detailed declaration of what individuals can wear and how much clothing they can distribute to members of their retinue. It begins with its most restrictive limitation—one imposed upon the bourgeoisie—and reiterates the necessity of distinguishing visually the wealthy, bannered knights from all others: "No bourgeois or bourgeoise will wear lesser furs or ermine and they will give up a year from Easter those that they now possess. They will not wear or be allowed to wear gold or precious stones or crowns of gold or silver." Similarly exclusionary provisions restrict the clothing of squires, garçons, and a knight's underlings: "No squire can have more than two suits of clothes per year ... garçons will have no more than one per year. No knight will provide his companions with more than two suits of clothes per year."[36] Much finer distinctions are drawn for the dress of the upper classes, where clothing is understood to reflect landed wealth: "Dukes, counts, and barons owning land worth six thousand pounds or more can have four suits of clothes made for them each year, and for their wives as well, but no more." Whereas knights and prelates alike are only allowed two suits of clothing per year, "knights owning land worth three thousand pounds or more or bannered knights can possess three suits of clothes per year, but no more. No damsel, except the chatelaines of ladies holding land worth two thousand pounds, will have more than one outfit per year."[37]

Despite differences in detail, the motivating factor behind each of these royal decrees is to establish clear and fixed boundaries for regulating physical bodies so that their status can be read accurately in the surface feature of clothes. Each royal ordinance cited here seeks to impose a match between dress and an individual's social worth, whether that worth be defined in land or otherwise, in large units (nobility versus all those of lower status) or fine gradations (knights in general versus knights holding lands of a specified value). And yet these regulatory measures reveal, despite their intent, the degree to which social status might be, at least in part, a production derived from luxury garments themselves, whether begged, borrowed, stolen, or rightfully acquired, a process in which class boundaries were both tenuously produced and easily transgressed, in this case according to what one wore.

The concerns of royalty and nobility in thirteenth-century France, however riven through conflict over other matters,[38] converge in these examples on the necessity of maintaining class hierarchies by regulating standards for appropriate dress. Sartorial extravagance had become a principal means of social definition for the French elite as evidenced both in practice and in the literary conventions of romance, as Gabrielle Spiegel, following Duby, has shown: "The greater the social challenge to the old nobility from the rising wealth of the urban bourgeoisie, the more necessary it became for the nobility visually to distinguish itself through the adoption of a distinctive mode of dress, comportment, and manners. It is hardly accidental that contemporary French romances lavish such exquisite concern on the details of aristocratic accoutrements and appearance or that the royal virtue most often extolled in aristocratic literature is that of largess to a warrior class for whom extravagance was rapidly becoming a form of social definition" (Spiegel, 21–22).

To be sure, French courtly literature of the twelfth and thirteenth centuries is replete with scenes in which luxurious and costly garments appropriately forge the public identity of kings and queens or knights and ladies who wear them. Perhaps most famous among these, the Arthurian romance *Erec et Enide* ends with an extended description of Erec's coronation in which his lavish robes, embroidered by fairies with images of the four liberal arts, provide material proof of his legitimate transformation into a reigning monarch. Chrétien de Troyes deploys the inexpressibility topos to convey the sheer opulence of the ceremony in which Erec receives, along with the royal insignia, a gold crown and scepter (vv. 6496–97), an extravagant "costly, elegant, and beautiful robe" with tassels bearing "four stones: two chrysolites on one side and two amethysts on the other, all set in gold" (vv. 6745–47). So ornate is this affair that it surpasses, we are told, the author's ability to convey its richness (vv. 6640–44).[39]

If King Erec is literally and appropriately "made" from his ornate royal robes at the end of the tale, so too do Enide's luxury garments transform her into the properly aristocratic and eroticized courtly beauty. Earlier in this tale of love and romance, a dramatic change of clothing marks the acceptable social transformation of this heroine, who sheds her lowly status as the daughter of an impoverished vavasor to become a wealthy countess through marriage. In preparation for her public presentation before the approving gaze of assembled male courtiers, she is attired in one of the queen's own dresses, worth more than a hundred silver marks. Thus is her own worn and tattered clothing, a simple *chemise* and torn overdress (vv. 403–5), replaced by a court dress suitable for the ruling elite:

Et le blïaut qui jusqu'as manches
estoit forrez d'ermines blanches;
as poinz et a la cheveçaille
avoit sanz nule devinaille
plus de .ijc. mars d'or batu;
et pierres de molt grant vertu,
yndes et verz, persses et bises. vv. 1575–81

(A tunic lined with white ermine, including the sleeves; at the cuffs and the collar there were, without exaggeration, more than two hundred marks of beaten gold and very precious stones of indigo and green, of deep blue and gray-brown.)

Signaling more than wealth and noble status, this couple's extravagant garments foretell Erec's requisite generosity as a successful monarch and Enide's potential gift giving as queen. Erec will be expected to follow the model set by King Arthur on the day of Erec's coronation, distributing garments widely:

> Ne tant n'osassent pas despandre
> Antre Cesar et Alixandre
> com a la cort ot despandu.
> Li mantel furent estandu
> a bandon par totes les sales;
> Tuit furent gitié hors des males,
> s'an prist qui vost, sanz contrediz. vv. 6621–27

(Caesar and Alexander together would not have dared to spend so lavishly as was done at this court. Cloaks had been removed from their trunks and spread liberally throughout the halls for anyone to take as he wished.)

Indeed, Erec has previously established his public reputation as a generous lord by distributing new clothes at Guivret's court in Tintagel:

> Povres mesaeisiez eslut
> Plus de cent et .LX.IX.
> Si les revesti tot de nuef;
> As povres clers et as provoires
> Dona, que droiz fu, chapes noires
> Et chaudes pelices desoz. vv. 6476–81

(He selected more than one hundred and sixty-nine poor suffering individuals and dressed them in a complete set of new clothes. To the poor clerics and priests he gave, appropriately, black-hooded cloaks lined with warm fur.)

Enide has been shown earlier giving royal vestments to the Church worth a hundred silver marks:

> Puis a ofert desor l'autel
> Un paisle vert, nus ne vit tel,
> Et une grant chasuble ovree;
> Tote a fin or estoit brosdee. vv. 2353–56[40]

(Then she placed on the altar a green silk cloth, the likes of which had never been seen, and a grand embroidered chasuble, completetly worked in fine gold thread.)

Within the frame of courtly romance, these gestures of lavish generosity along with the extravagant and costly clothes donned by the courtly couple are endorsed as an appropriate reflection of their noble status. The system of courtly *largesse* generally, so central to literary depictions of courtliness across a wide spectrum of social ranks, promotes, however, precisely the kind of conspicuous consumption among lower ranks that royal decrees sought historically to curtail. When the distribution of aristocratic wealth required by courtly generosity takes the form of clothing in particular, a problematic confusion of social ranks can easily result. Those very clothes, which serve so effectively as a visual marker of wealth and status among royalty and nobles, can function equally well, precisely because they are detachable goods, to confer visually a similar rank and status on non-nobles and non-royals.

Historically, concerted royal attempts to reserve a privileged mode of luxurious dress for the nobility alone were markedly unsuccessful. In 1301, when Philip the Fair entered Bruges with his wife, Joan of Navarre, the queen is said to have disparaged the many bourgeois women bedecked in silk, furs, and jewels by shouting, "I thought I was the queen here, but now I see there are hundreds of them!"[41] These comments, attributed to the queen, suggest an anxiety about the way that social status could be generated by luxury attire, as opulent clothes were used to make extravagant and visually powerful claims about social standing and individual worth. In the case of the hundreds of bourgeois queens witnessed by Joan of Navarre, costly decorative surfaces have thoroughly overshadowed distinctions of wealth and status figured in other terms. If luxury clothing can "make" Joan of Navarre into the reigning queen, it can just as easily mint bourgeois queens in her image.

Medieval Sermons and the Regulation of Gender

The losing battle waged through sumptuary legislation in thirteenth-century France was preceded by a similarly hopeless struggle on the part of prominent preachers and sermonizers, who began campaigning in the twelfth century to regulate courtly consumption on moral grounds. Whereas certain moralists in the High Middle Ages denounced the aristocracy's excessive consumption of food along with extravagant furnishings, luxury dress in particular was condemned in the twelfth and thirteenth centuries as a mark of undesirable attachment to the material world.[42] Most notable among these was the twelfth-century bishop of Paris, Maurice de Sully, followed in the thirteenth century by the widely traveled cardinal Jacques de Vitry, along with Dominicans Etienne de Bourbon, Humbert de Romans, and Gilles d'Orléans and the Franciscan Guibert de Tournai. Starkly different from the concerns expressed in sumptuary legislation, which takes dress as a significant indicator of social status, these sermonizers tend to see luxury attire as an insubstantial cover without social or spiritual significance.

Not unlike sumptuary legislation, however, moralizing efforts to regulate conspicuous clothing are adversely affected by the economic exchange and circulation of items of dress, in this instance not across class lines but between genders. What happens, for example, to the hierarchy of gender politics when garments representing substantial wealth are passed from men to women? And what ensues when women themselves begin to use items of clothing as currency in the courtly world, when women pass on to men those stereotypically feminine markers of lascivious excess? Clerical authors typically express concern that excessive expenditure on women's costly attire will bring financial impoverishment to the men in question and that men's participation in donning lavish clothes heralds their moral ruin. But what consequences accrue to the women involved? And who profits most from these sartorial exchanges?

Like many medieval sermonizers, Jacques de Vitry admonished his flock to renounce the seductive splendor of luxury goods precisely because they were transitory and to follow the example of Saladin, the sultan of Damascus and Egypt, who was said to have ordered that a small piece of cloth (*modicum tele*) be carried through his kingdom after his death with the proclamation that he could take with him nothing more than this shred of fabric.[43] More pointedly, for the courtly audience, an anonymous commentator on Psalm 38 questioned the spiritual value of lavish attire by asking rhetorically, "Ke sunt devenu, beles gens, vos riches vestiment, cist samit, cil ciclatum, cil mantel vair ne cil peliçun gris que vos avez ouz?" (What has happened, beautiful people, to all your rich clothes, your many silks and the various fur cloaks you had?)[44] Luxurious silks and furs, those items most highly prized in the courtly world for the status they conferred on the *beles gens* who owned them, were said to hold no lasting, otherworldly value.

The moralists' solution to this dilemma is often articulated in exhortations that opulent clothes and adornment should simply be removed, discarded, and summarily left behind. Medieval churchmen tend to make their case by targeting women, since, from the time of the Church fathers, women had been figured, like the character of Fortune in Reason's discourse, as purveyors of artful deception through their manipulation of superficial, decorative adornment.[45] Indeed, not uncommonly, medieval sermons extol individual women who divested themselves, often dramatically, of excessive garments. Jacques de Vitry reports that when St. Bernard's sister, finely clad in magnificent attire, attempted to visit her brother in the monastery, Bernard refused to see her because of her splendid apparel. In response, the sister, we are told, laid aside her vain ornaments and became a nun.[46] The preacher contrasts this newly religious woman with those who spend a great part of the day dressing to appear in public, adducing as a negative exemplum a passage from the courtly lyric "Bele Aelis." The fair Aleis, represented as adorning herself to meet her lover, has fallen under the devil's spell, according to Jacques de Vitry. This commentator actually alters the Old French song's reference to dressing up, making it allude to the archtempter. He changes the original, "Main se leva la bien faite Aelis; / Bel se para et plus bel se vesti" (Vitry, 253; The comely Aelis got up in the morning; she adorned herself beautifully and dressed even more beautifully), into "Quant Aeliz fu levee, et quant ele fu lavee, et la messe fu chantee, et deable l'en ont emportee" (Vitry, 114; When Aelis got up and washed and mass was sung and the devil carried her away). An extreme example of expressing spiritual humility by renouncing worldly clothes is recounted by Pierre de Limoges, who applauds the decision of an unnamed woman to have her tombstone carved with an image depicting herself stark naked. The tomb's inscription privileges the natural beauty of the naked body over the worthlessness of expensive clothes (Lecoy, 483). Since she was born naked and innocent, we are advised, she will exit the world dressed in nudity.

Both the unclothed, considered to be unsullied as newborns, and the modestly clad are rendered figuratively in medieval vernacular and Latin sermons as having traded material clothes for symbolic garments of spirituality. The Franciscan preacher Guibert of Tournai offered women who gave up worldly clothes a vast wardrobe of symbolic ornaments that promised to make them more beautiful,[47] echoing Tertullian's earlier call in his treatise on *The Apparel of Women* (*De habitu muliebri* and *De cultu feminarum*) for women to "cast away the ornaments of this world if we truly desire those of heaven."[48] Tertullian exhorts women further to "dress yourselves in the silk of probity, the fine linen of holiness, and the purple of chastity." And tying this symbolic dress more specifically to love he continues, "Decked out in this manner, you will have God Himself for your lover" (149).

Medieval commentators tend to follow Tertullian's treatise, reiterating his related claim that while lavish dress and adornments of gold, silver, and jewels connote human greed and ambition, women's specific use of makeup, the artful use of powders, ointments, and perfumes to enhance hair and skin, connotes lasciviousness (130–31). Thus does Maurice de Sully in the late twelfth century explain, "Celes qui leur cols et leur cheveuls descuevrent et oignent leur sorcilz et vernicent lor faces come ymage et lacent leur braz et leur costez et vont comme grue a petit pas, chiere levee que l'en les voie, cestes sont fornaises ardanz de luxure et sont mariees au deable et enfers est leur doaires, et si font meint ardoir entor euls par le jeu de luxure" (Those women who bare their necks and heads and grease their eyebrows and paint their faces like images, lace up their arms and bodices and walk with mincing steps like a crane, face uplifted so as to be seen, these women are burning fires of licentiousness married to the devil, with hell as their dowry. They make many around them burn through their lustful tricks; Zink, 373).

At issue in many medieval moralists' condemnation of luxury attire is much more than the ephemeral and artificial beauty that women create or the bodily lasciviousness that female adornment connotes. An equally significant threat of women's extravagant luxury dress for Tertullian's medieval followers lies in the seductive ability of lavish attire to contaminate men's dress as well. As Michel Zink has shown, the lover's passionate desire for the flesh (*luxuria*) is typically conceived by medieval vernacular sermonizers in terms of an equally compelling passion for costly adornment by both sexes (365–77). It is precisely because courtly love requires dressing in high style that Maurice de Sully condemns spring festivities, where *young men and women* gather to dance and socialize, as the work of the devil who can not only "le tans eschalfer / les jors enbelir, / les viandes amender" but also "le gent plus bel vestir" (Zink, 366; warm up the weather, create beautiful days, enhance the taste of food ... make people dress up in their finest clothes). One sermonizer locates the site of worthless luxury garments precisely in the bedchamber of *dames* and *barons*, "l'or et l'argent, le vair et lo gris, e les dames e les biau barons, e les povres deliz de la cambre" (Zink, 376; Gold and silver and furs along with ladies and barons and the simple delights of the bed chamber).

Innocent III extends Tertullian's warning against women who "anoint the face with cream, stain the cheeks with rouge, lengthen the eyebrows" as attempting "to perfect God's creation" (135), to say that "Every man is nothing but vanity. What can be more vain than to dress the hair, anoint the face, level the beard, paint the body, and make artificial eyebrows?" (61). To be sure, anxiety over the deceptive excesses of elite women's trailing gowns is registered in proverbs that typically cite women as the root cause of opulent decoration and dissembling, much as Reason decries Fortune's trailing dress: "Women's gowns are so long and so interwoven with dissimulation that one cannot discern what lies beneath" (Les robes de femme sont si longues et si bien tissues de dissimulation que l'on ne puet reconnaître ce qui est dessous).[49] Their dresses have become their bodies. And the further threat is that men who cavort with such women risk losing the ability to separate their own natural bodies from the contaminating and seductive trap of costly costume: "Those men and women who like prideful costume—two-tone gowns, robes with frontal slits and shoulder knots and long trains—should castigate themselves" (Lecoy, 441, n. 1; Se devraient chatier cil et celes qui ainment les orgueilleuses vesteures, les miparties, les entaillies, les haligotées, les grans trains). If in his *Art of Courtly Love* Andreas Capellanus warns Walter against "a woman who puts her trust in body-paint alone" (44),[50] he also explains that women should not choose a man "who perfumes himself *as women do* or who makes himself glossy with bodily adornment" (Walsh, 43; my emphasis).

The extravagant dress of courtly culture proves particularly troublesome for moralizing regulators of social custom in the High Middle Ages because it allows surface to merge with substance in a number of ways, occluding, most distressingly, what they presume to be natural differences between women and men. Clerical fear of women's seductive opulence carries the ultimate danger that men might no longer be visually distinct from women, since clothing and adornment can obscure biological difference, as we will see in Chapter 4. But moralizing efforts to demonize women as the chief practitioners of conspicuous consumption and thus retain a visual distinction between male and female bodies were no more successful than attempts through sumptuary legislation a century later to police a clear visual divide between members of noble and non-noble social ranks. In both instances clothing, marshaled in a vain attempt to define and delimit differential categories of either gender or social status, seems rather to collude in crossing the boundaries that define those categories. If luxury attire tends to erode rather than maintain distinctions of class and gender, love only aggravates the problem.

Clothes and the Regulation of Love

A number of medieval love treatises reveal what is at stake when love and luxury attire work in concert. Typically the male interlocutors in these accounts argue for social mobility, while their female respondents tend to defend established social rank. This relation, attested here and in other sources, has contributed to the scholarly view that the practice of courtly love was a means of social advancement for the disenfranchised squirine, landless young men seeking to secure their future social position.[51] Reading through the clothes of characters figured in these love treatises, however, suggests that an equally significant threat to the highly codified and highly gendered social hierarchies of courtly society might be found in women's effective deployment of luxury clothes in love.

To be sure, model female lovers are encouraged at times to shun luxury attire and find substantial "riches" in love itself. Speaking in this vein, Drouart la Vache offers what might be considered a secular version of Guibert de Tournai's promise of symbolic clothing for penitent women. He explains that love itself will enrich its female recipient far beyond the wealth that material gifts might provide:

Grans dons ne li demandera;
Mais sa richesse acroistera. vv. 4201–2

(She will not ask him [the male lover] for lavish gifts, but her wealth will increase.)

And yet, women are also often shown to benefit materially from love as the price of amorous indulgence for men is rendered in starkly material terms. The thirteenth-century *Art d'amours* warns male suitors that falling prey to the attraction of surface adornment can lead suitors into financial ruin: "Sachiez que aucun, soubz umbre et semblance d'amour, vous soubtrairont et feroit despendre voz vesturez et votre avoir, et iceulx vous devez eschiver. Pour leurs beaux cheveux, leurs belles vestures ne leurs precieux aniaus, ne les devez vous mie tant amer que vous en soiez deceüz" (Roy, 258; Know that some, under the guise of love, would carry you off and disperse your clothes and your goods. You must avoid them. You must not love them so much that you are deceived by their beautiful hair, their beautiful clothes, or their precious rings).[52] Drouart la Vache's *Livres d'amours* claims similarly that since the practice of love requires extensive giving and generosity, suitors risk impoverishment through *fole largesse*:

Amant richeces riens ne prisent,
Ains les gietent et les espardent,
Mais cil sont fol, qui ne les gardent;
Car, quant il l'ont tout hors geté,
Souvent chieent em povreté. vv. 356–60[53]

(Wealthy lovers do not value material goods but cast them away, distributing them widely. Yet they are foolish not to retain them because when they have given over everything, they often fall into poverty.)

In this view, the danger besetting certain lovers is not avarice, as Reason argued, but its opposite in excessive giving:

Qu'Avarice et Amours, ce samble,
Ne pueent demorer ensamble;
Ainçois le dy por vous deffendre
Fole largesse, qui despendre
Fait sans raison mainte richece. vv. 403–7

(It seems that Avarice and Love cannot exist together. I say this to prohibit you from giving foolishly and expending great wealth without reason.)

Women emerge in these accounts as stereotypical villains: greedy and deceitful schemers who seek to fleece their lovers, become rich from amorous gift giving, and thereby increase their social standing. Beware, Drouart warns male suitors, of women who constantly admire their friends' "robe tres fine" (v. 4274), those who say "toute ma robe est engagie, / mis joel et mes autres choses" (vv. 4276–77; All my outfits are used up, my jewels and other things too), or those who assert "il me faut .i. tel garnement" (v. 4280; I need a certain decoration). These women, Drouart counsels, are not asking for love but for "monnoie" (v. 4292). They seek clothes as a form of currency that will facilitate social mobility. Male suitors need to discern "quex amours est que on otroie, / Par dons, par joiaus, par monnoie" (vv. 4331–32; which kind of love one gives: love in gifts, in jewels, or in currency).

These accounts thus suggest that the practice of love and the acquisition of costly dress can provide women with a kind of financial leverage in heterosexual coupling. Indeed, when describing women in love as products of specific social classes, Drouart explains that some seek to rise in status:

Car les unes sont basses fames,
Les autres sont de noble affaire
Et les autres se wellent faire
Plus nobles que celes ne sont. vv. 698–701

(Some are women of lowly status, others are of noble rank, and still others want to become more noble than they are.)[54]

The man of higher nobility addressing a common girl in Andreas's *Art of Courtly Love* asserts, "Love seeks to adorn (*exornare*) his palace from any social rank, and desires all to serve in his court without distinction and without observing any class preference" (Walsh, 123). Thus does Love preside symbolically over a court outside the established court system, in which female as well as male lovers, both lowly and high-ranking, can in equal measure adorn and decorate its chambers with their elegant sartorial display (Walsh, 125). Drouart la Vache addresses the case of women specifically when he stages a conversation between a lower-class woman and a nobleman who explains:

Qu'Amours ne regarde linaige
...
Fame, qui est de bas affaire,
Est paraus a une contesse
En la court Venus la diuesse vv. 2966, 2974–76

(Love does not take lineage into account. . . . In the goddess Venus's court, a woman of lowly status is equal to a countess.)

Whereas women appear typically in French sumptuary legislation of this period as addenda to their husbands, bearing a rank and status identical to the man's, Drouart depicts women in love as individuals who can independently, if surprisingly, transform their social standing. If the royal ordinance of 1294 stipulates that dukes, counts, and barons "can have four suits of clothes made for them, and for their wives as well,"[55] Drouart portrays individual women in Venus's love court who can be elevated symbolically from "lowly status" to the prominence of a countess. Not only landless men, but women who dress up for love, can barter and work their way through love's court, moving toward a potentially higher social rank.

The Jealous Husband on Women, Love, and Clothes

This is precisely the concern expressed by the *vilain jaloux*, the boorish and bourgeois husband in Jean de Meun's *Roman de la Rose*, whose highly misogynous comments about women's undependability are designed to keep women in their place. The Husband's caustic remarks have typically been understood as antifeminist bombast against women's deception and disobedience.[56] They are that. And yet, reading the husband's virulent antifeminist outburst through the clothes of his excoriated wife reveals the extent to which his discussion of women's fickleness is imbricated with concerns of class status. Indeed, this bourgeois husband's failed attempts to control his wayward wife's attire replay, on a domestic scale, the losing battles waged by royal decrees, which attempt to enforce class rank, and by vernacular sermons, which hope to police gender identity through the regulation of clothes. At stake in this account is more than marital discord or spousal abuse. Like the authors of royal sumptuary legislation, this husband wants his wife to dress according to her social station and not drift toward elite status by wearing inappropriately costly clothes. His avowed desire to curb her licentiousness, consonant with the view expressed by moralists who see clothes as a superficial cover for a female body "naturally" in need of control and direction, suggests a deeper concern. Here the phenomenon of women "dressing up for love" connotes much more than indulging in the pleasure of artifice or preparing to seduce men and corrupt them morally. Courtly clothes in this instance forge a threateningly ambiguous sartorial body that allows the husband's wife to use excessively ornate feminine dress to gain crucial social mobility.

This unnamed wife's effective deployment of the very artifice and adornment used traditionally to deride women, then, productively reconfigures the terms of class and gender hierarchy that medieval sumptuary restrictions and moral dictates fight so hard to maintain. In "dressing up for love" this bourgeois wife can create a body that escapes her husband's misogynous categorizing and his domestic control while improving her social rank at the same time. The luxury garments that chagrin and torment him can leverage marital independence and social mobility for her. In this instance, lavish dress transforms the stereotypically "deceptive" woman into an effectively clothed social body.

Key to the Husband's attack on luxury dress is its association with love and sexual encounter. The Jealous Husband excoriates his wife for dressing up to seduce potential lovers in public rather than pleasing the husband himself in private:

Toutes vos osteré ces trufles,
qui vos donent occasion
de fere fornicacion,
si ne vos irez plus moutrer
por vos fere aus ribauz voutrer. vv. 9278–82

(You will take off all those adornments that give you the occasion for committing fornication. You will no longer go out and display yourself for wallowing with scoundrels.)

In this view, women who do "homage to Venus," as he calls it (v. 8995), take great trouble "to deck themselves out and look attractive" (v. 8987; se parer et cointer):

Et se cointoient et se fardent
por ceus boler qui les regardent,
et vont traçant par mi les rues
por voair, por estre veües,
por fere aus compaignons desir
de volair avec eus gesir. vv. 8997–9002

(They spruce up and apply makeup to fool those who look at them; and they go searching through the streets in order to see, to be seen, and to arouse in men the desire to lie with them.)

Although the riled Husband scornfully characterizes women who dress up and adorn themselves as prostitutes,[57] his remarks reveal how women's skillful manipulation of clothing can make them in fact "mistresses of their will":

Chascune a sus son chief corone
de floretes d'or ou de saie,
et s'en orgueillist et cointaie
...
Toutes estes, serez et fustes,
de fet ou de volenté, pustes;
car, qui que puist le fet estaindre,
volenté ne peut nus contraindre.
Tel avantage ont toutes fames
qu'eus sunt de leur volentez dames:
l'en ne vos peut les queurs changier
por batre ne por ledangier. vv. 9014–16, 9125–32

(Each one has on her head a crown of flowers, gold or silk as she pridefully spruces up . . All women are, will be, and have been whores, by design or in practice, for no man can constrain his desire/will, although he might eliminate the deed. All women have the advantage of being mistresses of their will. One cannot change your hearts, through beating or insult.)

But the husband's remarks send a curiously double message. While reitering the standard clerical fear of women's lasciviousness by casting his wife as a prostitute striding along town streets, the Husband also portrays this bourgeois woman as lounging inappropriately in the idyllic gardens of the courtly elite. Wearing expensive clothes to courtly dances, her head adorned with garlands of flowers, gold or silk (vv. 9014–15), she goes "singing and dancing through gardens and meadows" (vv. 9082–83) with young men, enjoying a life of leisure (vv. 9215–22). The Husband, by contrast, works, selling merchandise to Rome and Friesland (v. 8445). His misogynous rhetoric does not merely express the view of an enraged cuckold who rails against the evils of marriage and women's wiles. This man's remarks also denounce, more specifically, his bourgeois wife's participation in a life of love and leisure emblematic of the upper classes. She is, in his portrait of her, a bourgeoise overdressed for her class.

The Husband casts himself in an equally courtly register as a modified Pygmalion who would ideally dress and create a compliant and obedient female partner. The Jealous Husband complains specifically that he should be the master of his wife's desire precisely because he has clothed, shod, and fed her: "Que cil ribaut mastin puant, / qui flatant vos vont et chuant, / sunt si seigneur de vos et mestre, / don seus deüsse sires estre, / par cui vos estes soutenue, / vestue, chauciee et peüe" (vv. 9197–9202; These wretched, stinking scoundrels, who go around flattering and caressing you, are thus your lords and masters! I should have been their lord, I who support you, clothe you, buy your shoes and feed you). If the Husband, as a bourgeois Pygmalion, has thus fashioned his wife to be a properly obedient mate, she now redeploys that same clothing to create herself anew, beyond the limits of her class.

To be sure, the husband's concern appears to focus at times on the actual, material cost of luxury garments (vv. 9042–53) when he asserts that it is the monetary worth of lavish clothes more than the women themselves, their bodies, or the pleasure they offer, that attracts potential lovers:

Ces orz ribauz, ces pautoniers,
qui ne vos font se honte non!
...
Mes sachez, et bien le recors,
que ce n'est pas por vostre cors
ne por vostre donaiement,
ainz est por ce tant seulement
qu'il ont le deduit des joiaus,
des fermauz d'or et des noiaus
et des robes et des pelices
que je vos les con fos et nices;
car quant vos alez aus queroles
ou a vos assemblees foles,
et je remaign con fos et ivres,
vos i portez qui vaut .c. livres
d'or et d'argent seur vostre teste,

et commandez que l'en vos veste
de kamelot, de ver, de gris,
si que trestouz en amegris
de mautalent et de soussi,
tant m'en esmoi, tant m'en soussi. vv. 9204–5, 9223–40

(These dirty scoundrels, rascals who only dishonor you ... know this and take note: their delight is not in your body or the pleasure you offer, but only in the jewels, golden buckles and buttons, the robes and furs that I, like a fool, give you. For when you go to dances or to your silly gatherings and I stay home, like a drunken fool, you wear on your head gold and silver worth 100 pounds and insist on being dressed in camelot, gray fur, and squirrel, so that I am thoroughly distraught with ill-will and anxiety; I am tormented and beleaguered.)

The frustrated spouse here imagines gold-digging suitors, eager to profit from the expensive attire and jewels at his wife's disposal. And yet he also complains that she has benefited from receipt of costly clothes as gifts from her alleged lovers:

Mes or me dites sanz contrueve,
cele autre riche robe nueve
don l'autre jor si vos parastes
quant aus queroles en alastes,
Quar bien connois, et reson ai,
c'onques cele ne vos donai,
par amors, ou l'avez vos prise? vv. 9283–89

(But now tell me without lying, where, in the name of love, did you get that other costly new outfit which you wore the other day when you went to the dances? I know very well that I am right in thinking I never gave it to you.)

The clothes she has allegedly received as gifts are appropriate for amorous encounters at courtly dances, providing the unnamed wife with an opportunity to meet not just other men but nonbourgeois men.

The Husband's solution for dampening the social aspirations of his spruced-up wife is to remove her deceptively attractive clothes and reveal woman's true (and defiled) nature beneath. Thus does he impose sartorial restrictions reminiscent of sumptuary legislation, limits designed specifically in this case to punish his headstrong and sexually independent wife. He threatens to provide only pitiable clothes in the hope of constraining her amorous liaisons: "N'avrez de moi, par le cors Dé, / fors cote et sercot de cordé / et une toële de chanvre, / mes el ne sera mietenvre, / ainz sera grosse et mal tessue / et desciree et recousue" (vv. 9265–70; In God's name, you will have nothing from me but a coat and surcoat of coarse wool and a hempen kerchief, not finely woven but coarse and poorly made, torn and patched). The Husband's prior claim that clothes are just clothes, ornamental surfaces to be ignored (vv. 8867–74), pales significantly in light of this threat to reduce his wife's independence of mind and body by removing her access to luxury garments. The wearing of silks and brocades, it seems, can in fact effect a substantial change in this woman's social status.

This is not the Husband's overt claim. He argues instead against superficial adornment—whether violets, roses, lilies, or silk cloth (vv. 8997–99)—by asserting that women's deception hides a corrupted, fleshly body, characteristically ugly and vile. This debased female flesh, seductively disguised by false ornament and elegant attire, the husband defines baldly as "dung covered in silk," insisting that a dungheap is still a dungheap no matter how ornately it might be clothed:

Qui voudroit un fumier covrir
de dras de saie ou de floretes
bien colorees et bien netes,
si seroit certes li fumiers,
qui de puir est costumiers,
tex con avant estre soloit.
Et se nus hom dire voloit:
"Se li fumiers est lez par anz,
dehors en est plus biaus paranz;
tout ainsinc les dames se perent
por ce que plus beles en perent,
ou por leur laidures repondre,"
par foi, ci ne sai je respondre. vv. 8878–90

(Whoever might wish to cover a dungheap with silk cloth or cheaper silks of beautiful colors and shapes, it would still be a dungheap and would surely continue to stink, as it had before.[58] And if someone ventured to say that such a dungheap remained ugly on the inside, though it appeared more beautiful on the surface, much like women who dress up (*se perent*) so they will appear (*en perent*) more attractive by hiding their ugliness, I would not disagree / know how to respond.)

Reason, in the passage with which I began, makes a similar claim in decrying Fortune's appeal to lovers who see only her seductive opulence while remaining perilously ignorant of the befouled natural waste that her elegance conceals. Indeed, Fortune shifts constantly, Reason explains, between a lavish, gem-encrusted golden palace and its polar opposite: a dunghill, "Soit en palés soit en fumier" (v. 5857).

Robert de Blois's thirteenth-century tale of the courtly lovers Floris

Chapter 1

and Liriope, embedded in his larger didactic work (*Enseignement des princes, Chastoiement des dames*), draws on the metaphor of dung to argue that the allure of courtly beauty more generally—for men and women alike—can hide not only physical ugliness but also the stench of pride and vainglory:

Esgardez, con li fumerois
Apert beaux qu'est cuvers de nois
Qui le cuevre sus et entor.
La beautez cuevre la puor,
Mais adés est li per desous
Et laiz et puanz et idous.
Ausi est beautez orgoillouse;
Defors apert mout saverouse,
Mais per dedanz l'ordure gist. vv. 89–97

(Consider how the dungheap covered completely in snow can appear lovely. Beauty covers over bad odors but the underside remains nonetheless ugly, smelly, and hideous. Thus is beauty prideful; it appears delicious from the outside but filth lies inside.)

In these examples, dung as a product of base bodily functioning appears to be played off against its opposite in the artifice of beauty and the ornamentation of luxury attire. Attempts to dress up or adorn the courtly body in the hope of gaining honor, esteem, or improved social status will produce no better results, in this view, than similar attempts outside the courtly context, hypocritical efforts to dress dung in golden cloth and silk, as the Ménagier de Paris contends: "Et teles personnes ypocrites resemblent l'ort fumier lait et puant que l'en cuevre de drap d'or et de soie pour ressembler estre plus honnoré et prisié"[59] (Hypocrites resemble the foul, ugly, stinking dungheap that one covers with golden cloth and silk fabric to seem more honorable and more esteemed).[60]

As a way of combating such sartorial manipulations by women in particular, the Jealous Husband proposes that men have lynx eyes to pierce through the lie of surface decoration and aptly perceive the female body beneath:

Mes s'il eüssent euz de lins,
ja por les manteaus sebelins,
ne por sercoz ne por coteles,
ne por guindes ne por toëles,
ne por cheinses ne por pelices,
ne por joiaus ne por devices,

ne por leur moes desguisees,
qui bien les avroit avisees,
ne por leur luisanz superfices,
dom el resemblent ardefices,
ne por chapiaus de fleurs noveles,
ne leur semblassent estre beles. vv. 8901–12

(But if they [men] had the eyes of a lynx, women would never seem beautiful merely because of sable cloaks, surcoats, short tunics, head coverings, kerchiefs, dresses, or fur-lined tunics, because of jewels or other valuable objects, because of coquettish expressions, if one considered them favorably, or because of any sparkling adornments that make them look like art objects. And never because of garlands of fresh flowers.)

These lynx-eyed men would not mistake courtly garlands of flowers as an indication of elite social standing. Nor would they overvalue the artifice of costly, trailing gowns, characteristic of courtly nobility, which the husband asserts are useless to him. "Que me vaut ceste cointerie?" (What use/value is this finery to me?), the husband asks his wife:

Cele robe couteuse et chiere
qui si vos fet haucier la chiere,
qui tant me grieve et atahine,
tant est longue et tant vos trahine,
por quoi tant d'orguell demenez
que j'en deviegn tout forsenez?
Que me fet ele de profit?
Conbien qu'el aus autres profit,
a moi ne fet ele for nuire;
car quant me veill a vos deduire,
je la treuve si encombreuse,
si grevaigne et si ennuieuse
que je n'en puis a chief venir. vv. 8815–27

(This expensive, luxurious robe which makes you celebrate so while it grieves and troubles me. It is so long and trails behind you so, on account of which you become so prideful that I go crazy, how does it benefit me? No matter how much profit it brings to others, it only causes me harm. When I want to take pleasure with you, I find it so cumbersome, so troublesome and annoying, that I cannot come to the point.)

If this husband-lover tends to perceive women primarily as naturally sexed bodies regrettably concealed by clothes, his remarks also describe a dressed-up woman inseparable from her clothes, even at the most intimate moments.

Ornate Attire as Debased Nature

Indeed, the antifeminist comments by the Jealous Husband, Robert de Blois, Innocent III, and other moralists attempting to police what they see as an abuse of sartorial excess reveal the difficulty of maintaining a distinction between clothes and bodies in the courtly world. In fact, their moralizing complaints about luxury dress tend to confirm the extent to which the very categories of debased and ornate are often conflated in courtly culture. When Etienne de Bourbon questions the validity of women's long, trailing gowns he likens them tellingly to animal tails, asking rhetorically, "Comment les femmes n'ont-elles pas honte de porter un appendice que la nature a reservé aux brutes?" (Why aren't women ashamed to wear an appendage that nature has reserved for beasts? Lecoy, 440). The extensive taillike trains of women's luxurious robes in this instance become a sign of the natural, bestial world. Innocent III's *Treatise on the Misery of Man* decries the "horrible foulness" of facial makeup: "Artificial color cannot be compared to the natural. On the contrary, if the face is painted with artificial color it will be destroyed with a horrible foulness" (59–60).

Michel Zink cites preachers who speak regularly in the thirteenth century of "l'horrible pourriture de la corruption des fourures voluptueuses" for men and women alike (376), thus casting decorative artifice not in opposition to debased nature but as its twin. Innocent III similarly decries human vanity in dress by describing how rich robes turn into sackcloth as finery devolves into rottenness: "Silk and richly colored garments and fine linens decay like mud (*in limo putrescunt*); gold and silver, precious gems, and stones are like the potter's clay (*in luto sordescunt*). It is an evil thing that dignity and power are reduced to dust (*in pulvere*), that honor and glory sit on ashes (*in cinere*, 57). He continues, quoting Isaiah, "instead of perfume there will be rottenness (*fetor*); and instead of a girdle, a rope; and instead of well-set hair, baldness; and instead of a rich robe, a girding sackcloth" (Isa. 3: 16–24; Innocent, 58). Here the delights of sartorial excess move beyond the purely decorative or the fleetingly superficial into the natural, as artifice itself becomes a kind of degraded, decaying natural substance.

Earlier, of course, Tertullian had condemned the artificiality of women dying their hair as a kind of filth, much as he equated wearing wigs with uncleanness: "how can they make something attractive by means of filth?"[61] Cyprian too had critiqued virgins who defile their skin with lying cosmetics that "corrupt" the innocent woman's appearance and elicit "foul delight" in male onlookers (63). These examples suggest a more troubling fusion of decorative cover and debased flesh than the Jealous Husband's initial misogynous portrayal of women's adorned bodies as "dung covered in silk" would indicate. The husband imagines bodies from which the astute viewer might lift the deceptive cover to reveal the vile female filth beneath. On the contrary, these examples, along with the Jealous Husband's own extended remarks, suggest that extravagant court dress threatens to conflate garments and bodies so that one cannot separate the two any more than the watery vestments might be removed from the rocky terrain of Fortune's home.

The Jealous Husband's protracted tirade against jewelry, fabrics, and flowers as expensive, impractical surface ornaments that deceive potential lovers and bring shame to the cuckolded husband demonstrates in detail how these luxury items allow a dangerous slippage between figure and ground, a disconcerting blurring of body and clothes that can work to women's advantage. In proclaiming repeatedly his own lack of profit from his wife's fancy dress, this husband shows how it is *women* who profit considerably from extravagant clothing, how wearing luxury garments can increase women's sexual independence and social mobility. If dressing up allows ugly women to appear falsely beautiful, natural bodies to become "unnaturally adorned," and venomous women to seem alluring and attractive, as the husband contends, it also permits married women to appear unmarried (or at least sexually available) and servile wives to slip out from under their domineering spouses' control. The Husband's wholly misogynous remarks, cast in the tradition of Juvenal and others who condemn women as purveyors of artifice, intrinsically wily and deceptive, devilish and disobedient,[62] also provide a glimpse of women who ply these stereotypes to their advantage: women who exercise their will, assert marital independence, and seek increased social standing by fabricating a body from clothes.

Bodies Made from Clothes

A particularly striking example of the potentially transformative function of clothing appears in the satirical *Contenance des fames* from the early fourteenth century (before 1328). Another example of a clerical view on courtly extravagance, this brief account warns men not to give their hearts to deceitful and deceptive women,[63] like Fortune, we might imagine, as depicted in Reason's discourse or the wily wife that the Jealous Husband describes.[64] Yet in critiquing the undependability and changeability of such women, the *Contenance des fames* also reveals how women can fashion themselves productively through clothes. Here Eve-like seductresses who "suck pears and apples" (Orendroit poire ou pome succe, v. 102) remake their image throughout the day by dressing up and applying cosmetics.

Or est un pou descoulouree;
Ore sera toute fardee;
Or est sanz fart, or est sanz painte,
Chascun jour en maniere mainte
Ore se coife, or se lie;
Or se decoife, or se deslie. vv. 111–16

(Now she's a little pale, soon she will be completely made-up; then she's without powder, then without rouge. Every day in many ways she coifs her hair, she laces herself up; then she undoes her hair and unbinds herself.)

And yet, this dangerous temptress appears increasingly courtly as the description progresses. Her dress, in particular, features not only the veil and crown but more significantly the garland worn typically by courtly ladies:

Or a musel, or a nasiere,
Or a frontel, or a baniere,
Or a chapel, or a couronne,
Orendroit sa face abandonne
A veoir, et puis la requeuvre. vv. 117–21

(Now she wears a covering over her face, now just her nose, now her forehead only, now a garland, now a crown; now she unveils her face to be seen, and then covers it again.)[65]

This attractive woman will waste the time, the body, and the very soul of unfortunate men who either "love" or believe her, this poem warns: "Que qui aime et croit fole fame / Gaste son temps, pret corps et ame" (vv. 175–76). This cautionary tale about man's demise at the hand of a seductive, dressed-up woman reveals, however, a more alarming threat: that there is no tangible, fleshly body beneath her fancy clothes.

If the female protagonist in this account conforms in many respects to the Jealous Husband's portrait of a woman dressed up for love, her fancy garments cannot readily be removed to reveal a gendered fleshly body beneath. Different too from the opulent attire that temporarily covers Fortune's nude body, this heroine's courtly clothes are not a luxurious cover applied to degraded female flesh. Her body is rather made out of clothes themselves. When this sartorially fashioned woman stands at the door and opens her cloak, the admirers who look inside the doorway see not lovely skin or curving flesh but another garment, her belt: "Or va a l'uis, si se regarde / Se nesun de li se prent garde. / Son mantel par devant desploie / Pour ce qu'on voie la courroie" (127–30; She goes to the door to see whether anyone has noticed her, then opens her mantle to reveal her belt). If she doesn't have a mantle, she lifts the hem of her surcoat and one glimpses only more clothes, a nice tunic-dress or fur-lined tunic: "S'el n'a mantel, lieve le bout / De son sourcot, qu'on voie soubt / S'elle a bonne cote ou pelice" (131–33). This dressed-up woman takes us back to Reason's description of Fortune's water-clothed rock: a body that constantly sheds articles of clothing without revealing a clearly discernible or solid form beneath:

Mes el ne retient nule forme,
Ainceis se tresmue et reforme
Et se desguise et se treschange;
Tourjors se vest de forme estrange. vv. 5903–6

(It [the rock] does not retain any one shape. Rather it constantly changes and recasts itself, taking on a new shape as it metamorphoses. Thus does it continually dress itself in a different and unexpected manner.)

What "lies beneath" the woman's fine dress in the *Contenance* is not a natural body, whether appealingly seductive or rotten and vile, but still other lavish garments amassed in ample layers to forge a body made from clothes. Couched within this portrait of an ostensibly dangerous overdressed woman, then, we can see the sartorial image of another woman: a woman who apparently stands alone, independent of a male suitor or husband, a woman in courtly dress with no need of the requisite knight to protect her. A woman in love? Possibly. More certainly, a "mistress of her will." This woman is "dressed up for love," but not in the traditional sense of the term. Her endless layers of clothing fashion a sartorial body that challenges and troubles, as it also plays out, the established social and gender positionings of elegant ladies in love.

We have seen, in the course of this chapter, how various clerically derived discourses on the ills of extravagant dress and the dangers of conspicuous consumption contain important clues for understanding the function of clothing in courtly culture of the French Middle Ages. Taken together, Reason's attack on Fortune's lavish gown, the Jealous Husband's tirade against his wife's costly dress, and the anonymous author's depiction of the dressed-up woman in the *Contenance des fames* all denounce clothes as superficial adornment. Yet they also raise important questions for understanding how we might productively "read through the clothes" of courtly protagonists in medieval French literary texts to obtain a new perspective on courtly love.

Three issues that emerge from the foregoing discussion provide the framework for subsequent sections of this book. Part II discusses different ways that female protagonists in lyric and romance can deploy clothes to trouble and influence established paradigms of courtliness. Items of dress and adornment allow these courtly heroines to move subtly into the subject position of desiring lovers, but on new terms. In these instances, pleasure in love, figured through fabric and clothes, can reside in the closeness of touch rather than the distance of sight. Part III shows how reading through the clothes of courtly players poses a challenge to traditional medieval views of sexual difference and women's nature, while redefining the courtly parameters of men's nature as well. Taking clothes into account helps us see how medieval literary texts construct a range of sexual identities as spacings on a gendered sartorial continuum. Finally, Part IV considers the ways the importation of luxury goods to the west through crusade and mercantile exchange forges images of courtly aristocratic bodies as cultural crossing places that defy any simple polarization of east against west. Considerations of social rank and status, which I have addressed in this chapter, affect all three functions of courtly dress as configurations of the sartorial body reshape the terms of desire, gender, and place that we have come to accept as givens in the courtly world.

PART II

Reconfiguring Desire: The Poetics of Touch

Chapter 2
Amorous Attire:
Dressing Up for Love

Scholars who have discussed, debated, critiqued, censured, and often maligned the concept of courtly love since its inception in 1883 tend to agree, whatever their other disputes, on two things: that a literary work embodying the ideology of courtly love will necessarily depict, in some way, both a putatively heterosexual love—generally the unrequited or otherwise vexed passion of an aristocratic male suitor for a beautiful lady—and, secondarily, that the problematic passion will be situated within an idealized public sphere of refined court life in the early Middle Ages. Most scholars of courtly love would not readily characterize the stanza cited below as representative of the phenomenon of highly stylized desire first recorded in love lyrics from southern France at the end of the eleventh century and elaborated over the course of the next two hundred years in northern French tales of knights and ladies.

Indeed, the speaker in this thirteenth-century Provençal lyric is an indignant woman, not a lovelorn troubadour, and her complaint does not address the pain and hopelessness typically expressed by those male poet/lovers of the Occitan love song (*canso*) who decry their rejection at the hands of a beguilingly beautiful but insensitive beloved. On the contrary, this fictive female voice does not mourn the loss of love at all; her subject is, rather, clothes:

Ab greu cossire et ab greu marrimen
planh e sospire et ab perilhos turmen,
can me remire ab pauc lo cor no.m fen,
ni mos huelhs vire que gart mos vestimens
que son ricx e onratz
e ab aur fi frezatz
e d'argen mealhatz,
ni regart ma corona;
l'apostoli de Roma

volgra fezes cremar
qui nos fay desfrezar.¹

(In heavy grief, in heavy dismay, and in dreadful pain, I weep and sigh. When I gaze at myself my heart all but cracks, and I nearly go blind when I look at my clothes [rich and noble, trimmed with fine gold, worked with silver] or look at my crown. May the pope in Rome send him to the fire who untrims our clothes.)

While sharing the dolorous tone of the Occitan love song, this poem actually resembles most closely the genre of political poems known as the *sirventes* and provides, as such, one of the few examples of that genre of troubadour lyric articulated through a female speaker. Indeed, the poet signals the anomaly of this composition by calling it a *sirventesca*, a neologism that overtly feminizes the masculine noun *sirventes*. Although attributed in the manuscript to an unidentified P. Basc (whose gender remains uncertain), the poem has been included in the most recent edition of the women troubadours (*trobairitz*), where the editors classify it as a "woman's performance" to be considered, in their view, among the works of twenty or so known female poets who composed and sang in southern France between 1170 and 1260.² If linguistically, chronologically, and rhetorically the *trobairitz* form part of a poetic tradition in which courtly love was forged, their varied voices argue, in many ways, for a redefinition of courtly love itself. Critics of the *trobairitz* corpus have amply demonstrated how the hierarchy of sexual and linguistic power figured in the troubadour *canso* shifts significantly, and problematically, when women poets move into the subject position and begin to sing.³

However, this female speaker's insistence that clothing rather than love constitutes the source of her distress further complicates the displacement of the male lover's voice by the singing, courting *trobairitz*. The *trobairitz* typically call into question the dynamic of love service that structures troubadour lyric by asking, for example, whether women should court men, or how such singing or courting on the part of women will necessarily change the gendered hierarchy between the lady figured as feudal lord and her supplicant lover in the role of vassal.⁴ Yet the unnamed voice in P. Basc's poem suggests that clothing might be an equally crucial element in understanding the terms of the courtly love scenario and the lady's status within it.⁵

To be sure, the lavish attire of the *trobairitz* with whom we began, her clothing described as "rich and noble, trimmed with fine gold, worked with silver," locates her clearly within the courtly milieu of fictive aristocratic ladies.[6] However, this woman's lament, voiced through "heavy grief" and "heavy dismay" and in "dreadful pain" as she "weeps and sighs," provides a strong ironic echo of the typical Provençal poet/lover's dilemma. His heart also regularly all but cracks from grief, dismay, pain, and weeping as he pines for the haughty ladylove who refuses his suit.[7] The troubadour's doomed passion often results from his fatal gaze upon the female object of desire, in a complex rewriting of the Narcissus myth, as Bernart de Ventadorn's prototypical lines attest:

Anc non agui de me poder
ni no fui meus de l'or' en sai
que.m laisset en sos olhs vezer
en un miralh que mout me plai.
Mirailhs, pus me mirei en te,
m'an mort li sospir de preon
c'aissi.m perdei com perdet se
lo bels Narcisus en la fon. vv. 17–24

(Never have I been in control of myself or even belonged to myself from the hour she let me gaze into her eyes:—that mirror which pleases me so greatly. Mirror, since I saw myself reflected in you, deep sighs have been killing me. I have destroyed myself just as the beautiful Narcissus destroyed himself in the fountain.)[8]

When this stereotypical courtly lover gazes upon the beloved lady he sees his own image, magnified to perfection, but the irresistible woman-mirror-ladylove pulls him mercilessly to a mournful death.[9]

In a deft recasting of this ill-fated love scenario, the female singer/performer in the stanza we have been considering stares into a different kind of metaphorical mirror. Her gaze falls neither on the eyes of an unresponsive lover nor on a deadly image of self-love. When this poet looks at herself, she sees the horror of having expensive clothing denied to her because of sumptuary laws designed to restrict women's lavish dress.[10] Her pain results, not from loss of control, from loss of self or life, but from the more materially conditioned "harm and dishonor," as she explains (vv. 16–17; car nostres vestirs ricx / an nafratz e aunitz), wrought by friars and preachers who, in collusion with the king's stewards and ignoble husbands, have untrimmed women's dress, fiercely tearing from female attire its marks of decorative luxury, its "chains and buttons":

Coras que vengua lo rey nostre senhor
que es semensa de pretz e de valor,
per merce.l prenda c'auia nostra clamor

de la offensa que fan sieu rendador,
que.ls vestirs an naffratz
e desencadenatz
e dezenbotonatz,
...
a l'apostoli mandem un messatgier
que escumenie cosselhs e cosselhiers
e los fraires menors
en son en grans blasmors,
e los prezicadors
e selh de penedensa
ne son en malvolensa
e li autre reglar
c'o solon prezicar.
...
car vilanesca an fag, si Dieus be.m do,
e ribaudesca, nostre marit felo. vv. 23–29, 36–44, 47–48

(Whenever our lord the King may come (from him comes all merit) let pity move him to hear our outcry against the offense brought on by his stewards, who have torn from our clothing its chains and its buttons.... Let us ... ask the Pope in a message to excommunicate council and councilmen and the friars minor, who are greatly to blame for this, the preachers and penitentials who show their ill will in it, and other regulars accustomed to preach it.... For as God grant me grace—our ignoble husbands have done a vile deed.)[11]

As this lyric woman's voice mourns, her lament is for embroidery and silk; her "heart breaks" over the rich gold and silver threads she is no longer allowed to wear:

De ma camiza blanc'ai tal pessamen,
que era cozida de seda ricamen,
groga e vermelha e negra eyssamen,
blanca e blava, ab aur et ab argen.
Lassa, non l'aus vestir!
Lo cor me vol partir. vv. 56–61

(I grieve for my white blouse richly embroidered with silk—jonquil, vermilion, and black mixed together, white, blue, gold, and silver. Alas! I dare not put it on. My heart feels like breaking.)

Love is then not absent from this atypical lament, but substantially redefined.

My interest in beginning with the *sirventesca* is thus not merely to suggest that it should be included, along with the poems of the *trobairitz*, within the parameters of courtly love lyric. Rather I want to show how the focus on female attire offered in this poem will allow us to reconsider the larger phenomenon of courtliness as it has been defined in both medieval lyric and romance texts. Reading through clothes in this anomalous "love" song will help us begin to develop a more accurately gendered and historically specific notion of desire in medieval French culture.

Indeed, the words of this unnamed singer reveal the extent to which we have tended to look past the courtly lady's lavish garments to focus more intently on the image of a male suitor reflected in the courtly mirror. Taking her clothes into account will facilitate a shift away from the well-known poetics of Narcissus's helpless gaze to a poetics of touch, which figures female desire and pleasure in tactile terms. It will mean considering not only what female protagonists wear but also what they do with clothes. In this chapter I will investigate how courtly ladies in both lyric and romance deploy items of dress and adornment to fashion an amorous self in relation to touch rather than sight. In the following chapter, "Love's Stitches Undone," I survey examples of female protagonists who forge alternative subjectivities through clothwork as they embroider and sew.

If the focus on clothing in the anomalous woman's song cited above provides a significant alternative to the standard male love lament in troubadour lyric, an equally powerful staging of sewing and the embellishment of cloth offers cogent alternatives to other courtly figurations of love. Consider the distressed lovers Alixandre and Soredamor in Chrétien de Troyes's *Cligés*. In this canonical twelfth-century romance, the prolonged love laments that record the intense pain and anxiety of partners unable to declare their love openly come to a successful resolution with the exchange of the lady's *chemise*.[12] Queen Guenevere, serving as matchmaker for the distraught lovers, inaugurates a conversation between them by sending Alixandre a garment into which the heroine has purposefully sewn strands of her own hair:

Tant c'une chemise en a treite
De soie fu, blanche et bien feite,
Molt deliee et molt soutil.
Es costures n'avoit un fil
Ne fust d'or ou d'argent au mains.
Au queudre avoit mises les mains
Soredamors, de leus an leus;
S'avoit antrecosu par leus
Lez l'or de son chief un chevol,
Et as deus manches et au col. vv. 1145–54

(She pulled out a white silk *chemise*, finely made, delicate and soft. The threads in the seams were of gold or at least silver. On several occasions, Soredamor's own hands had done the work, stitching next to the gold thread in some places a hair from her head: on both sleeves and at the collar.)

Once Alixandre learns that the garment he wears contains strands of his ladylove's hair, the product of her careful handiwork becomes a highly fetishized replacement for the lady herself:

Liez est quant de s'amie a tant,
Car il ne cuide ne n'atant
Que ja mes autre bien en ait;
Ses desirriers doter le fait,
Nequedant il est an eise,
Plus de Cm foiz la beise.
Molt an fet tote nuit grant joie,
Mes bien se garde qu'an nel voie.
. . .
Tote nuit la chemise anbrace. vv. 1607–14, 1618

(He was delighted to possess this much of his beloved, since he never expected to have her in any other way. Although his desire made him fearful, when he was alone and at ease, he kissed the *chemise* more than a hundred thousand times. He took great joy from it all night, although he made certain that no one saw him.... All night he held the shirt in his arms.)

Most significantly for our purposes, it is the *chemise*, and in particular an account of how the *chemise was made* by Soredamor that breaks the interminable, pained silence of the lovers' prototypical courtly distress. Formerly at a loss for words in Alixandre's presence ("Que dirai ge, fet ele, primes?" v. 1372; "What shall I say first?" she asked), the lovestruck Soredamor initiates contact with her beloved by explaining, in response to Guenevere's prompting, "where this knight's shirt *was sewn*" (v. 1589; ou la chemise fu cousue). Her words, which fill him with such joy, do not detail her feelings or wishes, her regrets or hopes. They recount her work in sewing:

Cil qui de l'oïr a tel joie,
Quant cele li conte et devise
La feiture de la chemise. vv. 1594–96 (my emphasis)

(He [who] has such joy on hearing it, when she tells the queen how the shirt *was made*.)

In this courtly tale, love is declared literally and materially through an article of clothing. A silk *chemise* embroidered by one woman's hands is transferred to the knight/lover by the hands of a second woman whose key question, "how was the shirt made?" inaugurates the love affair.

Alixandre foolishly confuses the garment with the lady whose hair has been carefully threaded into it, as the narrator explains: "Bien fet Amors d'un sage fol, / Quant cil fet joie d'un chevol" (vv. 1621–22; Thus did Love make a wise man foolish, as the knight rejoiced over a strand of hair). Indeed, the narrator's denunciation of Alixandre's improper use of the *chemise* suggests that readers might understand the import of this love token differently. We might, in fact, give more weight to the heroine's work in making or adorning it. Indeed, Soredamor, whose name means "golden in love," has purposefully sewn herself into a garment, we are told: "Por savoir et por esprover / Se ja porroit home trover / Qui l'un de l'autre devisast" (vv. 1155–57; In order to know and establish if ever a man could be found who might be able to distinguish one from the other). That Alixandre lies in bed at night embracing the *chemise*, taking "delight, pleasure, and comfort in an object which itself holds no delight" (vv. 1616–17), certainly constitutes an act of fetishism on his part. But his conflation of embroidered cloth with the lady's body, his confusion of golden thread with her golden hair, also attests in an important sense to the skillful handiwork of a heroine who, in addition to being the beautiful object of desire, has created with her own hands a beautiful object to convey desire. Not unlike the demoisele d'Escalot, who expresses her love for Lancelot by attaching her sleeve to the banner on his helmet, this heroine has shaped in cloth—indeed, sewn into the two sleeves and collar of a *chemise*—a material version of herself that records female desire in courtly love.

Soredamor's sewing, taken together with the *trobairitz*'s insistence on the importance of women's clothing in forging love liaisons, encourages us to ask how gestures of dressing up, on the one hand, and clothwork, on he other, might offer alternative scenarios of lovemaking within established paradigms of courtliness. What is the significance of women deploying cloth in a wide spectrum of activities that range from sewing and embroidering to dressing and undressing themselves and others in the courtly milieu? In what ways do these alternative love scenarios fashion courtly women's bodies into sartorial bodies that might express forms of female desire otherwise missing from standard readings of courtly love?

The Mirror of Narcissus and Courtly Love Criticism

Since Gaston Paris first coined the term *courtly love* and canonized the process in 1883,[13] advocates of critical positions ranging from formalist and rhetorical to Marxist and sociological, from psychoanalytic to feminist, have demonstrated that despite its heterosexual presumptions, the courtly love affair was, in a variety of ways, an affair between men. From the pathbreaking work of Frederick Goldin on the courtly love lyric in the late 1960s[14] to the most recent analysis of Gaston Paris's formative study of the Old French *Lancelot*,[15] many commentators of the diverse and unwieldly phenomenon known as courtly love, whether working in lyric or romance, whether following the scholarly legacy of Paul Zumthor,[16] Erich Köhler,[17] Georges Duby,[18] Howard Bloch,[19] or Jean-Charles Huchet,[20] have outlined paradigms of courtly coupling in which men come together while leaving women out. Indeed, many of us, in attempting to correct the skewed emphasis of earlier scholarly interpretations that tended, at times, to overestimate the influence and authority of the courtly lady,[21] have pursued lines of argumentation that underscore, to varying degrees, Julia Kristeva's pointedly rhetorical question, "Woman, was she ever the main preoccupation of courtliness?"[22] From Christiane Marchello-Nizia's groundbreaking study of the courtly lady in romance as a "metonymy of her husband the king"[23] to Kathryn Gravdal's vivid demonstration of the subtle collusion between the male author and a male audience during scenes of sexual violence against women in Arthurian romance and Old French lyric *pastourelle*,[24] the scholarly answer to Kristeva's question has been a resounding "no." Roberta Krueger contends similarly that in courtly fiction "written by male clerics who supported the values of male aristocratic culture ... women's privileged status in the frame of romance accompanied her displacement from legal and social agency."[25] Peter Allen argues further that even in Andreas Capellanus's fundamental if problematic treatise on courtly love women "have virtually no existence outside of male rhetoric, fantasy and fear."[26]

Three recent analyses drive the point home most clearly, adding new and cogent ways of seeing how the key relationships addressed in courtly love involve men bonding with or reflecting other men. Sarah Kay's nuanced account of sociological and psychoanalytic approaches to troubadour lyric explains how these songs stage a crucial competition between knight and cleric in which the male *lauzengier* (rival poet/lover), not the *domna*, emerges as the key player in the courtly scenario.[27] The reading offers further proof of Kay's earlier argument that the Provençal *canso* constructs subjectivity as essentially masculine, allowing women to accede to the subject position only as alien, hostile, animalistic, morally corrupt or, more attractively, masculinized.[28] Simon Gaunt's analysis of the key courtly text in the romance genre, Chrétien de Troyes's *Chevalier de la charrete*, argues similarly that this founding romance, while ostensibly about love, does not celebrate the heterosexual bond between Lancelot and Guenevere or even a "bond between knights, but a bond between two clerks and their ability to determine the fate of fictional knights."[29] Even Gaston Paris's invention of the term courtly love itself has been shown recently to form part of a homosocial professional discourse at the end of the nineteenth century that attempted, according to David Hult, to tame and suppress the spontaneous and instinctual passions, coded as feminine, in favor of rule-governed scientific observation, analysis, and mastery.[30] Indeed, in a remarkably wide array of critical approaches brought to bear on courtly love in recent decades, scholars have developed a number of effective strategies that read, in essence, "for Narcissus" in the courtly scenario, demonstrating how courtly love often stages key relations between men, while allowing the lady to recede or vanish.

But have women disappeared so fully from the courtly landscape? Whereas we can readily agree with the many critical analyses that have read courtly love as, in different respects, an affair between men, we need not assume simultaneously that the lady has vanished entirely from view. If she is made to function alternately as a facade, a foil, a cipher, or a mirror for her narcissistic male counterpart, she never represents him completely or reflects him exactly. Rather, the lady participates in a relational dynamic of male and female interaction that, while helping to enshrine rigid gender identities, also undercuts them in surprising ways. Recent work on masculinity and sexuality in medieval culture has problematized issues of gender and status, encouraging us to consider the complexity and diversity to be discovered within standard expressions of courtliness.[31] Indeed, we have begun to see that within and around the courtly paradigm of unrequited male desire and putative devotion to women, other models of amorous encounter productively contest the premises of that heteronormative paradigm.

Resistant Readings; Feminist Readings

Roberta Krueger observed as early as 1988 that if the *Lancelot*, as a quintessential tale of courtly encounter, features women characters as desiring subjects who are systematically and "conspicuously written out of the text," the recuperation of female desire within this version of the Lancelot story also challenges female readers, medieval and modern, to "question and resist their narrative appropriation."[32] Even the most overt narrative repudiations of female "nature" in texts such as the *Roman de Silence* invite a critique of the romance's highly contradictory portrayals of sex and gender (126). Krueger argues further that the thirteenth-century spokesman for courtly etiquette, Robert de Blois, whose didactic poems advocate a detailed program for containing the lady's sexuality and safeguarding her chastity, sends a double message to female readers, who can also find within those pages an account of the erotic power that such a constrained female might wield (179–82). These analyses represent a strain of feminist scholarship, evident from the mid-1980s to the present, that builds on studies that record women's disenfranchisement under courtly ideology by looking for points of weakness within those very ideological structures. In *Bodytalk: When Women Speak in Old French Literature*, I argue, for example, that the objectifying portraits of highly fetishized courtly ladies are tempered when we listen to those bodies talk, because in speaking, the courtly heroine moves tenuously into the subject position and tells a different story from the one her otherwise stereotyped body underwrites.[33] In *The Master and Minerva*, Helen Solterer examines the specific genre of the woman's literary response, showing how a range of inscribed and authorial female voices from the thirteenth through the fifteenth centuries critiqued established clerical and masterly discourses about women.[34] Matilda Bruckner explains how the highly problematic voices of the women troubadours speak both within and against the lyric traditions already established by the Provençal troubadours.[35] Laurie Finke argues for a critical double positioning of courtly women in literary texts where female sexuality circulates as a kind of symbolic capital, while women are also often represented as authoritative literary patrons within an alternative economy of exchange.[36] Marilyn Desmond and Pamela Sheingorn show how Christine de Pizan's *Epistre Othea* challenges normative constructions of female sexuality and desire by exploring trans-species sexuality.[37] Roberta Krueger studies single women in the courtly landscape who, unfettered by family, spouse, or chivalric partner, complicate the stereotype of the lady defined in terms of a male partner.[38]

The heteronormative paradigm of amorous exchange in the courtly world is complicated further by a range of affective lesbian relations staged in a wide spectrum of medieval cultural artifacts.[39] Karma Lochrie has shown specifically how female mystical discourse can challenge and subvert the rhetorical traditions and topoi of courtly love, as many female mystics describe amorous union with Christ as a "frightening, violating, and debilitating experience," an emotional state quite beyond anything that conventional models of courtly love might adequately explain.[40] Barbara Newman has explained how three thirteenth-century women mystics, Hadewijch, Mechthild of Magdeburg, and Marguerite Porete, productively combined the literary discourse of courtly love with religious accounts of bridal mysticism to form an anomalous *mystique courtoise*, a brand of erotic expression and female desire that recasts conventional scenarios of courtly amorous coupling, often by conferring dual gender on both the lover and the beloved in question and thus broadening significantly the options for female subjectivity in love.[41]

These analyses do not deny the importance of historical women's lives, the real-life effects of misogyny and oppression, but see oppressive structures, however monolithic they may seem or claim to be, as necessarily fragile, permeable, and open to resistance.[42] It is precisely this type of reading that can allow us to move from the paradigm of Narcissus and the vanishing lady in lyric and romance, where courtly love has been most aptly characterized as an affair between men, to courtly love as an affair among women and men in which subject positions are less rigidly gendered and women can emerge from the locus of the fetishized body. If this move toward increased female subjectivity can be facilitated by resistant reading, resistant speech, and sparring response, the discourse of female patronage or mysticism, it can also be effected, I will argue here, when women dress up in courtly finery and shape themselves and their lives through clothes. But how can this be?

Courtly Costume: An Uncourtly Custom

Certainly courtly clothing does not typically enhance female subjectivity. On the contrary, the traditional scenario of the Occitan love lyric represents courtly clothes as an incidental cover for the alluring anatomy hidden beneath. Troubadour poets plead typically for permission to watch the lady undress, hoping to transform her public sartorial display into the suitor's private pleasure, as when Bernart de Ventadorn asserts, "Et ja no.m volh mais d'a sos pes mover / tro per merce.m meta lai o.s despolha" (I never wish to move from her feet until, through her compassion, she takes me to her boudoir—literally: *to the place where she undresses*; Nichols, no. 42: 41–42), or when Arnaut Daniel imagines the moment "qe.l seu bel cors baisan rizen descobra / e qe.l remir contra.l lum de la lampa" (When she unclothes her lovely body, kissing and smiling and I gaze on it against the lamplight).[43]

Authors of courtly romance, conversely, tend to fetishize their heroines either by describing clothed body parts as if they were naked or more commonly by burying female corporeality beneath extravagant layers of luxurious dress as a hallmark of refined court life.[44] Thus does Chrétien de Troyes describe the courtly Enide, sumptuously dressed according to the directives of the knight who has won her,[45] and displayed before the approving gaze of courtiers assembled to witness her official presentation at court:

Molt estoit riches li blïauz,
mes por voir ne valoit noauz
li mantiax de rien que je sache.
...
molt fu li mantiax boens et fins:
au col avoit deus sebelins,
es estaches ot d'or une once;
d'une part ot une jagonce.
et un rubi de l'autre part,
plus cler qu'escharboncle qui art;
la pane fut d'un blanc hermine,
onques plus bele ne plus fine
ne fu veüe ne trovee;
la porpre fu molt bien ovree,
a croisetes totes diverses,
yndes et vermoilles et perses,
blanches et verz, indes et giaunes,
...
Quant la bele pucele estrange
vit toz les chevaliers au range
qui l'esgardoient a estal,
son chief ancline contre val. vv. 1583–85, 1589–1601, 1707–10

(The tunic was very costly, but certainly the cloak was of no less value, as far as I know.... The cloak was beautiful and of fine quality, with two sable furs at the neck held by fasteners that contained more than an ounce of gold: on one side there was a hyacinth, on the other a ruby brighter than a flaming carbuncle. The lining was white ermine, the finest and most beautiful ever seen. The dark colored silk was finely worked in many little crosses of indigo and vermilion and dark blue, white and green, blue and yellow.... When the beautiful young woman from the distant land saw all the knights in order, looking at her with a fixed gaze, she lowered her head.)

Thus fashioned as a variant of Pygmalion's ivory statue, this romance heroine's innate beauty, received initially from Nature, is richly enchanced by courtly dress: "Car la robe tant li avint / que plus bele asez an devint" (vv. 1633–34). Yet she retains the key function, not unlike the Provençal *domna*, of reflecting her suitor's worth:

De ceste tesmoingne Nature
c'onques si bele criature
ne fu veüe an tot le monde.
...
Que diroie de sa biauté?
Ce fu cele por verité
qui fu fete por esgarder,
qu'an se poïst an li mirer
ausi com an un mireor. vv. 421–23, 437–41

(Nature bears witness that such a lovely creature had never been seen before.... What can I say of her beauty? In truth, she was made to be looked at, for a man could see himself reflected in her as in a mirror.)[46]

If courtly clothing only slightly conceals the desired body of the troubadour's fantasized *domna* or heavily drapes the courtly lady in the objectifying garb of Pygmalion's silent statue, why would the defiant woman's voice in the song with which this chapter began define women precisely in terms of just such lavish and ornate adornment? And why would she proclaim "a summer of love" as an attractive alternative for women constrained by the dictates of husband, preacher, and the king's stewards? The female voice asking that the decorative trimmings, the "chains and buttons," of elite women's clothing be restored, seems to envision both love and clothing in very different terms from the picture of courtly amorous encounter presented in troubadour lyric or Old French tales of chivalric adventure. Indeed, by insisting on drawing her portrait in clothes, the female advocate of this alternative kind of love asks pointedly what happens when the troubadour's lady moves to the other side of the courtly mirror and begins to gaze at and actively create the image reflected therein. This *trobairitz* suggests that the content of that courtly mirror and the very dynamic of the heteronormative love scenario it purportedly reflects can change significantly when ladies, stereotyped most often by courtly conventions as alluring and beautiful bodies or overdressed objects of desire, decide and even resolve to dress *themselves* in courtly finery.

In response to the enforcement of sumptuary regulations that she considers unjust, the offended *trobairitz* suggests two possible courses of action. She herself will eschew the legally sanctioned plain clothes and wear a pilgrim's cloak in protest:

Senhors, faitz me esclavina
que aitan l'am portar
can vestir ses frezar. vv. 64–66

(Lords, make me a coarse cloak; I prefer to wear that when my clothes have no trimmings.)[47]

She envisions other women refusing to wear veil or wimple to don instead the quintessential dress of courtly lovers in the thirteenth century: garlands of flowers:

Sesta costuma ni sest establimen
non tenra gaire, c'an fag novelamen,
...
qi o tractet sia marritz,
per que cascuna entenda
que non port vel ni benda
mais garlandas de flors
en estieu per amors. vv. 12–13, 18–22

(I will not observe this custom, this law they've just made.... May the law's author suffer to see every woman resolve not to wear veil or wimple but garlands of flowers in the summer for love.)

The garland of flowers mentioned here is especially key as an established icon of courtliness in romance texts from *Guillaume de Dole* to the *Roman de la Rose*, where leisurely, aristocratic lovers adorned in costly silks and elegant garlands often gather to sing or dance:

Ja mes, voir, en lieu ou ge soie,
ne verrai gent a tel solaz,
ne tante dame estroite a laz,
en chainses ridez lor biauz cors;
s'ont chevex ondoianz et sors,
chapelez d'or a clers rubiz.
...
et ces puceles en cendez,
a chapelez entrelardez
de biax oisiaux et de floretes. vv. 194–99, 203–4

(In truth I don't expect ever again to see people having such a good time, nor so many ladies in pleated tunics tightly laced about their beautiful bodies, with garlands of gold and bright rubies in their curly blond hair.... There were maidens in cendal silk whose garlands were interwoven with lovely birds and small flowers.)[48]

But the garlands evoked by the unnamed *trobairitz* produce a richly dissonant effect.

Love emerges tellingly in this unconventional poem as an expression of female resistance to marital, moral, and legal constraint, registered in garlands and other items of dress worn by women. As such, the *sirventesca* gives us a glimpse of an aspect of courtly love not often considered. For the politically motivated fantasy of renegade love figured in this *trobairitz* poem stands at a far remove from the obsessive passion that typically wracks the bodies of male troubadours, causing them to become sick and weak and to pale at the sight of their beloved while also ennobling their spirit or attesting to their intrinsic merit. Indeed, this alternative view of love in the *trobairitz* song charts a shift away from courtly love's typical obsession with the anatomically figured body—whether the suffering body of the troubadour lover in lyric and the lovestruck knight in romance or the fetishized body of the desired ladies whom they court; rather, it considers a social body formed from clothing that does not so much envelop or hide but actually creates the courtly bodies of both players in the love scenario.[49]

Clothes and Other Bodies

We have seen in Chapter 1 that courtly love often moves along a continuum from the naked to the dressed body, from the clerical presumption—reiterated in some literary formulations—that clothing conceals a natural, fixed, and biologically sexed body to the conception of a social body derived from the interaction of clothing and other cultural formations. If we follow Elizabeth Grosz's concept of the "social body" as "a cultural interweaving *and* a production of nature,"[50] we can begin to understand the unnamed *trobairitz* as actually forging a body from cloth. From this perspective, the embroidered silk and gold trimmings, for which the *trobairitz* of the *sirventesca* grieves, would not function purely as decorative adornments covering a sexed body beneath. Rather, her sumptuous courtly clothes, along with the veil, wimple, and floral garlands she mentions, could be understood instead as a kind of body in their own right, a type of embodied dress or garments that materially constitute the courtly lady's being. As this inscribed *trobairitz* explains it, in denying to women their accustomed sumptuous attire, the multiple offenders cited in her account have not only "harmed and dishonored our rich clothing" (vv. 16–17; car nostres vestirs ricx / an nafratz e aunitz) but the singer also pleads "that our persons are no longer shamed" (vv. 30–31; per que nostras personas/ ne van pus vergonhozas). To restore those persons will require restoring the clothes that shape and define them. It will mean, in this instance, reconstituting the shattered reflection of a woman who, when she gazes at herself, sees not the eyes, nose, mouth and skin that the troubadour poet typically adores but an altogether different portrait of femininity drawn in clothes rather than body parts:

can me remire ab pauc lo cor no.m fen,
ni mos huelhs vire que gart mos vestimens ... vv. 3–4[51]

(When I gaze at myself my heart all but cracks, and I nearly go blind when I look at my clothes.)

If the woman mirrored in the Occitan *sirventesca* does not conform to the courtly model of compliantly mirroring her suitor's worth and valor, she is nonetheless dressed up for love. Although love has changed, as desire, in this and other examples we have seen, is mediated through clothes that women assemble to fashion bodies formed more from fabric than from flesh.

Looking into the Lady's Mirror: Redefining Courtly Lyric

The glaring insufficiency of the Narcissus myth as a topos that might engage either the adored *domna* or the woman troubadour is revealed most directly in the *trobairitz* Lombarda's pointed critique of Bernart Arnaut's request that she be the mirror for his desire:

Mirail de Pres,
conort avez,
ges per vila no.s fragna
l'amor en qe.m tenez. (Bruckner, no. 21, vv. 17–20)

(Mirror of Worth, comfort is yours. Let the love in which you bind me not be broken for a villain's sake.)

Lombarda responds tellingly with a question:

E.l mirail on miraz
Car lo mirailz e no veser descorda
tan mon acord, c'ab pauc vo.l desacorda,
mas can record so q'el meus noms recorda
en bon acord totz mons pensars s'acorda;
mas del cor pes
on l'aves mes,
qe sa maiso ni borda
no vei, que lui taises. vv. 28–36

(And in which mirror are you gazing? For mirroring and absence so discord my chords that I can barely stay accorded, but, remembering what my name recalls, all my thoughts accord in good accordance; still, I wonder where you've put your heart; in neither house nor hut I see it; you keep it silent.)

She cannot sing as he does, to a mirror that putatively reflects her likeness while it actually records only his image and validates his worth.[52]

Lombarda here raises a crucial issue that informs indirectly a number of *tensos* featuring the *trobairitz*, asking whose portrait is at stake in these debate poems staged most often between a male and a female singer. How is the lady's worth or value to be determined; by what standard of measurement and according to whom? Indeed, Lombarda here calls into question the very process of mirroring that so often structures the courtly love lyric, shifting the ruling metaphor from sight to sound and thereby revealing how the troubadour's purported reflection is based on a double absence: both hers and his own. "Where are you?" she seems to be saying, "Where do you stand as a lover?" (v. 28; E.l mirail on miraz). For if he were truly reflected in her, he would have to stand before her, in front of her and in her sight. Yet she perceives absence, not reflection (v. 29; Car lo mirailz e no veser descorda), making his stance as a lover discordant, the product of a skewed reflection, or not a reflection at all but a tonal dissonance, a putative coming together of two chords which in fact do not resonate in tandem (v. 30; tan mon acord, c'ab pauc vo.l descorda) because this love is "off" key.

What, then, does this skewed reflection say about the lady's "worth," derived traditionally from mirroring him? How are we to assess her value? The established corpus of troubadour love lyric answers this question in terms of the woman's stunning physical beauty: it is the *domna*'s alluring and seductive body, her "delicate form, lovely eyes, soft glance, radiant face, and charming ways" that typically conquer the unassuming poet and inspire his extended lament, "Bela domna, .l vostre cors gens / e.lh vostre belh olh m'an conquis / e.l doutz esgartz e lo clars vis" (Bernard de Ventadorn, Nichols, no. 1, 49–51). Yet Lombarda indicates that the answer might lie elsewhere. And the inscribed female voice in P. Basc's *sirventesca* suggests pointedly that the courtly lady's worth might be assessed more aptly in terms of the clothing she dons to define and fashion her social identity. The courtly clothes she describes replace the troubadour's dichotomy of elegant attire/naked flesh with the image of a social body at once biologically derived *and* culturally fashioned—a body made from clothes that cannot be peeled away to reveal the more alluring substance of an objectified ladylove beneath.

Only a few of the twenty named *trobairitz* speak of clothing, but those who do invoke images of female attire to discuss the worth and power of women in a lyric genre concerned typically with establishing the social worth of men. In her *tenso* with Giraut de Bornelh, Alamanda defends the right of a jilted lady to be angry at Giraut because he openly courted another woman of lesser worth, someone who, in Alamanda's terms, "clothed or naked is not her equal" (Bruckner, no. 13, v. 60; Qe non la val ni vestida ni nuda). That the *domna*'s worth is assessed dually and perhaps differently when she is dressed and undressed recurs in the Comtessa de Dia's account of her betrayal by a lover/knight: "Ara vei q'ieu sui trahida / car eu non li donei m'amor / don ai estat en gran error / en lieig e qand sui vestida" (Bruckner, no. 3, vv. 5–8; Now I see myself betrayed because I didn't grant my love to him; I've suffered much distress from it, in bed and fully clothed). These women troubadours use metaphors of clothing and nakedness to signal how they have been constructed as objects of desire by troubadour admirers who traditionally have drawn the *domna*'s portrait, curiously in line with romance authors' constructions of courtly femininity, as bodies alluringly visible or seductively covered.[53]

Indeed, the *trobairitz*'s fleeting references to female attire outline two realms of amorous interaction in the courtly world, both typically governed by masculine desire: the public realm of the poet/lover's song and the private bedchamber of his fantasized erotic encounter. The Comtessa de Dia's solution to her dilemma addresses the second sphere, turning the courtly tables as she moves temporarily into the subject position and imagines herself to be playing the lover while her male suitor becomes the beloved. It is she who holds the naked knight in her arms and "in her power" while lying beside him: "Ben volria mon cavallier / tener un ser en mos bratz nut.... Bels amics, avinens e bos, / cora.us tenrai en mon poder, / e que iagues ab vos un ser / e qe.us des un bais amoros?" (Bruckner, no. 3, vv. 9–10, 17–20; I'd like to hold my knight in my arms one evening, naked.... Fair, agreeable, good friend, when will I have you in my power, lie beside you for an evening, and kiss you amorously?). This woman poet claims to hold power in the bedchamber by undressing the lover/knight who would typically wish to unclothe her.

The inscribed female voice in P. Basc's *sirventesca* takes the process one step further, reclaiming women's use of clothing as a means of fashioning self-worth in public. She asks the king to "see that our persons are no longer shamed: pray, have them restored to us, high, honored King [by restoring our rich clothes]" (vv. 30–33), and she hopes that women will resolve "not to wear veil or wimple but garlands of flowers in the summer for love" (vv. 20–22). Love, in this newly formed scenario, suggests the possibility of redefining the courtly lady's status, determined previously, in the main, as a mirror for the troubadour's worth or the courtly knight's honor, in terms of clothing that mirrors as it creates her fragile and partial subjectivity.

The point is made most cogently by the troubadour Giraut de Bornelh, who caustically laments the painful loss of his own ladylove, describing her independence from his hold in terms of her self-adornment and her singing:

Mas qui que.s laing
Qu'il ias'e.s baing
E iense sas colors,
E lui cresca dolors
Qu'es en latz et espres,
Jes Amors mais no.ill pes!
No m'es vis ben egaill
C'om desir e badaill
E viva consiros
E q'ella chan
D'autrui dolsas chansos.[54]

(But if a man complains that she rests and bathes and paints her face while his pain grows, because he is tethered and on fire, let him not care for love any more! For it seems to me hardly fair that a man should desire and sigh and live on, careworn, while she sings another's sweet songs.)

Here the lovesick prisoner of passion's flames has no purchase on the woman who "paints her face" and "sings" of another: another man and another kind of courtly love. This second scenario of love, drawn in shadow behind the troubadour poet's own narcissistic portrait, differs substantially from the traditional Occitan lament because the desired woman's body, fetishized and admired by the lover's gaze, has been replaced, much as in the *sirventesca*, by makeup and adornment fashioned by the singing lady herself. But does romance offer any such alternative, a possible counterpoint to courtly ladies like Enide who tend to be cast as Pygmalion's well-dressed statue?

The Mirror of Oiseuse and Courtly Clothing: Rethinking Romance

One thinks most immediately of Oiseuse, the iconic courtly maiden clad in "chapel de roses," rich brocades, silk cords, and lavish ribbons in Guillaume de Lorris's *Roman de la Rose* (v. 553). While the fawning Narcissus in this tale focuses his mistaken attentions on the details of fleshly beauty reflected in love's fountain: "Si vit en l'eve clere et nete / son vis, son nés et sa bouchete" (vv. 1481–82; He saw in the clear, clean water his face, his nose, and his delicate mouth), Oiseuse's sole purpose in the garden of earthly delights is "to dress herself up nobly," as the narrator explains: "Mout avoit bon tens et bon mai, / qu'el n'avoit sousi ne esmai / de nule rien fors seulement / de soi atorner noblement" (vv. 569–72; She led a pleasant life in May, since she had no care or concern for anything other than dressing herself up nobly). And Oiseuse corroborates further, "Rice fame sui et poissanz, / s'ai d'une chose mout bon tens / que a nule rien je n'entens / qu'a moi jouer et solacier / et a moi pigner et trecier" (vv. 582–86; I am a rich and powerful woman, and there is only one thing that gives me pleasure; I have no goal but to enjoy and amuse myself, to comb and braid my hair).

This is not a case of clothes making the woman, if we take that phrase to mean that clothes alone create social status despite the condition of the body they conceal. Rather, Oiseuse is made literally—and, more significantly, she fashions herself—out of the clothes that give her substance. A stunning example of Elizabeth Grosz's configuration of the social body, Oiseuse stands firmly at the intersection of natural and cultural modes. As a "pucele ... gente et bele" (vv. 523–24), this lady's body conforms to the standard physical head-to-toe depictions of courtly ladies like Enide, moving as it does from her blond hair to her tender skin, shiny forehead, and arched eyebrows, continuing further to her straight nose and green eyes and moving downward to her white chest and thin body:

cheveus ot blons come bacins,
la char plus tendre que poucins,
front reluisant, sorciex votis;
...
le nés ot bien feit a droiture
et les ieuz vers come faucons,
...
Sa gorge estoit autresi blanche
come la nois desus la branche
quant il a freschement negié.
Le cors ot bien fet et dougié. vv. 525–27, 530–31, 543–46

(She had hair as blond as a copper basin, flesh more tender than a baby chick, a shining forehead and arched eyebrows.... She had a straight, well-made nose, and gray-blue eyes like a falcon.... Her chest was as white as new-fallen snow on a branch. Her body was well-formed and svelte.)

Less typically however, the mirror into which this courtly beauty gazes reflects the noncorporeal aspects of her being as well, showing us a woman who has groomed and dressed *herself* elegantly:

Son chief trecié mout richement.
Por estre plus apertement
ot andeus cousues ses manches;
et por garder que ses mains blanches
ne halassent, ot uns blans ganz.
Cote ot d'un riche vert de Ganz,
cosue a lignel tot entor. vv. 557–63

(She had arranged her hair with a rich headband, had sewn up both of her sleeves, and wore white gloves to keep her hands from turning brown. She wore a tunic of rich green cloth from Ghent, bordered with decorative cord.)

The second mode of depicting Oiseuse, as a lady accomplished in fabricating a self from cloth and ornament, emerges abruptly at the precise moment when the narrator mentions the mirror she holds (v. 555; En sa main tint un miroër,).[55] Up to this point, our view of Oiseuse has been conditioned by the lover's gaze, underscored by the narrator's laudatory remarks about the beautiful body he has created: "Onques nule pucele n'ot / plus cointe ne plus desguisé, / ne l'avroie hui bien devisé" (vv. 550–52; There was never a young woman more comely or better arrayed; nor could I have described her properly). But the fictive Oiseuse uses the mirror to create another courtly self: that of a lady gazing at her clothed reflection, unaware, we are told, of anything beyond the mirror she holds to fashion that image: "Qu'el n'avoit sousi ne esmai / de nule riens, *fors seulement* / de soi atorner noblement" (vv. 570–72, my emphasis; She had *no care or concern except* to dress herself up nobly). The worth and status of this beauty do not result solely, or even principally, from the look of admiring suitors. If Oiseuse's name suggests leisurely repose,[56] she does not lounge passively as a beautiful object pleasing to the gaze of others but works actively to sculpt an image *pleasing to herself*, as we have seen: "Que a nule rien je n'entens / qu'a moi jouer et solacier / et a moi pigner et trecier" (vv. 584–86, my emphasis; I have no goal but to enjoy and amuse myself, to comb and braid my hair).[57] Indeed, Oiseuse resembles in many ways the autonomous single women charted by Roberta Krueger who exist independently of family, spouse, or male protector.[58] Poised tellingly at the edge of the courtly garden of delights, this well-dressed woman stands alone: powerful, capable, and pleasure-seeking. It is these qualities that her courtly mirror reflects,

Women's Clothes; Women's Pleasure

This bring us to the well-dressed lady in Jean de Meun's continuation of the *Roman de la Rose* (ca. 1168), who is instructed by La Vieille (indirectly through her speech to Bel Acueil) "*to look at herself* in the mirror" for the express purpose of "seeing whether she is well attired" (vv. 13499–500; Mes bien se soit anceis mireé savoir s'ele est bien atiree)[59] before "venturing out to weddings, processions, games, parties and dances, since in these places the god and goddess of love hold school and sing mass to their disciples":

Et face visitacions
a noces, a processions,
a geus, a festes, a queroles,
car en tex leus tient ses escoles
et chante a ses deciples messe
li dex d'Amors et la deesse. vv. 13493–98[60]

To be sure, La Vieille's advice to women in this section of the narrative echoes strongly Ovid's misogynous exhortations in the *Ars amatoria*, which encourage what he terms "naturally" deceitful women to trick, beguile, cajole, and trap the unwary suitor:

Et s'el n'est bele de visage,
plus leur doit torner conme sage
ses beles treces blondes chieres
et tout le haterel darrieres,
quant bel et bien trecié le sant;
c'est une chose mout plesant
que biauté de cheveleüre.
Torjorz doit fame metre cure
qu'el puist la louve resembler
quant el vet les berbiz enbler;
car, qu'el ne puist du tout faillir,
por une en vet .m. assailir,
qu'el ne set la quele el prendra
devant que prise la tendra.
Ausinc doit fame par tout tendre
ses raiz por touz les homes prendre. vv. 13545–60

(Now if she does not have an attractive face, she must cleverly display her beautiful and priceless blond tresses and her neck, when both are well-groomed. Beautiful hair is a very pleasant thing. A woman must always take care to imitate the she-wolf when she goes out to steal ewes. In order not to fail utterly, the wolf must attack a thousand to capture one, since she doesn't know which one she will get before she has taken and held it. Thus should a woman spread her nets everywhere in order to catch all men.)

In La Vieille's account, emphasis falls in particular on the artificial enhancement of individual body parts to deceive male admirers:

Et s'el reperdoit sa couleur,
don mout avroit au queur douleur,
procurt qu'el ait ointures moestes
en ses chambres, dedanz ses boestes,
tourjorz por sai farder repostes.
Mes bien gart que nus de ses hostes
nes puist ne santir ne voair:
trop li en porroit meschoair.
S'ele a biau col et gorge blanche,
gart que cil qui sa robe tranche
si tres bien la li escolete
que la char pere blanche et nete
demi pié darriers et devant,
s'an iert assez plus decevant. vv. 13275–88

(In case she loses color in her complexion, which would weigh heavily on her, she should make sure always to have jars of moisturizing cream in her rooms, so that she can apply makeup in secret. But she must be very careful not to let any of her guests notice or see her; that could cause her great trouble. If she has a lovely neck and white chest, she should be sure that her dressmaker lower the neckline so that it reveals a half foot of her fine, white flesh, in front and back. Thus she will deceive more easily.)

As Ovid's antifeminist words are displaced onto a female speaker in the *Roman de la Rose*, however, the timeworn topos of women as artful deceivers begins to shake loose from its misogynous moorings and to offer alternative possibilities for figuring the lady's worth and status.[61] La Vieille's goal in this speech, as Sarah Kay has shown, is to preserve women's access to pleasure in the face of male exploitation.[62] Even though the stated purpose of such physical enhancements is to enable women to be seen, coveted and in demand,[63] it is significant that these women put *themselves* on display and that their acts of beautification are designed to take the lady out of an enclosed and controlled space, "Et gart que trop ne sait enclose"

(v. 13487), allowing her to move through the public sphere in a way not equally characteristic of the beautiful Enide. Whereas the well-clad Enide is carefully led by Guenevere before the king and his entourage of admiring knights, "L'une a l'autre par la main prise, / si sont devant le roi venues" (vv. 1658–59), where all she does is blush (vv. 1710–14) before being handed off to the king himself, "par la main l'a dolcemant prise" (v. 1717), the ladies counseled by La Vieille are enjoined to move independently through the streets, gesturing broadly with their limbs and their clothes, moving their shoulders, walking with a lively step (vv. 13502–10). They gather up their cloaks and open their arms wide so that both the body *and* its clothing will be deployed to greatest effect, by a beauty who fashions herself through clothes:

Et s'ele est tex que mantel port,
si le doit porter de tel port
qu'il trop la veüe n'anconbre
du bel cors a cui il fet onbre;
et por ce que li cors mieuz pere,
et li teissuz don el se pere
...
a .II. mains doit le mantel prandre,
les braz eslargir et estandre,
soit par bele voie ou par boe;
et li souviegne de la roe
que li paons fet de sa queue:
face ausinc du mantel la seue,
si que la penne, ou vere ou grise,
ou tel con el l'i avra mise,
et tout le cors en apert montre
a ceus qu'el voit muser encontre. vv. 13525–30, 13535–44

(If she is the sort to wear a cloak, she should wear it so that it will not significantly impede the view of her lovely body which it shades, so that the body and the cloth decorating it will [both] be apparent ... she should take the cloak in both hands and stretch out and extend her arms, whether on nice streets or muddy ones, and remember the wheel that the peacock makes with its tail. She should do the same with her cloak, so that she displays openly, to those whom she sees walking around her, both her body and the lining of squirrel, costly fur, or whatever she has put there.)

Here clothing is not principally looked upon by the aspiring suitor but more specifically manipulated by the woman who looks out at the spectator from a body she has arranged, assembled, and displayed, a body she has fashioned from cloth. As Iris Marion Young has explained for clothing of the contemporary era, "Some of the pleasure of clothes is the pleasure of fabric and the way the fabric hangs and falls around the body. Straight skirts with slits may give thigh for the eye, but the skirt in all its glory drapes in flowing folds and billows when you twirl."[64]

To be sure, the association of women with the beguiling deception wrought by makeup, adornment, and excessive decoration forms part of a misogynous tradition found in Ovid and Juvenal and systematically elaborated by the Church Fathers from Tertullian on.[65] However, the force and power of women's adornment looks quite different when read from the point of view of female subjects who use clothing to remake themselves in an image very different from the Provençal *domna* created to reflect the troubadour's worth or the courtly lady of romance whose beauty should ideally reflect the knight's honor.

At least one medieval translator of Ovid's *Ars amatoria* confirms this view. Having chosen, uncharacteristically, to include the section devoted specifically to instructing women in the ways and wiles of dressing up to attract male suitors, this author appends the following note to his translation of Ovid's instructions to women: "Il est prouffitables pour les hommes, car par icel ilz puent savoir les cautelles et decepcions des femmes, et ainssi ilz se puent mieux garder; aussi est il pour les femmes prouffitablez, car par icelui elles puent vaincre les hommes et mectre dedens leurs loys" (v. 281; It [this third book] is useful for men because they will learn from it the ruses and deceptions of women against which they will better be able to defend themselves. But it is also useful for women because with it they can conquer men and bring them under their control [literally, under their laws]).[66] For men in the courtly tradition this advice can caution against the power of female dress as an effective weapon in the battle of the sexes. But for courtly women it can suggest a path to increased social mobility and status.

This is the point made by the *trobairitz* in the *sirventesca* who hopes that women adversely affected by sumptuary legislation will don garlands of flowers and indulge in love. For this female singer, submitting to the dictates of dress, ornament, and adornment means, in some measure, conforming to the laws of women as a group. Indeed, she calls for collective action among the community of noblewomen, alluding specifically to "*our* rich clothing" and "*our* persons," asking elite women as a group to protest unjust laws by dressing in appropriately amorous attire, thereby recasting the image reflected in the mirror of courtly love. The exhortation is especially significant as a call to arms in which the clothes of courtly ladies will replace not only the more traditional armor of knights suiting up for combat but also the metaphorical garb of soldiers in love's army as conceived in the early pages of Andreas Capellanus's treatise: "We must now see what persons are suited to bear the arms of love" (Est nunc videre quae sint aptae personae ad amoris arma ferenda).[67] We have seen what power this newly hewn armor, fashioned of fabric, can provide its female bearers who, like Oiseuse and the women advised by La Vieille, stand on the other side of the courtly mirror.

The Mirror of Courtliness Reconfigured

Following the lead established by the *trobairitz* who performs P. Basc's *sirventesca*, we can see how the courtly corpus in its broadest definition, and even in standard exemplars of the phenomenon, contains cogent alternatives to reading for Narcissus, alternative scenarios in which the courtly lady herself looks into the mirror of love and redefines the terms of the courtly equation. Rather than a reflected image of an embodied self, a beautiful seductive face, and an alluring but elusive body, these courtly ladies see a generative force of clothing that they use productively to make and mold a social body. Rather than being fashioned by a gaze that remains distanced from and mastering its object, such as the gaze of Arthur's knights on the beautiful Enide or any number of courtly ladies who are created, Pygmalion-like, from the desiring look of their male admirers, this social body results from a kind of looking that more effectively blurs the border between self and other. Iris Young has explained how this second form of gazing, which she denotes as "touch," can exist in the reciprocal relationship between women and clothes: "By touch I do mean that specific sense of skin on matter, fingers on texture. *But I also mean* an orientation to sensuality as such that includes all senses. Thus we might conceive a mode of vision, for example, that is less a gaze, distanced and mastering its object, but an immersion in light and color. Sensing as touching is within, experiencing what touches it is ambiguous, continuous, but nevertheless differentiated" (182–83).[68]

More specifically, Young characterizes this reciprocal touching gaze that can connect women and clothing as an alternative form of embodiment and a variant form of love: "When I 'see' myself in wool," she explains, "it's partly the wool that attracts me, its heavy warmth and textured depth.... History documents the measurement of nobility and grace through fabric. Women have been imprisoned in this history, have been used as mannequins to display the trappings of wealth." But "feminine experience," Young continues, "also affords many of us a tactile imagination, the simple pleasure of losing ourselves in cloth," a self formed within and not apart from clothes. "Some of our clothes we love for their own sake, because their fabric and cut and color charm us and relate to our bodies in specific ways—because, I almost want to say, they love us back" (183). Despite their clear material value, clothes in Young's scenario do not function primarily as monetary substitutes, "In these relations my clothes are not my *property*, separate things with identifiable value that I might bring to market and thus establish with others relations of commodity exchange that would keep a strict accounting of our transactions. I do not possess my clothes; I live with them" (184), or within them.[69]

Reading Through Clothes

If we take our cue from Young's insightful comments and attempt to reread the social status and function of courtly ladies *through their clothes*, we will find that courtly love looks very different from the standard paradigms provided by the troubadour lover who stares longingly into Narcissus's mirror or by the valiant knight whose honor and prowess are admirably reflected in the beauty of his ladylove. Whereas the iconic courtly figure of Dame Oiseuse, for example, has traditionally been seen as the stereotypical incarnation of courtly Beauty and *luxuria*, the image of irresistible seduction that marks the gateway to the male lover's fantasized pleasure, Oiseuse can also provide a model for reading courtly ladies who actively fashion their social image before a mirror that reflects not the adoring lover's status but the lady's chosen clothes.

As Young explains for women in the contemporary era, "Women take pleasure in clothes, not just in wearing clothes, but also in looking at clothes and looking at images of women in clothes, because they encourage fantasies of transport and transformation" (184). In the case of medieval courtly ladies, we might amend Young's observation to include women like Oiseuse, the *trobairitz* in P. Basc's *sirventesca*, or the women addressed by La Vieille, who transform themselves while looking in the mirror. Here, as in Young's formulation, the adored object becomes, to a degree, the looking subject: a subject gazing at her own clothes rather than someone else's. And she is a working woman in an important if anomalous way, a woman working with cloth to fashion a self for her pleasure. Certainly the inscribed female protagonists mentioned here are not free to do as they please in shaping the concept of femininity,[70] but the terms of the construction alter significantly when they move from being a mirror reflecting the male lover's worth to women looking at themselves in the mirror. Young's analysis of the special relationship between women and clothing does not evade cultural constructions of femininity that remain capable of oppressing and exploiting women. Indeed, as Judith Butler has explained at length, we cannot avoid the cultural construction we are in.[71] But much as Butler advances the possibility of disrupting established cultural codes by making gender trouble within their fixed sexual hierarchies, Young argues for a similarly disruptive effect through certain deployments of clothing: "The unreal that wells up through imagination always creates a space for the negation of what is, and thus the possibility of alternatives.... It may not be possible to extricate the liberating and valuable in women's experience of clothes from the exploitive and oppressive, but there is reason to try" (186–87).

One could make a similar argument concerning the relation between women and sewing in the medieval French context. Certainly, the image of the oppressed women silkworkers in Chrétien de Troyes's *Yvain* comes to mind most immediately, where imprisoned and impoverished young women are made to sew and embroider in an exploitative workhouse for minimal pay (vv. 5219–5331).[72] Although such realistic details are rare in romance narratives, we do hear of Galeron working as a seamstress to support herself during her far-flung adventures in *Ille et Galeron* (v. 3140).[73] We learn in passing of Joan of Arc being a highly capable seamstress, having learned the trade from her mother.[74] In addition to these examples of sewing as waged work, we find highborn women sewing as part of a requisite model of elite life. The narrator in the *Bien des fames* lists among the attractively civilizing influences of courtly women (v. 39) the making of men's tunics: "Fame fet fere les blïaus, / Si fet fere les homes biaus / Et ascemés et gens et cointes" (vv. 63–65; It is woman who has tunics fashioned that make men attractive, noble, and comely).[75] The heroine of the *Roman de Silence* is enjoined by Lady Nature to go to her room and sew, as a way of substantiating both her "natural" gender and her position as a courtly lady (v. 2528).[76] Lienor's testimony in the *Guillaume de Dole* draws, in part, on a related stereotype of women's passivity and helplessness as they "sit and sew," only to overturn it with a heroine equally adept at the fine points of legal discourse.[77] At the other end of the spectrum, the mute heroine Philomena conveys the story of her brutal rape and physical mutilation by "writing" or "working" the account of her violation into a tapestry that enables her to communicate and bond with her sister.[78] Similarly, Soredamor's sewing, in the example with which I began, helps us to see how this particular form of women's work, although allied precariously at times with the decorative and thus, by implication or extension, with the adornment and fetishizing of women, can also be deployed by female protagonists as an alternative to the highly codified and dissatisfied lament of lovesick partners within the courtly world.

The spectrum of possibilities that lie between the extreme functions of both clothing and clothwork—as either potentially liberating or fundamentally oppressive to women—is well documented in the vast corpus of French courtly literature. None of the examples we have seen thus far of women dressing up for love is free of restrictive overtones, whether the long shadow cast by Pygmalion's ivory doll or the misogynous intertexts for La Vieille's comments. Yet in many instances, the gestures of women dressing up for love or working on luxury cloth succeed in redefining the relation of their bodies to the courtly space surrounding them. If those bodies are depicted at times in terms of their visual appeal and attractiveness to a controlling heterosexual male gaze, there are other moments in which the stultifying visual dynamics of male desire born and nourished from his sight of the beloved are accompanied by and sometimes displaced by female desire expressed through the tactile contact of fabric and clothes. The full force of this alternative paradigm of tactile loving emerges in the subgenre of women's song known as the *chanson de toile*.

Chapter 3
Love's Stitches Undone:
Women's Work in the chanson de toile

A remarkable passage in Gautier d'Arras's *Ille et Galeron* (ca. 1167–78) provides a particularly cogent example of the way sewing, like female attire itself, balances tenuously on the line between empowering and entrapping medieval heroines. Having fallen helplessly and hopelessly in love with the tale's hero, Ille, the heroine, Ganor, decries her fate by explaining that she has been sewn into her clothing by the artful stitches of the Goddess of Love. Amours, here figured as a woman, binds the unsuspecting female lover in the trap of courtly garments, carefully laced and woven with dolorous threads that seem at first simply to mimic the perilous nets that more typically entrap male lovers in the courtly world:

Lasse, quel bliaut me vesti
Amours, quand Ille m'acointa!
Ele coisi, ele enpointa,
de dolor fist la gironee
qui m'a trestote avironee.
De lons sospirs, de griés espointes
fist les coustures et les pointes;
le cors du bliaut de pesance
qui me destraint sans esperance
Amors meïsme le tissi. vv. 6262–71[1]

(Alas! What a tunic did Love dress me in when Ille met me. She sewed and pricked, making the skirt that surrounded me out of sadness. She made the stitches and the pinpricks out of long sighs and dolorous jabs. She made the bodice of the tunic, which squeezes me without hope, from sorrow. Love herself sewed it [this garment].)

This account of Love's sewing appears initially to do little more than engulf an image of women's work within the traditional male love lament, reinforcing amorous paradigms in which Loves strikes, pricks, and binds a helpless victim. Ille, for example, assailed and battered by love's metaphorical arrows, has voiced such a lament of woeful captivity earlier in the tale:

Mais ne sui pas del tot a moi,
et cil qui mie n'est a soi
n'*oevre* pas tot si com il veut,
ains fait sovent dont mout se *delt*.
E! las, caitis, com je me duel!
Je faç tot el que je ne voel.
Amors, qui m'ocit et enserre,
devroit on le mesfait requerre,
qu'ele m'a mis en ceste briçe;
...
E! las por coi m'en sui je plains?
Et ne poroit pas ester estains
li max qui si me trait et tire. vv. 1345–53, 1369–71 (my emphasis)

(I am not at all myself [or in control of myself], and he who has no self-control cannot act fully as he wishes. Rather, he does things that cause him pain. Alas, I'm dismayed by what a weakling I am. I'm doing precisely the opposite of what I would like. One should attribute the evil deed to Love, who has ensnared me and is killing me; she has put me in this prison. ... And Alas! Why am I complaining? The ill that drags me and tears me apart cannot be stemmed.)

To be sure, the amorous distress of female protagonists in romance narratives is sometimes made to follow this male model. At one point, Ille's beloved Galeron utters a highly syncopated version of the hero's dismayed lament (vv. 1378–98), and Soredamor echoes more fully the lengthy complaint of her suitor Alixandre in Chrétien de Troyes's *Cligés* (vv. 865–1038).

By contrast, the account of Ganor's emotional distress and physical discomfort, cast in terms of Love sewing the heroine into a psychologically weighty *bliaut gironee*, adds a significant material element to other, more standard passionate effusions. In this instance, the rhetorical force of Love's prison, figured allegorically and abstractly in Ille's earlier complaint, now resides in a tactile image of women's handwork, grounding female desire and passion specifically in the materiality of fabric fashioned into clothing. In Ille's lament, suffering derives from the sight of a beloved whom the male lover can see but not touch. The male suitor's desire emerges here as a force entirely outside himself and beyond his will (vv. 1345, 1350). Moreover, as the term *oevrer* is played off against *doloir*, the painful sentiments of love emerge in this account as inherently antithetical to the actions and activities of men in the courtly milieu: "Et cil qui mie n'est a soi / n'*oevre* pas tot si com il veut / ains fait sovent dont mout se *delt*" (vv. 1346–48, my emphasis).

Ganor's desire, by contrast, resides close to home, in the garments touching her skin. It is recorded in material, decorative work of sewing and embroidery that aristocratic women often perform, work typically designated in Old French texts by the very term *oevrer* that sets Ille at odds with love. Rather than being "pulled and torn" by the abstract "ills" that plague the male lover in this tale, Ganor is pricked and prodded by the very clothes she wears, feeling sadness in her skirt and weariness in the bodice of her tunic. As Love sews these emotions into the heroine's clothes, her gesture signals the possibility that representations of clothwork might be used more generally to express female desire in the courtly world. The corpus of Old French women's songs known as the *chansons de toile* further develops the affective function of cloth and clothwork only hinted at here. An extended look at the *chansons de toile* will reveal how love's traditional stitches, represented by the Goddess of Love's sewing in *Ille et Galeron*, are undone and resewn by singing women who fashion alternative love scenarios through clothwork.

The *chansons de toile* are unique among the varied genres of women's song in the Old French and Occitan traditions because a number of them feature a lovely lady, object of the male lover's desire, who not only sings songs of love but also sews.[2] Consider *Bele Yolanz en chambre koie*, a mother/daughter dialogue that sets the story of the daughter's love for an unnamed knight within an elaborate context of sewing, spinning, embroidery and cutting cloth:

Bele Yolanz en chambre koie
sor ses genouz pailes desploie.
Cost un fil d'or, l'autre de soie.
Sa male mere la chastoie;
—Chastoi vos en, bele Yolanz
...
—Mere, de coi me chastoiez?
Est ceu de coudre ou de taillier,
ou de filer, ou de broissier,
ou se c'est de trop somillier? vv. 1–5, 11–20; p. 96[3]

(Lovely Yolanz in a quiet room unfolds silk fabric across her knees. She sews with one golden thread, another of silk. Her cruel mother chastises her: "I reproach you for it, lovely Yolanz." . . . "Mother, why do you reproach me? Is it because of the way I sew or cut or spin or embroider? Or is it because I sleep too much?").

The song *Bele Aiglentine*, which opens similarly with the portrait of a woman in love who sings and sews, ties clothwork to desire more specifically through a heroine who works both fabric and words. Initially, the key term *esploita*, repeated in the refrain, refers to Aiglentine's sewing:

Bele Aiglentine en roial chamberine
devant sa dame *cousoit* une chemise.
Ainc n'en sot mot quant bone amor l'atise.
Or orrez ja
conment la bele Aiglentine *esploita*. vv. 1–5; p. 161

(Bele Aiglentine in a sumptuous room *was sewing* a shift in front of her lady, yet the lady knew nothing of the sweet love that burned inside her. Now you will hear how Bele Aiglentine *worked* [my emphasis].)

Later in this song, the term *esploita* doubles for the verb *dit*, used to delineate the heroine's skillful lovetalk. When Aiglentine entreats her lover directly in stanza 6, we are told:

Bele Aiglentine s'est tornee de ci,
et est venue droit a l'ostel Henri.
Li quens Henris se gisoit en son lit.
Or orrez ja que la bele li *dit*.
Or orrez ja conment la bele Aiglentine *esploita*. vv. 33–38; p. 162

(Bele Aiglentine left and went straight to Henri's house. Count Henri was asleep in his bed. Now you will hear what the lovely lady *said* to him. You will now hear how lovely Aiglentine *worked* [my emphasis].)

That women's work in the *chanson de toile* often revolves around three key actions of sewing, desiring, and singing is made especially clear in another version of Bele Yolanz, *Bele Yolanz en ses chambres seoit*, where *cosoit* rimes with both *voloit* and *chantoit*:

Bele Yolanz en ses chambres seoit.
D'un boen samiz une robe *cosoit*:
a son ami trametre la *voloit*.
En sospirant ceste chançon *chantoit*. vv. 1–4; p. 77

(Bele Yolanz was sitting in her chambers, *sewing* a gown of beautiful silk which she *wanted* to send to her lover. Sighing, she *sang* this song. [my emphasis].)

This scenario of a female singer/lover/sewer differs significantly from the standard pattern of the male trouvère in the *grand chant courtois*, which Paul Zumthor aptly characterized a number of years ago as a tautological equation between the acts of loving and singing, such that the meaning of *aimer* is synonymous with *chanter*.[4] For the women figured in the *chansons de toile* I have been discussing, however, the acts of loving and singing are equally imbricated with sewing. Even the songs in this corpus that do not overtly describe their female protagonists as literal seamstresses can best be understood, I believe, in relation to the icon of women working on cloth that the term *chanson de toile* conveys.

But what has sewing got to do with women in love? Why is it that eight of the twenty or so songs normally included in the corpus of the *chansons de toile* locate the young woman's tale of love specifically within a frame of embroidering and sewing?[5] Why is Bele Aye's love lament wrapped in an image of this heroine's clothwork?

Siet soi bele Aye as piez sa male maistre.
Sor ses genouls un paile d'Engleterre,
[et] a un fil i fet coustures beles.
Hé! Hé! amors d'autres païs,
mon cuer avez et lié et souspris. vv. 1–5; p. 159

(Bele Aye is seated at the foot of her cruel governess. Upon her knees, some English cloth which she sews beautifully. Alas! Alas! My distant lover, you have captured and bound my heart.)

What links the opening line of *Fille et la mere*, where "mother and daughter are seated, embroidering gold crosses with golden thread," to the subsequent evocation of Aude's love for Doon, "Aude made such perfect love with Doon"?

Fille et la mere se sieent a l'orfrois.
A un fil d'or i font orïeuls croiz.
...
Tant bon'amor fist [bele] Aude en Doon. vv. 1–2, 4; p. 158

Why is the love that burns Bele Aiglentine framed by a portrait of this courtly beauty sewing a *chemise* (vv. 1–3; p. 161), as we have seen?

Commentators on the *chanson de toile* have seriously underestimated the potential significance of such questions, remarking dismissively that medieval poets could not be expected to embroider much on the simplistic scenario of women embroidering, or asserting offhandedly that in these women's songs, where fabric features prominently, "l'étoffe en est mince" (there is little material).[6] Not uncommonly, definitions of the *chanson de toile* as a genre omit any consideration of clothwork altogether, producing statements such as "The anonymous songs depict their heroine as beautiful, seated in a chamber, unhappy and in love."[7] She is not seen as sewing. From Pierre Bec's characterization of the genre as a doleful lament "placed on the lips" of a young woman to Michel Zink's description of the inscribed female singer as a seated young girl who gets up only to go to bed with her lover, the heroines of this genre of woman's song have been read principally as lovelorn damsels, sighing and pining away in high towers as they "exhale their grief."[8] Even Pierre Jonin, an otherwise careful and sensitive reader of the *chanson de toile*, understands the female protagonists in these songs to have no life apart from love: "Love and love alone gives meaning to the young woman's existence."[9] All too often, the inscribed female singers in the *chanson de toile* have been made to appear stereotypically passive and ineffectual, lovely and looked at. To be sure, these female singer/lovers recount their misfortunes along with their desires, but there is much more to the love stories they tell than pained lament.

Singing or Sewing a Love Song?

Critical debate on the *chanson de toile* has tended to focus primarily on the question, "who's speaking, male or female?" in this genre of women's song, addressing the inherent difficulties of women singer/lovers assuming a subject position traditionally reserved for the male suitor.[10] Since seven of the twenty *chansons de toile* appear only as lyric insertions within romance texts authored by men, and five have been attributed to the male poet Audefroi le Batard,[11] while only nine are found in a collection of anonymous songs called the *Chansonnier de Saint Germain-des-Prés*, the question of authorship remains highly problematic. Critics have debated whether Old French "women's songs," as they are perhaps erroneously called, were in fact composed by historical women or by men ventriloquizing a woman's voice.[12] Are these lyric pieces to be taken primarily as *chansons a toile*, as they are called in the thirteenth-century *Roman de la violette*, that is, folk songs sung at one time by historical women while they worked? Or should we understand this corpus more fictively as songs that merely portray women sewing, as the designation *chansons de toile*, provided in another thirteenth-century text, *Le Lai d'Aristote*, would suggest?[13] Certainly there is some validity to Edmond Faral's assertion that when Guillaume de Dole's mother "sings" her song in the romance by the same name, it is not a woman singing but Jean Renart, the romance author, speaking for his female character.[14] And yet, what is the significance of this double-voiced authorship? Do we want to go as far as Zink in arguing that the *chansons de toile* merely offer the illusion of women singing used by the male poet to craft playful rhetorical scenarios, whether in romance or lyric?[15]

Scholarly efforts to determine a clearly gendered voice in the *chanson de toile*, whether arguing in favor of historical women worker/singers or of all male poet/composers, have generally assumed too strict a distinction between historical women and fictive female speakers and too rigid a divide between categories of gendered authorship. In fact, we are faced instead with the possibility that female subjectivity might be structured rhetorically in the *chanson de toile*, both in terms of female speech and through the varied depictions of women's work that accompany it. Indeed, if the act of singing "like men" appears fraught with cultural contradictions for women in medieval love lyric, the activity of women sewing presents no such cultural paradox. Whereas male and female poets of medieval France share, in different ways, the paired functions of singing and loving, in these songs only women sew. It is important to read the images of women sewing and lamenting that have become prototypical of the *chanson de toile* against depictions of material objects in the courtly household—whether gowns, coverlets, or bed curtains—that attest both to women's skilled handwork on cloth and to their successful work in love.

If Bele Yolanz, Bele Aiglentine, Bele Aye, and Bele Aude seem at first to be statuesque courtly beauties, as their epithets suggest—lovely and desirable aristocratic ladies seated demurely in the *chambre des dames*—they are also shown to be working: sewing, spinning, and shaping cloth. These doubled portraits in the *chanson de toile* bring to mind the vexed cultural positioning of the young women in Iris Marion Young's essay "Throwing like a Girl,"[16] whose status as objects of desire vies uncomfortably with their attempts to perform physical skills. Young explains how girls who grow up in a sexist society tend to throw a baseball as if they were in a beauty pageant. Girls who are conditioned by cultural expectations to be looked at and surveyed, Young contends—whether as the admirer's catch or the rapist's prey—move with difficulty from their prescribed role as object (of desire or derision) into a subject position required to complete the action of throwing a ball effectively. It is less a question of physical strength, muscular ability, or even training that makes girls "throw like girls," in Young's analysis. She cites instead a cultural positioning that constructs girls prototypically to be the object of another's gaze, whether admiring or predatory: "the modalities of feminine bodily existence have their root in the fact that feminine existence experiences the body as a mere thing—a fragile thing, which must be picked up and coaxed into movement, a thing that exists *as looked at and acted upon*" (my emphasis).[17] Whereas the female body has the physical ability to throw the baseball "like boys do," we tend to imagine it as more circumscribed and static. So too have literary critics tended to read female performers in the *chansons de toile* in terms of the dominant western cultural paradigm of the embodied beauty. It would not be surprising, in terms of Young's analysis, that we have paid less attention to the possible significance of these heroines' involvement in clothwork.

The analogy is not exact because, unlike modern sports, medieval sewing is not coded as a stereotypically male endeavor, but singing a love song is. Indeed, if female protagonists in the *chanson de toile* occupy, in many respects, the doubled stance of subject and object that Young finds so problematic in "Throwing like a Girl," these lyric voices also significantly transform, through their stereotypically "women's" work, the cultural status often assigned to that uneasy positioning. To understand this important shift will require that we alter our own critical focus, that we move away from asking whether women in the *chanson de toile* can sing successfully "like men" or only problematically "like ladies" and investigate instead the significance of the fact that these skilled, working women know how to "sew like girls."

We do not yet have an adequate conceptual framework for understanding the *chanson de toile* as a form of lyric composition distinctly different from the songs of the trouvères or the troubadours to which they are poetically indebted and closely linked—much less as a genre that could effectively stage alternate subject positions for its female protagonists. Indeed, what has been least explored is how the women figured in the *chansons de toile* are not only singers but also workers in a number of key ways, including but not limited to sewing. Once we shift the focus of our inquiry from "who's speaking?" to "who's sewing?" we will begin to understand the importance of clothwork and other kinds of work that move the lyric beauties of the *chanson de toile* toward subjecthood. And we will begin to appreciate the complexities of what has been assumed by many to be a straightforward and simple, if not simplistic, lyric genre. In fact, I will argue here that sewing provides a crucial model for understanding how the inscribed female voices in the *chanson de toile* significantly recast the traditional male lover's lament. Perhaps it is time to reconsider the substance (*étoffe*) of the *chanson de toile* in terms of the very fabric that gives the genre its name.

Textured Topics: What Women Have to Sing About

If we return for a moment to the thirteenth-century narratives that contain some of the best-known examples of *chansons de toile*, we will begin to get a sense of the rich diversity and highly varied texture of these women's songs. In the *Roman de la violette*, written in 1227–29, the author, Gerbert de Montreuil, follows the pattern with which we are familiar, describing the heroine, Euriaus, who "delicately adorns a stole and amit" while she sings a "chanson a toile" (vv. 2296–2301).[18] The single stanza that follows depicts a heroine, much like the other women we have seen, who "sits alone and enclosed" as she laments an absent lover (vv. 1–7; p. 166). But when Henri d'Andeli tells how a young woman sings "a verse from a *chanson de toile*" in his *Lai d'Aristote*, the song so designated differs significantly from the model set by Euriaus or Yolanz.[19] The seated woman detailed here is forcibly enclosed by a jealous husband who beats his wife for singing of a far-off love (vv. 3–9, 13–15; p. 86).[20] *Le Roman de la Rose ou de Guillaume de Dole* highlights a third key element of the *chanson de toile* when the hero's mother, after explaining that *chançons d'istoire* were sung in former times by groups of aristocratic women as they embroidered, sings the mother/daughter dialogue *Fille et la mere* to exemplify the genre.[21] This kind of woman's song recasts the lone stance of the isolated heroine like Euriaus in a more communal setting where women work and sing together.

These few examples record the wide range of thematic scenarios that characterize songs that historically have been pulled together under the overarching rubric of *chanson de toile:* women sewing while lamenting a lost lover, women complaining of mistreatment by an abusive husband or father, and mothers and daughters conversing as they work. Two songs, *Bele Amelot* and *Bele Yolanz en chambre koie*, exhibit all three characteristics, while most others display one or two key features.[22] It is crucial, then, to understand how a *chanson de toile* can be built around any one of these elements, and further how songs that feature women sewing might be related to tales of women physically abused or to conversations between mothers and daughters.

Songs Pieced and Woven Together

The *chansons de toile*'s thematic diversity is matched by an equally challenging complexity in form and structure, attesting to an eclectic genre that defies easy classification. The songs have been called "lyrico-narratif" because they combine elements of a lyric lament in the first person with a more linear story of lovers, often in the third person.[23] The dialogic relation that results between the recurrent refrain and the evolving story line is amplified further in those songs used as lyric insertions in longer narratives. There, the words and actions of romance protagonists play off against those of characters figured in the songs they sing.[24] Other intertextual resonances occur when dance tunes combine with songs performed to inscribed audiences, enclosing the lyric mode within a narrative frame that can liberate and expand its story.[25] Some women's songs are pieced together from lines borrowed or recast from other genres, many only to be broken down in turn and inserted piecemeal, or like a patchwork, into romance narratives.[26] The formal structure of the songs themselves combines the courtly lyric couplet and refrain with features more typical of the epic genre: ten-syllable lines joined by assonance.[27]

These kinds of rhetorical hybridity are further amplified in the *chanson de toile* by a hybridity of voice. If we consider, for example, that in *Guillaume de Dole* the "woman's song" *Bele Aiglentine* is sung to the court by a Norman knight and that two songs by Audefroi le Batard also appear without attribution in the collection of anonymous songs in the St. Germain manuscript, it becomes apparent that gendered designations of authorship are actively undermined in this corpus of songs as quickly as they are generated.[28] Indeed, Zink uses *Bele Aleis* to show how the lyric voice shifts unpredictably in the *chanson de toile*, noting that the refrain is often placed in the mouth of the male lover rather than the beloved described in the preceding stanza.[29] Bele Euriaus in the *Roman de la violette* sings a stanza from a *canso* by the troubadour Bernart de Ventadorn in a way that prompts Maureen Boulton to comment that "these lines, although composed by a man, are in perfect accord with the sentiments and circumstances of the woman who sings them."[30] And yet, we confront here the conundrum of a man, the romance author Gerbert de Montreuil, singing for a woman (his female character Euriaus) who is using the words of a man (Bernart de Ventadorn) to "sing as a woman" (if we accept Boulton's formulation).

Thus does the uncertain position of lamenting women in the *chanson de toile* begin to sound like the conundrum of Tancredi, the heroic knight/lover in the Rossini opera *Jerusalem Delivered*, analyzed by Hélène Cixous in her collection of essays *Coming to Writing*.[31] Musing on the difficulty of interpreting the gender of Tancredi, whose role as the chivalric hero is designed to be played by a woman (sung by a female voice), Cixous asks, "Is Tancredi a woman ending or a man beginning to be a woman in order to be a man?" and similarly, "Where does man begin woman begin continue?"[32] Not unlike the Rossini opera, the medieval *chansons de toile* raise similarly complex questions about gender identity and subjectivity.

Indeed inscribed voices in other *chansons de toile* tend to multiply and cross gender lines in many ways. As I have argued elsewhere, *Bele Yolanz en ses chambres seoit* begins as a song sung by a woman, but that purported female voice modulates, over the course of the poem, to include a range of possible speakers who seem to repeat, recast or appropriate the initial speaker's words.[33] The poem's opening stanza attributes the refrain unequivocally to its heroine, stating that:

En sospirant ceste chançon chantoit:
—Dex, tant est douz li nons d'amors:
ja n'en cuidai sentir dolors. vv. 4–6; p.77

(Sighing, she sang this song: "God, how sweet the name of love is; I never thought I would feel pain from it".)

But the poem's second stanza problematizes such a clear-cut attribution by inserting the narrator's descriptive commentary into the woman's supposed speech:

Ne pot ester, a la terre s'assiet.
Dex, tant est douz li nons d'amors:
(ja n'en cuidai sentir dolors). vv. 10–12; p. 77

(Unable to stand, she sits down. God, how sweet the name of love is. I never thought I would feel pain from it.)

When Bele Yolanz's words are interrupted by the narrator's account of her physical condition, the refrain that follows hovers uncertainly between two speakers. Does it issue from the mouth of the heroine, as it seemed in the first stanza, or from the mouth of a third person narrator? The highly ambiguous "A ces paroles et a ceste raison" of the third stanza suggests yet another possibility, that this same refrain may have been spoken by the newly arrived lover: "A ces paroles et a ceste raison,/ li siens amis entra en la maison" (vv. 13–14; p. 77; With these words and this thought her lover entered the house). It seems, further, that someone other than the heroine is responsible for pronouncing the ostensibly feminine words at the end of the third stanza where Bele Yolanz is said to be speechless: "ne pot parler, ne li dist o ne non" (v. 16; Unable to speak, she said nothing).

Who, then, is mouthing this refrain? Is the woman's song in this instance also always a song by someone else? Are other voices somehow hers too? It is not uncommon in the *chanson de toile* for the heroine to speak of herself in the third person. Bele Aiglentine addresses her lover Henri, for example, as follows:

—Sire Henri, velliez vos ou dormez?
Ja vos requiert Aiglen[tine] au vis cler,
se la prendrez a moullier et a per. vv. 39–41; p. 162

(Sir Henri, are you sleeping or awake? The fair-skinned Aiglentine wants to know whether you will take her as a wife and companion.)

In the *Lai d'Aristote*, Alexander's mistress attempts to seduce the philosopher Aristotle by singing a rondeau in which she figures simultaneously as the desiring subject and the beautiful blond object of desire:

C'est la jus desoz l'olive.
Or la voi venir, m'amie!
...
Or la voi, la voi, la voi,
La bele blonde! A li m'otroi! vv. 303–4, 307–8; p. 51

(Down there under the olive tree, I see her coming, my beloved! ... Now I see her, see her, see her, the beautiful blond! I give myself to her.)

In the case of *Bele Yolanz*, we have generally assumed that the voice of the song's seemingly ungendered narrator, who constructs the beautiful female object of desire in the opening stanza ("La Bele Yolanz ..."), remains distinct from the voice of the female singer who speaks directly to her mother, lover, and messenger (or to us) in the more lyric portions of the poem. And yet, in line with the other examples we have seen of the tendency for the woman's voice to float in this genre, these unassigned words could also belong in some loose and indefinite sense to the female singer herself. We might imagine that in the nonlyric sections of the *chanson de toile* the heroine tells her love story in the third person, much as Nicolette disguised as a minstrel tells her tale of love to the unassuming Aucassin in the thirteenth-century chantefable.[34]

Singing of themselves in the third person, female protagonists in the *chanson de toile* play the role of *je* and of *il*, female beloved and male lover, in a way that destabilizes the traditional subject/object positions of trouvère love lyric. Indeed, the female protagonists in the *chanson de toile* can be seen to sing both parts in a number of different ways, moving subtly between male and female subject positions. But as long as we continue to assess these songs by asking, "who's speaking, male or female?" we will misread the real force and complexity of this dynamic gendered interaction. And we will miss the dense and rich fabric of shifting identity formations in the *chanson de toile*.

Sewing and Women's Work

It is, I think, the metaphor of sewing that must be invoked here to explain exactly how the women's songs in this tradition are able to recast significantly the relationship of the singing subject to the adored object in the courtly love lyric. Bele Yolanz's lament, set in a lyrico-narrative frame, is more than circular and self-referential. It wraps around a tale of developing affection enabled and facilitated by a singing woman who, different from the troubadours, trouvères, and even the *trobairitz*, makes love happen.[35] If we look again at the shifting voice of Bele Yolanz, we can see that the song provides us with two distinct, but subtly entwined, portraits of the beautiful courtly lady. The first depicts Bele Yolanz as the sighing, pining lady in love, enclosed in her chambers, stereotypically immobilized, much as critics have tended to read her. When her beloved arrives, this beauty lowers her chin deferentially and falls silent:

Bele Yolanz en ses chambres seoit.
...
En sospirant ceste chançon chantoit:
...
Cele lo vit, si bassa lo menton:
ne pot parler, ne li dist o ne non. vv. 1, 4, 15–16; p. 77

(Lovely Yolande was sitting in her chambers.... Sighing, she sang this song.... She saw him and lowered her chin. Unable to speak, she said nothing to him.)

But woven within this portrait of frozen and mute beauty we see another Yolanz, one who actively pursues women's work—in the form of sewing a gown of silk—and subsequently secures the affections of her beloved: first by preparing to send him the finished gown as a love token, then by extending her beautiful arms to embrace him and hold him close, and finally by declaring her love for him and kissing him assertively:

D'un boen samiz une robe cosoit:
a son ami tramettre la voloit.
...
Bels douz amis, or vos voil envoier
une robe par mout grant amistié.
...
En sospirant ses bels braz li tendi:
tant doucement a acoler l'a pris
...
mais de fin cuer vos aim et senz trechier.

...

Bele Yolanz lo baise estroitement. vv. 2–3, 7–8, 21–22, 26, 33; pp. 77–78

(She sewed a gown of sumptuous silk which she wanted to send to her lover... "Beloved, I want to send you a gown as a token of love." ... Sighing, she extends her beautiful arms toward him and draws him toward her tenderly.... "I love you completely and sincerely." ... Lovely Yolande kisses him assertively.)

The courtly beauty has moved over the course of this woman's song (and indeed at times from one line to the next) from being the adored object of desire to adopting a less familiar pose as a desiring subject. Her lament has substantially transformed the static pose of a distressed, seated woman in the opening line (v. 1; en ses chambres seoit) into an active exchange of sentiment and physical embrace shared by two lovers seated together: "En un biau lit s'asient seulement" (v. 32; p. 78; They sat together alone on a lovely bed).[36] Indeed, women's work in this poem consists in the allied actions of singing, loving, and sewing: successfully joining two partners in love, bringing together the threads of two disparate lives, sewing them together in a union modeled effectively on the act of attaching embroidery thread to cloth, of joining two threads together or of sewing one piece of fabric to another.

As this kind of union, rendered as "sweet love" in the refrain of *Bele Yolanz en chambres seoit* ("God, how sweet is the name of love") takes effect, it becomes increasingly difficult to discern clearly who might be the subject and who the object of such amorous interaction. In fact, a number of the lines that we have attributed to Bele Yolanz and others that have been assigned typically to her beloved might just as readily apply to the opposite partner. If the act of extending "her" arms, "En sospirant ses bels braz li tendi," could grammatically denote an action taken by the male lover, so too the final embrace in which "he stretches her out on the bed" (v. 34; p. 78; a tor françois enmi lo lit l'estent) could, grammatically, be attributed to the beauty herself as "she stretches him out on the bed." Women's work in sewing and singing brings courtly lovers together in a way that unsettles the dyadic constructions of masculine suitor and feminine beloved perpetuated by trouvère lyric.

This does not mean that female singers in the *chanson de toile* move unproblematically into the subject position, as the portraits of Bele Beatrice and Bele Aiglentine show most clearly. Aiglentine's work, first detailed as sewing (vv. 1–2; p. 161) and later expanded to include speaking, as we have seen (vv. 36–38), also includes the concerted actions of "leaving" her house and "going" to Henri's house for the express purpose of declaring the love she has earlier revealed to her lady (vv. 19–21, 39–41; see above, p. 91).[37] These substantial indications of women's work directed toward facilitating the love relationship do not lead, in this instance, to the unqualified success of Bele Yolanz in joining with her lover. Rather, this song stages a more conventional denouement in which Henri literally takes possession of a bride whom he "Si enporta la bele en son païs/ et espousa: riche contesse en fist" (vv. 47–48; p. 162; Carries off, marries, and makes into a rich countess). The song ends with an altered refrain that expresses Henri's joy at having secured *la bele*: Grant joie en a / li quens Henris quant bele Aiglentine a. (vv. 49–50; p. 162; Count Henri felt great joy when he got/had the lovely Aiglentine). But this new refrain, which appears only in the last of eight stanzas, must be read against the insistent announcement of the preceding seven: "Or orrez ja / conment la bele Aiglentine esploita." Indeed, the *bele* who is carried off by Henri in the song's final stanza is not fully defined by the hierarchized paradigm of courtly coupling that the closing lines suggest. Rather she is, like Yolanz, at one and the same time the beautiful object to be looked at *and* the sewing/singing subject who crafts a beautiful object with her hands. We have glimpsed other versions of this heroine earlier, female singers in the *chanson de toile* who sew in a room with other women much as Bele Aiglentine here sits with her lady and her mother (vv. 2, 9), working with her hands and her words to craft a lasting relationship with a man she has loved: "Je ai amé .i. cortois soudoier, / le preu Henri, qui tant fet a proisier" (vv. 20–21; p. 162; I loved a courtly soldier, valiant Henri, who is so highly praised).[38] When Bele Aiglentine takes up the position of the desiring, speaking subject in this song, it is neither as the male poet who traditionally sings the courtly love lyric nor entirely as the conventional ladylove. Indeed, these singer/heroines play both parts at once and in so doing forge a third option for female subjectivity.

La Bele Beatris follows a similar pattern when, at song's end, the courtly Hugues is said to "have" his beloved Beatrice: "And the courtly, educated Hugh got his ladylove" (v. 114; p. 133; Et Hugues ot s'amie, ki fu cortois et duis). And yet the coming together of these lovers has been fully engineered by Beatrice herself, who begins in a now-familiar pose: seated in a chamber, crying and lamenting her fate while at the same time sewing (vv. 1–2; p. 130; An chambre a or se siet la bele Beatris, / gaimente soi forment, en plorant trait ces fis). The lament, which continues throughout the poem, is accompanied, however, by Beatrice's repeated initiatives, which culminate in a mutually fulfilling, shared passion: she sends a messenger to retrieve Hugues (vv. 29–32) and communicate her proposal of marriage (v. 45), and she declares to him directly her desire to be carried off (v. 68), with the result that:

Grant joie et grant desduit orent a l'essambleir.
Tant *s'antreaimment* entre aus loialment sens fauceir,
ke l'uns l'autre ne veult son voloir refuseir. vv. 80–82; p. 132

(They took great joy and pleasure in meeting. They loved each other so completely, truly and without deceit that neither wanted to deny the other's desire.)

As with Bele Aiglentine, the indications of how Beatrice works to facilitate the love relationship must be taken into account and read against the narrator's reference in the song's closing line to a more conventional dynamic in which the male suitor unilaterally "has" his *amie*. Here, as with the other *chansons de toile* I have discussed, Beatrice's clothwork turns profitably into love work.

Mothers and Daughters Sewing Love Together

So too in those songs containing a mother/daughter dialogue, the conversation between women often serves as a model for how lovers might come together in a nonhierarchical relationship, staging before us a community of women who join forces while sewing and speaking long before the lovers are conjoined. In *Bele Yolanz en chambre koie*, with which I began, the heroine who sews also insistently pursues love through actions that are largely verbal rather than physical, repeatedly asserting her unmitigated commitment to taking a lover outside of marriage against the advice of her concerned mother:

—Se mes mariz l'avoit juré,
et il et toz ses parentez,
mais que bien li doie peser,
ne lairai je oan l'amer. vv. 26–29; p. 96

(Even if my husband had sworn, along with all his relatives, that my actions displeased him, that would make no difference to me. I will never renounce this love.)

In the course of the dialogue between mother and daughter that structures this song, Bele Yolanz, initially seated and waiting in her chambers (*Bele Yolanz en chambre koie*, v. 1; p. 96), becomes, through a chain of repeated references to sewing, cutting, spinning, and embroidery that dominate the first, third, and fourth stanzas, an intransigent, determined, and outspoken advocate for another kind of love. It is her continued and persuasive lament that transforms the mother's resistance into support and opens the way for the couple's love to flower. As the two women sew and speak together, the mother's position alters significantly from opposition, voiced in the refrain, "Chastoi vos en, bele Yolanz" (I reproach you for it, Lovely Yolanz) to consent, in the final line: "Covegne t'en, bele Yolanz" (v. 30; p. 96; Do what suits you, Lovely Yolanz). If this heroine remains "bele" to the end, her beauty is reconfigured as belonging to a sewing, working, singing woman who, rather than being pursued by a lamenting and helpless suitor, pursues a renegade and unconventional love for him.

Similarly, the song entitled *Fille et la mere*, which stages a mother and daughter embroidering together, charts a progression from the young woman who *makes* crosses with golden thread (vv. 1–2; p. 158; Fille et la mere se sieent a l'orfrois. / A un fil d'or i *font* orïeuls croiz) to that same woman *making* "sweet love" with her beloved, Doon, in the refrain (v. 8; p. 158; Tant bon'amor *fist* bele Aude en Doon). Initially, the mother's advice appears to pit the productive activities of sewing, spinning and embroidering against fruitless loving, as she counsels her silent daughter to forget love and learn women's work instead:

—Aprenez, fille, a coudre et a filer,
et en l'orfrois les oriex crois lever.
L'amor Doon vos covient oublier. vv. 5–7; p. 158

(Learn to sew and spin, daughter, and to embroider golden crosses. You should forget about loving Doon.)

However, the refrain that closes both stanzas of the song underscores the daughter's success in making love work. While remaining the beautiful object of the narrator's gaze and our own, this courtly lady is also sewing and forging a love liaison.

Bele Amelot, the only heroine of the *chanson de toile* shown to spin rather than sew, exhibits a singular determination not to marry without love, reminiscent of Yolanz's commitment not to abandon love for a loveless marriage. Amelot's repeated cry in the song's refrain, "Deus, doneis m'a marit Garin, / mon dous amin" (God, give me my sweet love Garin as a husband), records both a fear of an arranged marriage that would lack affection between partners and a commitment to pursuing an impassioned love match:

Per Deu, meire, trop dout prandre signor:
c'est un merchiez dont se plaignent plusors.

Car si ne m'aimmet et il ne rait m'amor,
leis lui vivrai a honte et a dolour. vv. 31–34; p. 103

(In God's name mother, I am so afraid to marry. It's an undertaking that many complain of. If he does not love me nor I him, I will live alongside him in shame and dismay).

Indeed, the initial lament of this *bele*, "soule an chambre," becomes a rallying cry that the concerned mother supports and executes, acting in concert with her daughter against the husband's plans for an arranged marriage:

Amelot ot ceu ke sa meire dist,
ke ces peires li veult doneir marit.
...
La meire vit son enfant angossous.
Trop bial li dist: -Fille, rahaitiez vos.
Garin ameis, si l'averés a spous. vv. 49–50, 61–63; pp. 103–4

(Amelot heard her mother say that her father wanted to marry her off ... Seeing her child distressed, the mother said to her, "Daughter, console yourself. You love Garin and will have him for a spouse".)

It is because of the mother's intervention, here seated (*s'asiet*, v. 25) with Amelot as the daughter spins, much as Bele Aude sits sewing with her mother (*se sieent*, v. 1), that the lovers in this song succeed in coming together: "La meire ... c'ansamble mist et l'amie et l'amin" (vv. 67, 69; p. 104; The mother brought the beloved and her lover together). If *Fille et la mere* shows how Aude succeeds in "getting" Doon in the end, Bele Amelot triumphs similarly in securing Garin: "Amelot tot enisi / ot Garin son amin" (vv. 71–72; p. 104; Thus did Amelot have her lover Garin). Once again, women's clothwork sets the stage for women's work in love as the lifeless beauty of trouvère lyric begins to seek, pursue, entreat, and effectively secure a mutually shared passion. If trouvère lament often records unfulfilled and prolonged male desire, the women who sew in the *chanson de toile* sing of love that works, like needles through cloth, pulling desirous partners into mutual embrace.

Beauties Who Wear Clothes or Make Them?

To stage women sitting, sewing, and loving also reconfigures the established courtly relationship between women and clothes, in which women's bodies are elegantly dressed up and ornamented as objects of desire constructed by a male gaze.[39] Descriptions of lavishly attired women abound in romance texts of the twelfth century in particular, but they persist in thirteenth-century courtly tales and emerge most strikingly in the romance that contains five inserted *chansons de toile*, *Le Roman de la Rose ou de Guillaume de Dole*.[40] These "countesses sheathed in samite silk and cloth of gold" and "maidens in cendal silk" whose "graceful bodies and firm little breasts were greatly admired" are the courtly beauties whom knights desire, adore, and pursue. By contrast, the *chansons de toile* often recast the lovely lady's embellished and seductive body into a working body, unreceptive to the suitor's desiring gaze. Indeed, when women's body parts are mentioned within the portraits of these female singer/sewers they are covered, not alluringly shapely, and covered specifically by the cloth that the heroines handle and work. Bele Aye has "Sor les genouls un paile d'Engleterre / [et] a un fil i fet coustures bele" (vv. 2–3; p. 159; On her knees, a cloth from England in which she makes beautiful stitches). In *Quant vient en mai*, Bele Erembors seated at the window has on her knees colored cloth (vv. 7–8; p. 93), as does Yolanz (v. 2; p. 96). The standard description of the fetishized courtly woman's delicate white hands is also replaced in these songs by the suggestion of hands that work the needle and pull the thread:

An chambre a or se siet la bele Beatris,
gaimente soi forment, en plorant trait ces fis. vv. 1–2; p. 130[41]

(Bele Beatrice is seated in a golden chamber. She laments loudly and crying, pulls/draws out the threads of her work.)

Through its portraits of women sewing the *chanson de toile* brings into clear relief a key fact that the paradigm of the elegantly dressed courtly beauty occludes: the rich and sumptuous cloth used to dress up ladies in the courtly world is often worked and embellished by women themselves.

So too do these singing/sewing women recast at times the convention of courtly men offering articles of costly clothing as tokens of love.[42] When Bele Yolanz sews a garment for her *bels douz amis* (vv. 1–3; p. 77; *Bele Yolanz en ses chambres seoit*), we can see how the working women of the *chanson de toile* do more than simply displace the male suitor as the desiring subject of the love song. She has literally produced the garment that will bring the lovers together, sewing her desire into the cloth that will seek to establish love on new terms. Having first fashioned her lover's gown, she will now thread her sentiments together with his in an amorous interchange more delicate and complex than the trouvère's commercialized quid pro quo of clothes tendered to buy love.[43] Bele Yolanz's song concludes with an image of the union she has successfully engineered, framed again by clothwork: the ladylover kisses her *amis* assertively as the two are seated together on a beautiful, rich bed (vv. 31–32; p. 78). The lovers' bed, often enclosed by decorated "cortines"[44] or covered with rich silks ("pailes") and figured here as a site of alternative lovemaking, is shown in other *chansons de toile* to result from skilled work by women's hands. When Bele Erembors is joined by her lover Raynaud at the close of *Quant vient en Mai*, the pair sit next to one another on "a bed decorated with embroidered flowers" (vv. 31–33; p. 94).[45] Thus do the images of women sewing and embroidering together in the opening lines of a number of *chansons de toile* often resonate with closing lines that further evoke women's skilled handwork in love and on cloth.

Other Philomenas?

The complex positioning of these beautiful working women recalls the function of the Old French Philomena, as I have analyzed her in *Bodytalk: When Women Speak in Old French Literature*. The female protagonist in that romance moves from the position of the beautiful object of male desire into the subject position as she weaves a beautiful tapestry to be looked at and adored. Instead of the heroine's beauty being fashioned by the Pygmalion-like gaze of interested suitors—or, in Philomena's case, an inflamed rapist—beauty here results from clothwork done by women's hands. The women's work that helps rewrite the courtly love story in this unconventional romance is not limited to Philomena's weaving and embroidery but crucially includes its narrative counterpart in her sister's shockingly brutal actions of cooking.[46] The two women work together with their hands to resist a system that trades, entraps, and violates them in the name of love.

Less violently, female protagonists of the *chansons de toile* often depicted as lovely ladies sewing also perform related forms of women's work used specifically to rewrite the lyric love lament. Whether through imploring, beseeching and insisting, arranging for messengers, kissing and hugging, or openly declaring love, they set the terms for a love redefined: a love based, in this case, on shared pleasures. If only eight of the twenty or so examples of the *chanson de toile* actually feature sewing, all are clearly marked as *chansons de toile* because women's work, in some form, forges a resolution to the love dilemma. It is in this that the *chansons de toile* remain most distinct and distinguishable from the lyric traditions of the troubadours, trouvères, and *trobairitz*. Whether these women's songs work toward the union of committed lovers against an insensitive husband or the joining of lovers themselves in marriage, the *chansons de toile* expand from an initial portrait of a woman often enclosed, seated, and singing alone to tell the tale of a woman determinedly engaged in concerted efforts to bring two lovers together, sharing a relationship that often defies easy recognition of who holds the subject position and who plays the object of desire.

Women Working to Make Love Work

In *Oriolanz*, not only is the heroine not shown sewing but the first five stanzas of this song bear all the marks of the standard trouvère lament. This female singer invokes her "beautiful, sweet lover Helier" while sighing, weeping, recalling past encounters, and recounting current dreams of him.[47] Indeed, as her voice asserts that nothing can relieve her suffering, for she has only longing (vv. 25–26; p. 81), and that difficulty in obtaining the beloved only feeds and increases one's desire (vv. 32–33; 81), this female singer replays precisely the distraught male suitor of the *grant chant courtois*. Nothing in the first thirty-five lines of this putative woman's song would mark it as a *chanson de toile*. It is only in stanza 7 where "la bele" breaks the pose of the sighing, isolated female singer by raising her lowered head and taking Helier into her arms that the *chanson de toile* begins in earnest:

La bele sosleva son vis:
voit ke c'est Heliers ses amis.
Baisier et acoler l'a pris,
si l'a entre ses beax bras mis. vv. 43–46; p. 82

(The beauty raised her head and saw that it was Helier, her beloved. She hugged and kissed him and took him in her lovely arms.)

Only with this woman's gesture do the couple abandon themselves to pleasing games of love, free to pursue their passions despite the wagging tongues of *losengiers*:

Assez i ot jué e ris.
. . .
Oriolanz li dist: —Amis,
malgré losengeors chaitis
estes vos or de moi saisiz.

Or parleront a lor devis
et nos ferons toz noz plaisir. vv. 47, 50–54; p. 82[48]

(They frolicked in laughter and playfulness ... Oriolanz said to him, "Beloved, despite the miserable lying gossipers, you have attained me. Now they will say what they wish but we will indulge ourselves in every pleasure".)

As a genre the *chanson de toile* lends a wide range of meanings to the term *esploita*, used in the *Bele Aiglentine* to designate the heroine's conjoined efforts at clothwork, singing, and lovemaking. If Oriolanz, like Yolanz in *Bele Yolanz in chambre koie*, purposefully initiates physical contact with Heliers, bringing to fruition a union of shared pleasures, much as Aiglentine travels in person to secure Henri or as Beatrice sends a messenger to fetch Hugues, the unnamed bele in *En un vergier* successfully entreats God to deliver her beloved Gui to her (vv. 25–29; p. 86). As a result of her plea, the *amis* suddenly materializes (v. 33; p. 87), transforming the seated princess who initiated this song into an amorous couple sitting together under the branches of a fruit tree (vv. 3, 34–35; pp. 86–87). The kind of women's work that makes love possible in *Bele Ydoine* is the heroine's determined insistence, reminiscent of the unwavering resolve exhibited by Yolanz and Amelot, that she will have no husband or lover other than the one she has chosen:

—Sire, pour Dieu merci, ci n'a mestier d'estrainte.
Se ne l'ai a seigneur, de duel serai estrainte. vv. 116–17; p. 118

(Sir, in God's name, such restrictions are useless.... if I cannot have him as my lord, I will die of grief.)

Again, as with Aiglentine and Beatris, the heroine's success in engineering the match of her choice (v. 171; p. 120) is set within a more traditional context. In this instance the *bele* is won by a most valiant suitor. Although Ydoine choses Garsile outright and dictates that choice to her reluctant father, the father sets up a tournament to prove the suitor's worth. And Garsile wins the prize:

Tout le tornoi veinqui, la pucele a conquise.
Et li rois li dona, si l'a a feme prise.
En sa terre l'enporte, a haute honor l'a mise. vv. 166–68; p. 120

(He won the tournament, conquered the maiden. The king gave her to him and he married her. He took her away to his country and held her in high esteem.)

These lines delineate the conventional substrata of courtly love, most evident in romance narratives where knights fight for possession of the beautiful, fetishized lady. It is against this background of hierarchized amorous encounter that this *chanson de toile* poses an alternative model for joining lovers together.

For Ysabel, much like Yolanz (in *Bele Yolanz en chambre koie*), the kind of work that will facilitate future union between lovers is located specifically in a conversation between women who tailor the standard love scenario to their liking. In an interesting variant on the mother/daughter dialogue, Ysabel speaks to a woman servant whose advice helps transform the sighing, plaintive beauty (v. 6) into a woman both loved and in love. Ysabel explains that

—Se je savoie .I. cortois chivelier
ke de ces armes fust loeiz et prisiez,
je l'ameroie de greit et volentiers. vv. 22–24; p. 98

(If I knew of a courtly knight who was praised and valued for his skill in combat, I would love him with all my heart.)

In response, the woman servant (*damoselle*) maps out a scenario of mutually shared affection that will thwart the objections of the lady's low-class husband (*vilain signor*, v. 14):

—La moie dame, je sai .I. chivelier
ke de ces armes est loeiz et prisiez:
ameroit vos, cui c'an poist ne cui griet. vv. 27–29; p. 98

(My lady, I know of a knight who is praised and valued for his skill in combat and he will love you, no matter who it grieves or pleases.)

Two final examples offer still other venues for women's work in *chansons de toile* that do not feature sewing. Bele Argentine, who is *cortoise*, accomplished, esteemed, and above reproach (vv. 71–75; p. 145), finds herself banished by a husband whose love has turned sour (vv. 43–47; p. 144). Sobbing, sighing and weeping uncontrollably, this mother of six sons defies the prototypical epithet of the courtly beauty to travel, despite her distress, to Germany where she enters the service of the empress:

Quant se pot radracier, dolente s'achemine.
Del cuer va sospirant et de plorer ne fine.
...
Tant a la dame erré et sa voie tenue,
qu'en Alemaigne droit est la bele venue.
Tant fait qu'en la court est l'empereour veüe.
Devant l'empereris s'est si bel maintenue,
qu'a son service l'a volentiers retenue. vv. 58–59, 64–68; p. 145

(As soon as she could stand, the lady began walking in sadness, sighing deeply and sobbing incessantly.... The lovely lady walked so far following this course that she arrived at the imperial court in Germany. There she displayed such good manners that the empress gladly took the lady into her service.)

Love and marriage prevail at the end of the song when Argentine's sons help to reconcile the capable and independent lady/mother with her reformed husband such that "Si c'onques puis n'i ot descort ne felonie" (v. 123; p. 147; Never again was there dispute or disagreement).

Bele Doette stands alone among the independent *chansons de toile*—those that are not lyric insertions—in not carrying the reader/listener toward a final union of lovers or mates.[49] But women's work is not absent from this singular song. Bele Doette, whose lover Doon has been killed in a joust, resolves to become a nun, wear a hair shirt, and found an abbey for chagrined lovers:

Bele [Doette] prist s'abaïe a faire,
qui mout est grande et adés sera maire.
Toz cels et celes vodra dedanz atraire
qui por amor sevent peine et mal traire. vv. 38–41; p. 91

(Bele Doette began building her abbey, which is large and will continue to grow. She hopes it will attract those who know how to endure pain and suffering for love.)

The song's paired refrains capture the twin portraits of this *bele*. The first, an image of Doette sitting by the window awaiting Doon's return, a passive beauty who might well be heard to lament "E, or en ai dol!" stands in sharp contrast to the Bele Doette engaged, in the opening lines of the song, in reading a book (v. 2).[50] The latter figure might more likely have been seen to build an abbey and oversee its operation, as indicated in the additional refrain of the last three stanzas: "Por vos devenrai nonne en l'eglyse saint Pol" (vv. 31, 37, 43; pp. 90–91; For you I will become a nun at Saint Paul's church). Although this woman's work cannot repair her own lost love, it is work dedicated to loyal lovers who have themselves worked to make love succeed (vv. 34–35).

Women Enclosed and Beaten or Sewing Their Way Toward Open Spaces

If the women who sit and sew in the eight *chansons de toile* that give the genre its name appear typically to be enclosed and often isolated in a remote chamber, many of the women who sing in the other songs of the corpus complain of forced enclosure by husbands or fathers. In those poems that focus typically on a woman unhappily married or facing the possibility of a loveless match, the female singer laments her fate at the hands of an unacceptable partner while working nonetheless to secure the man she prefers. Bele Ysabel has been driven from her country by gossipmongers and liars (*medissans*) into the hands of an insensitive husband who encloses her in a high tower (vv. 1, 5; p. 98). Although Oriolanz is not married, she too suffers from the claims of *felon et losengier* (traitors and gossips) who have driven her lover far from the high chamber where she pronounces her lament (vv. 1, 4–5; p. 81). Amelot, isolated in her chambers, fears the impending marriage that her mother advises and her father plans (vv. 31–34, p. 103; see quote, p. 105). Yolanz "en chambre koie" (v. 1; p. 96), who sews as does Amelot, defies her dismayed husband by courting the conte Mahi (vv. 21–25; p. 96).

For these women, the chamber represents both the possible restrictions of enclosure imposed by a domineering husband and a potential opening onto another world of women's work and community that can lead to satisfaction in love. Three of the four songs mentioned here include dialogues between women at work (Yzabel, Amelot, Yolanz) that facilitate the ladylover's movement away from the husband toward a more satisfying union. I would include in this category *Bele Aiglentine* and *Bele Beatris*, although their work is not designed to secure a beloved as an alternative to a loveless marriage. Both must negotiate the obstacle of pregnancy: Aiglentine must arrange for Henri, father of her unborn child, to marry her, and Beatris must avoid an arranged marriage and ensure that the father of her child, Hugues, becomes her spouse.

But enclosure in its most extreme version can mean physical abuse and severe beating, as four songs attest. In punishment for her protracted lamenting over an absent lover, Bele Ydoine is severely beaten by her father and locked in a tower where she remains for three years.

—Or aura, dist li rois, bateüre prochainne,
puis la ferai serrer ens en la tour autainne
. . .
Trois ans fu la pucele en la tour enserree. vv. 66–67, 84; pp. 116–17

("She will be beaten at once," said the king. "Then I will have her enclosed in a high tower." . . . The maid was locked in a tower for three years.)

Like Ysabel and Amelot, this young woman persists in her resolve to attain her beloved against impressive odds. Here the father's beating only intensifies her complaint and leads to loss of consciousness, as she explains to her distant lover:

Ci sui pour vostre amour enserree a grant painne,
ne puis seur piés ester, tant sui souprise et vainne. vv. 93–94; p. 117

(Because of my love for you I have been enclosed here and suffer greatly. I cannot stand; I am so overcome and weak.)

The narrator concludes: "A cest mot chiet pasmee, sanz vois et sanz alainne" (v. 95, p. 117; With these words she fell into a faint, voiceless and without breath). The unnamed heroine in *En un vergier* falls similarly in a faint after being beaten by her husband for loving Gui:

Tant la bati qu'ele fu perse et tainte:
entre ses piez por pou ne l'a estainte
...
La bele s'est de pameson levee. vv. 15–16, 25; p. 86

(He beat her so long that she became blue and discolored. He nearly killed her at his feet.... The beauty revived from her faint.)

Even Argentine, banished if not beaten by her philandering husband, collapses physically from the emotional distress (vv. 57–59; p. 145). The loss of consciousness that results from physical abuse of the women in these love stories resonates oddly with the more traditional swoon of women in love such as Bele Yolanz, who faints from distress over her *ami*'s absence (v. 10; p. 77); Amelot, who faints from the distress of having to marry against her will (v. 55; p. 103); or Doette, who faints when receiving the news of Doon's untimely death (v. 14; p. 90).

The suffering endured by Ydoine and the heroine in *En un vergier* by contrast substantially transforms the lovely, white courtly lady's body by staining it graphically with color. When Ydoine is beaten by her father:

Tantost fait la pucele despoillier et desçaindre;
tant la bati d'un frain la ou la puet ataindre
que toute sa char blanche li fait en vermeill taindre.
Puis la fait enserrer en la tour et remaindre:
ensi la cuide bien chastoier et destraindre. vv. 70–74; p. 116

(He had the young woman undress and remove her belt. He beat her so hard with a horsewhip wherever he could reach that her white skin was completely colored red. Then he locked her in a tower and left her there, as a way of punishing and correcting her.)

As the *vermeill* of this description modulates into the color *perse* invoked in the other accounts of beaten women, we are reminded tellingly of the red, blue, and violet hues often associated with the luxurious silks that women in romance narrative are said typically to wear. In *En un vergier*, we are told that the vile husand, when hearing his wife's lament:

Entre el vergier, sa corroie a desceinte.
Tant la bati q'ele en fu *perse et tainte*. vv. 14–15; p. 86[51]

(entered the garden, took off his belt, and beat her until she was *blue and discolored*.)

Bele Emmelos recounts that:

A li s'en vint, parmi les dras de soie
la bati tant, que por un poi
ne l'a morte lez le rapoi
...
Tant li debat sa char qu'ele *persoie*,
si qu'en cent leus li desront et peçoie. vv. 21–23, 25–26; p. 154

(He [her husband] came to her and beat her so harshly amid her silk garments that he nearly killed her in the bushes.... He flogged her flesh so much that it turned blue and broke open in a hundred places.)

In two cases documented here, the assailant must negotiate the women's clothing—Ydoine's father makes her undress before beating her skin red and Emmelos's husband must lift her silk garments before beating her blue—displacing the woman's clothes from a body that begins itself to resemble fabric, the colored fabric that women sewing in other *chansons de toile* fashion with their hands.[52]

These women too, though vilely brutalized and attacked, succeed, as we have seen, in making love work. Ydoine and Garsile come together in sweet, mutual love (v. 170), Gui appears and comforts the heroine in *En un vergier* (v. 33), and Emmelos and Guis "love each other intensely" (v. 53). The battered bodies of women in these songs point tellingly to the cloth worked and embellished productively by women who sing and sew in other *chansons de toile*, as the brief two-stanza song *La Bele Aye* shows cogently. Staging both paradigms in contrasting narrative moments, this song sets the heroine's accomplished skill at sewing the "coustures beles" that she adds to "un paile d'Engleterre" in the poem's first stanza against her utter helplessness when being beaten in the second stanza for loving a distant man:

Siet soi bele Aye as piez sa male maistre.
Sor ses genouls un paile d'Engleterre,
[et] a un fil i fet coustures beles

...

Aval la face li courent chaudes lermes,
q'el est batue et au main et au vespre,
por ce qu'el aime soudoier d'autre terre. vv. 1–3, 6–8; p. 159

(Bele Aye sat at the feet of her mean mistress with a silk cloth on her knees that she stitched beautifully with thread. . . . Warm tears rolled down her face because she is beaten, morning and night, for loving a soldier from afar.)[53]

Indeed, this brief song cogently encodes the complex doubled position occupied by a number of singing women throughout the *chansons de toile*, courtly heroines balanced precariously between the poles of working subject and object of desire, often located in an enclosed chamber that might either facilitate women's work and lead to fulfillment in love or entrap and restrain the beautiful lady against her will. At times the fragile line between male desire for and denigration of women snaps, and the beloved object of affection and adoration becomes the object of abuse. In addition to staging this tenuous balance, the *chansons de toile* also point to a way out of enclosure and entrapment through women's work, here emblematized most concretely in sewing and clothwork. Those eight poems that depict women sewing and spinning represent a larger sphere of women working, sometimes together, sometimes alone, whose lyric laments contain key elements that substantially redefine the terms of the courtly love scenario. Women in the *chansons de toile* work at choosing a partner they prefer, pursuing a desired match, designing terms of mutual affection, and engineering a successful union so that love takes place on new ground.

At stake, then, in this corpus of women's song is more than whether women singers of love songs can accede to the subject position and proclaim their love as male singers do because these women's love laments are work songs too. Indeed, one crucial issue addressed by the *chansons de toile* is how women, when given the right to pursue love as desiring subjects, might proceed to shake up the very system of courting and loving that courtly lyric has traditionally enshrined. As Bele Emmelos, beaten literally to a pulp by her husband's heavy hand, explains to her lover Guis returned from afar:

Amis, por vos les maus amoie
que me faisoit li dus quant vos nomoie;
et dit de vos amer n'ai loi.
Or me sormainne a estreloi. vv. 38–41; p. 155

(Dear one, for love of you I relished the blows that the duke inflicted as I called your name. He says I do not have the right to love you and mistreats me to excess.)[54]

If women had the right to love the right man, the *chansons de toile* suggest, not only might beating cease but the very terms of loving from afar, of sighing, pining, lamenting, and wishing all for naught might be fashioned into more effective actions of pursuing, insisting, arranging, managing, hugging, kissing, and passionately embracing. As the trouvère's self-referential and solitary lament thus evolves into a physical conjoining of two lovers wrapped in mutual pleasure, those bruised and bleeding female bodies, constructed in vivid imitation of colored fabric, might also become able bodies that could take up cloth and clothwork as they sewed their way to a more satisfying union. We can see the stark contrast between these two highly gendered positions on love described in more general terms in Drouart la Vache's *Art d'amours*. While the male partner explains how love thrives on difficulty, pain, and separation, the beloved lady says love flourishes when the lovers are together. His assertion, "Que se je l'avoie a grant paine, / A meillor gré je la penroie / Et plus chiere assez la tenroie. / Amant ausi qui s'entrevoient, / Por plus chierement se conjoient / Et s'entraimment plus ardamment / Que s'il se veïssent granment" (vv. 3382–88; If I gained it through great hardship, I would value it more and I would hold it more dear. Thus lovers who see one another only intermittently value those encounters more dearly and love one another more ardently than if they saw one another more often), contradicts her insistence that "Or voit chascuns, si se deduise / A fame qui li soit prochaine: / Si n'averont pas tant de paine / Et se porront recomforter, / Souvent ensamble deporter" (vv. 3370–74; Therefore, everyone knows that if he takes pleasure with a woman who is nearby, in that way, the couple will not feel so much pain. Rather, they can comfort one another and enjoy being together frequently). The kind of male lovesickness evoked in the man's statement derives typically from sight. The male lover falls hopelessly and helplessly in love with a physically beautiful woman whom he watches from a distance, only to increase his desire by watching her further and wanting her more, in keeping with Drouart's dictum, "Amors croist par *veoir* souvent" (v. 3366, my emphasis). But seeing is not loving for the working women of the *chansons de toile*. Their songs stage the possibility of alternative scenarios where lovers touch like threads sewn through cloth.

Pulling Strings: How Women Singers Renegotiate Love

If the metaphorical threads of the Old French *Philomena* convey concerns with lineage and rivalry between father and son in particular, as Nancy Jones has shown compellingly, the more tangible threads of the *chanson de toile* bring partners together in love.[55] The threads used to weave and embellish the fabric of these songs resemble most aptly the conjoined threads worked by Bele Yolanz in the example with which I began:

Bele Yolanz en chambre koie
sor ses genouz pailes desploie.
Cost un fil d'or, l'autre de soie. vv. 1–3; p. 96

(Bele Yolanz, in a quiet room, unfolds silk fabric across her knees. She sews with one golden thread, another of silk.)

The joining together of these two threads, and indeed the joining of cloth and thread that typifies the act of sewing generally, often working in tandem with the paired voices of mother and daughter (in the five *chansons de toile* that stage a mother/daughter dialogue), provide an alternative model for the courtly love story: a model of coming together, of union with a new twist.

If the women featured in the *chanson de toile* sometimes speak "for each other," they do not speak in place of one another, as Jean Renart is said to have done for Guillaume's mother in *Le Roman de la Rose ou de Guillaume de Dole*. The rhetorical world of these heroines does not presume that only one voice at a time can occupy the position of speaking subject. Rather, these conjoined women's voices provide a model of subjectivity that begins to accomplish what Luce Irigaray has said we who live now need crucially to do: to establish difference on the level of the subject; not the hierarchized difference between subject and object, male lover/female beloved of trouvère lyric, and not a difference predicated on sight, on the male subject viewing the beautiful object of desire.[56]

The subjectivity figured in the *chanson de toile* is modeled instead on the basis of touch through sewing: the coming together of thread and cloth. Whether in the sewing songs, where women thread their way toward a desired lover's embrace, or in the songs of triangulated affection, where women work in other ways to join loving bodies together, the *chansons de toile* refigure the subjectivity of the singing, loving lady through the exercise of women's work. In thus transforming the status of the desired female body through clothwork, the *chansons de toile* encourage us to reconsider the range of possible subject positions for male bodies in courtly love encounters as well.

Indeed, within this poetics of touch it is difficult to know, as Iris Young has explained for the phenomenon of touch more generally, who's touching whom or when one stops touching and starts being touched, where one voice ends and another begins. This is the model of subjectivity figured in the fabric of the *chanson de toile*, one that does not reify sexual difference or the categories of male and female but asks, more in line with Hélène Cixous's query in "Tancredi Continues," "When does woman begin when does one become other when continues when pursues when finally touches finally embraces?"[57]

PART III

Denaturalizing Sex: Women and Men on a Gendered Sartorial Continuum

Chapter 4
Robes, Armor, and Skin

Floris et Lyriope

In Robert de Blois's thirteenth-century tale *Floris et Lyriope*, the standard plot of Narcissus's demise, in which falling in love means overvaluing one's own beauty and plunging to a vainglorious and prideful death, provides the frame around another tale of courtly coupling in which clothes, not beauty, make all the difference. To be sure, Narcissus explains the danger of beauty at the end of this text:

C'est la chose que plus m'ocist.
Puis que je l'ain, amer me doit.
Ne cuit pas que ma beautez soit
Tele que lo dongier me face
De moi amer. vv. 1682–86

(It's the thing that's killing me: loving him means I must love myself. I didn't think that my own beauty would ever put me in danger of self-love.)[1]

In terms reminiscent of the Jealous Husband's tirade against dung covered in silk,[2] Robert de Blois's clerically inflected narrative explains that the ugly underside of beauty is the *ordure* of pride, hidden and covered over but lethal:

Ausi est beautez orgoillouse;
Defors apert mout saverouse,
Mais per dedanz l'ordure gist
Qui la beauté trop envillist. vv. 95–98[3]

(Beauty is prideful. Although it appears very appealing from the outside, filth lies within beauty and debases it.)

Although this portion of *Floris et Lyriope* insists on the importance of being able to discern glittering surface from putrid substance, the lives of the courtly couple featured in this love story reveal how courtly garments can function in place of the anatomical body, as love facilitates a significant uncoupling of sex from gender. In the very process of denouncing the dangers of love, the narrator of *Floris et Lyriope* also reveals its most cogent feature: that courtly love has the potential of significantly troubling distinctions of sex and gender, specifically through the deployment of clothes.

Roberta Krueger has shown how *Floris et Lyriope* forms part of the larger intertextual compendium of Robert de Blois's *Enseignement des princes* and his *Chastoiement des dames*, which together pursue a project of moral indoctrination. The anomalous love story of *Floris et Lyriope*, contained within this didactic frame, works, however, against Robert de Blois's moralizing program, Krueger argues, and significantly undermines both the sexual and social categories he sets up in the surrounding works.[4] Of special import for my purposes is the crucial role played by clothing in this process of destabilization. The clothes at issue in *Floris et Lyriope* are not lavish silks and brocades featured in many other courtly narratives. At stake here is a simple unisex outfit (*robe*), unspecified and unadorned. The key function played by this single article of clothing in the story of courtly love uniting Floris and Lyriope highlights the importance of looking beyond luxury attire in the courtly world to other forms of dress. It prompts us to consider how other robes, chivalric armor, and even luscious skin might construct a range of sartorial bodies in courtly literary texts, not in terms of immutable sex differences but as spacings on a sartorial continuum.[5] Such gendered spacings can produce, at different moments, "different densities of sexed being"[6] within individual players in courtly love scenarios, calling into question the dominant heteronormative paradigms that typically unite knights and ladies in courtly coupling.

In many ways, courtly narratives play out a crucial tension, current in a number of medieval discourses, between traditional sex-based identities and a range of less rigidly conceived gender identities. Joan Cadden offers abundant evidence that medieval scientific texts, which expressed a profound and compelling discomfort with "displaced" gender identities and attempted to impose a two-term system of gender difference, also acknowledged the existence of middle terms such as hermaphrodites, eunuchs, women dressing as men, and homosexuals. In so doing, these early medical texts outlined a system based on degrees of sexual difference that posed a significant challenge to any strict either/or categorization of the sexes.[7] Roberta Krueger has shown how a number of didactic treatises and courtesy manuals that appear in northern France in the thirteenth century also attest to an uncertainty about the fixity of sex roles even as their moralizing authors attempt concertedly to enforce traditional categories of gender.[8]

Susan Crane has argued that "despite the dominance of a hierarchized conception of gender difference (in medieval romance narratives from the English and French traditions), romance also represents gender contrarily as unstable, open to question, and in danger of collapse."[9] Simon Gaunt has demonstrated how gendered identities presented as "natural phenomena" are highly flexible and repeatedly negotiated in a wide range of Old French and Occitan texts from lyric and romance to epic, fabliau, and hagiography.[10] Indeed, even the paradigmatic chaste knight in Old French Grail romances significantly troubles the masculine subjectivity of chivalric heroes by renouncing desire, as Peggy McCracken has shown.[11] And the passive reception of God's authoritative texts often used as a model of literary activity by women visionaries has proven to be potentially transgressive, in Susan Schibanoff's reading, when borrowed by male Christian writers who would then be both authorized by God and marked by same-sex encounter.[12] The range of affective lesbian relationships, staged in a diverse array of medieval texts, further complicates the heteronormative paradigm of amorous exchange in the courtly world.[13]

Literary accounts of cross-dressing provide other potential alternatives to conventionally gendered subject positions in courtly love liaisons. Although a number of transvestite heroines in historical, pseudohistorical, hagiographical, and literary sources enact only temporary or comedic alternatives to heterosexual amorous union, their tales record important cultural anxieties about the presumed fixity of gender roles.[14] Texts from the thirteenth century in particular disrupt established patterns of courtly lovemaking with a wide range of male and female cross-dressing scenarios.[15] Best known among them perhaps is the highly misogynous *Roman de Silence*, whose heroine's exemplary actions while attired as a knight and minstrel invite the reader to question the text's earlier unmitigated condemnation of women's nature.[16]

With these varied scenarios of troubled gender assignment as a backdrop, this chapter explores how clothing in the form of robes, armor, and even skin can forge a range of gender and social identities for couples in courtly literary texts. I want to demonstrate, in brief, that even though the ideology of courtly love seeks to regulate sexual practice through compulsory heterosexuality by dressing bodies in gender-specific clothing, that same clothing often produces gender identities that fall beyond the sex-based binary terms of male and female. I will begin by considering the deceptively simple love story staged in *Floris et Lyriope* as a point of entry into understanding the more complex interactions between gender fluidity

124 Chapter 4

and love service in the stories of Lancelot and Guenevere. Chapter 5 focuses specifically on the issue of women's nature and examines how courtly clothing can offer models of "embodied dress" that help redefine the parameters of both maleness and femaleness in Old French love stories.

Perfect Lovers

The basic love plot of *Floris et Lyriope* epitomizes the standard courtly paradigm in which details of refined living provide the setting for the male lover's intense physical distress. We are told from the opening lines how a "gentilhomme courtois," known for his *largesse*, skill in *chevalerie*, and extreme courtliness, marries a "bele, courtoise dame." The union of these courtly parents produces a predictably lovely daughter, Lyriope, the paragon of female courtly virtue: so white, so blond, and with all the requisite facial features—a smooth, white forehead, arched, dark eyebrows, gray-green eyes, nose of a perfect length, small ears, slightly full red lips, small white teeth (vv. 227–44). No one can escape the effect of her beauty:

Nuns hons, tant fut religïous,
Que de li ne fust covoitous
Et por s'amor ne foloiast. vv. 219–21

(No man, no matter how religious he may be, can avoid desiring her and falling madly in love with her.)

Floris, the product of an equally courtly family (vv. 316 ff.), falls for Lyriope, appropriately, at court where:

De toz amans est ce la guise.
Per bel samblant, per bel ator,
Per cortoisie, por douçor,
Per envoisier, per joie faire,
Lor est avis qu'il doient plaire. vv. 391–95

(Lovers learn that they must please through their attractive appearance, lovely dress, through courtliness and gentility, by giving themselves over to amusement and joy.)

Within this courtly setting, Floris suffers the devastating effects of Ovidian love described by Andreas Capellanus. Wounded by the sight of Lyriope's beauty (vv. 376–77), which traverses his eyes to pierce his heart (v. 412), the lover is assailed by the very features that earlier defined the lady's courtly perfection: her lovely forehead, eyes, face, nose, and mouth now produce a sweetness that maims (vv. 418–27) and a joy that could kill (v. 431). As the fire of love inflames and consumes the enthralled and powerless lover (v. 433), we are led to the inevitable conclusion that haunts the classical troubadour *canso*: no man can love without pain (v. 439). Love's symptoms reside specifically in bodily dysfunction:

Toz li sans du cors li fremit.
D'angoise l'estuet tressüer,
Trimbler, et la color müer.
Et li cuers si li tressailla,
C'onques un soul mot ne perla. vv. 479–83[17]

(The blood throughout his body trembles; anxiety makes him sweat, worry, and turn pale. His heart palpitates so much that he cannot utter a word.)

And yet the cure for this lover's distress is found nowhere in troubadour lyric, *The Art of Courtly Love*, or standard twelfth-century tales of love and romance.

Rather, Floris will overcome the ill effects of his vexed passion and succeed in courting Lyriope only by wearing his twin sister's clothes. Florie, who resembles her brother in physical appearance, differs from him only by sex, we are told:

Que tuit cil qui perler ouoient
De lor beauté se mervoilloient.
S[i] furent si d'une semblance
Que nuns n'i savoit dasavrance
N'en piez n'en mains n'en cors n'en vis
Fors que tant, ce dit li escris,
Qu'en une samblance et figure
Avoient diverse nature. vv. 326–33

(Everyone who heard of their beauty was amazed. They resembled each other so much that no one could tell them apart on the basis of their feet, hands, body, or face, except that, the written record says, behind their single appearance, they were of two diverse natures.)

Emphasis here falls less on their biological distinctiveness, their "different natures," than on the indistinguishable character of their "semblance," which effectively prevents viewers from perceiving a difference between them. The siblings thus easily change places, Floris masquerading as a woman in order to live at court in close proximity to his beloved Lyriope and thereby avoid dying of love (v. 835). A brief phrase marks the exchange, which leads progressively to a more substantial transformation. The process depends on borrowed garments:

"Ta robe," fait il, "me donras,
Et tu la moie vestiras.
Lai irai en guise de toi.
Tu remaindras en leu de moi." vv. 830–33

("Give me your robe," he [Floris] said [to Florie], "and you will wear mine. I will go there appearing to be you and you will stay here in my place.")

The generic term "robe" generally refers to an ensemble or "outfit" that, for members of the courtly world in twelfth- and thirteenth-century France, would typically include a *chemise, bliaut, surcot* (in some instances), and also a mantle. After the twins switch clothes, we learn that Floris "is transformed in a very short time; previously a 'he,' now he's a 'she,' and the young lady is a young man":

Bien est en pou d'oure muez.
Or ains fu il, or est il elle
Et damoiseaux la damoisele. vv. 877–79

The transformation enables Floris to stay in Lyriope's company as a "maiden," smiling with her, holding hands, lying in her lap, touching her skin:

Sovant mout doucemant li rit.
Sovant en son giron se couche,
Sovant a sa char nue toche
Et sovant la prant per la main. vv. 909–12

(He often smiles at her sweetly, often lies in her lap, touches her naked skin, and often takes her hand.)

The two kiss and embrace with all the sweetness of love's pleasure (vv. 931–32), which prompts Lyriope to declare:

Onques mais n'an oï novales
Que s'entramassent dous puceles.
Mais n'ameroie pas, ce croi,
Nul home tant con je fais toi,
Ne tant, ce cuit, ne me plairoit
Li baisiers, s'uns hons me baisoit.
Li tien baisier me sont si douz,
Si plaisant et si saverous. vv. 1010–17

(I have never heard of two maidens loving each other so much. But I don't think I will ever love any man as much as I love you. Nor would a man's kiss please me as much as your kisses, which are so sweet, agreeable, and delicious.)

One might be tempted to take this statement as an indication that Lyriope, believing what she sees, is fully deceived into thinking that this man is a woman. And yet, if Floris's kisses are not those of a man any more than are his garments, and if, as the text relates, "he's now a she" (v. 878), one must ask, what precisely creates or determines gender identity in this tale of courtly coupling?

The foregoing passage is arresting for several reasons. Whereas the narrator later roundly condemns the figure of Narcissus (representing both the classical character and the eventual son of Floris and Lyriope who bears the same name) for confusing surface and substance, mistaking his beautiful reflection for a fleshly body, Lyriope is nowhere chastised for making a similar "error." In her prolonged courtship with Floris dressed as Florie, Lyriope is taken in by the visual illusion produced by the hero's borrowed robe: her presumed failure to recognize what the text refers to as Floris's hidden manly nature bears no dire consequences. On the contrary, it is precisely *because* of the mismatch between body and cover that the lovers' union is able to develop and flourish. Indeed, courtly love, in this scenario, seems to thrive on, if not require, a lack of alignment between sexed bodies and the garments they wear. In this instance, Lyriope falls in love with a woman, whom she loves more than she could love any man. She then continues to love this same individual once he resumes his identity as Floris. What lies beneath the gowns of these courtly lovers—the anatomical differences contributing to their "diverse nature"—appears in this sense to be of little consequence.

More important in this narrative of love and romance is the *robe* that facilitates and marks the crucial gender crossing that makes love possible. If the incorporation of the Narcissus myth into this tale serves to warn potential lovers against the dangers of assuming that a compellingly beautiful exterior necessarily represents an equally beautiful body, the story of Floris and Lyriope's amorous encounter argues, on the contrary, that when it comes to love, the body cannot always be distinguished from its more superficial manifestations. Narcissus's error in this version of the tale is to mistake a surface reflection for a corporeal being: "He thought the water was a body" (v. 1610; De l'aigue cuide que cors soit), we are told, and "that body seemed so beautiful to him" (v. 1613; Tant beaux li samble toz li cors) that he not only looked at it but tried to touch/kiss it as well (v. 1627; L'aigue regarde, l'aigue baise). And yet, when Lyriope encounters the beautiful Floris wearing his sister's *robe*, she responds to his/her advances, much as Narcissus does to his own reflection, embracing the visual image of the beloved other:

Quant la bele de gré l'embrace
Et baise sovant en la face. vv. 938–39

(Embracing it/him/her willingly, kissing its/his/her face often.)

But whose face is this, a man's face or a woman's? The twins, Floris and Florie, we have been told, have identical faces along with their indistinguishable bodies, hands, and feet (v. 330). The distinction between male and female, essential to Robert de Blois's condemnation of the narcissistic evils of beauty, appears not to apply to the protagonists in this tale of courtly amorous encounter.

Indeed this story of courtly coupling appears, in many ways, to have broken sex loose from gender, refusing the necessity of aligning the two. It explores instead the possibility of a spectrum of gendered subject positions, based on a conception of the courtly body as more sartorial than anatomical. Indeed, this tale of heterosexual courtly love is bracketed by an initial amorous encounter between two women, "dous compaignes" (v. 963)—Lyriope and the cross-dressed Floris—and a closing episode featuring two young men—Narcissus and his reflection cast as an active male lover:

Et bien le sai et bien le voi
Qu'il fut velontiers avec moi,
Car quant je voil l'aigue baisier
Vers moi lo voi lors apruchier.
Il m'aimme, je n'an dot noiant
Qu'il i pert bien a son samblant.
Quant mes braz en l'aigue li tant,
Il me tant les siens ausimant.
Et quant je ris, je lo voi rire,
Et quant je sopir, il sopire.
Quant je plorois, plorer lo voi. vv. 1665–75

(I see and know perfectly well that he joins me gladly. As I begin to kiss the water, I see him draw nearer to me. He loves me, I have no doubt; it shows in his appearance. When I extend my arms toward him in the water, he extends his toward me. When I laugh, I see him laugh and when I sigh, he sighs. When I cry I notice he is crying.)

To be sure, all the love relationships depicted in this short piece are decried and condemned by a moralizing voice that sees love of any kind as ultimately self-destructive, a return to the dung that hides beneath deceptive courtly beauty or a descent into the foul depths of woman's nature, which we witnessed in Chapter 1.

And yet the story of the love tryst between Lyriope and Floris, occasioned by the hero's donning his sister's robe, provides a scene of heterosexual union that is infused with a range of negotiable gender identities. Floris, dressed as a woman, first declares his/her love for Lyriope by casting her/himself as the star-crossed lover, Piramus, drawn from a story that the couple are reading together:

Dist: "Dame, certes, se je estoie
Piramus, je vos ameroie,
Et se vos jur per toz les sains
Que je ne vos ains mie moins
Que cil fit la bele Tysbé.
Or me dites vostre pansé!" vv. 992–97

("Lady," he said, "truly, if I were Piramus, I would love you and thus do I swear to you on all the saints that I love you no less than he loved the beautiful Thysbe. Now give me your response.")

Then, as we have seen, Lyriope's answer eschews the heterosexual register altogether, declaring the uncanny strength of the bond that unites the two of them as *pucelles* and insisting that she could love no man so ardently or appreciate his kisses (vv. 1010–17). Floris himself proclaims further:

Quant nos en nostre fole amor
Sentons andui si grant douçor.
Mout est cele douçor plus granz,
Plus saverouse et plus plaisanz
Que cil ont qui ainment a droit. vv. 1030–34

(When we, in our mad passion, both feel such intense pleasure, this pleasure is so much greater, more agreeable, and more delicious than the pleasure felt by those who love *a droit*.)

One begins to wonder indeed whose pleasure is in question here: the love between two young women or the desire joining a woman and a man. Floris's further remark only compounds the ambiguity:

Se li une de nos estoit
Uns damoiseaux, nostre solas
Ne porroit nuns dire sanz gas. vv. 1035–37

(If one of us were a young man, no one could speak of our delight without boasting.)

Changing Floris to a *damoiseau* would produce a heterosexual couple; but if Lyriope, as an equally viable referent for "l'une de nos," were to become a *damoiseau* (much like Florie, who has, we recall, taken on her brother Floris's identity when they exchanged "robes"), the resulting couple would feature two men.[18]

This key scene of courtly love and cross-dressing marks but one point on a gendered sartorial continuum that structures the narrative of *Floris et Lyriope*, moving from the representation of an amorous liaison between *deux pucelles* that opened the story to the joining of two "male" lovers in the account of Narcissus that closes the tale, and passing along the way through any number of variably gendered combinations seen in the preceding examples. The spectrum of gendered possibilities advanced here raises a number of probing questions that make this tale much more than a simple account of cross-dressed lovers. Floris's line "if one of us were a young man" makes us wonder, for example, what it might take to transform Lyriope into a *damoiseau*. What are the terms of the production of gender in the courtly world? What are the implications of the kind of gender fluidity suggested in the foregoing examples for the normative sexuality promulgated by the ideology of courtly love? Certainly clothing plays a key role in shaking gender loose from its anatomical moorings in this tale. Here, a single undistinguished and undetailed "robe" makes the entire love story possible. Indeed, reading through clothes in *Floris et Lyriope* encourages us to ask how other forms of courtly dress might offer the means of negotiating gender positions for both men and women along a sartorial continuum. The issue becomes complicated when we shift from the relatively simple coming together of two young lovers featured in *Floris et Lyriope* to the more elaborate interaction between Lancelot and Guenevere in the *Prose Lancelot* and the *Chevalier de la charrete*, where amorous encounter is governed by the imbrication of feudal homage and love service.[19]

The Courtly Dress Code: How Clothes Make the Woman a Man. Or Do They?

The ideological complexity of courtly homage was brought into relief most clearly a number of years ago in a scholarly dispute over how to decipher the sex of two figures appearing on the seal of a southern French nobleman, Simon de Mondragon.[20] The somewhat maverick historian of courtly love, John Benton, charged that the celebrated historian of feudal society, Marc

Bloch, had crucially misidentified the two figures the seal represents. Where Bloch saw a scene of love service, an armored knight kneeling in supplication to his revered courtly lady, Benton saw an image of feudal homage and investiture: a knight kneeling in reverence before his feudal lord. The key to Bloch's putative misidentification, according to Benton, lay in the clothing—literally, the dress—worn by the standing figure on the seal. In the absence of facial hair, armor, or any other distinguishing features of masculinity, Bloch assumed, we are told, that the figure wearing a long robe was a woman. He thus dubbed the image "the lover's homage."[21]

Benton reminds us that civilian dress for aristocratic men in the twelfth and thirteenth centuries was in fact the kind of gown pictured on the seal, a unisex garment that could have been worn by either men or women.[22] The identity of the kneeling knight remains uncontested by both historians, who seem to presume that as long as a courtly figure is dressed in armor, whether in a visual image or in a literary text, one can readily recognize and identify him as a proper knight. But as soon as this male figure is "disarmed" (*desarme* in Old French) and divested of that key marker of masculinity, his gender comes into question: he looks in fact more like an aristocratic woman. In this instance, a determination of sexual difference could not be made on the basis of biology or anatomy. More important, even if we could establish what some might term the "natural sex" of romance characters, such verification would provide no sure clues to the system of gendered identity in the courtly world. The ideologies of gender and social status promulgated in French courtly texts of the twelfth and thirteenth centuries pointedly discourage any such line of inquiry on the part of medieval and modern audiences alike.[23]

Rather, the complex mechanisms of service and subservience that characterize French courtly society, as depicted in medieval literary texts, offer a richly fluid system of social interaction between women and men. The very position of the courtly lady, like that of her literary precursor in the Provencal *domna* of southern French lyric poetry, makes of her a third or hybrid gender, as Sarah Kay has cogently explained.[24] This lady is a woman who remains sexually female while possessing the social status of an aristocratic man, "from the poetry of Guilhem de Peitieu onwards, imagery derived from feudalism makes the *domna* the lover's lord and credits her with masculine powers such as making war, appearing in court and granting territories" (91–92). The *domna* of the southern tradition, so often emblematized by a masculine form of address (*midons*; my lord), is by definition a woman clothed in the social robes of a man. Provençal lyric represents the feudal *domna* as having a constructed gender that derives from the social status imputed to it. So too, the courtly lady of northern French romance is of "mixed" gender and status. Nominally vested with the authority of a feudal lord, as she receives putative homage from the knight in her service, this fictive woman occupies a cultural position balanced precariously between that of lady and lord: she must be a woman to receive the amorous advances of her heterosexual suitor, but she plays the seemingly empowered lord to his supposedly subservient vassal.[25] At the very core of courtly culture, then, cross-gendered performances are the norm, since social status, not anatomical sex, actively conditions gender identity.[26]

Whereas both Benton and Bloch seem compelled to choose one of two fixed gender norms, male or female, in identifying the figures on Simon de Mondragon's seal, the very ambiguity of the visual icon they interpret resists such a reliance on a fixed, natural or biological body. In this courtly scenario, clothing has replaced anatomy as the prime indicator of gender identity. The body constructed by that clothing undermines rather than underwrites the belief that sexual difference is fixed and primary.[27] Taking the courtly body as a sartorial body, a clothed, cultural product, we can begin to see how the image on Simon de Mondragon's seal indicates many more possible gender identities than the two signaled by Bloch and Benton. In addition to reading this representation of courtly exchange as a knight kneeling to his lord or a knight kneeling to a lady who is playing the lord in the game of love service, Old French literature provides a number of other options that one might use to assess the seal's image. Foremost among them is the description of the love service between two companions at arms, Lancelot and Galehaut, in the thirteenth-century *Prose Lancelot*. When Galehaut takes Lancelot as his lord in love, saying that he is given over "body and soul" (8: 483) to this man whom he loves more than any other man can (8: 81), we find him playing the helpless and lovesick *fin amant* to Lancelot's more unforgiving and distant "ladylove."[28] In terms of the iconography on Simon de Mondragon's seal, this relationship would yield a knight doing service to another knight who is also, culturally speaking, a lady miming the role of a lord.[29] And what about the figure kneeling in armor? This sartorial marker of medieval maleness effectively occludes any clear determination of sexual difference. As literary texts from the *Tournoiement as dames* to the *Roman de Fauvel* suggest,[30] the very fact that armor so thoroughly hides the anatomy assumed to be protected beneath it makes this specifically "male" medieval costume the perfect mode of cross-dressing for women wishing to switch genders in the social sphere.

The social hierarchy at work in both pictorial and literary representations of courtly culture in twelfth- and thirteenth-century France can then be said to draw its gender boundaries socially such that "the dominant notions of gender depend not upon the supposedly manifest difference of the genitals but upon the precarious differentiation of the 'same,'" as Peter Stallybrass has argued for certain texts of the English Renaissance.[31] Looking to medical discourses of medieval and Renaissance Europe, he finds that "the body" in these later texts "is itself shaped and imagined through discursive categories which problematize inside and outside, male and female.... Gender was manifestly a production, in which boundaries were produced and transformed rather than biologically given" (19).[32] But how can heterosexual lovers come together in the adulterous liaisons that we have understood to be fundamental to courtly coupling if their bodies are not clearly sexed as male and female? How, we might ask, do clothes make the "man" (whether he is a knight, a lord, or a lady) and the "woman" (whatever her ascribed social and sexual status) in court culture?

The Church's Dress Code: How to Keep Men from Becoming Women

From the twelfth century on, churchmen in France sought to regulate dress as a means of constructing and enforcing rigid boundaries of gender identity for knights, courtiers, and clerics.[33] St. Bernard, well known for having railed against the luxurious extravagances of Abbot Suger's artifacts at St. Denis, also launched a pointed attack against the sartorial excesses of what he termed "old" or secular knights in comparison to the celestial knighthood he sought to promote. In 1130, his *In Praise of the New Knighthood* critiques the chivalric tendency "to devote such expense in labor and fighting for no purpose except death and sin" by attacking the costly and unnecessary accouterments of war:

"You deck your horses with silk, and plume your armor with all manner of rags. You paint your saddles and shields with emblems. You adorn your bits and spurs with gold and silver and precious stones. And in all this glory you gallop in shameful frenzy and mindless stupidity to your own death!"[34] And further, "Why... do you blind yourselves with effeminate locks of hair, and trip yourselves up in long and flowing tunics with cumbersome sleeves in which you bury your tender, delicate hands?"[35] The problem with these excesses, as Bernard makes clear, is not only wasteful expense but the blurring of gender categories that they suggest: "Are these the trappings of a warrior, or are they not rather the *trinkets of a woman*?" (my emphasis here and following).[36]

Around 1140, the Norman monk Oderic Vitalis blamed the general degeneration of aristocratic manners among the Norman upper classes on the influence of womanish effeminacy: "Our wanton youth is sunk in effeminacy, and courtiers, fawning, seek the favours of women with every kind of lewdness. They add excrescences like serpents' tails to the tips of their toes where the body ends, and gaze with admiration on these scorpion-like shapes. They sweep the dusty ground with the unnecessary trains of their robes and mantles; their long, wide sleeves cover their hands whatever they do; impeded by these frivolities they are almost incapable of walking quickly or doing any kind of useful work. They shave the front part of their head, like thieves, and let their hair grow very long at the back, *like harlots*."[37] He compares these contemporary degenerates to their predecessors at the court of William Rufus, "effeminates" who "parted their hair from the crown of the head to the forehead, grew long and luxurious locks *like women*, and loved to deck themselves in long, over-tight shirts and tunics."[38] Even these "tight shirts" appear to depart somehow from the contours of the "naturally" sexed male body to construct an anatomy seen as foreign and other, that is, female. Earlier, St. Anselm's biographer, Eadmer (d. 1124), complains that from roughly 1096, "almost all young men at court wore long hair *in the manner of girls*; they combed it thoroughly each day and then walked around lasciviously, taking small steps."[39] Anselm himself is said to have preached against the effeminacy of long hair on Ash Wednesday around 1096 and succeeded in cutting short the hair of men in the congregation who repented this excess (1080). Whereas these efforts were made in the name of stemming moral decay, it is significant that they equate moral degeneracy specifically with a collapse of gender boundaries that must be reinstated to preserve the social order.

When the prior of Vigeois (1184) denounces the excesses of checkered and speckled robes and full, floor-length mantles, he critiques them in particular for having been contaminated by a feature belonging to the opposite sex, "long trains *like those worn by women*."[40] Clerics too came under attack and were charged, among other vices, with taking even greater care in their appearance than women: "You will see them in public with hair *as curly as women's*, clean shaven, their skin softened by cosmetics, their head uncovered and shoulders bare, with arms waving, wearing gloves, lightly shod, their robe split to the hipline, and to ensure that no part of their outfit falls out of balance, you will see them constantly checking their mirror."[41]

The danger posed by such transgressions of moral boundaries goes much further than the question of self-indulgence or excessive spending. The equally threatening danger, voiced indirectly in the ecclesiastical pleas for curbing luxury garments among knights, noblemen, and clerics alike, is the collapse of what is presumed to be the God-given sexual difference between women and men. William of Malmesbury makes the case overtly when describing "one of these long-haired men who, *forgetting their natural sex*, like to transform themselves by taking on the appearance of a woman."[42] Knights who wear "trinkets," young men with long hair and trailing gowns, clerics with soft skin and bare shoulders risk looking, in an echo of the ambiguous figure on Simon de Mondragon's seal, more like women than men. And yet, that ambiguously defined charge of "effeminacy," so often leveled by medieval churchmen against those who, through cross-dressing, were seen to deny their biological sex, finds no ready equivalent in the depiction of romance heroes. However blatantly Arthurian knights may cross the gender line into the socially defined domain of femininity, their behavior is not measured against an anatomical standard. In the earliest tales of courtly coupling, "natural sex" seems not to be at issue.

Armor and Skin: The Status Quo of Sexual Difference

If courtly ideology, as it appears in tales featuring Lancelot and Guenevere, typically constructs the elite social body in two discrete and easily recognizable categories—male and female—it locates that sexual difference for men in particular in distinctive dress and clothing. Indeed, the properly socialized body in Arthurian romance results from encasing the male anatomy so fully in armor that no skin shows. Knights are by definition "totes armez," as is Méléagant, whose arrival in the opening scene of the *Chevalier de la charrete* establishes the standard of chivalric dress that persists throughout this romance and continues in the thirteenth-century *Prose Lancelot*: "A tant ez voz un chevalier / qui vint a cort molt acesmez, / de totes ses armes armez / Li chevaliers a tel conroi / s'an vint jusque devant le roi" (Then a knight arrived at court well attired, in full armor, and thus equipped he approached the king).[43] The first time we see Lancelot in the *Charrete*, though unhorsed and disoriented, he is nonetheless a "chevalier," "*tot armé*, li hiaume lacié / l'escu au col, l'espee ceinte" (vv. 318–19; fully armed, helmet laced up, shield around his neck and sword belted on). In the closing battle with Lancelot, Melegant remains "toz armez" (v. 3538), his body parts fully contained within an armored surface: "Molt estoit genz et bien aperz / Melïaganz, et bien tailliez, / de braz, de janbes, et de piez, / et li hiaumes et li escuz / qui li estoit au col panduz / trop bien et bel li avenoient" (vv. 3540–45; Méléagant was noble and fit with well-formed arms, legs, and feet. His helmet and the shield hanging from his neck suited him perfectly).[44] The knightly body in this scenario is deemed comely and attractive to the extent that it is controlled and constrained (*taillie*); limbs and head, trunk, hands, and feet remain invisible to the eye, which reads only the armored casement surrounding the flesh.[45]

Conversely, visible flesh not only invites wounding but marks a knight's formal defeat. Thus does Lancelot end his battle with the *orgueilleux* in the *Charrete* by removing the opponent's helmet to expose his head: "si li fet le hiaume voler / del chief, et cheoir la vantaille; / tant le painne, et tant le travaille / que a merci venir l'estuet" (vv. 2740–43; He flung the helmet off his [opponent's] head, causing the visor to close and tormented him and made him suffer until he was forced to surrender). The final battle of the *Charrete* shows Lancelot defeating Méléagant by first exposing his head to view: "Lancelot vient, si li deslace / le hiaume, et la teste li tranche" (vv. 7086–87; Lancelot approaches, unlaces his [Méléagant's] helmet and decapitates him). Typically, knights in the *Prose Lancelot* are considered "desarme" and dangerously close to death once their helmet is gone: "et cil a poor qui a la teste *desarmee*" (1:143; The knight, whose head was uncovered, feared for his life).[46] Unprotected flesh connotes chivalric shame as Lancelot explains on one occasion: "ce seroit trop grant honte, se je m'en aloie *desarmés*" (2: 306; It would be an intolerable shame for me to go without armor). Indeed, when we encounter this knight stripped of his armor and most all his weapons, we confront a man "stripped bare" (pur le cors, 2: 306) we are told, though he remains fully clothed. Thus the courtly knight's masculinity and social status derive from the fact that his specific body parts are encased and literally unseen. He is gendered masculine precisely to the extent that his anatomical sex is concealed and unverified. He is a knight and a man, curiously, to the degree that he has no clearly sexed body.

Consequently, the courtly knight can switch genders with relative ease. The most vivid example of this phenomenon is provided by Gauvain's assertion in the *Prose Lancelot* that he would give anything to secure Lancelot's liberation from prison and forever have such a valiant man with him/for himself[47]: "Je voldroie orendroit estre la plus bele damoisele del mont saine et haitie, par covent qu'il m'amast sor toute rien toute sa vie et la moie" (8: 94; I would like to be the most beautiful damsel in the world, in perfect health, provided that he love me more than anyone else for the duration of his life and mine). Gauvain here imagines himself in the role of the beautiful *demoiselle*, a female object of desire loved and adored by Lancelot, that is, in the role typically allotted to Lancelot's official ladylove, Guenevere. I consider Gauvain's suggestive comment in this scene to be a key example of the unmarked transvestism that traverses the *Prose Lancelot*, as I have argued elsewhere.[48] Gauvain's imagined and rhetorical cross-dressing functions as a gender performance, in Judith Butler's definition of the term; it constitutes an expression of gendered subjectivity that does not presume or depend upon a natural alignment of anatomical sex, gender identity, and gender performance.[49] Gauvain qualifies as a knight and a man at the very moment he casts himself in the role of Lancelot's ladylove principally because of the armor he wears.

The courtly lady, by contrast, gains social status "as a woman" to the extent that her flesh is exposed to view.[50] A passage from the *Prose Lancelot* juxtaposes male and female modes of dress as follows: "si voient venir .II. routes de chevaliers *tous armés*, si i a .X. chevalier en chascune route et ... chevauche une dame moult cointement achesmee de palefroi et d'autre ator; et fu vestue d'un samit vermeil, cote et mantel a pene d'ermine; si fu *toute desliie* et ele estoit de merveilleuse biauté" (7: 385; They saw two columns of fully-armed knights approach, ten knights in each column and ... a lady approached on horseback, equipped very attractively with a palfrey and other accouterments, dressed in a red silk gown and a cloak lined in ermine. She [her head] was completely uncovered and of wondrous beauty). The lady's costume is characteristically open (headdress undone: *deslie*) so that her beautiful face can be seen.[51] Even though the standard portrait of the courtly "dame" often describes her as clothed in *cotte* and *mantel*, it also typically delineates her plump breasts, alert nipples, and curving thighs as if she were standing naked before us. Much is made, typically, of the white skin that covers the elite lady's face and neck, chest, and hands.[52] It is not that this lady is unclothed per se but that skin itself constitutes the aristocratic woman's typical garment.

Guenevere, as a temporary prisoner of King Bademagu in Gorre, is defined, in the *Charrete*, in terms of flesh alone when Bademagu assures Lancelot of her safekeeping by stating that no one has touched her *char*: "La reine a boene prison / que nus de *char* a li n'adoise / neïs mon filz cui molt an poise" (vv. 3362–64; The queen fared well in prison; no one touched her [literally: her flesh], not even my son, for whom it was difficult). An extreme version of this characterization of femininity as skin and flesh is found in the courtly temptress of the *Charrete* who, as the starkest contrast to the "chevalier toz armez," appears to us instead to be "tote descoverte" (v. 1067). Later described as "descoverte jusqu'au nonbril" (v. 1082; uncovered down to the navel), this nearly ravished woman reveals disturbingly how the courtly association of female attractiveness and visible skin might rest in fact on a principle of women's vulnerability to attack,[53] even when they are fully clothed.

This is, indeed, what the *coutume de Logres* confirms: that the company of armed and armored knights, bound to one another through ceremonies of homage and dubbing, are authorized by the customs of Arthur's realm to trade unarmored women and ravish them if they please: "Mes, se ele conduit eüst / uns autres, se tant li pleüst / qu'a celui bataille an feïst / et par armes la conqueïst, / sa volente an poïst faire / sanz honte et sanz blasme retraire" (vv. 1311–16; If she was in the care/company of one [knight] and another wanted to fight with him and win her in combat, he could do with her as he pleased, incurring no blame or shame).[54] The terms of this relationship are clarified in an especially striking passage where the disobedient son refuses to give up his claim on an unnamed *pucele* and explains that to relinquish the woman he escorts would be tantamount literally to losing his armor: "Einz iert de mon escu la guige / ronpue et totes les enarmes, / *ne an mon cors ne an mes armes* / n'avrai je puis nule fiance, / ne an m'espee, n'en ma lance, / quant je li lesserai m'amie" (vv. 1720–25; The strap of my shield and its handles would be broken; I would no longer have any confidence in my body, arms or armor, not in my sword or my lance, if I gave my ladylove to him). The courtly knight's armor cannot function properly unless he has a lady in tow (vv. 1716–19). For him to be armored effectively, she must be uncovered and physically vulnerable, in need of chivalric protection. If knights in the Arthurian world are "made" literally when a lord confers upon them the armor that creates their social body, ladies, who experience no such ritual investiture, are defined by the absence of any equivalent garment.[55] Instead of armor, it is the lady's skin that confers social status upon her; and her status is that of an objectified body to be traded by armed knights.[56]

Roughly midway through the *Prose Lancelot*, Lancelot's female guide subtly oversteps this allotted role and draws a strong rebuke from "the most perfect knight." Having begun the journey through the forest as the lovely and deferential Arthurian lady who "takes pains to serve and praise" (1: 317) the knight in her company, this damsel suddenly switches rhetorical modes and begins to solicit Lancelot's amorous attention as a lover: "De totes les choses le semont de quoi ele le cuide eschaufer, si se deslie sovent por mostrer son vis et son chief qui de tres grant bialté estoit et chante lais bretons et autres notes plaisans et envoisies, et ele avoit la vois et haute et clere et la langue bien parlant et breton et françois et mains autres langages" (1: 317; Everything she said to him was designed to heat him up; she repeatedly unlaced her headgear to reveal her very beautiful head and face as she sang Breton songs and other pleasing and seductive tunes. She had a high, clear voice as her tongue pronounced words in Breton, French, and many other languages). This alluring maiden who has taken pains to unveil her skin is nonetheless not reduced to skin alone, for she has moved tentatively into the subject position, actively constructing a possible love scenario between herself and the hapless Lancelot, "Et quant ele voit un bel lieu plaisant, si li mostre et dist: 'Veez, sire chevaliers, dont ne seroit il bien honis qui tel lieu passeroit avec bele dame ne avec bele damoisele sans fere plus?'" (1: 317–18; Showing him a lovely place by the roadside, she said, "Look sir knight, don't you think that anyone who passed by such a place, while traveling in the company of a beautiful lady or maiden, and didn't act further, would be dishonored?").

Though couched in properly courtly syntax, this damsel's request appears thoroughly unladylike. It provides a cogent example of bodytalk, as I have defined that phenomenon, in which fictive females can be seen to resist, through the speech attributed to them, the very stereotypes of femininity that their gendered anatomy is designed to convey.[57] Lancelot immediately brands such resistant speech as unacceptable within a courtly code that does not allow ladies to speak this way, "Je n'avoie pas apris que pucele parlast en tel maniere" (1: 318; I never knew a maiden could speak in such a way). Curiously, no equivalent censure follows Gauvain's crossover speech, which casts him in the role of Lancelot's ladylove, or Galehaut's unproblematic depiction of Lancelot as his lord in love (8: 81, 483). Yet the damsel accompanying Lancelot in the forest cannot as readily step into the crossgendered role of the desiring subject. Her movement off the pedestal of courtliness into a more sexually aggressive, combative, and knightly pose meets with considerable resistance.

Later in the scene, the young woman guide undresses and slips into bed next to the timorous and incredulous Lancelot, who repeats his earlier rebuke, this time more specifically in terms of physical aggression, "Kar onques mes n'oï parler de dame ne de damoisele qui volsist prendre chevalier par force" (1: 323; I've never heard of a lady or damsel who tried to take a knight by force). "Ladies" don't make sexual advances; "ladies" don't attack with force. That is to say, in effect, that ladies don't wear armor; they can't cross-dress as knights. Unmarked transvestism practiced by females is actively policed by a courtly code that sees men as relatively bodiless while consigning women to the realm of skin. Whereas knights can play at being armored men or robed women in the Arthurian world, ladies themselves cannot as easily cross the gender lines dictated by courtly culture. Ladies, according to the dominant rules of courtliness, should wear only one outfit, a loose and flowing gown which, diametrically opposed to the knight's armor, is tied typically to her exposed and gendered flesh. The lady escorting Lancelot through the forest has injudiciously stepped over the hypothetical line dividing armor from skin. In cross-dressing metaphorically as a knight she has made gender trouble in the courtly world.[58] And yet this is precisely the dilemma posed by the quintessential courtly lady, Guenevere, who so often eschews proper courtly conduct[59] and by the hybridized Provencal *domna* before her.

Unisex Dress: Where Genders Cross and Knights Become Ladylike

We can see from the preceding examples that whereas the courtly code attempts to impose strict gender identities by insisting that "knights are knights" and "ladies are ladies," because knights wear armor and ladies do not, such a highly polarized regulation of sexual difference falters from its very inception. The fact that ladies can, though with difficulty, break through the limiting restrictions of their beautiful skin and that knights can, much more readily, shift into the hybrid status of lady/knight, conveys a more fluid relationship between armor and skin than the traditional strictures of courtly coupling would suggest.

Indeed, the terms of masculinity and femininity can shift and recombine in surprising constellations that are figured along a continuum from armored, invulnerable subject to naked, vulnerable object. In one scene alone we watch the perfect knight Lancelot travel across the full spectrum of socially defined modes of dress and their assigned gender identification: he passes from the standard masculine armor to the unisex court garb of *mantel* and *chemise*—until falling finally into the category of lowest, most embodied status when he takes on the quintessential marker of femininity as the courtly code defines it: white flesh. When Lancelot arrives at the temptress's castle in the *Chevalier de la charrete* and exchanges the military shield, which hangs typically around the knight's neck (*l'escu au col*), for a courtly mantle that the lady places around his shoulders, "Quant cele li ot au col mis / le mantel" (vv. 1019–20; When she placed the cloak around his neck and shoulders; and further vv. 1000, 1012–13), he becomes as vulnerable to attack as the temptress herself. His thin mantle offers no protection against armed assailants: "et li quarz qui l'a assailli / fiert si que le mantel li tranche, / et la chemise et la char blanche" (vv. 1144–46; And the fourth one to attack him struck so as to slice through his cloak and *chemise* and through his white flesh). The subsequent seduction scene reveals Lancelot as even more fully denuded (*desnüer*, v. 1205) in a way that recalls the temptress's own state of being "tote descoverte" earlier in the tale.[60] In that fleeting moment when we are allowed to glimpse what lies beneath this knight's clothing, however, we see not the body of a man but the vulnerable, uncovered body of the aristocratic woman, "la char blanche," and concomitantly lowered social status.

More commonly in the *Prose Lancelot*, however, knights cross-dress overtly, moving with ease and no loss of status into the socially prescribed realm of "ladies." Key to this process is the fact that knights change clothes regularly in romance narrative. Their numerous arrivals and departures are marked by elaborate rituals of hospitality that include the shedding of armor and the donning of elegant garments worn at court,[61] that is, the kind of unisex aristocratic dress worn by the standing figure on Simon de Mondragon's seal. In the *Prose Lancelot*, Hector is greeted by a *pucele* who removes his armor and offers instead a garment identical to her own indoor dress, clearly distinct from the battle armor that only men can wear. The *pucele* "le fait desarmer desus une moult bele queute pointe; et ele misme le desarme. . . . Si li aporte la puchele .I. court mantel, si li met au col" (8: 303; On a beautiful coverlet, she had his armor removed; she removed it herself . . . and brought him a short cloak which she placed around his neck and shoulders). In disarming and undressing the knight, she removes the insignia of his chivalric maleness and clothes him as she clothes herself, erasing sexual distinctions between armor and skin. This visual "feminization" of the knight who steps off the battlefield to enter the world of courtly extravagance is made especially clear in the encounter between the duc de Clarence and his female cousin. After a valet removed the duke's shield and armor, "est issue une damoisele d'une chambre qui porte sor son col un mantel d'escarlete et li dux le voit molt bien venir. . . . Lors li met la damoisele le mantel al col et maintenant rest entree en la chambre dont ele estoit issue" (1: 181; The duke saw a damsel, wearing a dark-colored wool cloak around her neck and shoulders, emerge from a room. The damsel placed the cloak around *his* neck and shoulders and reentered the room from which she had come). In this instance the mantle passed from lady to knight does not only resemble a woman's garment; the mantle he dons belongs in fact to her. The description of the knight Bors arriving at Bademagu's court "vestuz d'unne robe d'un samit vermoil foree d'ermine dont il avoit cote et mantel" (4: 374; dressed in a red silk gown lined in ermine with a tunic and cloak lined in ermine) offers a close reflection of the queen, Guenevere, "vestue d'unne robe de porpre qui toute estoit batue a or, si en avoit cote et mantel forré d'ermine" (4: 385; dressed in a rich, dark-colored gown, completely worked in gold, with a tunic and cloak lined in ermine).[62]

What lies beneath the knight's armor in courtly romance, then, is not sexual difference but the sexual ambiguity of a social body that can move quite readily between genders and between social stations. Even in combat, the body parts of fighting knights remain remarkably gender-neutral. Descriptions of "les bras," "les espaules," "li cors," "li dos" (1: 337; arms, shoulders, body, back), "la char, li os" (2: 127; flesh, bones), "la teste" (1: 344; the head), do not in any way tie these bodies to a gendered anatomy. The armor that constructs the properly socialized body in the courtly world seems rather to connote both masculinity and its fundamental mutability. Knights can dress as men (in armor) or cross-dress as women (in robes) without risking effeminacy or diminished social status.

Even the putatively male suit of armor itself proves less gender specific than it originally appears. When the Dame du Lac first arrives at King Arthur's castle to request that the young Lancelot be dubbed a knight, she insists on supplying his apparel: "Or vous requier je dont que vous chest mien vallet qui chi est me faites chevalier de teus *armes* et de teil harnois com il a" (7: 267; I ask that you make this young man, here before you, into a knight, with the arms and armor that he now has). One of her horses carries "*la robe* au vallet dont il devoit estre chevaliers et une autre ruebe a porter" (7: 265; the robe he should wear to become a knight and another to carry with him) in addition to a shield, helmet, and sword. When Arthur replies that he can only create a knight out of his own robes and his own arms, not hers: "Mais en che que vous me requerés avroie je honte, se jel faisoie, car je n'ai pas a coustume que je fache nului chevalier se de mes *robes* non et de mes *armes*" (7: 267; It would be dishonorable for me to do as you request; I have only made knights using my own robes, arms, and armor), the Lady of the Lake responds, "Et bien sachiés que chis vallés ne puet estre chevaliers ne ne doit d'autres *armes* ne d'autres *robes* que de cheles qui chi sont" (7: 268; Be assured that this youth cannot become a knight using any arms, armor, or robes other than these).

At stake in this scene are many issues: who will make Lancelot a knight? A man (the king) or a woman (his surrogate mother, the Lady of the Lake)? And what clothing will be used to make the young Lancelot into a knight? But clearly the knightly self that is fashioned from this clothing will not derive from arms and armor alone. The unisex robes are as much a part of Lancelot's putatively male outfit as they are for knights wearing armor elsewhere in Arthurian romance. Lancelot, when fighting with Griffon, is said to have "tote sa robe ... ensanglentee" (2: 305; his robe completely bloodied), and Galehaut on another occasion explains to Lancelot that he set out with a band of knights "armé desos lor robes" (1: 36; wearing armor under their robes).

In addition, the helmet that fully covers the knight's head often veers surprisingly close to an evocation of the aristocratic lady's typically white skin. The *orgueilleux* who suffers defeat at Lancelot's hand in the *Charrete* is said to have "la vantaille et la coiffe blanche" (v. 2908; a white visor and head covering), just as Lancelot and Méléagant later locked in battle sport "les hiaumes et les haubers blans" (v. 3613; white helmets and hauberks). As these metallic items of chivalric dress are described using the color attributed characteristically to the aristocratic lady's skin, the courtly dichotomies that construct male and female bodies, as well as those that fashion knights and ladies as distinct and clearly separate categories, begin to erode. The range of possibilities for sexual difference no longer stops at two. Even the most masculine of knights such as Gauvain can occupy, at times, an indeterminate social space between dichotomous extremes, which foils any attempt to peg "him" as purely female or wholly male. Whereas courtly love attempts to convince us that sexual difference is biologically conditioned, the very phenomenon of courtliness also reveals tellingly that sexual difference in King Arthur's world, constructed as it is by courtly costume, does not involve a fixed choice between only two options, male and female. This does not mean that body parts are absent or insignificant in court culture. Indeed, they play a key role in the homage ceremony; but in the move from feudal homage to courtly love service, body parts tend to lose their gendered specificity.[63]

Homage Refashioned in Courtly Clothes:
Lancelot as Ladies' Man or Lady/Man?

The ceremony of feudal homage focuses on two body parts in particular: the mouth and hands. A feudal vassal typically vows to become the "man" (*homme*) of his lord, and more specifically to be "un homme de bouche et de mains" (a man of the mouth and the hands).[64] This medieval ritual differs from courtly love service in that homage joins the hands of two men, while courtliness unites the hands of a woman with those of a man. But can we really tell the difference? Lancelot, the perfect knight, the anomalous quester, the conundrum of courtliness personified, is said to be "bien tailliés" (well-formed) with a "pis espés," "col gros" (thick chest, fat neck); but he also bears the more typically feminine features of a noble lady: "bochie petite" (small mouth) and "mains longues et plaines et soés a baillier" (1: 128–29; long, smooth hands, soft to the touch). Indeed, his remarkable "bouche vermeille" (red mouth) prompts an unnamed *demoisele* to remark that "onques mais a son esciant dame ne damoisele ne vit si bel" (4: 134; as far as she knew, she had never seen a lady or young lady as beautiful as him). Elsewhere Lancelot is said to have the perfectly proportioned neck of a noble lady: "De son col ne fait il mie a demander, car s'il fust en une tres bele dame, si fust il assés couvenables" (7: 73; No need to ask about his neck. If it had belonged to a beautiful woman, it would have suited her perfectly). This knight has, moreover, long, straight arms that end not in a man's hands but those of a lady: "les mains furent de dame tout droitement" (7: 73).

What does it mean to say that Lancelot has the mouth, neck, and hands of a lady, while also asserting that he has the hips and stance, the chest and shoulders of the perfect knight? What kind of hybridized sexual and social status is suggested here? We have certainly moved well beyond the temporary cross-gendered identities staged in *Floris et Lyriope*. In the context of the *Prose Lancelot* itself, these allusions to a lady's face and hands provide a striking contrast to the more rugged description of Lancelot recuperating from combat at the dame de Malehaut's castle. Lying "naked on a bed," Lancelot is said to have a swollen face, battered and bruised by the chainmail of his hauberk. More specifically, his neck is flayed and his wrists hugely swollen and covered with blood: "le vis enflé et batu et camoissiés des mailles, le col et le nes escorchié ... les puins gros et enflés et plains de sanc" (8: 33). Indeed, the typical knight's neck and hands take such a beating during combat because they are crucial to his successful self-defense: the hands wield the sword and lance while the neck, as we have seen, bears the weight of the shield, hung from a leather strap (8: 107). Elsewhere, Lancelot's capable and heroic hands lift the tombstone at the Doloreuse Garde (7: 332). If the fighting knight's hands and neck are typically concealed beneath protective armor and thus invisible (7: 222–24), they emerge during the ceremony of dubbing. In Lancelot's case we are told twice that at the moment when Lancelot became a knight he was fully armed "except for his head and hands" (8: 111, also 7: 286; tous armés fors de mon chief et de mes mains). Yet Lancelot becomes a knight in a highly anomalous manner.

The scene of his dubbing by Queen Guenevere constitutes the most significant rewriting of the ceremony of homage, in which the vassal becomes his lord's "homme de bouche et de mains." Indeed Lancelot explains to Yvain that he does not want to be a knight "de la main le roi" (7: 286; by the king's hand).[65] Rather, with his hands and neck bare he will become, it seems, "a knight of the queen's hand." And in fact in response to the young Lancelot kneeling before her, Guenevere first "takes him by the hand" and asks him to rise (7: 285) and then "pulls him up by the hand" (7: 286). The gesture reassures Lancelot: "il est moult a aise, quant il sent a sa main touchier la soie toute nue" (7: 286; He was pleased to feel the touch of the queen's naked hand against his own). As these naked hands touch, not only is the homage ceremony eroticized but the traditional bonding between men—the ceremony that makes one man another man's man—shifts significantly. Guenevere extends her courtly and delicate hand to touch. Is it the hand of a knight or is it, as we have seen before, the "hand of a lady" (7: 73)?

In this instance the ideology of courtly love that tries concertedly to control the social body by constructing it according to a binary logic of masculine and feminine also shows how such rigid categorization, figured in terms of armor and skin, proves woefully inadequate. Lancelot has none of the social vulnerability that characterizes the physically beautiful and delicate *demoiseles* whose bare hands are traded among armed knights in the Arthurian forest.[66] Nor does he exhibit the vulnerable *char blanche* of his predecessor in Chrétien's tale.[67] The prose hero's masculinity is not feminized in a way that would reduce his social or sexual status. Rather, his hybrid existence as the atypical but quintessential courtly knight further challenges the categories of masculinity and femininity already called into question by Gauvain's rhetorical cross-dressing and Lancelot's own layered performance as Galehaut's lady/lord in love. Indeed, the very phenomenon of courtly love, which, in the examples we have seen, tends to blur distinctions between lord and ladylove, between a man's hands and a woman's or the mouth of a knight and that of a lady, undermines the importance of being able to identify the sex of who is kneeling before whom in courtly encounters.

Sexuality as Spacings on a Gendered Sartorial Continuum

The examples we have seen from the twelfth- and thirteenth-century tales of the archetypical courtly lover, Lancelot, reveal, in specifically medieval terms, that the constituent elements of gender cannot be made to signify monolithically, that maleness and femaleness, masculinity and femininity, are not impermeable or mutually exclusive categories. Even within the heteronormative model of Arthurian romance, which tries relentlessly to construct men as knights and women as ladies, we find ample evidence that gender might better be understood as "queer" in Eve Sedgwick's definition of the term: that is, that the constituent elements of sexuality move within "an open mesh of possibilities, gaps, overlaps, dissonances and resonances, lapses and excesses of meaning."[68] This does not mean that the categories of male and female have disappeared altogether,[69] any more than Peter Stallybrass's contention that gender depends upon a precarious "differentiation of the same" might suggest that the ability to differentiate has thoroughly vanished.

Indeed, we have seen how the "mesh" of sexuality's component elements remains more open for men than for women in the Arthurian world, where the ideology of courtliness polices female sexuality with greater rigor. But those key moments in which courtly ladies do veer problematically across the gender divide, those moments not of literal but of metaphorical cross-dressing, outline a range of possible scenarios that courtliness tries to suppress: that ladies could be knights—that they could court men, make sexual advances, refuse the terms of the courtly contract, dress in armor and do battle. If this kind of behavior is unbecoming to the properly socialized Arthurian lady and denigrated by the courtly code, which claims it inadmissible for ladies to cross the gender line in such ways, courtly romance shows us nonetheless what might happen if ladies did "dress" as knights, just as knights can fashion themselves as ladies.

Yet the productive troubling of gender categories is not limited to romance narrative alone. Even medieval ecclesiastical discourses that attempt to set male apart from female monolithically as armored knight and metaphorically naked lady cannot help but bring the two extremes together, emphasizing instead how knights and ladies appear more accurately, like the varied protagonists in *Floris et Lyriope*, as spacings on a gendered sartorial continuum, as figures exhibiting many different densities of sexed being, depending to a significant degree on what they wear. A particularly striking example of the rhetorical difficulty of insisting that knights cannot be ladies appears in a sermon delivered by the Dominican preacher Gilles d'Orléans in 1273 that rebukes Parisian women for being simultaneously too knightly and too seductive.

"En apercevant une de ces femmes, ne la prendrait-on pas pour un chevalier se rendant à la Table Ronde? Elle est si bien équipée, de la tête aux pieds, qu'elle respire tout entier le feu du démon. Regardez ses pieds: sa chaussure est si étroite, qu'elle en est ridicule. Regardez sa taille: c'est pis encore. Elle serre les entrailles avec une ceinture de soie, d'or, d'argent" (Upon seeing one of these women, wouldn't one take her for a knight of the Round Table? She is so well-equipped, from head to toe, that she breathes the devil's fire. Look at her feet: her shoes so narrow, she looks ridiculous in them. Look at her waist; it's even worse. She has squeezed her innards with a silk belt of gold and silver).[70]

A woman as a knight of the Round Table? Because she is so well "equipped"? And her equipment consists, in this case, of a belt made of silk, gold, and silver and a knight's armor. How is it, this sermon asks specifically, that this "miserable" and lowly (female) creature dares to wear the "armor" of a knight: "D'ou vient qu'une misérable and fragile créature ose se revêtir d'une armure pareille...?" (438). But what precisely is that armor made of by this preacher's own definition? None other than courtly armor's gendered opposite: skin, more precisely the skin of a woman, revealed on her open chest by a plunging neckline. The preacher continues: "C'est à Paris surtout que règnent ces abus. C'est là qu'on voit des femmes courir par la ville toutes décolletées, toutes *espoitrinees*" (It's in Paris that these abuses are especially prevalent. There, one sees women running through the city completely uncovered, their chests bare; 438, my emphasis).

In attempting to protect knights from the contamination of effeminacy, this thirteenth-century preacher attests to the necessary permeability of both social and sexual status. His own speech constructs that most feared and evocative hybrid: the lady/knight, figured in this instance as a non-noble woman wearing a sash fit for a king *and* as a knight of the Round

Table whose armor is fashioned from the delicate skin of a lady's chest. Is she a man or a woman? Is he a woman in disguise? S/he bears the cultural mark of both armored knight and skin-clad lady, with flesh as delicate as it is steely. This constructed flesh cannot be used to determine sexual difference. This skin is armor too; it marks thereby that crucial zone of flexibly gendered subjectivities that lies at the heart of courtliness.

Chapter 5
From Woman's Nature to Nature's Dress

The Fall into Clothes

Old French tales of courtly coupling typically contain cast-off phrases that situate the medieval act of falling in love as a privileged inheritor of the prelapsarian moment of falling into sin. In these instances, the biblical fall into gendered, sexualized flesh is rewritten as an elevation into pleasurable, heterosexual courtly passion. The thirteenth-century *Roman de la poire*, which provides the most thorough rewriting of the Adam and Eve story, announces that:

Des puis qu'Adan mordi la pome,
ne fumes tel poire trovee;
bien orroiz com s'est puis provee.
En la poire mors sanz congié.
. . .
Tel force avoit qu'ele pooit faire
a son ami joie et doulor.

(Never since Adam bit the apple has such a pear been found. Now you will hear how it has been proven; I bit the pear without respite. . . . It had such power that it could give its beloved joy and sadness.)[1]

A bite of this apple is a bite into love, offered by an Eve-like courtly "dame" who seductively peels the pear with her ivory and silver teeth, touching it occasionally with her lips and tongue (vv. 415–35), thus launching this male lover's encounter with pleasure and passion. *Le Lai de l'ombre* contrasts Adam's downfall more specifically with the obverse, elevating phenomenon of courtliness itself:

N'avint puis qu'Adam mort la ponme,
Si bele cortoisie a honme.

(Never since Adam bit into the apple has such courtliness belonged to any man.)[2]

Chrétien de Troyes's twelfth-century *Perceval ou le conte du Graal* offers a further development of the paradigm. The archetypical courtly lady, Guenevere, appears as a new Eve, a courtly version of the woman drawn from Adam's side:

Dame, voir, ele est tant courtoise
Et tant est bele et tant est sage
C'ainc Diex ne fist loi ne langage
Ou l'en trovast si bele dame.
Des que Diex la premiere fame
Ot de la coste Adan formee,
Ne fu dame si renomee. vv. 8176–82

(In truth, lady, she is so courtly, so beautiful and wise, that God has created no language or religion that could account for such a beautiful lady. Never since God formed the first woman from Adam's side has there been a lady of such renown.)[3]

This elegant Eve, credited with the rise of civilized behavior, stands as a source of courtliness from which all good descends:

Ausi ma dame la roïne
Tot le mont ensaigne et aprent;
Que de li toz li biens descent
Et de li vient et de li muet. vv. 8186–89

(Thus does my lady the queen instruct and teach everyone. From her all virtue descends; it originates with and stems from her.)

In these examples, courtly narrative situates itself as offering, in some sense, a new version of the age-old tale of sexual differentiation, a rewriting of the story that once told how woman's distinctly different and beguiling "nature" caused man to fall.

Indeed, well-dressed ladies in the courtly world often issue a challenge to the gestational history of the Edenic fall as a fall away from innocence into fleshly sin and sexual differentiation, a fall marked, on women especially, by deceptive and superficial clothing. Medieval interpreters of Genesis often speak specifically of the fall from Eden as a fall into luxury dress and material extravagance, as Howard Bloch has shown.[4] In the misogynous formulations of Christian thinkers from Paul to Clement of Alexandria, Tertullian, Jerome, and others, clothes were associated with the material, fleshly nature of women and thus denounced as corrupting while also being linked to the immaterial and decorative often decried as feminine, as we saw in Chapter 4. Some medieval moralists liken the trailing fabrics of elite women's long gowns to extended serpents' tails or showy peacock feathers, denouncing luxury attire as bestial excess by those "qui, cum caudas suas extendunt, turpitudinem ostendunt."[5] In the late twelfth century, Innocent III rails against the dangers of women's ornate dress by citing Isaiah's condemnation of the haughty daughters of Zion who "walk with outstretched necks, glancing wantonly with their eyes, mincing along as they go, tinkling with their feet."[6] As punishment the Lord will not only "lay bare their secret parts," Innocent continues, he will also "take away the finery of the anklets, the headbands and the crescents; the pendants, the bracelets, and the scarves; the headdresses, the armlets, the sashes, the perfume boxes and the amulets; the signet rings and nose rings; the festal robes, the mantles, the cloaks, and the handbags; the garments of gauze, the linen garments, the turbans and the veils." Eve's fall is read specifically by Innocent III as a seduction into the bejeweled opulence of the devil, since, according to Ezekiel 28: 12–17, the devil in the Garden of Eden was bedecked with decorative gems and precious metals. As God told Lucifer, "You were in Eden, the Garden of God; every precious stone was your covering, carnelian, topaz and jasper, chrysolite, beryl and onyx; sapphire, carbuncle and emerald; and wrought in gold were your settings and your engravings" (52).[7]

The repeated and seemingly off-hand allusions to the first couple included in Old French tales of courtly love provide an insistent reminder that these stories are not in fact recounting the narrative of man and woman's fateful fall into flesh or clothes. They are pointedly telling a different tale, one that recasts the foundational account of sexual difference and woman's beguiling nature. Indeed, these stories feature couples who are lavishly dressed in layers of clothing that tend to blur, rather than demarcate, their putatively natural sexual differences. For courtly lovers, falling in love can indicate a fall into a different kind of clothing that does not indelibly mark femininity or masculinity, maleness or femaleness. Neither does it underwrite the distinct and secondary status of woman's highly vexed "nature."

To be sure, sentiments echoing this clerical view of women and love as beguiling and dangerous are found in a range of vernacular literary texts, in particular the *Queste del Saint Graal*, where temptresses repeatedly entice chivalric questers, and in the *Prose Lancelot*, where Guenevere herself is characterized as a serpent.[8] Yet, even in this corpus of tales, known as the Arthurian Vulgate Cycle, many female bodies are wrapped within a larger vernacular tradition that reveres courtly ladies as paragons of civilized virtue: intensely worthy and incomparably meritorious. Exemplary in this role is Guenevere herself, as described in the *Prose Lancelot*:

"La roine regarde le vallet moult doucement et il li, toutes les fois qu'il puet vers li mener ses iex covertement, si se merveille moult dont si grans biautés puet venir com il voit en lui paroir, ne de la biauté sa dame del Lac ne de nule qu'il onques veist mais ne prise il rien envers chestui. Et il n'avoit mie tort, se il ne prisoit envers la roine nule autre dame, car che fu la dame des dames et la fontaine de biauté. Mais s'il seust la grant valor qui en li estoit, encore l'esgardast il plus volentiers, car nule n'estoit, ne povre ne riche, de sa valor." (Micha VII, 274)

(The queen looks tenderly at the young man and he at her. Whenever he can glance imperceptibly in her direction, he wonders how she could be so stunningly beautiful. The beauty of all the women he had ever seen, including his Lady of the Lake, held no value for him in comparison to hers. And he was not mistaken to value the queen above all others since she was the lady of all ladies and the fountain of beauty. But if he had known the great worth she possessed, he would have looked at her all the more willingly. No one, rich or poor, could equal her worth).

Here, the courtly Guenevere, whose Eve-like "nature" is figured later in the tale as deceptively serpentine, eludes the conventional and debilitating characterization of a dangerously seductive woman. The snake is now a courtly beauty.

More specifically, a number of courtly love stories contain portraits of women's nature refigured paradoxically as an embodied dress. This view of bodies forged from clothes and flesh alike opens the important possibility of redefining the relation between women and men in the courtly world, not in terms of the stark sexual differences between Adam and Eve set out in Genesis, but as spacings on a gendered sartorial continuum. This chapter will focus on the various ways that courtly love scenarios challenge misogynous conceptions of women's nature derived from the Genesis story, offering instead portraits of sartorial bodies that disrupt and undermine the very concept of clothes that might be assumed to cover a naturally sexed body. A closing section on Marie de France's *Lai de Lanval* will explain how the unconventional gendered subjectivities staged in that brief narrative offer models for reconfiguring not only courtly women's "nature" but men's nature as well.

Nature's Dress

Perhaps the most apt model for understanding courtly clothing as "embodied clothing" is found in the icon of Nature's dress. Detailed in the opening passage of Guillaume de Lorris's *Roman de la Rose*, this garment is worn by an allegorical female protagonist in a natural state. And yet her very nature is to be dressed up. Her beautiful gown provides a decorative surface that literally cannot be displaced from its wearer's body. In spring, we are told, the earth fashions a suitably new dress for herself, not from the lavish silks, brocades, or golden buckles typically worn by courtly lovers, but from natural grasses and colored flowers:

El tens enmoreus, plain de joie,
el tens ou toute rien s'esgaie,
...
lors devient la terre si gobe
qu'ele velt avoir novele robe,
si set si cointe robe feire
que de colors i a .c. peire;
l'erbe et les flors blanches et perses
et maintes colors diverses. vv. 48–49, 59–64

(In the amorous season, full of joy, the season when everything rejoices.... The earth becomes so vainglorious that she wants a new outfit; and she knows how to make a robe so ornate that there are a hundred kinds of colors in it, of grass and flowers in white and blue and many other colors.)

Although Nature's gown is "cointe" (v. 61) and elegant, a lovely and decorative garment imbued with the lively colors used to tint luxury fabrics, this dress is fashioned when the woods recover their own natural greenery and when bushes and hedges adorn themselves:

Que l'en ne voit buisson ne haie
qui en may parer ne se veille
et covrir de novele fuelle.
Li bois recuevrent lor verdure. vv. 50–53

(One sees no bush or hedge that does not wish to adorn itself with new leaves. The woods regain their verdure in May.)

Nature wears this robe in the season of love.[9] And love itself, personified in this text through the allegorized God of Love, is a masculine figure who wears a garment with similarly naturalized decoration. Made entirely of *floretes* rather than silk, the God of Love's robe bears intricate images of animals and birds that are worked in flowers rather than thread:

Qu'il n'avoit pas robe de soie,
ainz avoit robe de floreites,
fete par fines amoreites.
A losenges, a escuciaus,
a oiselez, a lionciaus

et a betes et a liparz
fu sa robe de toutes parz
portrete, et ovree de flors
par diverseté de colors. vv. 876–84

(He did not have a silk outfit but one made of tiny flowers formed into delicate love tokens. The gown was covered all over with images of diamond shapes, small shields, birds, lion cubs, leopards, and other animals. The whole was worked in flowers of many colors.)

Distinct from the courtly dress of Deduit, the garden's founder, who wears a silk robe embroidered with birds worked in gold, "D'un samit portret a oisiaus, / qui estoit toz a *or* batuz" (vv. 818–19, my emphasis; heavy silk [samite] decorated with birds and hammered gold), the God of Love's gown displaces the purely artful and decorative gold (*or*) evoked in Deduit's portrait with the equally artful but also natural *flor*, "Flors i avoit de maintes guises, / qui furent par grant sens asises" (vv. 885–86; There were many kinds of flowers placed with great finesse). We are given no indication that the God of Love's gown might serve to cover or conceal a material body.[10] Rather, the garment itself constitutes both body and clothing of this figure. In fact, we find only a fleeting reference to the God of Love's exquisite physical beauty obscured amid a lengthy account of the character's clothes (vv. 873–75). The God of Love's elegant courtly attire is no more separable from a physiological body than is Nature's robe from the earth itself.

Nature's dress, along with the God of Love's garments, is then not a gown or cloak in the traditional sense of attire that can be put on and removed at will. Rather, Nature's robe should be understood as a kind of body, what we might call a naturally artificial body, or perhaps an embodied dress. And, most significantly, this alternative model of "women's nature" is not limited to women. It provides thus a cogent response to medieval moralists' derogatory view of woman's debased nature—deriving from Eve's *luxuria*—or to the Jealous Husband's association of women's natural bodies with dung.[11] What Guillaume de Lorris offers us in the icon of Nature's dress is a woman "naturally" adorned—that is, dressed in her nature but also in fancy and elegant clothes bearing the attribute *cointe* so often used to define the lavish attire of well-dressed courtly ladies.

Thus does Nature's elaborate gown in Guillaume's romance provide an important alternative to medieval interpretations of the Edenic fall in which woman is held responsible for a descent into lavish clothes while woman's nature remains tied to unclothed and debased flesh.[12] Once freed from its traditional association with a fallen body needing cover, women's nature in courtly literary texts can be figured through garments like Nature's own, both luxurious and material, highly decorative but not necessarily superficial. Furthermore, material display can break free of its imposed association with women alone. Indeed, the bodies of both male and female protagonists in courtly love stories can be fashioned on the model of Nature's dress.

Another Nature, a Different Dress: Alain de Lille's *De Planctu Naturae*

Such is not the case with the representation of Nature's robe in Alain de Lille's twelfth-century *Plaint of Nature* (ca. 1160–65), which states specifically that Nature's "linen tunic, with pictures from the embroiderer's art, concealed the maiden's body beneath its folds,"[13] much as her "underclothing ... lay concealed beneath the outer garments" (104). Indeed, what is emphasized throughout this earlier account of Nature's splendid robe is the accomplished artistry that skillfully represents, without substituting for, elements in the natural world. Resembling more closely Deduit's robe in the thirteenth-century *Roman de la Rose*, Nature's dress in this account, "woven from silk-smooth wool" (85), features pictures of birds: "On it, as the eye would image a picture seen in a dream, was a packed convention of the animals of the air" (86), later joined by fish as well (94 ff.). If, as the text tells us, "these living things, although they had there a kind of figurative existence, nevertheless seemed to live there in the literal sense" (94), they only seem to do so because of the artist's genius. Artistic craft also accounts for the verisimilitude of images that decorate the lower part of Nature's boots in Alain's description: "By the pictures' genius shades of flowers, falling little below truth and reality, were there with their charm" (105). Indeed the nearly real images on Nature's fabulous garments dazzle the viewer with "a presentation *akin* to a stage production" (104, my emphasis), but clearly fixed nonetheless in the realm of artifice. Different from Nature's embodied dress in Guillaume de Lorris's *Roman de la Rose*, the plants and animals adorning Nature's cloak in Alain's account are not to be confused with her material substance. In fact we learn that Nature's tunic has been rent by violent men who have torn her clothes to shreds and stripped her naked (142),[14] maintaining the crucial distinction between body and cover that much early medieval moralizing literature promotes.[15]

By contrast, Guillaume de Lorris reminds us, through the powerful courtly icon of Nature's dress, that the natural can itself be decorative and that artifice can be one's natural state. Thus does Nature's "embodied dress" provide an especially apt model of the sartorial body in courtly romance, displacing women's "nature" from the realms of the sexualized flesh and pure decoration into a hybrid arena in which courtly women and men alike can fashion a different nature from clothes.

Woman's Nature Redefined: Creating Naturally Artificial Bodies

Medieval love treatises offer at times additional models for such a reconceptualization of the courtly body through their insistence that the "nature" of women and men in love should be artful and their adornment fully "natural." The anonymous *Art d'amours* counsels specifically that women should fashion a body out of clothes and surface ornament, a created body that would effectively replace their naturally given one. When advising women to "conceal any fault of the body" as much as possible and to improve their faces by deploying "secret arts," this treatise advises women to create the effect of artifice being natural, at least in the eyes of the lover who must remain ignorant of any artifice deployed in the process.[16] If done successfully, such "women's art" actually transforms the artificial into the natural from the viewer's perspective: "Il loit aux dames elles coucher sanz leur cheveulx pignier puis qu'il sont bien mis en coiffe. Et plus doivent faindre que leurs cheveulx sont ainsi bien ordenés leur vient de nature et non pas d'art, ne d'usage de pignier" (Roy, 240; He [Ovid] advises women to go to bed without combing their hair if it is well coiffed. More importantly, they must pretend that their hair is so well arranged that it comes to them *by nature* and not by artifice or the use of a comb).

Knights too, we are told, should display an artful corporeality. As one female interlocutor in Andreas Capellanus's *Art of Courtly Love* says to her suitor, "Your calves are on the contrary podgy, bulging, round and stunted, and your feet are as broad as long and gigantic to boot" (79). Natural biology has little place in this woman's version of courtliness where knights should, she contends paradoxically, "be naturally endowed with slim, long calves and neat feet, whose length exceeds their width, as if moulded by a craftsman" (79). The ideal knight's body, in this account, should be an artificially natural object, that is, naturally formed as only art can do. This knight's thin legs and the lady's impeccable hair in the preceding examples defy easy classification as "simply natural" or "purely artificial." Within these model love scenarios, at least, the ornamental and artistic allure of body parts belonging to men and women alike tends to fuse with their more fleshly substance. At these moments, artifice has become naturalized as a material that can create rather than merely decorate the courtly body.

In an example closest to the icon of Nature's dress, the *Art d'amours* enjoins women to "adorn themselves as much in clothes as in showing their natural beauty" (Les dames se doivent aourner tant en vesteures comme en leurs beautés monstrer; Roy, 236). The text illustrates this precept by drawing on a model from Nature, describing a plantlike woman, desired by amorous suitors precisely because the work that goes into decorating her body produces a natural, vinelike beauty: "La vigne, quant elle est bien labouree et deuement, si rent fruit, et aussi fait la terre. En telle maniere la femme, quant elle est bien aornee et ascenee, si appert belle et plaisant, pour laquelle beaulté elle est plus tost des hommes convoitié et amee" (Roy, 236; The vine, when it is well cared for, bears fruit, as does the earth. In such a manner, woman, when she is well adorned and turned out, appears beautiful and pleasing. Because of this beauty, she is all the more desired and loved by men).

Love and the luxury garments required to practice it thus fashion women with a sartorial artifice that becomes an integral part of their fleshly bodies. Indeed, metaphorically these clothes produce organic results; they are said to bear fruit. The women dressed in them possess a hybrid status perhaps best rendered by the oxymoronic phrase that appears in many romance narratives: "made from nature," that is, artificially fabricated but also naturally created. The image seems odd until we consider any number of courtly heroines in literary texts known for their excessive sartorial display. In fact, it is the detailed cataloguing of the romance heroine's perfect beauty that ironically often provides an alternative model for imagining "naturally artificial" bodies for players of both genders in courtly love scenarios. Indeed, like Nature's embodied dress, the exquisitely crafted but still fleshly bodies of many female protagonists emerge before us as fashioned, decorated, and lavishly bejeweled, but curiously also natural.

The portrait of Blanchefleur in Chrétien de Troyes's *Perceval ou le Conte du Graal*, for example, moves from the natural world of colorful birds through an extensive account of her elegant clothing to culminate in an image of this heroine as handmade, fabricated by a "main d'ome":

Et la pucele vint plus cointe
Et plus ascemee et plus jointe
Que esperviers ne papegaus.

Ses mantiax fu et ses blïaus
D'une porpre noire, estelee
D'or, et n'estoit mie pelee
La penne qui d'ermine fu.
D'un sebelin noir chenu,
Qui n'estoit trop lons ne trop lez,
Fu li mantiax al col orlez.
...
Le front ot haut et blanc et plain
Come s'il fust *ovrez a main*
Et que *de main d'ome ovrez* fust
De pierre ou d'yvoire ou de fust. vv. 1795–1804, 1815–18 (my emphasis)

(The maiden approached, more gracious, more comely, and more elegant than sparrow hawk or popinjay. Her mantle and tunic were of dark silk starred with gold. The cloak's ermine lining showed no sign of wear. It was decorated at the collar with black and white sable, neither too long nor too wide.... She had a high, white, and smooth forehead, *as if it had been worked by hand, sculpted by a man's hand* from stone, ivory, or wood.)

As the description continues, the decorative red lips and white skin of this heroine "made by hand" contrast sharply with the oft-cited comparison of Blanchefleur's beauty to drops of blood on the snow. To be sure, later in the tale, Perceval observes the "natural color" (v. 4189) that a wounded goose has left behind and sees therein the beauty of his beloved's face:

Que li sanz et la nois ensamble
La fresche color li resamble
Qui ert en la face s'amie,
Si pense tant que il s'oblie,
Qu'autresi estoit en son vis
Li vermels sor le blanc assis
Com ces trois goutes de sanc furent,
Qui sor le blance noif parurent.
En l'esgarder que il faisoit,
Li ert avis, tant li plaisoit,
Qu'il veïst la color novele
De la face s'amie bele. vv. 4199–4210.

(Together the blood and the snow reminded him of the fresh color on his beloved's face, and he considered this until becoming lost in thought, musing that the rosy color was placed on her white face much as these three drops of blood appeared on the white snow. As he looked, he realized with pleasure that he was seeing the fresh color of his beloved's beautiful face.)

But the initial portrait of Blanchefleur's exquisite beauty, heavily laden with references to costly silks with golden details, to ermine and sable, compares "the red on white" of her face to handmade colors of heraldic imagery, artificial colors painted on shields or sewn on the cloth of chivalric banners:

Et miex avenoit en son vis
Li vermeus sor le blanc assis
Que li sinoples sor argent. vv. 1823–25

(A red hue set on a white background was more becoming on her face than vermilion on silver.)

While this heroine is said at times to be more elegant and comely than sparrow hawks or parrots, and while she possesses the "widely spaced eyebrows, smiling gray eyes, and straight nose" that are standard features in portraits of courtly ladies (vv. 1819–22), the ensemble of these naturally derived elements creates an overall effect of sculpted beauty. In the end, this courtly beloved emerges as more naturally beautiful than a hand crafted statue. She is a natural woman exquisitely fashioned from "stone, or ivory or wood" by a "main d'ome" (vv. 1817–18).

So too the famed heroine Lienor in *Le Roman de la Rose ou de Guillaume de Dole*, attired "elegantly enough to present herself before a king at court" (vv. 4421–22), has hair arranged by Nature to create the effect of a shining gold helmet. Having arrived at court to engage a judicial opponent, Lienor removes her hooded cloak and accidentally strips away a layer of distinctively female clothing—the wimple, figured here in curiously chivalric guise as a helmet with ventail and *hordeïs*:

Ele prent dou mantel l'atache;
que qu'el l'oste dou col et sache,
si l'enconbra si li mantiaus
qu'ele hurte as premiers cretiaus
qu'ele avoit fet en sa touaille.
Le hordeïs et la ventaille
enporta jus o tot le heaume,
voiant les barons dou roiaume,
si que sa crigne blonde et sore
son biau samit inde li dore
par espaulles et pres dou col. vv. 4717–27

(She took hold of the cords that fastened her cloak. As she pulled the cloak from her shoulders, it caught in the folds she had made in her wimple, so that helmet and visor and hood all came off. Noblemen of the realm saw her shining blond hair cover her beautiful indigo silk [gown] with gold on her shoulders and at her neck.)[17]

But Lienor's gesture of disrobing reveals curiously yet another helmet, this one made of golden hair:

Ele haoit tant son solas
que ne li chaloit de trecier;
mes, por ses chevols adrecier,
ot drecié sa greve au matin
d'une branche de porc espin,
et si ot fet front de heaumiere. vv. 4730–35

(She was so unconcerned with her own pleasure that she had not bothered to braid her hair; she had merely combed it that morning, parting it with a porcupine quill, in a way that looked like a helmet.)[18]

And this hybrid helmet/hair has been made especially visible by Nature herself, we are told, who has artfully pulled back from the lady's eyes yet another form of headgear—a garland, typically made of flowers—to provide a better view of the heroine's "lovely [helmeted] forehead":

S'ot chapelet a la maniere
as puceles de son païs,
s'ot flocelez aval le vis
de ses biaus chevex ondoianz.
Li chapelez li fu aidanz,
qui li fu un poi loig des iex;
et Nature, por veoir miex
son biau front, li ot tret arriere. vv. 4736–43

(She was wearing a garland according to the fashion of maidens in her region. Her beautiful wavy hair fell around her face. The garland, set back from her eyes, was very becoming. Nature had pulled it back in order to show off her beautiful forehead.)

As a golden helmet is confused with golden locks of the heroine's hair or as a frontal helmet doubles for her forehead, this account of Lienor's extraordinary beauty moves continually between registers of natural, corporeal features and fabricated garments. It ends tellingly with the chaplet, which is, in many courtly accounts, literally made from natural elements, an elegant, decorative garland fashioned from leaves and flowers. To be sure, Blanchefleur and Lienor differ significantly from the allegorical figure of Nature because they are flesh-and-blood heroines in love. And yet, like Nature's embodied dress, their stunning courtly beauty emerges repeatedly as both given and fabricated.

The final portrait of Lienor further underscores this uncanny sartorial corporeality when her beauty is rendered in terms of elaborately embroidered silk cloth. As highborn ladies from all over the city "come most willingly to adorn and dress" Lienor for her coronation, the new empress is robed in a gown cut from cloth made by a fairy and lavishly embroidered by a queen of Apulia with the story of the Trojan War and Helen's kidnapping (vv. 5324–51). This splendid garment, resulting from the work of several women, adorns an even more gorgeous Lienor, whose exquisite physical features are said to surpass the workmanship that distinguishes her extraordinary clothes. But even as the narrator makes this claim, the direct object "la" representing the beautifully crafted *robe* segues imperceptibly into a description of the heroine's face. Praise for her visage ("sa chiere") becomes entwined rhetorically with praise for the costly workmanship ("l'ouvraigne chiere") of the garment itself:

Mout se pot bien consirer d'autre
robe vestir, qui celë ot.
Nus ne *la* voit qui ne *la* lot,
que trop en ert l'ouvraigne chiere.
Mes chascuns prise plus sa chiere. vv. 5356–60 (my emphasis)

(Whoever had this gown could readily forgo all others. No one who saw her/it did not praise her/it, since the workmanship was so fine. But everyone esteemed her face more.)

No less fabricated is Enide's face, transformed by the lavish robes that Queen Guenevere gives her, at Erec's behest, for presentation at court in *Erec et Enide*. After donning the extraordinarily ornamented and costly *bliaut* and *mantel* that Guenevere provides, Enide's "*chiere* is not drab," we are told, "because these garments, which become her so well, make her even more beautiful":

Or n'ot mie la chiere enuble,
car la robe tant li avint
que plus bele asez an devint. vv. 1632–34

The initial portrait of Enide, daughter of an impoverished vavasor, records an exquisite, unenhanced beauty, conferred by Nature alone:

Plus ot que n'est la flors de lis
cler et blanc le front et le vis;
sor la color, par grant mervoille,
d'une fresche color vermoille,
que Nature li ot donee,
estoit sa face anluminee. vv. 427–32

(Her forehead and face were brighter and whiter than the lily, her face lit up amazingly by a fresh rosy color that Nature had given her.)[19]

Once she is remade as an established courtly lady, however, Nature's handiwork combines with delicate clothwork in the evocation of a lavishly fashioned beauty. We hear first in the courtly portrait that Enide's luxurious attire has been "worked" with embroidered colored designs and golden threads:

Molt fu li mantiax boens et fins:
...
La porpre fu molt bien ovree,
a croisetes totes diverses,
yndes et vermoilles et perses,
blanches et verz, indes et giaunes.
Unes estaches de cinc aunes
de fil de soie d'or ovrees
a la reïne demandees. vv. 1589, 1598–1604

(The cloak was beautiful and of high quality.... The dark silk was worked in a variety of little crosses in indigo and vermilion and dark blue, white and green, blue and yellow. The queen asked for some ribbons five yards long worked in golden silk thread.)

Then two *puceles* adorn her hair with a golden garland also "worked" in many colored flowers:

Un cercle d'or *ovré* a flors
de maintes diverses colors
les puceles el chief li metent. vv. 1639–41 (my emphasis)

(The maidens placed a circlet of gold on her head worked in many different colored flowers.)

The adjective "ovree" returns at the end of a detailed account of this heroine's luxurious garments when the beauty decked out in silks and furs, gold and gems, with "two clasps of enameled gold and a topaz" decorating her neck, reemerges from her dressing chamber so comely and beautiful that one could not find her equal in any land. Responsibility for creating this extraordinary beauty is granted not only to Guenevere, Erec, or the *puceles* who have dressed Enide in the sumptuous clothes that have, in a sense, "made her," but also to Nature, who has "worked" her material, much as the silk cloth and gold that create this courtly lady have also been "ovre":

Deus fermaillez d'or neelez,
an un topace anseelez,
li mist au col une pucele,
qui fu tant avenanz et bele
que ne cuit pas qu'an nule terre,
tant seüst l'an cerchier ne querre,
fust sa paroille recovree,
tant l'ot Nature bien *ovree*. vv. 1645–52[20] (my emphasis)

(One maiden placed around her neck two small clasps of enameled gold set around a topaz. The young woman was so comely and beautiful that I do not believe her equal could be found anywhere, no matter how thoroughly one knew how to search—so well had Nature formed/worked her.)

This courtly lady embodies the combined power of love and luxury goods to create heroines whose fabricated and ornate garments have been naturalized to denote beauty both made and innate.

Even Oiseuse, the noble lady who constantly creates her own richly attired self, poised elegantly at the entrance to love's garden in Guillaume de Lorris's *Roman de la Rose*, displays a created beauty that rivals natural elements. The initial description of her flesh tender as a baby chick and soft as fleece, her eyes gray as a falcon, with skin white as new-fallen snow, segues into an account of the courtly lady made entirely from clothes as she holds a mirror, arranges her hair like a treasure, has her sleeves sewn, dons white gloves, primps and combs for her own pleasure (vv. 522–86). She is made from nature but also from clothes, as her hybrid garland attests most cogently. It contains both natural roses and decorative golden thread: "un chapel de roses tot frois / ot desus le chapel d'orfrois" (vv. 553–54). As "frois" (fresh) rhymes here with "orfrois" (golden embroidery), we witness another version of the lady "made by Nature." The work implied here of fashioning roses into a decorative headpiece resonates further with earlier references to working cloth, especially with the artificial flowers embroidered in colored threads on Enide's golden garland.

To assert, in varied ways, as these texts do, that courtly heroines are "made" artificially from nature is to defy, in an important sense, the Edenic gestational narrative of natural sexual difference, which relies on a foundational view of women's given "nature" as fleshly, disobedient, and secondary to man's.[21] If the lavishly clothed courtly heroine stands as a complex cultural hybrid whose naturalness is fabricated, it becomes much more difficult to discern what might constitute her "nature." Once staged within the fictive parameters of courtly narrative, these latter-day Eves no longer bear fleshly bodies neatly separable from clothing that might conceal, decorate, or adorn a corrupted or debased female "nature" beneath. In these examples of courtly encounter, clothing itself tends to become naturalized. As a result, reading through clothes in courtly love scenarios can offer new possibilities for understanding gender differences apart from those constructed according to the strictly dichotomous paradigm of naturally sexed male and female bodies and its antifeminist corollary, which further characterizes those female bodies as adorned with corrupted clothing.

Love's Clothed Body in *Cligés*

A particularly striking example is provided by Chrétien de Troyes's *Cligés* where Love, dressed in the garments of an aristocratic lady, disrupts perceptible distinctions between naked flesh and lavish attire, emerging before us as another version of Guillaume de Lorris's lady "Nature." When the besotted Alixandre, suffering the telltale pain, anxiety, sleeplessness, battering, and wounding (vv. 608–700)[22] of lovesickness, attempts to explain how Love has penetrated his body when no wound is visible on the surface (vv. 687–88), he invokes, predictably, a metaphorical arrow lodged in his heart. This arrow bears golden feathers that make it a *coveted* treasure, so priceless that Alixandre would not exchange "its shaft and its feathers" for Antioch itself.[23] This arrow makes him rich:

Dex, con tres precïeus avoir!
Qui tel tresor porroit avoir,
Por qu'avroit an tote sa vie
De nule autre richesce anvie?
Androit de moi jurer porroie
Que rien plus ne desirreroie,
Que seul les penons et la floiche
Ne donroie por Antioiche. vv. 785–92

(God, what a precious possession! Why would a man who could have such a treasure covet any other riches in his lifetime? I personally could swear that I would desire nothing more. I would not give even the feathers and the shaft for all of Antioch.)

And yet, that same materially valuable golden arrow also connotes the utterly natural features of the courtly hero's ladylove. The priceless feathers, which are not artificially gilt but golden by nature, also adorn the head of the lady that Alixandre encountered a few days earlier. His valued treasure has become her golden tresses:

Li penon sont si coloré
Con s'il estoient tuit doré,
Mes doreüre n'i fet rien,
Car li penon, ce savez bien,
Estoient plus luisant ancores.
Li penon sont les treces sores
Que je vi l'autre jor an mer,
C'est li darz qui me fet amer. vv. 777–84

(The feathers are so brightly colored, as if completely gilded, but no gilding was involved. You can be certain that the feathers themselves [naturally] were even more lustrous. The feathers are the golden tresses I saw the other day at sea. This is the arrow that causes me to love.)

The metaphor of the lady/arrow performs a number of crucial tasks. Attributing incomparable worth to the courtly beloved by assessing her value in terms of material treasure, it also underscores love's ability to enrich its followers and elevate their fortunes in a nonmaterial sense. As Alixandre puts it:

Et quant ces deus choses en pris
(Qui porroit esligier le pris
De ce?) que vaut li remenanz,
Qui tant est biax et avenanz,
Et tant boens, et tant precïeus,
Que desirranz et anvïeus
Sui ancor de moi remirer. vv. 793–99

(And since I hold these two things in such high esteem—who could estimate their value?—what is the rest worth? That countenance is so beautiful and comely, so fine and precious, that I am eager and anxious to gaze at myself again in it.)

The courtly lover is here catapulted into wealth and riches by a natural treasure, a female body bearing the requisite courtly attributes that Nature provides, such as a "cler vis / Com la rose oscure le lis" (vv. 809–10), but along with features valued in relation to costly gems: a "countenance, made by God, so clear that no emerald or topaz could mirror it":

El front que Dex a fet tant cler
Que nule rien n'i feroit glace,
Ne esmeraude, ne topace? vv. 800–802

This is not the image of runaway avarice and unbridled greed for material possessions that Reason fears in her account of lovers coveting Fortune's seductive gown. The effect of love in this instance is not to choose the material over the natural but to naturalize decorative gold and gemstones of the material world while also rendering natural beauty as artifice. Such is also the effect of Guillaume de Lorris's description of Nature's lavishly beautiful dress and the *Art d'amours*'s evocation of plantlike ladies who blossom and bear fruit through the application of decorative adornment, as we have seen.[24] But the image of Love's arrow in *Cligés* does more.

We hear of the snow-white skin visible on the neck and bosom of this courtly heroine. Yet the "whole of the arrow" remains hidden from view because it is clothed in a lady's *chemise* and *bliaut*:

Molt volantiers, se je seüsse,
Deïsse quex an est la floiche:
Ne la vi pas, n'an moi ne poiche,
Se la façon dire n'an sai
De chose que veüe n'ai.
Ne m'an mostra Amors adons
Fors que la coche et les penons,
Car la fleche ert el coivre mise:
C'est li bliauz et la chemise,
Dont la pucele estoit vestue. vv. 840–49

(If I knew how, I would willingly describe the shaft, but I did not see it. I am not to blame if I am unable to describe the form of something I have not seen. At the time, Love showed me only the notch and the feathers because the arrow was placed in the quiver. That is, inside the tunic and *chemise* the maiden was wearing.)

In this account, then, both Love and the ladylove, represented jointly by the fateful arrow, are conceived of as inseparable from clothes. The icon for love itself in this romance is a sartorial body.

And as clothes here become a necessary component of the image of amorous coupling, gender assignments begin to elide. Although the items of courtly dress depicted in this passage—the *chemise* and *bliaut*—are tagged as "lady's clothes," these garments form part of the unisex dress worn by knights as well as ladies in the courtly world. The standard ensemble of garments in twelfth- and thirteenth-century France, known collectively as the *robe*, is worn by elite men and women alike in literary accounts. It includes a loose-fitting quasi-undergarment termed a *chemise*, which is mostly covered by a loosely draped tunic (*bliaut* or *cotte*), followed by a floor-length mantle. Very different from the close-fitting and sex-differentiated attire that developed in fourteenth-century France, the courtly garb from the High Middle Ages actually did little to distinguish women from men. On the contrary, the unisex dress of the courtly elite could readily be used to promote and facilitate cross-gendered identities, as we have seen in Chapter 4. Indeed, the complex allegorical image of Love as a clothed lady/arrow presented in *Cligés*, the lady/love, dressed in unisex *chemise* and *bliaut*, stands before the desiring male lover, but she also exists inside him, as part of him. This clothed lady/arrow is said to be lodged deep inside his heart (vv. 685–86.)

Indeed, the allegorical portrait of courtly love presented in *Cligés*, which initially disrupts our ability to discern golden feathers from the lady's hair and then conflates the allegorical figure of Love with the lady's clothes, finally also makes it difficult to distinguish visually the male lover in this account from the ladylove. If elsewhere in this tale of courtly coupling Alixandre and Soredamor play highly gendered roles of knight and lady, their relationship is figured at this moment by a clothed body that suggests the possibility of subtle gender crossing in love. It also indicates the potential for reconfiguring both woman's *and* man's "nature" in amorous encounter. The further implications of the kinds of sartorial bodies suggested by the foregoing passage from *Cligés* and by the combined images of Nature's dress and the God of Love's garb in the *Roman de la Rose*, are played out more fully in Marie de France's version of the Lancelot story, the *Lai de Lanval*.

Redefining Gender in the *Lai de Lanval*

The twelfth-century *Lai de Lanval* stages the courtly love story in the realm of a particularly intriguing female protagonist who would defy any number of definitions of female "nature." This opulently clad *pucele* bears all the marks of the courtly lady, although she is most often tagged as an otherworldly fairy.[25] When Lanval first meets her, she lounges like a temptress, scantily clad on a sumptuous bed, but she behaves subsequently more as a knight, a king, and a lord than a lady, whether civilizing or dangerous. Her court, set apart from the established locus of King Arthur, relies on an elaborate exchange of lavish garments in a world governed by women whose wealth derives principally from ornate and decorative textiles.[26] Her deployment of these material resources within an alternative courtly economy, more prized and valued than Arthur's own, according to the hero Lanval's assessment of it (v. 300), significantly upsets the traditional distribution of gendered subjects in the courtly world.

Courtly clothes function in this environment more like the naturally artificial garment of Nature's dress than Fortune's opulent gown as Reason depicts it. Although this love story features an ornately dressed lady, distinguished by the abundant wealth of her abode, the love she offers does not rely primarily on luxury garments to display status ostentatiously or to connote female lasciviousness. Falling in love, in this brief tale, thrives in a context of luxury dress without the labor, pain, and loss represented by Reason's arrows,[27] without the concomitant dangers of falling into poverty or covetousness that Reason fears, and without blaming man's fall on woman's deceit and *luxuria*. This lady is a temptress of a different kind.

Indeed, the *Lai de Lanval* offers a cogent alternative to misogynous prescriptions of women's "nature" often conveyed by clerical discourse while also reconfiguring traditional gender assignments in the courtly love scenario. We find here an account of heterosexual coupling within an economy of wealth, opulence, and generous giving that facilitates an unconventional love between a knight who often resembles a lady and his amorous partner who is courtly but quite unladylike. Neither subject position is determined by a biologically given "nature" but is fashioned from lavish garments that forge a range of courtly identities along a gendered sartorial continuum.

The tale opens with a standard depiction of *largesse* at King Arthur's court, figured as a site where knights in armor and ladies in finery play games of love while the wealthy king distributes lavish gifts of land and women to his deserving vassals:

A la Pentecuste en esté
I aveit li reis sujurné;
Asez i duna riches duns
E as cuntes e as baruns.
...
Femmes e teres departi. vv. 11–14, 17

(The King stayed there [at Logres] during Pentecost, in the summer. He gave rich gifts to counts and barons . . . and distributed women and lands.)

This beneficent king's wealth is offered in stark contrast to the *pucele*'s material abundance, which derives not from land or the traffic in women but from luxury cloth. The ladylove's tent, we are told, is worth more than any king could afford:

Suz ciel n'ad rei kis esligast
Pur nul aveir k'il i donast! vv. 91–92

(There is no king on earth who could buy it, no matter how much he offered.)

The coverlets on her bed cost as much as a castle:

Ele jut sur un lit mut bel—
Li drap valeient un chastel. vv. 97–98

(She lay on a beautiful bed; the bedclothes were worth a castle.)

And to pay for the trappings of her horse alone would require the sale of royal or comital lands:

Riche atur ot el palefrei:
Suz ciel nen ad cunte ne rei
Ki tut le peüst eslegier
Sanz tere vendre u engagier. vv. 555–58

(The palfrey had such rich trappings that no earthly king or count could have afforded them without selling or mortgaging land.)

To be sure, the King Arthur of other courtly narratives could boast of similarly impressive and costly goods; but they are not mentioned here.

What we hear instead is that Arthur's traditional *largesse* has failed. Lanval, who has received no financial support from the normally generous king, finds himself literally without sufficient resources (vv. 30–32), the victim of a system of courtly *largesse* gone awry. It is the unnamed *pucele* in this account who fulfills the traditional role of a courtly king, offering an endless source of goods and riches:

Ja cele rien ne vudra mes
Que il nen ait a sun talent;
Doinst e despende largement,
Ele li troverat asez. vv. 136–39

(Never again would he want for anything; he would have what he desired. However generously he might give and spend, she would provide what he needed.)

The metaphorical authority accorded nominally to the Provençal *domna*, who hypothetically plays the part of the feudal lord, is here enacted literally by a feudal lady who controls substantial material resources in the form of cloth. It is in the latter context that this reputedly anomalous and "uncourtly" tale situates the love plot.

Andreas Capellanus's twelfth-century treatise, the *Art of Courtly Love*, typically credits the lady with the ability to instill requisite courtly attributes in her male suitor, thereby dressing him metaphorically in courtliness: "the man who demands the love of any woman of character, especially one of more noble rank, must be exalted by considerable reputation and *invested* with all possible courtliness."[28] But the *Lai de Lanval* reveals how actual material dress might serve as a key to the amorous couple's place in the sexual and social hierarchies of court life. Lanval, for example, though he bears the conventional epithet of *chevalier* throughout the story, is nearly always without a horse and never wears armor.[29] Instead, the *pucele*'s servants dress him as they dress themselves, in *riches dras* that literally replace the armor of knights at Arthur's court with the fabric that characterizes this competing courtly economy of feudal and amatory allegiance:

Celes ki al tref l'amenerent
De riches dras le cunreerent;
Quant il fu vestuz de nuvel,
Suz ciel nen ot plus bel dancel! vv. 173–76

(The women who had brought him to the tent dressed him/armed him/equipped him/ in rich fabric/clothes. When he was dressed anew, there was no more handsome youth in all the world!)[30]

What are we to make of this curious and unconventional icon: A knight armed in cloth?

The image is significant for a number of reasons. In addition to marking visibly an ideological shift from the feudal economy of King Arthur's court to the textile-based economy of the *pucele*'s alternative court, Lanval's "new" clothing signals the possibility of considerable play in the highly gendered roles of the courtly knight and lady.[31] Although this lady secures a standard commitment of love service from Lanval—"Jeo ferai voz comandemenz" (v. 127; I will follow your command)—she behaves, in many ways, more like a knight than a lady. It is she who sets out purposefully on horseback in search of her beloved (v. 112) and she again who, soon after finding him, initiates the lovesuit (v. 116). This lady/knight later testifies in the accused Lanval's defense and deftly secures his release (playing in some sense Lancelot to his Guenevere or Tristan to his Iseut). In the celebrated final scene, the capable and noble *pucele* sweeps Lanval off his feet and carries him away on her horse. She couldn't be more different from Reason's image of the courtly lady Riches who is assailed, ridden at a gallop, and spurred by amorous attackers. Dressed elegantly as a courtly lady but performing actions typically reserved for kings, lords, knights, and male suitors, this *dame* significantly upsets expected gender hierarchies of courtly coupling.

So too does Lanval's borrowed attire call into question the very status and function of men's courtly clothing. The wide-ranging implications of this hero's seemingly feminized chivalric dress are rendered most cogently in a single phrase uttered by his ladylove during their tryst, "Ne vus descovrez a nul humme!" (v. 145). We hear most immediately in this cautionary note the standard courtly admonition to keep the amorous liaison secret: "Do not let anyone know about this." As the *pucele* explains it:

De ceo vus dirai ja la summe:
A tuz jurs m'avrïez perdue,
Si ceste amur esteit seüe. vv. 146–48

(I will tell you why: you would lose me forever if this love were known.)

Indeed, the narrator later uses the verb *descovrir* to describe Lanval's anguish at having revealed the love affair, "Descovert ot la druërie" (v. 336). And yet we learn that Lanval has revealed much more than love by speaking to Guenevere openly, or *a descovert*, as he calls it. Indeed he has alleged that the queen, and by implication the putatively luxurious world of King Arthur's court, is literally worth less than the most miserable servant girl in the *pucele*'s realm:

Bien le sachiez a descovert:
Une de celes ki la sert,
Tute la plus povre meschine,
Vaut mieuz de vus, dame reïne. vv. 297–300

(You might as well know everything: any of the young women in her service, even the poorest girl, is worth more than you, my lady queen.)

Lanval here reveals, to the horror of Guenevere and Arthur alike, the existence of a competing courtly system where the material effects of courtly *largesse* and generous giving of luxury clothing in particular can seriously undermine expected sartorial and behavioral markers of knight and lady. In this alternative courtly economy, populated primarily by women, knights do not necessarily wear armor—indeed they dress "like ladies"—and ladies, armed in cloth alone, can behave like knights.[32]

But the phrase, "Ne vus descovrez a nul humme" also sends us back to the initial depiction of the *pucele* in this tale, an eroticized damsel stretched out on lavish bedclothes inside her ornate tent, a paragon of seductive beauty undressed, "tut descovert":

Dedenz cel tref fu la pucele:
Flur de lis e rose nuvele,
Quant ele pert al tens d'esté,
Trepassot ele de beauté.
...
Un chier mantel de blanc hermine,
Covert de purpre alexandrine,
Ot pur le chaut sur li geté;
Tut ot descovert le costé,
Le vis, le col, e la peitrine:
Plus ert blanche que flur d'espine! vv. 93–96, 101–6 (my emphasis)

(The maiden was inside the tent. Her beauty surpassed the lily and the young rose which appear in summer.... She had thrown over herself a precious cloak of white ermine covered with Alexandrine silk because of the cold. But her entire side was *uncovered*, her face, neck, and chest. She was whiter than the hawthorn flower.)

As with so many courtly ladies, often depicted as "nue en sa chemise," this woman's beauty resides in her sumptuously white skin, seductively bared among the *riches dras* and costly mantle that both clothe and reveal her body.[33] Could her admonition to Lanval about keeping their love secret also refer to dress and clothing as it does in the preceding quote? Could the phrase "ne vus descovrez a nul humme" also be a kind of instruction regarding his appropriate dress, suggesting figuratively, while not saying so literally, "Don't undress; don't take off these clothes I have given you, these *riches dras* that mark you as my lover and my vassal rather than one of Arthur's armed retinue"?[34] Operating on several narrative registers simultaneously, the word *descovrir* could then suggest that the prohibited act of revealing the couple's secret love and making a full disclosure to Guenevere (by speaking to her *a descovert* and unmasking the naked truth, as Lanval does unwittingly) *does not* necessarily mean that this knight will have to lose his ladylove. Neither will he be required to relinquish the garments he has received from her. Since Lanval's ornate dress constitutes a new kind of armor, cut from cloth rather than metal, retention of it does not, it seems, depend on keeping a vassalic oath to the overlord, as the model of feudal service would dictate. Indeed, we witness here an alternative model of love service in which Lanval can break the oath he swore earlier to his ladylord and still keep the garments that mark him unmistakably as *her* vassal in love.

The final scene in the *Lai de Lanval* contains perhaps the most crucial moment of undressing, although the verb *descovrir* does not figure in the depiction of the ravishingly beautiful *pucele*'s arrival at King Arthur's court.

As the object of the assembled barons' attention and Lanval's desire, the *pucele* lets her mantle fall away from her body so that onlookers can see her more fully:

Sun mantel ad laissié cheeir,
Que mieuz la peüssent veeir. vv. 605–6

(She let fall her mantle, so they could see her better.)

But this *bele* has not come only to be seen and adored. Her task is specifically to talk to King Arthur, "Ele vient ci a tei parler" (v. 537), to acquit Lanval of the charges leveled against him and deliver him physically from a court where he has been unable to secure monetary support or judicial aid (vv. 38, 68, 466). Indeed, when this stereotypically courtly beauty opens her mantle, we not only see her body, admired by all; we also hear her voice. She speaks deftly of both love and vassalage, redirecting the viewer's gaze from her exquisite beauty to Lanval's accused body:

Quant il l'orent bien esgardee
E sa beauté asez loëe,
Ele parla en teu mesure
Kar de demurer nen ot cure:
"Reis, j'ai amé un tuen vassal;
Veez le ci: ceo est Lanval!" vv. 611–16

(When they had looked her over fully and thoroughly praised her beauty, she spoke, having no desire to wait, "King, I have loved one of your vassals. You see him here: It is Lanval!")

This heroine provides a particularly striking example of the phenomenon I have termed bodytalk, in which the speech attributed to female protagonists in Old French texts disrupts the stereotypes of femininity that their fictive bodies otherwise underwrite and promote.[35] In this instance, however, when the classic romance beauty, fetishized object of everyone's gaze, speaks from that gorgeous body, her words are enriched by a contributing factor of clothes that facilitate cross-gendered positioning in love. The elaborately dressed *pucele* speaks here not as a dolled-up beauty but as a well-dressed knight, providing legal defense for the helpless accused party in a feudal trial:

"Si par mei peot estre aquitez,
Par voz baruns seit delivrez!"
. . .
N'i ad un sul ki n'ait jugié
Que Lanval ad tut desrainié. vv. 623–24, 627–28

("If he can be acquitted by me, let him be freed by your barons!" ... There was not one among them who thought she had not successfully defended/exculpated Lanval.)

Having come on horseback to save her beloved from impending danger, this knight errant remains nonetheless a beautiful *pucele*:

Quant par la vile vint errant
Tut a cheval une pucele.
Et tut le siecle n'ot plus bele! vv. 548–50

(A maiden came riding through town on horseback; there was none more beautiful in all the world.)

Whereas Erec wins the sparrow hawk contest in Chrétien de Troyes's *Erec et Enide* because his lady qualifies as the most beautiful woman in the world, this lady/knight errant, richly attired in a mantle of "purpre bis" (v. 571), carries the sparrow hawk herself (v. 573) while retaining throughout the claim to being "la plus bele del mund" (v. 591). Thus does this heroine play both parts at once, an anomaly recorded here when the standard "head to toe" catalogue of feminine beauty is tellingly inverted. This lady/knight's portrait proceeds irregularly from bottom to top, beginning with her hips and ending with her head:

Le cors ot gent, basse la hanche,
Le col plus blanc que neif sur branche;
Les oilz ot vairs e blanc le vis,
Bele buche, neis bien asis,
Les surcilz bruns e bel le frunt. vv. 563–67

(She had a gracious body with a low waist. Her neck was whiter than snow on tree branches. She had gray eyes and white skin, a beautiful mouth and a fine nose, brown eyebrows and a lovely forehead.)

Still, any man gazing upon her beauty would be heated up:

Il n'ot un sul ki l'egardast
De dreite joie n'eschaufast! vv. 583–84

(Not a single man who looked at her could avoid feeling warmed by joy.)

But this beguiling and dressed-up beauty does not menacingly tempt her knight to fall away from chivalric duty or vassalic loyalty, as the more Eve-like Enide is reputed to do. This lady's seductive appeal, fashioned from the silks and brocades of luxury dress, secures instead her knight's health, well-being, and legal exoneration from criminal charges. Here beauty actually saves a knight imperiled by false accusations. Lanval's claim, "I am saved when I see her" (v. 600), offers a telling alternative to the troubadour lament for a lady who might ideally cure and free him of lovesickness, if only she would consent to his requests. This lady/knight, by contrast, literally saves Lanval from charges of treason, which would legally carry a penalty of death. She offers a provocative mix of gendered identities, which make her less an icon of woman's nature or sexual difference than a model of more fluid sexual differences. We associate her and the love she offers less with dangerous Edenic seduction or with the ethereal spring breezes, leaves, and flowers of the natural world than with the material opulence of luxury cloth.

Throughout the trial, this lady/knight is defined by lavish cloth deployed uncharacteristically in the service of chivalric rescue. Prior to her arrival at King Arthur's court, two female messengers dressed in "cendal purpre" (v. 475; dark-colored, lightweight silk) ask that the king's chambers be hung with lavish silks in preparation for the lady's stay:

Reis, fai tes chambres delivrer
E de palies encurtiner
U ma dame puisse descendre:
Ensemble od vus veut ostel prendre. vv. 491–94

(King, prepare your rooms by hanging silk curtains where my lady can stay. She wants to take lodging with you.)

Two more *puceles* "de gent cunrei" follow, also dressed in ornate silks, "vestues de deus palies freis" (v. 511), which announce the "manteus de purpre bis" (v. 571) the lady herself will wear. More than anything else, the beauty of luxury dress marks this capable liberator; her armor is made of *pailes* and *cendal*.[36] In this context, the elegant courtly attire characteristic of a woman's community becomes equally appropriate for knights needing to be rescued and ladies cast in the role of armored saviors.

As Lanval takes up the part generally played by a courtly damsel in distress, the beautiful object of desire moves into the subject position, riding off as a knight, though dressed in female finery, with a man mounted behind her:

Fors de la sale aveient mis
Un grant perrun de marbre bis,
U li pesant humme muntoent,
Ki de la curt le rei aloent.
Lanval esteit muntez desus.
Quant la pucele ist fors a l'us,

176   Chapter 5

Sur le palefrei, detriers li,
De plain eslais Lanval sailli!
Od li s'en vait en Avalun,
Ceo nus recuntent li Bretun,
En un isle ki mut est beaus.
La fu raviz li dameiseaus! vv. 633–44

(A large stone had been placed outside the hall where heavy men (i.e., armored knights) mounted before departing from the king's court. Lanval had climbed onto the stone, and when the young woman came through the gate, Lanval leapt, in one bound, onto the palfrey, behind her. He went to Avalon with her, as the Bretons tell us, to a beautiful island. Thus was the young man carried off/seized/ravished.)

This is not an Arthurian knight or suitor, laden and heavy with armor, who would typically fight to win possession of his ladylove, but a lightweight man, a ravished and ravishing *damoiseau* wrapped in the rich garments (*riches dras*) of a woman's world, another court, and a different kind of love. The ornamental dress, so characteristic of this lady's realm, promotes a love without waiting and lament, a love without pain and deceit.

As this decidedly courtly if anomalous couple ride off (v. 231), they leave behind the traditional world of King Arthur's court, which has become a site of false accusations (vv. 327, 353) and heteronormative prescriptions for courtly coupling. Guenevere's pointed attack on Lanval reveals the limitations of amorous affairs at King Arthur's court, now replaced by the more welcome terrain of the ladylove's equally courtly abode (vv. 183, 490, 533). When the rebuffed and angered Queen Guenevere charges Lanval with preferring the sexual favors of young men to the pleasures of women, she posits two gendered categories in stark opposition to one another:

Lanval, fet ele, bien le quit,
Vus n'amez gueres cel deduit.
Asez le m'ad hum dit sovent
Que des femmes n'avez talent!
Vallez avez bien afeitiez,
Ensemble od eus vus deduiez. vv. 277–82

("Lanval," she said, "I think it is true that you have no interest in that pleasure. Men have told me often enough that you have no desire for women. You have frequented young men; you take pleasure with them".)

Lanval responds by claiming a mutually shared love for a lady whose *value* far surpasses the queen's:

Mes jo aim e si sui amis
Cele ki deit aveir le pris
Sur tutes celes que jeo sai.
...
Une de celes ki la sert,
Tute la plus povre meschine,
Vaut mieuz de vus, dame reïne,
De cors, de vis e de beauté,
D'enseignement e de bunté! vv. 293–95, 298–302

(I love and am loved by a lady who should be prized above all others I know. . . . Any of the young women in her service, even the poorest girl, is worth more than you, my lady queen, in body, face, and beauty, in learning and goodness.)

What Lanval does not say to his courtly and royal interlocutor, who divides the world neatly into heterosexual and homosexual lovers, is that his love for the unnamed *pucele* challenges the exclusivity of these very categories. The courtly Lanval is enamored of a lady/man to whom he plays the damsel/knight. The two cannot readily be distinguished by their dress. Neither do they occupy traditionally gendered positions in social, legal, or amorous exchange.

Left behind at Arthur's court as well is the medieval model of "women's nature" derived from the lascivious Eve-like seduction now embodied, uncharacteristically, by Guenevere herself.[37] Posed in the role of Potiphar's wife, later taken up, for example, by Eufeme in the *Roman de Silence*, King Arthur's wife has seduced the unsuspecting Lanval and, when rebuffed, charged him with dishonoring her:

Lanval, mut vus ai honuré
E mut cheri e mut amé;
Tute m'amur poëz aveir.
Kar me dites vostre voleir!
Ma druërie vus otrei:
Mut devez estre liez de mei! vv. 263–68

(Lanval, I have honored you, loved you, and held you dear. You can have all my love; just tell me your wishes. I pledge my love to you; you can take delight in me!)

Indeed, of the two charges leveled against Lanval—treason against Arthur for propositioning Guenevere and boasting of his *amie*'s unsurpassed value—the former drops out of the narrative altogether, and Guenevere along with it. We are left at the trial scene with one woman: the finely attired lady/knight summoned to save the beloved she has dressed like herself, fashioning him in her ornate image while she adopts his chivalric pose. Falling in love in this courtly scenario is an elaborate process of falling into cross-gendered clothes. This fall effectively recasts the Genesis narrative's account of falling into clothes, which divides the world into two discrete sexes and allocates the secondary, degraded position to women's depraved nature. By contrast, clothes in this account, like Nature's dress or the watery garments that constantly shape and reform Fortune's home in Reason's tale, help us to move away from limiting misogynous prescriptions of woman's nature to an understanding of sartorial bodies that allow both genders substantial room in which to move. The varied subject positions available to knights and ladies in the *Lai de Lanval* could perhaps best be described not as sexed bodies but as spacings on a gendered sartorial continuum that calls into question the very category of the natural and its suitability to account not only for courtly women's nature but for the nature of courtly men as well.

PART IV

Expanding Courtly Space Through Eastern Riches

Chapter 6
Saracen Silk:
Dolls, Idols, and Courtly Ladies

A Saracen Love Story

The first volume of the thirteenth-century Lancelot-Grail Cycle, the *Estoire del Saint Graal*, contains a curious story of King Mordrain's doll. It is, at one and the same time, a story of conversion and a love story, both set within a larger tale of the transfer of the relic-like Holy Grail from the Middle East to Great Britain by the Chosen Quester, Galahad. The conversion story of King Mordrain caught the imagination of the *Estoire*'s anonymous author, who extends the earlier account provided in the *Queste del Saint Graal*, committing fully one-fifth of the *Estoire* to chronicling the Saracen king's many and varied hesitations before finally converting to Christianity. The tale of Mordrain's life-size doll, which occupies one such moment, stages an unexpected and uncanny version of the Pygmalion story, as a Saracen king falls passionately and obsessively in love with "une ymagène de fust amierveilles de grant biautet en guise d'une femme" (a wondrous wooden image of great beauty in the form of a woman).[1] Theirs was the strongest love ever, we are told. And, like the Ovidian Galatea, this woman is lavishly clad: "Si estoit viestus d'une riche reube (les plus riches) qui li roys pooit trouver et les plus pressieuses" (Hucher, 2: 318; She was dressed in rich garb, the most costly and most precious that the king could find).

But different from her Roman predecessor, who comes to life when Venus intervenes, this statue of a woman, cut from wood instead of ivory, remains an adored but lifeless image. And different too from Pygmalion's ongoing amorous attachment to his beloved in Ovid's tale, Mordrain's fifteen-year love affair with the lady doll comes to a starkly brutal end. Conversion intervenes. Josephus, the Christian bishop, explains to King Mordrain (called Evalach before conversion) that he must cast out a "desloyal semblance" of the woman statue he has kept hidden in a locked room where he goes "to sin": "A ceste hymagène gisoit li roys carnelement et de si grand amour l'avoit amée bien quinze ans ... il voloit aler à l'ymagène pour faire son péchiet et sa desloyalité" (Hucher, 2: 318, 320; The king lay carnally with this image and loved it/her passionately for 15 years.... He liked to go to the image to sin and misbehave). When Mordrain finally relents, deciding to embrace the naked Christ instead of his well-dressed ladylove, he throws the female figure into the fire and incinerates tellingly not only the wooden statue but also her clothes: "la robe que ele avoit viestue et li fus dedens" (320).[2] Paganism dies, taking luxury dress along with it.

Of further significance, the site of Mordrain's ill-fated love affair is the city of Sarras, imagined in this context as the origin of all Saracens, and located somewhere between the historical Cairo (here called Babiloine) and Salamander.[3] It is in this eastern locale that King Mordrain's carnal excess (*péchiet*) becomes a form of idolatry through his purported worship of a pagan lady idol (*ymagène*). But the Saracen king's dual sins are recorded, as we have seen, through the oriental opulence of luxury clothes attributed to a lady's "riche reube." Thus does the love story entwined with the account of Mordrain's conversion record a western Christian condemnation of what is called Saracen religion by rejecting eastern wealth, and more precisely by spurning the lavish clothes used to adorn the foreign, infidel beloved.

And yet if we read through the clothes of Mordrain's doll in the *Estoire*'s version of the Pygmalion story, the dreaded and threatening Saracen idol begins to look remarkably like the revered courtly lady herself. In fact, Mordrain's wooden paramour, finely dressed in "a splendid gown, the richest and most precious," contains within it a snapshot portrait of the western, Christian courtly lady, whose hallmark in the French literary tradition is precisely to be "richement parée." We have seen how heroines such as the courtly Enide bear this epithet, along with beauties ranging from the allegorical Cortoisie in the *Roman de la Rose*, who is "richement vestuz" (Lecoy, v. 820),[4] to Oiseuse described as "bien paree et atornee" (v. 567) or the unnamed *trobairitz* in Chapter 2, whose clothes are "rich and noble, trimmed with fine gold" (vv. 4–6). The robes of courtly heroines are not only expensive and luxurious. They are cut more specifically from eastern silks and often adorned with gems like those imported to France throughout the twelfth and thirteenth centuries along trade routes through Italy from the Middle East and beyond.[5] If Perceval's beloved Blanchefleur wears a *mantel* and *bliaut* of Byzantine silk called "purple"—"une porpre noire, estelee / D'or" (vv. 1799–1800)—Lanval's lady dons a costly mantle of white ermine covered with Alexandrine silk from Egypt: "un chier mantel de blanc hermine, / Covert de purpre alexandrine" (vv. 101–2).[6] Other heroines are said more generally to wear "pailes d'Orient."[7]

If we have in many ways understood the court setting for medieval love stories to be identifiably western, European, and Christian, the tale of Mordrain's doll suggests that some of the most immediately recognizable features of courtly identity—those conveyed by the sartorial opulence of luxury dress—are often marked in literary accounts as deriving in fact from eastern and often non-Christian lands rich in costly textiles. And love itself in the western court is structured, far more than we have imagined, by evocations of lavish goods that have moved westward through mercantile exchange and crusading plunder from an ambiguously defined but linguistically demarcated "orient." The transfer of luxury goods into western court culture that is recorded in Old French accounts of courtly love does not serve an incidental, exotic, or merely decorative function. While luxury silks, precious metals, and costly gemstones are used in romance texts to display the requisite wealth of European courtly players, they also mark that purportedly western identity as utterly dependent for its visual recognition and social definition on goods bearing, paradoxically, the names of eastern cities: Baghdad, Damascus, and Phrygia, as well as Constantinople. Seen through the lens of clothing, courtly versions of Pygmalion's dolled-up beauty, then, challenge us to rethink the spatial politics of courtly love: its putative westernness as a phenomenon both geographically and culturally distinct from the Muslim east, although it remains clearly linked in some literary accounts to a Byzantine heritage.[8]

The description of Pygmalion's coveted ladylove in Jean de Meun's *Roman de la Rose* is a case in point. In addition to a brief mention of domestic woolens and imported furs, it features an extensive catalogue of luxurious eastern silks and gemstones, although their precise origin remains occluded:

Puis les li roste, et puis ressaie
con li siet bien robe de saie,
cendauz, melequins, hatebis,
indes, vermeuz, jaunes e bis,
samiz, diapres, kameloz.
. . .
Autre foiz li reprent corage

d'oster tout et de metre guindes
jaunes, vermeilles, verz et indes,
et treçoers gentez et grelles
de saie et d'or, a menuz pelles;
...
une courone d'or grellete,
ou mout ot precieuses pierres. vv. 20915–19, 20932–36, 20940–41

(Then he removes those clothes from her and tries silk dresses instead, a dress of light weight cendal, or thin *melequin*, or a *moiré* in indigo, vermilion, yellow, or brown, or a dress of heavy samite, silk brocade, or wool.... At another time he is moved to take off everything and put on head ornaments of yellow, vermilion, green, and indigo, or comely, thin ribbons of silk and gold with seed pearls ... a delicate little crown with many precious stones.)

The light-weight *cendal* (from Arabic "sundus") mentioned here denotes a supple silk taffeta deriving, along with the thicker, more luxurious and heavier *samit*, from Syria and Asia Minor. The decorative floral brocade called *diapres* in this description originates from Baghdad, as do a number of silks named frequently in other courtly romances: *siglaton, baldequin,* and *tiraz*.[9] The lavish fabrics draped on the body of Pygmalion's ladylove, along with the imported gold, pearls, and precious gems that further adorn her, mark a substantially porous cultural border between east and west, allowing oriental opulence to infiltrate and define not only courtly elegance, but also the practice of love.

Reading through clothes in this instance will allow us to take into account the symbolic and imaginative roles that such ornate eastern fabrics and jewels play in fashioning the literary identities of protagonists in a range of courtly love stories. It will acknowledge at the same time the material history of those luxury goods as part of elaborate medieval systems of trade, pilgrimage, and crusade. Eastern luxury goods came into France during the twelfth and thirteenth centuries via these three principal channels. Accounts of their transfer recorded in chronicle and crusading narratives tend to be cast in terms of the oppositional geography that pits east against west in the story of Mordrain's doll.[10] Courtly romances, however, often provide a much more nuanced view, fashioning literary lovers whose putatively western courtliness already contains a highly variegated sartorial east within it. Reading through clothes in this chapter will enable us first to acknowledge where the rich clothes and adornments of courtly players come from, and then to ask how courtly romances put these luxury goods into play. In Chapter 7 we will see more specifically how the hybrid heroine of the Byzantine romance *Floire et Blancheflor* refashions western institutions of courtly love and Christianity by using the material opulence and decoration so often coded as pagan and eastern.

I do not wish to argue here that courtly literary texts enact a kind of exotic orientalizing of otherwise western subjects. Nor does the phenomenon I want to chart conform to the related tendency noted by Jean Frappier in the twelfth-century *romans d'antiquité*, which "modernize" classical figures and locations to conform to feudal cultural norms. Frappier cites as examples the literary fabrication of the Greco-Macedonian king Alexander as an epitome of courtly perfection and *largesse*, the arming of the Trojan Enéas as if he were a feudal knight, and the portrait of Caesar as a model courtly lover in the thirteenth-century *Hystore de Julius Cesar* by Jehans de Tuim.[11] Frappier argues that these portraits are not ineptly anachronistic but successfully westernized, adapted to contemporary French tastes for the familiar, while staged among more exotic, fantastic, and foreign details of décor, architecture, and costume.

And yet the analysis breaks down at the very point where clothing comes into play. In describing the lavish attire of the queen of Egypt in the *Hystore* as typical of the "roman courtois," indeed comparable to that of "une très haute dame d'une cour médiévale" (48) such as Iseut, Frappier suggests that the European medieval author has dressed the Egyptian queen in clothes reflecting a western courtly identity. The passage in question, however, describes medieval items of dress that owe their recognizably "French" character to imported eastern luxury goods including silk, gold, and precious gems: "*robe de soie tresgetee a or*, manteau fourre d'hermine entremelee de zibeline, avec des *pierres precieuses en guise de 'tassels' et deux emaux pour fermer l'attache*, bliaut avec une traine longue d'une aune, *ceinture d'argent et d'or, garnie de saphirs et de rubis*" (48; my emphasis). Frappier's comment is revealing because it tells us just how enmeshed these eastern goods have become in fashioning our own scholarly conception of the western court, but in a way that does not acknowledge the implications of their inclusion. This is a particularly striking example of how we have read past the full range of clothing's functions in Old French texts. It is significant, for my purposes, that the sumptuous clothes specified here are not just costly or ornate luxury goods. Although their exact provenance in the foregoing example is not named, we will see in the texts studied below how these luxury goods and lavish adornments, silk fabrics and gemstones in particular, are often marked specifically as being from an "orient" that ranges geographically over an expanse from Constantinople to Egypt, Persia, and India.

Saracen Princess or Well-Dressed Lady?

It is a commonplace of medieval studies that the Saracen princess in Old French literary texts occupies, in many respects, a liminal space between cultures, often embodying the western ideals of beauty and elegance modeled by her European counterpart. The heroine of the thirteenth-century *chantefable Aucassin et Nicolette*, for example, originates from a "vile a Sarasins" (2) but bears skin so white that the daisies look black by comparison (14).[12] This "flor de lis" (13) not only appears to residents of her estranged father's court in Carthage to be "a gentille femme de haut lignage" (34), she also displays the more corporeal "cler vis, gent cors, vair yeux, beau ris" (24) of a western courtly lady.[13] The Saracen princess Orable in the epic *Chanson de Guillaume* is a "dame d'Aufriquant," subtly transformed through conversion and marriage into a "reine gente" (vv. 202–7, 660) bearing the typically courtly "cler vis" and "char blanche."[14] The highly westernized portraits of these female protagonists seriously complicate the oppositional logic that otherwise pits Christian knights from France against demonized Saracen rivals.[15] Indeed, the position of Saracen princesses "between cultures" of east and west is as complex as their function as "gifts" in a system that governs the exchange of women in Old French epic, as Sarah Kay has shown.[16] If the Saracen princesses studied by Kay often perform as subjects and objects simultaneously, as gifts given and manipulators of those very gifts, they also stand as hybrid heroines who call into question the dichotomous religious categories of eastern paganism and western Christianity that the epics featuring them promote.

More important for our purposes, however, is the courtly lady of romance texts, who further complicates the polarized geography of east and west in Old French literature. She does so specifically through her clothes.[17] Oiseuse, the gatekeeper of love's garden in Guillaume de Lorris's *Roman de la Rose*, wears a gown of *samit* (vv. 859–62). Her chaplet or decorative head garland is fashioned with *orfrois*,[18] *aureum phrygium* or gold thread from Phrygia, which also adorns the lavish silk gowns worn by the allegorical figure Richesse and many others (vv. 1051, 1054, 1056–58). The black inlay decorating the band of gold on Richesse's richly trimmed collar derives from a technique of enameling developed in Egypt (vv. 1059–61). Even the colors embroidered on the heroine's luxurious robes in Chrétien de Troyes's *Erec et Enide* signal the eastern provenance of costly dyes, indicating, among other hues, blue tints termed "yndes" (from India) and "perses" (vv. 1698–1701; from Persia).[19] If these references to eastern sites tend to lose their full geographical resonance when they pass into generic usage as terms for "indigo" or "blue," as in Jean de Meun's account of Pygmalion's ladylove cited above, the Old French words themselves retain the rich allusions to cross-cultural exchange, travel, and trade.[20] The generic term "pailes" (from *pallium*) denotes costly silk fabric and the spectrum of luxury goods fashioned from it: tents, tapestries, wall hangings, bed curtains, and coverlets, as well as luxury garments, frequently characterized by the adjective "d'orient."[21] These silks sometimes carry a more specific designation of provenance such as "paile d'ynde," "paile grigois," or "paile alixandrin" (silks from India, Greece, Alexandria). Courtly figures draped in these costly fabrics become, at one and the same time, decorative icons of the excessive wealth accumulated in western European courts in the French Middle Ages and visual maps pointing to the non-European sites that provided the sumptuous goods used to mark the elite social status of courtly lovers in literary accounts.

Courtly *Largesse* and Saracen Wealth

The hybrid positioning of courtly ladies between east and west is recorded perhaps most tellingly in the gown of "Saracen silk" worn by the stately allegorical figure of Largesse in Guillaume de Lorris's *Roman de la Rose*. Representing the importance of courtly generosity against the forces of avarice, Largesse is said to wear "a fresh, new outfit" made not of indigenous wool, but of "porpre sarazinesche":

Largesce ot robe tote fresche
d'une porpre sarazinesche. vv. 1161–62

Porpre refers literally to purple silk originally produced for the Byzantine emperors, although it later came in many grades, ranging in color from magenta to brown. The term "Saracen" in the Old French context usually denotes "pagan," more specifically Muslim. In the *Cycle du Roi*, Charlemagne fights Saracens, who are synonymous with pagans, Joinville brands the Islamic world "païennie" in his account of the Fourth Crusade, and Innocent III exhorts Christians to attack Saracens as "pagans" in the Fourth Lateran Council of 1215.[22] And yet "Saracen" also becomes synonymous in the medieval cultural imagination with individuals who are "rich" from mercantile exchange. In the *Estoire*, for example, Matagran like Mordrain before him is tagged as practicing idolatry (141), but this infidel's identity resides equally in his stunning wealth. He is cast as a prototypical and generic "Saracen" because of his rash promise to make Josephus a "rich man" by offering the Christian bishop a treasure of material and mercantile goods: precious metals, costly gemstones, and luxurious silks: "Jou vos ferai rice homme à tousjours.... Si ai assés, dist *li sarrasin*, or et argent et pières présieuses et grant plentet de dras de soie et vaissielemence d'or et d'argent, tant que plus n'en voel, en est-çou grant riquèce?" ("I will make you a rich man forever.... I have enough gold, silver, and precious stones, and a great many silk cloths and gold and silver dishes, more than I could ever want," said the *Saracen*. "Aren't these great riches?" Hucher 3: 212–13; Ponceau 2: 497; my emphasis). Joinville's account of the Fourth Crusade tells similarly how the comte de Brienne, lord of Jaffa, appropriated golden and silk fabrics from "Saracen" caravans, using the term less to indicate religious affiliation than to signal ample mercantile wealth: "sarrazins qui menoient grant foison de dras d'or, et de soie" (Le Goff, 179–80).

Indeed, when set in the material context of textiles, travel, and trade, the meaning of "Saracen" used in Old French romance texts extends far beyond a strictly religious connotation of "paganism" to include a geographical meaning based on the material displacement of eastern luxury goods westward. "Saracen" lands in this context connote an opulent *place*—albeit an ambiguous and ill-defined expanse of lands—some Muslim, others Christian, lying vaguely to the east, beyond the borders of western Europe and stretching from Constantinople to Egypt, while also including southern Spain. The concept of "Saracen lands" most often recorded in medieval romance narratives comprised a highly diverse and often Hellenized orient whose geographic parameters were as imprecise as its specific religious affiliation. Since Byzantines were often viewed in the medieval cultural imagination as schismatics, their refusal to acknowledge the pope's authority often branded them as "less than Christian." Jacques Le Goff reports that at the time of the Second Crusade the bishop of Langres, intent on conquering Constantinople, urged Louis VII to declare that the Byzantines were not in fact Christians (179). These sentiments persist through the Fourth Crusade when Robert de Clari defends the western sack of Constantinople because the city's residents who refused allegiance to the pope in Rome were Christian "in name only" (180). From this perspective, the adjective "sarazinesche," based on "sarasin," although often used in the French Middle Ages to denote Muslims and other non-Christians, reflects more accurately its derivation, according to Greimas, from an Arabic word that itself meant "Oriental" in general, *including* Greek and Byzantine.[23]

The full range of meanings inherent in "Saracen silk" emerges perhaps most tellingly in the *Roman de la Rose* through the association of the allegorical Largesse with Alexander the Great. As a female model of courtly generosity, Largesse descends, we are told, "dou lignage Alixandre" (v. 1128), thus perpetuating the medieval tradition of linking courtly splendor to Alexander the Great's famed generosity, first recorded in Geoffrey of Monmouth's pseudohistorical chronicle about the kings of Britain (ca. 1136). In that account, King Arthur's court is said to surpass "all other realms in the multitude of its riches, the luxuriousness of its décor, the nobility of its inhabitants," and in its courtiers' "extravagant dress."[24] Yet such opulence was imported to France in the Middle Ages not only from the famed Constantinople but also from the lands of Alexander's empire that had been held since the seventh century in Muslim hands.[25] Indeed, by the twelfth century Alexander's name had become associated in the west with the city he founded at Alexandria, known as a major exporter of silk cloth termed by the Italian merchants responsible for its transport "panni alexandrini" (Lombard, 93).

Much like the "porpre sarazinesche" worn by Largesse in the *Roman de la Rose*, repeated allusion to the *paile alexandrin* that adorns courtly heroines throughout the western romance tradition resonates in two registers simultaneously, evoking not only the lavish opulence of France's ostensible heritage of generous giving from the Macedonian-Greek king but also the equally stunning wealth of medieval trade with Muslim sources of "Saracen silk" in Egypt and the Levant. As early as the eleventh century both Islamic and Byzantine silks were available in the Latin west, which received great numbers of these costly fabrics, the majority probably of Byzantine provenance, as Anna Muthesias has shown.[26] Of further importance, however, there was at this time considerable exchange between Byzantium and the Islamic world in the field of silk weaving, and their products were not readily discernible from one another.[27] Techniques of murex dyeing, used to make the highly regulated imperial Byzantine "purple," were available in Muslim countries along the Syro-Palestinian coast and in Tyre as well as in Alexandria, Egypt, by the late twelfth century.[28] The main axis of trade during this period moves from western and southern Europe to Muslim as well as Byzantine countries and back. Eastern luxury items, transported to Europe by Italo-Byzantine merchants, moved north into France via western traders who obtained them in exchange for woolen textiles produced in northern Europe. Italians are known to have traded eastern luxury silks at the fairs in Champagne as early as 1170, carrying English and Flemish wools back to Italy and then eastward.[29]

Cloth Trade at the Fairs of Champagne

The city of Troyes specifically was a highly prosperous commercial center that traded domestically produced wool, linen cloth, and wine to Italian merchants in contact with the east at least from the time of the Third Crusade (1189–92; Dubois, 696–703).[30] Fairs held in the towns of Troyes, Provins, Bar-sur-Aube, and Lagny developed in the course of the twelfth century from local argicultural markets into international commercial centers, in large part because of policies established by the counts of the region to provide housing and safe conduct (*conduit*) for merchants coming from Italy and other parts of Europe.[31] Certainly by the thirteenth century Italian merchants were regularly carrying "fine cloth, silks, horses and other goods imported from the Levant" into the fairs of Champagne.[32] Italians imported from Muslim lands spices, perfumes, ivory, textiles, and oils (Lopez, "Trade," 275). Sources from the twelfth century, which provide detailed records of cloth being exported from Champagne, only hint at products coming into northern France. But ample evidence exists that merchants from Champagne engaged in active trading with eastern markets. Commercial exchange with Egyptian Jewish merchants, who had been trading with northern Europe since the ninth century, focused principally in the eleventh and twelfth centuries on textiles and spices.[33] As early as 1131, merchants of Count Thibaut de Provins were trading in London and sending their cloth to all of Europe and the Levant (Chapin, 73–74). Northern French merchants from Troyes, Provins, Lagny, and other northern towns are attested in Genoa between 1180–1225, where trade with the Near East had been reopened by the Third Crusade. In 1191, cloth from Provins is sent to Genoa and transported from there to Constantinople (Chapin, 258). By the twelfth century, Robert Lopez argues, southern French seaports become more independent of feudal lords and the Capetian kings of the thirteenth century try to channel commerce through Aigues Mortes (Lopez, "Trade," 284), which under Louis IX becomes a direct line to Syria and the orient.[34] French colonies in Syria at this time exported large quantities of heavy silks, including gold and silver brocades, to the west.[35]

Muslim trade, which reached its peak between the ninth and eleventh centuries, provided silk from Turkestan, the south Caspian area, and China, ivory and gold from Africa, spices and gems from India, rubies from Yemen, and emeralds from Egypt (Lopez, "Trade," 281). Nearly all silk, cotton, and the best color dyes came to medieval Europe from the Levant and Africa

(328). Lombard locates the main textile zones of the Muslim orient in the Middle Ages at Le Fars (in modern-day Iran), Hurzistan (near Baghdad), and Egypt (Lombard, 90). Damascus produced rich brocades and silks of all kinds (92). Tyre, Antioch, and Tripoli specialized in moiré silks and brocades (93). Baghdad was known for the rich brocaded "baldachinus" and *tiraz* garments ornamented with luxurious embroidery in Arabic script (90, 219).

Production of silk textiles does not begin in France itself until 1470 and grows rapidly only after silk-weaving crafts are established at Lyons in 1536. Even though after the mid-eleventh century many European countries could grow silk and make silk cloth, no European products rivaled the quality of Byzantine silks.[36] Western copies, which imitated Byzantine and Muslim motifs and designs, remained inferior, since Byzantine silk production techniques were not fully known in the west. Although Louis le Pieux manufactured "purple" in his own gynacaeum, it was deemed a poor second to imperial fabrics from Constantinople (Lopez, "Silk," 42). Even after the production of western copies, demand for the eastern originals did not decrease.[37]

To be sure, the increasing availability of lavish cloth in twelfth- and thirteenth-century Europe does not tell the full story of its representation in literary accounts of courtly love. Luxury cloth and the garments fashioned from it might have been deployed rhetorically in any number of ways by medieval romance authors. My interest lies in showing how material fabrics, specifically luxury goods coming into western Europe from the time of the First through the Fourth Crusades, were used in literary accounts to signal the wealth and status of courtly elites in a way that defines courtliness and courtly love visually as cross-cultural phenomena.

Courtly Identity and Eastern Textiles

The infant Fresne, for example, in Marie de France's *lai* by the same title, appears on the doorstep of a nunnery wrapped in a "paile roé" imported from Constantinople, which, along with the inscription on the ring hanging from her arm, is said to guarantee her noble lineage:

En un chief de mut bon chesil
Envolupent l'enfant gentil,
E desus un paile roé;
Ses sires li ot aporté

De Costentinoble, u il fu:
...
Bien sachent tuit vereiement
Qu'ele est nee de bone gent. vv. 121–25, 133–34.[38]

(They wrapped the noble child in a piece of fine linen and then placed over her a silk brocade that her father had brought from Constantinople, where he had been ... so that everyone would know in truth that she was of noble birth.)

The silk coverlet from Constantinople is specified further as a distinctive and personalized mark of this particular western European family. Fresne's mother calls it "*nostre* palie" (v. 474), indicating that the family's French identity is established and recognized through the deployment of foreign silk. But more importantly for our purposes, the eastern tokens attesting to Fresne's western nobility in this tale also facilitate love. It is because of the imported cloth and ring that the star-crossed lovers can finally come together and marry.[39] It is similarly a courtly ladylove clad in "purpre alexandrine" who engineers and guarantees the success of the love story in the *Lai de Lanval*. The hero's unnamed paramour, who seems in many ways to be from another, magical realm, actually wears garments of dark silk that tie her directly to Alexandria: "Un chier mantel de blanc hermine, / Covert de purpre alexandrine" (vv. 101–2; a costly mantle of white ermine, covered in Alexandrine silk). In Marie de France's *Guigemar*, too, the vehicle responsible for the successful union of troubled lovers bears the mark of eastern provenance. An ornate and magical boat features, along with a bed of gold and ivory and a silk coverlet threaded with gold, a coverlet of imported *sabelin*[40] backed with "purpre alexandrin" (v. 182). In *Floire et Blancheflor* the very telling of the courtly love story emanates from a richly hybrid silk coverlet dyed with color from India and containing Arabic banding, an eastern luxury item that surpasses in quality the best silks coming to France from the Greek city of Thessaly:

En cele cambre un lit avoit
qui de pailes aornés estoit.
Molt par ert boins et ciers li pailes,
ainc ne vint miudres de Tessaile.
Li pailes ert ovrés a flors,
d'indes tires bendes et ours.
Illoec m'assis por escouter
.II. dames que j'oï parler.
Eles estoient .II. serours;
ensamble parloient d'amors. vv. 37–46

(In that room, there was a bed adorned with a lovely and expensive silk coverlet. No better had ever come from Thessaly. It was embroidered with flowers and decorated with bands of indigo and gold *tiraz* fabric. I sat down and listened to two ladies who were sisters speaking of love.)

The *tire bendes* mentioned here suggest the adoption in the west of Levantine traditions of decorative cloth. Janet Snyder has shown how sculptural representations of courtly attire in the early twelfth century in France contain specific ornamental details that may have been borrowed from eastern textiles. She points in particular to the flat border bands bearing carved geometric patterns that adorn the *mantels*, *bliauts*, and *chemises* worn by many figures in jamb statues on Gothic cathedrals between 1130 and 1165. Snyder argues that these decorative details of western elite dress recall Islamic *tiraz* fabrics in which patterned silk tapestry bands alternate with strips of linen (Snyder, 8–18, 38, 60ff., 92). In the exquisite coverlet evoked in *Floire et Blancheflor*, bands of indigo alternate with strips of gold cloth. And although no such Levantine features characterize the site of indulgent lovemaking in *Erec et Enide*, that famous encounter too takes place on a highly syncopated version of the lavish quilt described in *Floire et Blancheflor*:

An une chanbre fu assise
Desor une coute de paile
Qui venue estoit de Tessaile. vv. 2402–4[41]

(In a bedchamber, Enide was seated on a silk coverlet from Thessaly.)

If repeated allusions in courtly narratives to the foreign sites of Constantinople, Alexandria, and Thessaly, among others, have often passed unnoticed before the eyes of sensitive readers, it is largely because courtly love stories have so thoroughly defined themselves in terms of the east.

Indeed, the opening pages of the twelfth-century *Cligés* explain how the very practice of *largesse* at King Arthur's court derives from the transfer of "saracen" luxury goods to the west. When the emperor of Greece and Constantinople (v. 47), the latter termed "Costantinoble la riche" (v. 123), sends his son, Alixandre, to become one of King Arthur's knights (vv. 110–13), he amply provisions the youth with "furs, horses, and silk cloth" (vv. 140–41) from the imperial treasury, instructing him specifically to spend this eastern wealth generously at Arthur's court. In so doing, the wealthy emperor of Constantinople describes a necessary conversion of eastern riches into the currency of courtly exchange, lauding the inestimable value of the *largesse* that his son, laden with eastern treasure of gold, silver (v. 107), and precious clothes will soon exemplify:

> Or est li vaslez bien heitiez
> Et cortois et bien afeitiez,
> Quant ses peres tant li promet
> Qu'a bandon ses tresors li met
> Et si l'enore et li comande
> Que largement doint et despande
> Et si li dit reison por coi:
> "Biax filz, fet il, de ce me croi
> Que largesce est dame et reïne
> Qui totes vertuz anlumine,
> Ne n'est mie grief a prover.
> A quel bien cil se puet torner,
> Ja tant ne soit puissanz ne riches,
> Ne soit honiz, se il est chiches?
> Qui a tant d'autre bien sanz grace
> Que largesce loer ne face?
> Par soi fet prodome largesce,
> Ce que ne puet feire hautesce,
> Ne corteisie, ne savoir,
> Ne gentillesce, ne avoir,
> Ne force, ne chevalerie,
> Ne proesce, ne seignorie,
> Ne biautez, ne nule autre chose." vv. 181–203

(Now the courtly and well-mannered young man is pleased because his father promised to lavish treasure upon him, thus honoring him and exhorting him to give and spend generously. And he explained why: "Believe me, son, that *largesse* is the lady and queen who illumines all virtue. This is not difficult to prove. When good fortune comes to someone, no matter how powerful or rich, wouldn't he be ashamed to be stingy? Who has so many goods not bestowed by luck that he could fail to praise *largesse*? *Largesse* alone can make you a good man, more so than rank, courtliness, knowledge, noble manners, material goods, strength, chivalry, prowess, lordship, beauty, or anything else.")

This aspiring knight's generous giving of Saracen treasure to King Arthur's entourage documents the material transfer of eastern silk to feudal use that is recorded more subtly in Largesse's silk gown. Both accounts raise the issues of place and space as underexplored aspects of courtly love.[42]

Place, Space, and Orientalism

Whether the luxury goods that create the cultural hybridity of courtly players result from gift giving, as in the example from *Cligés* cited above, or from mercantile exchange or the plunder of crusading armies, as we will see below, opulent adornment of the courtly lady's lily-white flesh evokes a complex alliance between court life in western Europe and an expansive and hybridized "orient" that mitigates the more polarized view of east-west relations promulgated in the *Estoire*. There, the quasi-historical, quasi-mythical city of Sarras emerges as the centralized "capital" city of the indeterminate lands to the east of France, while Camelot provides the centralized hub for activities in King Arthur's geographically dispersed and highly imaginary realm.[43] Michelle Szkilnik has shown how the conversion ideology of the *Estoire* depends on a westward movement, evacuating the east of people, relics, and other costly goods. It is through the transfer of substantial eastern wealth—material as well as spiritual—that King Arthur's realm becomes established as a sanctified promised land rivaling Palestine (16–17). The tale of King Mordrain's conversion charts this displacement under cover of a failed love story: the Saracen king throws over his Galatea-like ladylove and moves westward to King Arthur's court.

But in fact the purported opposition between Christian west and pagan east erodes as quickly as it is drawn. Michelle Warren has shown how the city of Sarras, a site cast in the *Estoire* as an eastern stronghold of paganism, is also said to be under Champenois authority: its king, Mordrain, we are told, was born in Meaux.[44] Conversely, Arthur's capital, Camelot, emerges in the *Estoire*'s version of French history as a former Saracen city (Hucher III, 195; Ponceau II, 479). In this sense, the prose romances chart, according to Warren, "a sacralized version of expansionist settlement that never in fact leaves home" (182).[45] Indeed, a number of literary accounts of courtliness, whether in the *Roman de la Rose*, the *Prose Lancelot*, or the *Estoire*, help reveal the extent to which distinctions of "foreign" versus "domestic" spaces make little sense in fictive representations of court culture, based as they are on highly imaginative and culturally diverse geographies that span east and west, while also ranging from historical courts in Capetian and Angevin France to fictive Arthurian courts in England and Brittany. The putative east/west divide is especially complicated by the Frankish aristocratic diaspora of the eleventh and twelfth centuries in which French nobility migrated to crusader states or other eastern venues for expansionist purposes. Glenn Burger reminds us more specifically of the extent to which the crusader "east" was itself characterized by a complex mix of "foreign" Europeans, members of crusading orders (Hospitaliers, Teutonic knights, Templars) permanently based in the Middle East and knights from the Christian states of Outremer such as Cyprus or earlier Antioch or Jerusalem, which contained "native" populations of Greeks,

Jews, Armenians, Muslims, and others ruled by Frankish elites.[46] Robert Bartlett cites the Joinville family of Champagne as a particularly apt example of the "adventurous, acquisitive and pious aristocracy on which the expansionary movements of the High Middle Ages are based."[47]

Indeed, many aristocratic Frankish families at this time, and especially those located in Champagne, occupy complex dynastic households that stretch readily between western Europe and the Levant. Contact between them is recorded on rare occasions in the transfer of valuable material objects including gemstones, silver and gold utensils, cloth, and clothing. The succession document for Eudes, count of Nevers, a vassal of Louis IX who died in Acre in 1265, lists among the count's valuable possessions items familiar to the reader of courtly romance. Along with numerous rings, two sapphires, a cameo, silver goblets, some of which are embellished with precious gems and enamels, and silver knives and platters, we find household items such as bed sheets, embroidered tablecloths, silver and gold needles, and hand towels. But more interesting in the context of courtly love are items of clothing that include "couvre-chefs," gloves, new stockings and hose and shoes, "une viez corroie d'or a pelles, et un chapel d'or a pierres et a pelles" (an old golden belt with pearls and a golden garland set with precious gems and pearls).[48] These articles are accompanied by a wide array of valuable fabrics, including woolens, linens, and silks. The imported eastern silks include in this instance "iiii quarriaus de soie," "une coute pointe de cendal vermoill," and "cote et serecot, et corset de tireteinne perse, forré de cendal vert" (191, 194; four squares of silk; a coverlet of lightweight red silk; a tunic including a blouson of blue silk, lined with green silk taffeta) and cloth from Tyre and Tartary. These silks stand alongside linen purchased in Troyes and cloth said to belong to Eudes's wife, the duchess of Burgundy: "la toile qui fu achetée à Troies, que Simon Ysanbars acheta, dont il i ot x pièces; x pièces de toile, de la toile la duchoise de Borgoinge, xxxvii aunes de toile, en un remenant et xxv aunes en ii autres remenanz" (191; Linen purchased in Troyes, bought by Simon Ysanbars, of which there were ten pieces; ten pieces of linen from the duchess of Burgundy, thirty-seven yards of linen in one remnant and twenty-five yards in two others). The travels of Count Eudes eastward, on crusade to the Holy Land, have thus repatriated in a sense costly silks previously carried to the west, while transferring to the east, as did Venetian merchants in another venue, cloth obtained at the fairs in Champagne.

Placing this document alongside the courtly narratives I have been discussing suggests that the display of imported and costly silks in tales of love, whether they are presented as coming from distant venues termed vaguely "oriental" or attributed to cities bearing specific eastern names, records a *relational* rather than an oppositional dynamic between the French "homeland" and points east. Indeed, the symbolic value given to pitting east against west in certain clerical discourses, crusading narratives, chronicles and perhaps most importantly in our own postmedieval scholarship has led to the reification of an ostensible east/west divide not supported by the cross-cultural contacts evidenced in the transfer and exchange of valuable cloth and costly items of dress.[49]

What we witness in courtly literary texts' fascination with eastern opulence is not in this sense a straightforward form of orientalism as Edward Said has defined it, a vacillation between the familiar and the alien used to characterize the orient as the "other" while appropriating it at the same time. Nor do we see here a racialized geography used only to fabricate an imaginary, superior west.[50] On the contrary, many Old French narratives of courtly love chart a reverse movement, as we have seen, an economic infusion of the Christian west evidenced by a highly visible display of costly fabrics still bearing the telltale names of Baghdad, Alexandria, and Constantinople. By associating "pailes d'orient" with a domestic site of courtly lovemaking or positing "porpre sarazinesche" as a fundamental marker of courtly *largesse*, medieval French narratives chart a necessarily expansive and hybrid terrain for courtly love. They represent it as a western locus that can only be defined by its easternness, a site where the amorous identity of courtly nobility relies on the Saracen splendor of eastern luxury attire, acknowledged repeatedly as coming from a different "place," whether Baghdad, Constantinople, or Phrygia, but displayed as culturally requisite to French courtliness.

When seen in this light, courtly love emerges as a cultural hybrid in the sense that Robert Young uses the term—to indicate a cultural formation exhibiting a seemingly impossible simultaneity of sameness and difference.[51] In this instance, the French aristocracy emerges as engaged in crusading efforts against an oppositional "other" in eastern lands while also being substantially defined by the effects of material imports from that same "other" at court. This is not a case of generating hybrid cultures that result from a long history of confrontation with a dominant power that attempts to control, remake, or eliminate the subordinate partner. In economic terms, it is the European west that has been fashioned by material goods crossing its borders. Indeed, in terms of luxury fabric, the east has already begun to define the west from within.

Courtly Treasure

Romance texts of the twelfth and thirteenth centuries typically invoke the treasure trove of eastern luxury goods to describe prized and highly valued courtly beauties. Many of the heroines we saw in Chapter 5, whose sartorial bodies are forged from Nature and clothes simultaneously, are also made more specifically from eastern silks and gems. From Blancheflor, described in her lover's lament in *Floire et Blancheflor* as a "precïeuse jeme" (v. 729), to Soredamor, depicted as "tres precïeus avoir" (v. 785), we hear the ring of Mordrain's doll clothed in "li plus precieuses reube." Indeed, it would not be difficult to imagine the words here uttered by the courtly Cligés coming instead from the Saracen king Mordrain, who desires no other "riches" than his own precious treasure, his beautiful and beloved statue "in the form of a woman" dressed in "the richest and most precious [robe] the king could find." His love had no equal, we are told; his ladylove too remains valuable beyond comparison.

The image is played out further in romances like Jean Renart's *Roman de la Rose ou de Guillaume de Dole*, where the heroine, Lienor, who "surpasses all others just as gold surpasses all other metals" (vv. 1417–20), is designated by her brother as "mon tresor" (v. 1115). But the figure of Richesse in the *Roman de la Rose* provides the most extreme and extended example of the paradigm. Her extravagant, costly, and imported attire stands in stark contrast to the simple, innate, and domestic attractiveness of her allegorical opposite: Biaute. Perfect unadulterated Beauty in this account displays the typical courtly lady's face: light and smooth with thin, well-aligned features (vv. 1002–3) but with the added insistence that this lady's face remains free of makeup or artifice:

N'estoit fardee ne guigniee,
car ele n'avoit mestier
de soi tifer, ne afaitier. vv. 1004–6

(It was not powdered or made up, since she had no need to adorn or decorate herself.)

This "dame de haut pris" (v. 990), who figures among the "nobles genz de la querole" (v. 986), conveys the unadorned beauty of body parts that reflect the natural world. Biaute shines bright as moonlight; her skin is tender as dew and white as the lily (vv. 992, 995–96, 999–1001). Lady Richesse, by contrast, evokes the world of imported courtly wealth, paraded ostentatiously in expensive luxury garments decorated with incomparable embroidered images, golden fasteners, precious stones, and jewels. Her hair is adorned with a golden crown set with rubies, sapphires, emeralds, and other foreign gems:

Richece ot d'une porpre robe,
nu tenez ore pas a lobe,
que je vos di bien et afiche
qu'il n'ot si bele ne si riche
el monde, ne si envoisie.
La porpre fu toute enfroisie,
s'i ot portretes a orfrois
estoires de dus et de rois.
D'une bende d'or naelee
a esmaus fu au col orlee
mout richement la ceveçaille,
et s'i ot, ce sachiez sanz faille,
de riches pierres grant planté,
qui mout rendoient grant clarté. vv. 1051–64

(Riches had a dark silk gown. Don't think this an exaggeration because I tell you truly and assure you that nowhere in the world was there a gown so beautiful, so costly, or so attractive. The silk was decorated with gold embroidery that portrayed the stories of dukes and kings. The collar was very richly adorned with a band of gold and black enamel. And be assured that there were also many precious stones emitting flashes of brilliant light.)

Richesse emerges here as pure treasure, an extreme portrait of the valued and valuable courtly lady who seems, in this instance, to have no natural body at all:

Richece ot sus ses treces sores
un cercle d'or: onques encores
ne fu veüz si biau, ce cuit.
Li cercles fu d'or fin recuit,
mes cil seroit bons devisierres
qui vos savroit conter les pierres
qui estoient, ne deviser,
que l'en ne porroit pas priser
l'avoir que les pierres valoient
qui en l'or asises estoient.
Rubiz i ot, saphirs, jagonces,
esmeraudes plus de deus onces. vv. 1085–96

(On her blond tresses, Riches had a golden circlet. Never since, in my opinion, has such a beautiful one been seen. It was made of pure gold, carefully worked. But it would take a good storyteller to describe for you all the stones that were in it. It was impossible to estimate the worth of the stones that were set in the gold. There were rubies, sapphires, amethysts, and more than two ounces of emeralds.)

Indeed, amid lengthy descriptions of her costly accouterments we hear nothing of this lady's skin, nose, eyes, or body shape. Whereas Biaute's blond hair sparkles unaided like the moonlight, Richesse's golden locks can only be made to shine with the help of an ornate and intricately worked crown whose stones light up her head and face:

Tel clarté des pierres issoit
qu'a Richeice en resplandissoit
durement le vis et la face,
et, entor li, tote la place. vv. 1103–6

(Such brilliance issued from the stones that the face and head of Riches sparkled, along with everything around her.)

As an influential lady of great *hautece*, "de grant pris et de grant afaire" (vv. 1018–19), she wears not just a domestically valued gown but the "richest silk gown in the world" (vv. 1051–55). Her extravagant "porpre robe," embroidered in gold thread with stories of dukes and kings (vv. 1056–61), evokes at one and the same time the "porpre sarazinesche" donned by the courtly Largesse and the rich and precious "robe" worn by Mordrain's doll. Richesse's gown of purple silk, paralleled only by her lovely belt, "the richest one worn by any woman" (vv. 1065–66), suggests, along with wealth and status, that this courtly lady's dazzling and seductive beauty is acquired and foreign rather than natural and homegrown.

How, then, to account for all those courtly heroines who are said repeatedly to be created and fashioned by Nature? In fact, in many instances, Nature's handiwork often crafts courtly beauties whose worth and status can only be understood and evaluated in terms of objects of foreign trade, whether gold, silver, ivory, or silk. In the case of Soredamor, Nature made her teeth, but they resemble silver and ivory (*Cligés*, vv. 813–24). Blancheflor has "iex vairs rians / plus que gemme resplendissans" (*Floire et Blancheflor*, vv. 2879–80; smiling gray eyes, more brilliant than gemstones). Philomena has eyes "plus cler qu'une jagonce" (v. 146; clearer than an amethyst), and her seductive vermilion lips are redder than "samiz vermauz," silk dyed with costly cochineal (*Philomena*, vv. 153–55). In these and other depictions of elite courtly beauty we have seen, elements of the earth's botanical bounty rely curiously on the visual power of imported eastern goods to record their grounding in the natural world. Similarly, Soredamor's face displays the color of roses and lilies, while her light-colored forehead outshines an emerald or topaz (*Cligés*, vv. 798–802). Laudine's "naturally fresh" coloration covers a neck that rivals in brilliance the most highly polished crystal (*Yvain*, vv. 1480–81, 1486–87). Blancheflor's lily-white skin surpasses the most costly fur, "plus blanc le front que n'est hermine" (*Floire et Blancheflor*, v. 2876).[52]

These courtly portraits, then, accord value to elements of the natural world, associated traditionally with desired features of western beauty, in terms of material goods imported from the east. Imported luxury fabrics, precious metals, and gemstones are deployed in these accounts not so much to convey a sense of exoticism or foreign travel but to represent wholly indigenous courtly protagonists, even though their portraits rely again and again on eastern details. This infusion of the east into idealized representations of western courtliness did not go unnoticed by medieval clerical writers, who decry and condemn it.

Clerical Fear of Foreign Luxury

Indeed, it is sometimes difficult to distinguish the general clerical antipathy toward conspicuous consumption from a deep-seated but largely unstated anxiety about the ambiguously "foreign" east from which these goods derive. María Menocal has shown that, even before the menace of Averroism in the thirteenth century, the "foreign devil, with his material temptations and promises of a better life in this world . . . was an Arab."[53] Peter the Venerable, she argues, "like many others before and after him, feared that the combined material, cultural, and intellectual seduction of Arabic culture, plainly visible in a number of different spheres, would ultimately be destructive of the Christian values it was his duty, and in his interest, to preserve" (41). Worst of all, she says, was "the insidious acculturation provoked by the material advantages and cultural chic of the foreign influence," including new styles in clothing (41). Western clergymen, she contends, were both seduced by and critical of imported material opulence.

We saw in Chapter 1 how a strong clerical undercurrent in a number of courtly narratives, following the tradition of the Church Fathers and medieval preachers of the twelfth and thirteenth centuries, denounces opulence, extravagance, and artifice as both too material and too insubstantial: as a mark of the tangible (if transitory) material world, and as an indication of the superficial artifice often associated with women. More precisely, when Saint Bernard insists that members of the "new knighthood" avoid the idolatry of material possessions by shunning "every excess in clothing and food," he specifies further that "silk" is the costly clothing in question, along with decorations of "gold and silver and precious stones."[54] Bernard further contrasts the religious fervor and disciplined behavior that metaphorically adorn the contemporary Temple of Jerusalem with the excessive display of Solomon's masterpiece: "Truly all the magnificence of that first temple lay in perishable gold and silver, in polished stone and precious woods," along with "beautiful colors," "shining marble," and "gilded paneling," "jewels," and "ancient golden crowns" (101). The new knights renounce the ornate adornments of the old temple because their mission, as Bernard explains it, is to strike fear in the enemy rather than to "incite cupidity" (100). For Bernard, then, the seductive pull of costly fabrics, gems, and precious metals leads to a kind of idolatry born of cupidity (100) that resonates with the *Estoire*'s depiction of Mordrain's doll as sinfully indulgent and corrupting.

The association of luxury items with eastern cultures in the preceding analysis suggests that vociferous moralizing attacks against excessive adornment and indulgent attire in the High Middle Ages might also contain a veiled condemnation of those ill-defined and little-understood "eastern" cultures more generally. If so, it is fear of the eastern "other" that is then displaced onto dressed-up courtly ladies. In the case of Mordrain's doll, the religious corruption borne of excessive riches typically represented in the medieval western imagination by the wealthy Saracen shifts pointedly from the Saracen king himself to the Saracen fabric adorning a female love partner. As so many amorous ladies in the courtly world, she has become the carrier of pagan riches and foreign indulgence. Esteemed and lauded in Guillaume de Lorris's courtly *Roman de la Rose* as the force of generosity (*largesse*), the lavishly clad lady is condemned in the *Estoire* as a dangerous infidel and further decried in Jean de Meun's continuation of the *Rose* as fickle Fortune. Tellingly, in Jean's account, Reason denounces Lady Fortune as a perilous temptation to innocent lovers, not only because she is unpredictable, but also because she is foreign. Fortune's abode—that rocky cliff, which constantly reclothes itself in new and varying form, draws the charge of being specifically a "forme estrange," in Reason's view. That is, the extremes to which Fortune swings are surprisingly unknown and, in that sense, foreign. But it is significant that this "foreign" place bears the telltale features of eastern wealth that we have witnessed elsewhere as an excessive show of gold, silver, and gemstones:

Mout reluit d'une part, car gent
i sunt li mur d'or et d'argent,
si rest toute la couverture
de cele meesmes feture,
ardanz de pierres precieuses. vv. 6069–73

(In one part, Fortune's palace shines brightly, for the fine walls are of gold and silver, and the entire roof is made the same way, aglow with precious stones.)

More overtly, the Jealous Husband condemns the artificial decoration of women trying to improve upon the natural beauty of God's creation, citing the decorative metals and poor quality silks they might use along with "other objects" considered specifically "foreign" to indigenous beauty:

Si quiert biauté des creatures
que Dex fet de plus vils figures,
con de metauz ou de floretes
ou d'autres estranges chosetes. vv. 9029–32

(Therefore she searches for the beauty of created things in the most vile things that God made, such as metals, inferior silks, or other foreign things.)

The allegorical figure of Ami explains further in this scene that contact with "the foreign" through pilgrimage or travel generates avarice, envy, fraud, and all other vices responsible for sowing discord among couples. In ancient times, by contrast, when:

N'estoit lors nul pelerinage,
n'issoit nus hors de son rivage
por cerchier estrange contree;
...
Riche estoient tuit egaument
et s'entramoient loiaument.
Ausinc pesiblement vivoient,
car naturelment s'entramoient,
les simples genz de bone vie.
Lors iert amor sanz symonie,
l'un ne demandoit riens à l'autre. vv. 9471–73, 9491–97

(At that time, there was no pilgrimage; no one left his own shores to search for foreign lands.... All were rich in the same way, and they loved each other loyally. Thus they lived in peace, for these simple, good people loved each other naturally. At that time there was no simony in love; one did not demand anything from another.)

If Reason refers more cryptically to Fortune's abode as strangely "foreign," caustic remarks by the Jealous Husband and Ami locate the source of the corrupting desire for opulence and wealth specifically in other, distant and possibly non-Christian lands.[55]

One finds the sentiment expressed as early as Tertullian's treatise *The Apparel of Women* when, in condemning the artificial adornment of female bodies decorated with gold, silver, jewels, and costly clothes, he explains that "the only thing that gives glamour to all these articles is that they are rare and that they have to be imported from a foreign country."[56] He continues: "For, just as certain things, which are distributed by God in individual countries or in individual regions of the sea are mutually foreign to one another, so in turn they are considered rare by foreigners ... the rarity and singularity of an object which always finds favor with foreigners stirs up a great desire to possess it for the simple reason of not having what God has given to others" (127–28). Tertullian's comments, along with remarks in the *Rose* about vices coming from foreign travel and pilgrimage, suggest that the medieval clerical concern with luxurious indulgence in material goods may extend far beyond a denunciation of female-derived conspicuous consumption and the threat of effeminacy it poses to male adherents that we saw in Chapter 4.

Pious Thievery and Crusading Consumption

The substantial economic transfer of luxury goods along trade routes from the Levant and Egypt through Italy into France during the High Middle Ages is paralleled by an equally important transfer into western Europe of precious relics and other luxurious booty from eastern cities during the crusades. Both processes involve the conversion of eastern wealth for western use—whether courtly or religious. Both are most amply attested in the literary scenarios of the Grail narratives, which chart the transfer of costly eastern relics of putative spiritual value to the Arthurian world, as we have seen. The purpose of the Grail questers in both the *Queste* and the *Estoire* is to transport a holy Christian relic from the eastern realm of Sarras to Great Britain.[57] But the Grail itself displays in many respects the material luxury and opulence often coded in romance narratives and crusade chronicles as eastern. In the *Queste del Saint Graal*, the enigmatic Grail vessel, imported into Britain, remains enclosed in a golden coffer studded with precious gems (277; "une arche d'or et de pieres precieuses qui covroit le saint Vessel").

In Chrétien's *Conte du Graal*, the mysterious vessel at the Fisher King's Grail castle sparkles with fine gold and precious gems surpassing all others:

Li graaus qui aloit devant,
De fin or esmeré estoit;
Prescïeuses pierres avoit
El graal de maintes manieres,
Des plus riches et des plus chieres
Qui en mer ne en terre soient;
Totes autres pierres passoient
Celes del graal sanz dotance. vv. 3232–39

(The Grail, which came first, was of fine, pure gold, adorned with many kinds of precious stones, the richest and most costly to be found on sea or land. Without a doubt, the stones on the Grail far surpassed all others.)

More commonly in the *Queste*, however, the Holy Grail appears wrapped, like Mordrain's doll and like the stereotypically richly garbed courtly lady, in "Saracen silk." In its initial appearance at King Arthur's court we find "Li Sainz Graal covert d'un blanc samit" (15) and later at the Grail Castle "covert d'un vermeil samit" (255, 273). If these "rich robes" recall the luxury attire of King Mordrain's Saracen idol, they are not cast off but used to clothe the revered Arthurian relic, creating an icon of desired courtly sanctity that shares the visual opulence of the dolled-up secular lady.

Historically it is Constantinople, rather than the quasi-mythical Sarras, that functions in the western medieval imagination as a treasure trove of unsurpassed relics and an icon for astounding wealth and lavish material display. The city retains that mythic status in the west throughout one hundred years of crusading activity, although the circumstances and political stakes of economic transactions in the Byzantine territory shift considerably during that time. Eastern imports of gold, gems, and silks to Europe, which began to arrive in substantial quantities from the time of the First Crusade, increase significantly with the return of booty from Constantinople in the Fourth Crusade. However, this gemlike city resonates in European accounts throughout the High Middle Ages as a paradigm of eastern splendor. Odon de Deuil, who accompanied Louis VII on the Second Crusade in the mid-twelfth century, records Constantinople's remarkable richness in material goods and religious relics, while the Arab geographer Edrisi reports first-hand that Constantinople surpassed in opulence and grandeur all cities in the Roman empire.[58] In the second half of the twelfth century, a Spanish Jew, Benjamin of Toledo, links Constantinople's stunning wealth to the extensive array of international merchants trading in costly cloth and gems:

"Merchants come there from all parts of the world. The Greeks possess gold and gemstones in abundance; their clothes are made of fabrics covered with embroidered decoration in gold" (34). French chroniclers of the Fourth Crusade attest similarly to the extreme wealth found in Constantinople and the luxurious booty obtained there. Remarking on the wondrous amounts of gold, silver, and jewels encountered by French crusaders, Robert de Clari declares that "not even Charlemagne or Alexander found so much booty in one city."[59] Villehardouin notes similarly that "never was there so much taken from a city."[60]

Although historians continue to debate the most appropriate means for calculating the amount of booty obtained, chronicle accounts provide a compelling picture of western crusaders overwhelmed by their impression of boundless eastern luxury goods, treasure, and wealth. Villehardouin describes the crusaders' initial reaction to the visual splendor of Constantinople as follows: "Or poez savoir que mult de cels de l'ost alerent à veoir Costantinople, et les riches palais et les altes yglises don't il avoit tant, et les granz richesces (que onques nule vile tant n'en ot). Des saintuaires (reliques) ne convient mie à parler; que autant en avoit-il à ice jor en la vile cum el remanant dou monde. Ensi furent mult comunel li Grieu et li François de totes choses, et de mercheandises et d'autres biens" (110; Now know that many members of the army went to see Constantinople, the rich palaces and tall churches, which it had in abundance, along with the vast riches (no city ever had so many). It's difficult to talk about the relics; that day in the city there were as many as in the rest of the world. Thus did the Greeks and the French share much in common, including commodities and other goods).[61] Constantinople in these accounts emerges as a lavishly clad city, a gem, a site of eastern splendor beautifully dressed in costly adornment.

And members of the crusading army begin to resemble the problematic "pilgrims" condemned by the allegorical figure of Ami for importing foreign luxury goods into France. Villehardouin notes that in Constantinople, along with other cities, the amount of booty (*gaienz*) taken by "the army of pilgrims and Venetians" surpassed description, making those who had been poor, rich and joyous: "Cil qui avoient esté en povreté, estoient en richece et en delit" (146). These western travelers have, in a sense, taken on the "wealthy" identity attributed in the *Estoire* to the stereotypically "rich" Saracen, Matagran, whom Josephus attempts to convert. Villehardouin's detailed account of the spoils from Constantinople catalogues the very luxury items that typify Matagran's ample "Saracen" wealth: "D'or et d'argent et de vasselement et de pierres precieuses et de samiz et de dras de soie, et de robes vaires et grises et hermines, et toz les chiers avoirs qui onques furent trové en terre" (146; Gold, silver, silverware, and precious gems and samite and other silks, outfits of fur and ermine, and all the costly goods that could ever be found in the world). In a romance context, when the courtly hero Ille returns to France after having defeated the Greek army in *Ille et Galeron*, he appears "garnis de grant avoir," specified further in terms that will be replayed in Matagran's Saracen loot and later accounts of crusader booty: "assés a d'or et d'argent, / de dras de soie en son tresor / et de vaisselemente d'or" (vv. 4942–44; He has plenty of gold and silver, silk cloth, and golden tableware in his treasury).[62] Once they begin to trade and transport the luxury items of foreign wealth, western warriors and crusaders depicted in romance narratives and vernacular chronicle alike begin more than ever to resemble their dreaded, rich Saracen rivals, with one key difference. They function within Christian ideology to transport and convert eastern wealth into the currency of belief.

One account of the Fourth Crusade defends the plunder of Constantinople as a means of protecting valuable relics from pagan takeover. The *Hystoria Constantinopolitana*, written in 1205 by a Cistercian monk of the Alsatian abbey at Pairis, records the sack of Constantinople during the Fourth Crusade as a form of pious thievery, defending the plunder of the rich Christian city as a means of translating costly relics to the west.[63] The account supplements Villehardouin's description of Constantinople's incredible wealth with a justification for transferring these incomparable riches to western Europe: "This people, proud because of its wealth, should be humbled by their very pride.... It certainly seemed proper that this people, which otherwise could not be corrected, should be punished by the death of a few and the loss of those temporal goods with which it had puffed itself up; that a pilgrim people should grow rich on spoils from the rich and the entire land pass into our power; and that the western Church, illuminated by the inviolable relics of which these people had shown themselves unworthy, should rejoice forever" (91).

Curiously, this Christian apology for robbing "so great a wealth of gold and silver, so great a magnificence of gems and clothing, so great a profusion of valuable trade goods" (107) contains an unexpected love story between Constantine and a beautiful maiden that provides another twist on the story of Mordrain's Saracen doll. The narrator of the *Hystoria* tells how Constantine's conversion to Christianity was marked, not by rejecting love or opulence but by converting a ladylove—here in the form of a city—to riches, through the very kind of costly embellishment that Mordrain is required to destroy. In the wake of Constantine's famous donation, we are told, the emperor of the Greeks and Romans conferred on Peter his throne in Rome, traveled to Greece, and settled in the city called *Bisancion*. That night, Constantine dreamt of a wizened old woman whom he resuscitated through prayer, on the advice of Pope Sylvester, transforming her into a "beautiful maiden who excited a chaste love in his eyes" (101–2). In the role of a Christian Pygmalion, Constantine performs a kind of amorous investiture, adorning the ladylove with a royal cape and a diadem on her head (102), making her "queen among all the cities of Greece" (102). The Christian leader of the eastern empire thus rejuvenates and converts a pagan Roman site into a bejeweled and queenly lady. Further description reveals that this "lady" grows rich from historical plunder, receiving treasures previously pillaged from ancient Troy:

Rich Greece gave her distinguished and wealthy
Citizens, and it offered the *lady* trophies of ancient rapine
And plunder still gory with Phrygian blood:
The immense ransom which Pergamum [Troy] had paid;
The utensils of ancient people, gilded and set with gems;
And ancient bars of silver, heavy with weight. (108)

This lady, decked in elegant clothes and a jeweled crown by a chaste Pygmalion-like lover, is literally a treasure trove of Christian Greek and earlier pagan Roman wealth that the chronicle's hero, Abbott Martin, and other pilgrims will seize as "opulent treasure" (129) destined for western Christendom:

So God, for hidden reasons, I believe,
Enriched Constantinople long ago with multitudinous spoils
So that as soon as they were secure within the walls,
The happy victors could then bear away all that earlier folk had plundered. (108–9)

Significantly different from Mordrain's Saracen lady doll, this "chaste" beloved is eastern but Christian. She is also a place, not a statue, a site known specifically for the opulence and splendor that connote the quintessential "Saracen" in the *Estoire*. In transferring this "lady's" wealth to the western Church, crusader monks attempt to convert riches originating in a pagan past into "sacred articles" from God (120). Whereas the Saracen King Mordrain destroys his "beautiful maiden" by fire, obliterating her rich and precious attire, these crusading monks capture and hold the lavish wealth of

Constantine's ladylove, displacing her valuable riches from pagan Troy and foreign Constantinople to the western Church. Their gesture legitimates in a Christian sphere the substantial importation and use of foreign wealth that had suffused western court culture and fictional accounts of its lavish generosity and boundless opulence for more than a century. Indeed, by the time Abbott Martin records his version of Constantine's love story, the gemlike opulence of the emperor's ladylove has already been displaced onto the statuesque bodies of courtly beauties in Old French romances, whether Soredamor as a golden-haired treasure or Lienor as Guillaume's courtly treasure. These courtly heroines emerge before us as complex cultural hybrids, white-skinned beauties wrapped in eastern luxury clothes: they are French nobles whose elite identity depends on visible recognition of textiles that transpose Saracen sites of Constantinople, Damascus, Baghdad, and Egypt into the space of western court life.[64]

In one sense, these female bodies map loci of cultural convergence, crossing places, that can undermine the representation of a monolithic, demonized orient. They also prevent a thorough domestication of the eastern "other." Rather, the beautiful, lavishly clad heroines of courtly romance demarcate courtly space as a complex "borderlands" in the sense that Gloria Anzaldúa uses the term: not to evoke a frontier dividing a putatively advanced culture from a distant and primitive one, nor a zone that synthesizes opposites into a homogeneous or domesticated form. The courtly beauty can neither be assimilated into the Saracen princess nor held wholly distinct from her. She occupies in this regard the double feminist positioning of "both/and" that characterizes Anzaldúa's "borderland"—a site that stages and displays, without resolving, tensions inherent in cultural differences.[65] In terms of the literary setting for courtly love, these female bodies/borderlands reveal the internal heterogeneity of the western court while unmasking its imaginative and elaborate constructions of the east as an "orient" both distinct from and inherent in the west. Most specifically, the hybrid bodies of dressed-up courtly ladies show that an important part of the medieval west's imagined orient derives from the east's own very literal material contributions to court life. The courtly lady's elegant white limbs wrapped in Saracen silk enable us to see that literary documentation of the western European crusading impulse to convert the pagan "other" also records an equally formative reverse transformation affected not by knights on horseback or through clerical exhortations to serve God but by the transfer of silks, gems, and precious metals from east to west.

Chapter 6

Bringing the Orient Home

To be sure, western narratives of courtly love function in many respects as European discourses of displacement, tending to absorb cultural differences and mystify social relations between east and west as they forge ahistorical amalgams.[66] But these tales of love also do more. At key moments, they reveal a relation between east and west that does not depend on the oppositional and hierarchized categories of home and abroad, self and other, traveler and native.[67] Reading through the clothes of amorous players in the western courtly world reveals a kind of spatial politics within some courtly romances that allows metaphorical imaginings of a foreign culture to combine productively with the material conditions of its own history. If the luxury clothes that delineate aristocratic players in fictional tales of western European court culture bear the names and cultural markings of their eastern provenance, those lavishly clad aristocratic bodies tell a tale of economic transfer that clerical writers attempt to halt or at least transmute into a Christian frame. Clerical efforts to curtail the "easternization" of knights and ladies wage a losing battle against the eager secular embrace of imported opulence. If King Mordrain's conversion requires that he immolate the pagan ladylove and her costly clothes, his gesture does not erase all traces of eastern extravagance in the western court to which he migrates. On the contrary, those lavish garments live on in the courtly world, at the cultural center of courtly love, having already become a requisite feature of the white-skinned *dames* and *demoiseles* so endlessly coveted and courted by chivalrous men who burn with passion rather than burning the telltale remnants of Saracen silk.

Chapter 7
Golden Spurs:
Love in the Eastern World of Floire et Blancheflor

The mid-twelfth-century tale of *Floire et Blancheflor* is a deceptively simple love story. To judge from the protagonists' names alone, Floire and Blancheflor appear at first to incarnate the quintessential innocent delight and natural simplicity of love's garden: two flowers, male and female, joined from childhood in sweet embrace. They seem a perfectly balanced metaphor for the flowering of heterosexual desire in the western courtly tradition. But they are not. Blancheflor, born of the kidnapped daughter of a French knight on pilgrimage to Compostela, falls in love with the Muslim king's son in a hybrid locus both western and pagan: his father's court in Andalusia. When Blancheflor is sold by the boy's parents to foreign merchants trading in cloth and gold and then transported to the Egyptian city of Babiloine (Cairo),[1] the courtly hero's quest begins. Yet as the site of amorous encounter shifts in this romance to distant venues and pagan cultures, the love depicted is no less courtly. It follows in many respects the requisite literary conventions we have come to associate with the romance genre, although often with a significant twist. In this instance, the courtly, western, flowerlike protagonists are a mixed-race couple whose love is born and flourishes in Saracen sites beyond French borders.[2]

In one sense, this Byzantine romance sets the familiar chivalric plot of abduction and rescue squarely within the reductive geographical dichotomy of pagan east and Christian west that structures many Old French crusading narratives and conversion stories.[3] The hero Floire is said to rescue his ladylove from captivity in an "estrainge contree" (v. 3296) and bring her back to "son païs" (v. 3289).[4] When the courtly couple return to the hero's homeland and rule side by side as king and queen of Andalusia, Floire converts to Christianity and requires his subjects to do the same. And yet, Floire's anomalous status as a model Muslim courtly lover and Blancheflor's unconventional role as an enslaved Christian courtly lady complicate pat dichotomies of race and religion that would otherwise tend to cast these lovers in stark opposition. The hybrid venue of southern Spain, as geographically western but religiously Muslim, and the site of Babiloine, as physically eastern but culturally courtly, reveal the extent to which the more standard ideological location of courtly love in a western court setting actually relies, to a remarkable degree, on cultural elements far beyond European borders. Both Muslim Spain, where the love is born, and Babloine, where it later flourishes, are revealed to be equally productive sites of courtly encounter. Moreover, both venues are characterized by the kind of lavish Saracen wealth that the converted King Mordrain was forced to leave behind with his lady idol in the *Estoire*. Love, luxury goods, and religious conversion go hand in hand in these complex hybrid locales that overtly fold the pagan and mercantile east into feudal, amorous, and religious conventions of the courtly west.

The east/west paradigm used to structure parts of this romance becomes further complicated as the entwined tales of love and conversion are set within a frame of mercantile travel and luxury trade. Different from the narratives of courtly love discussed in Chapter 6 where Saracen silks, gold, and jewels from the east are subtly embedded into the fabric of western court life, this story, which derives in part from the Arabian *Thousand and One Nights*, details a practice of trading luxury goods between east and west. The lovers' journey—from southern Spain to Fatimid Egypt and back again—traces commercial axes of cloth exchange in the twelfth century, crossing between two medieval sites of silk trading: Andalusia, already an important silk-producing region by the tenth century, and Egypt, one of the main textile zones of the Muslim orient.[5] Indeed, Floire's quest to free a captive beloved is more mercantile than chivalric;[6] it features a hero laden with precious silks and costly fabrics, a Lancelot turned cloth merchant while searching for his ladylove. Although Floire suffers from the standard symptoms of courtly lovesickness—he pines and frets, cannot eat, laugh, play, sleep, or drink (vv. 397–99)—this hero undertakes his quest with the avowed purpose of "buying and selling" (por vendre et por acater, v. 1526) in the traditionally male space of travel and trade that Blancheflor eventually enters and transforms. At tale's end, in one manuscript version at least, Blancheflor plays Pygmalion to Floire's Galatea, refashioning her suitor amorously and religiously through an unexpected deployment of luxury goods.

As courtly lovers are displaced geographically to Spain and the orient, the familiar gendered hierarchies structuring relations between devoted suitor and beloved lady, chivalric savior and captured dame also begin to shift. We witness in this seemingly simple tale a strikingly rich array of gendered subject positions in love. The semiheroic savior, Floire, plays a Lancelot of uncertain gender. Said repeatedly to resemble physically the lovely Blancheflor, this hero is in fact eventually mistaken for a woman—Blancheflor's western friend and companion, Gloris, in the emir's harem, partly because the beardless youth has a face prettier than any *damoisele* in the emir's tower (vv. 2587–88). But the misidentification occurs, interestingly, when the emir's chamberlain sees what he presumes to be the two "women," Gloris and Blancheflor, lying together "bouce a bouce" (v. 2599). Indeed, before the ambiguously gendered Floire arrives to "rescue" Blancheflor from the pagan ruler's embrace, the heroine herself is said to have already enjoyed "perfect love" with this same woman, Gloris: "Ainc mais si grans amors ne fu / com a Blancheflor vers Gloris / et ele a li, ce m'est avis" (vv. 2594–96; Never was there such a great love as Blancheflor had for Gloris nor Gloris for her, in my view).[7] If Floire's gender as a "man" in love with Blancheflor is revealed when he is forced to disrobe and bare his chest, thereby ending his temporary masquerade as a harem girl, the affectionate bond between Gloris and Blancheflor endures as a symptom of yet another possible love story, complimentary to, but not disruptive of, the heterosexual coupling in the dominant narrative.

And even there, recognizable features of the courtly love plot are invoked only to be skewed. It is Blancheflor, rather than the male lover, who dresses up her beloved at the end of the tale, endowing him with items of luxury dress that are as rich, as pagan, and as eastern as the "riche roebe" that the *Estoire*'s King Mordrain is dramatically forced to burn. The demonized emir in Babiloine, who provides a mercantile version of the unscrupulous abductor, Méléagant, crosses over at times to assume the opposing role of the enamored courtly suitor. He wants in the end exactly what the courtly rescuer Floire desires: to marry the woman he calls, in western amorous rhetoric, "son amie" (vv. 2614–18, 2725–26).

It is thus not simply a question in *Floire et Blancheflor* of embellishing a courtly love plot with exotic elements from the east or of transforming an oriental tale into a "roman français" by adding Arthurian themes or features of the *matière de Bretagne*.[8] Although often read as an idyllic, charming, and unproblematic love story,[9] *Floire et Blancheflor* results from a complex literary mixing of elements found in Graeco-Roman or Byzantine romances, more indigenous French materials, biblical antecedents, traditional Arabo-Persian tales, and passages from the *Pilgrim's Guide to Compostela*.[10] The resultant anomalous tale, which positions the perfect courtly couple within an expansive geography, overtly defies the pat binarism of east and west. Indeed, reading through clothes and costly adornments in *Floire et Blancheflor* reveals that courtly love thrives amid border crossings of many kinds. While often disrupting oppositional structures of race and religion, amorous coupling in this tale also challenges rigidly dichotomous formulations of gender and sexuality.

To be sure, sexist stereotypes of traded and entrapped women are intricately entwined with racist and crusading impulses that govern portions of this love story. The Egyptian emir's harem in Babiloine offers a phantasm of the presumed eastern delight in incarcerating sexually submissive women, not unlike nineteenth-century colonial stereotypes of the harem that feature "supine concubines, lush interiors, water pipes and an atmosphere of indolence and decadence."[11] The concerted orientalism informing these aspects of the tale cannot account for the specificity and diversity of the numerous cultures invoked in the course of this richly hybrid courtly narrative. Like many postmodern Euro-American discourses of displacement, the twelfth-century love story of *Floire and Blancheflor* tends at these narrative moments to absorb difference and create ahistorical amalgams,[12] constructing the pagan courts in Andalusia and Babiloine as an unspecified "other" against which French courtliness defines itself. It is also true, however, that the orientalizing surface of this romance is constantly disrupted by a cast of hybrid characters who repeatedly subvert dichotomies of race and religion, geography, gender, and sexuality.

The whole of this many-layered love story is further complicated by a costly golden goblet that tells its own story of love, abduction, and rescue. When Blancheflor is literally sold by Floire's parents to foreign merchants for ample quantities of eastern luxury goods—gold and silver, "pailes, mantiaux and bliauts" (silk cloth, mantles, and tunics), the parents receive, as payment for the tale's heroine, a material object of great value, neither Christian nor Muslim: an extraordinarily costly golden goblet from ancient Troy (vv. 491–504).[13] This stunningly beautiful and priceless cup, derived initially from the "treasure of a rich Roman emperor" (vv. 442–43), was carried by Aeneas from Troy to Lombardy as a love token for his "amie" Lavinia (vv. 503–6).[14] It bears on its surface, amid gold and enamel detailing, a Graeco-Roman love story in three dimensions—the judgment of Paris and the rapt of Helen. In delicate enamelwork, Vulcan adorned the goblet with images of the Trojan War, the Greek attack, and "comment Paris ses drus *l'en maine*" (v. 458, my emphasis; how Paris led away his beloved), prefiguring the way Floire will later take Blancheflor from the emir in Egypt in a rhetorical echo of the earlier rapt, "Flores s'en va, s'amie *en maine*" (v. 3287, my emphasis; Floire departs, leading away his beloved).[15] The precious and costly *coupe* inspires Floire to act, much as the mere sight of Guenevere incites Lancelot to feats of prowess that enable him to rescue her in Chrétien de Troyes's *Chevalier de la charrete*.

And yet, the goblet's material value also plays a significant role in securing the imprisoned Blancheflor, as we shall see. Although the goblet's story may be Graeco-Roman, its material composition resonates with the luscious profusion of gemstones and precious metals coded elsewhere in the tale as part of eastern opulence and foreign trade negotiations. Indeed, the story of this courtly lady's complex disappearance and rescue is made to resonate both with the ancient tradition of the rapt of Helen and with a more contemporary mercantile narrative that, in the end, can allow the often commodified courtly lady in fiction to deploy valuable commodities herself. As depictions of love in this tale stretch beyond western Europe, they point toward a putative Trojan and Graeco-roman past while also foregrounding a medieval Muslim, Egyptian present based on commercial travel and trade in luxury goods.

A Courtly Tale in Eastern Dress

Floire et Blancheflor opens with a number of recognizably courtly topoi infused with eastern features that map an ever-expanding setting for courtly love. Here, a familiar account of medieval textual transmission from clerical written work to oral love story is staged physically on a ground of costly eastern silk. This story, designed to teach aristocratic listeners and noble lovers of both genders about love ("Molt i porrés d'amors aprendre," v. 6; Here you will be able to learn a great deal about love), was recounted initially, we are told, by two beautiful and knowledgeable women. One of them had learned the story from a cleric who had earlier read it in written form. But she in turn delivers her version of the story orally while seated on an expensively adorned silk coverlet, embroidered with flowers, not unlike those occupied by satisfied lovers in the *chanson de toile*:

En cele cambre un lit avoit
qui de paile aornés estoit.
Molt par estoit boins et ciers li pailes,
ainc ne vint miudres de Tessaile.
Li pailes ert ovrés a flors. vv. 37–41

(In the room there was a bed adorned with a lovely and expensive silk coverlet. No better had ever come from Thessaly. It was embroidered with flowers.)[16]

This quilt, which surpasses all those from the Greek province of Thessaly, also bears specifically Muslim features, as we have seen: "D'indes tires bendes et ours" (v. 42; bands made of indigo and golden *tiraz* fabric). And indeed, like successful lovers in the *chanson de toile*, Floire and Blancheflor later declare their mutual passion while seated together on a "cortine de soie" (vv. 2453–54). They do so, however, not in a western court setting but amid the lavish splendor of an Egyptian emir's palace. As the lovers come together, so too do east and west join, according to a pattern that has been set in motion during the young couple's childhood games at the Muslim court in Andalusia. There they enjoyed a stereotypically courtly "joie d'amor" (vv. 240, 240b) in a pagan king's garden that bears the requisite features of the western love locus: trees and flowers in constant bloom, birds singing of love (vv. 243–49). The same young lovers who read "pagan" (presumably Ovidian) love stories (vv. 231–32) in this courtly Muslim garden also write love poems at school in gold and silver letters on luxurious ivory tablets (vv. 257–66). From the outset of this tale, courtliness and courtly love exist in a hybrid zone where the "distant" east inhabits the heart of the courtly west, as eastern riches are used to define western traditions of love and courtliness.

A Mercantile Adventure Story

As the tale progresses from Muslim Spain to Babiloine, Floire's assumed identity as a traveling trader brings into stark relief the Levantine contours that often subtly shape a number of courtly love stories, as we have seen in Chapter 6. In this instance, the voyage itself, staged along medieval trade routes between Spain and Egypt, reframes the standard romance adventure plot of abduction and rescue as a quest based on trade. When Floire sets out to retrieve his captive ladylove, he goes armed by his father specifically with "ciers pailes et or et argent, / biax dras et mules en present" (vv. 1137–38; costly silks, gold and silver, beautiful cloth, and mules as gifts). The intrepid Floire asserts, "comme marceans le querrai / .VII. somiers avoec moi menrai, / les .II. cargiés d'or et d'argent / et de vaissiaus a mon talent, / le tiers de moneés deniers, / car tos jors me sera mestiers, /et les .II., sire, de ciers dras, / des millors que tu troveras (vv. 1141–48; I will search for her as a merchant, taking seven pack horses with me, two of them carrying gold and silver, and silver utensils to my liking, the third packed with coins, since I will always need those, and two, sir, loaded with costly cloth, the best you can find). He will carry this cargo along with an ample supply of furs and the king's chamberlain "car bien set vendre et acater / et au besoing consel doner" (vv. 1157–58; because he knows how to buy and sell, and when necessary, to give advice). Thus has the courtly quest become a mercantile quest based specifically in cloth trade with the east.

We know that throughout the thirteenth century Spain exported silks to Christian and Muslim countries along the Mediterranean Basin and to Egypt. Maurice Lombard explains that Syrians, who had come to southern Spain as early as the eighth century, some settling in Niebla (where Floire's family resides),[17] introduced the production of *tiraz* silks in a number of sites. By the tenth century luxurious brocaded silks were being sent east from the Andalusian towns of Almeria, Malaga, and Baza, among others (Lombard, 96). But commerce in luxury cloth went two ways. Egypt itself manufactured silk cloth in the Middle Ages, especially silks brocaded in gold, along with wool and linen (94). When the town of Damietta near Alexandria was taken by crusaders in 1219, the invaders discovered large quantities of silk held by Egyptian merchants (94). Lombard explains further that Christian pilgrims visiting holy sites would take home "Syrian" silks, including moires and brocades produced in Tyre, Antioch, and Tripoli (93). The already hybridized historical site of Muslim Spain, where the love story of *Floire et Blancheflor* begins, thus garners additional richness through contact with Saracen cultures to the east via the commercial exchange of lavish cloth. The courtly love story played out in *Floire et Blancheflor* is itself wrapped in this cross-cultural transport of sumptuous and costly fabric.

From the moment Floire leaves his father's court in search of Blancheflor, the courtly hero's hallmark passion is played out in a setting of goods and services traded for gain. The lovesick Floire, whose prototypically intense "doel and ire" (v. 402) prompted him earlier to contemplate suicide (v. 540), now becomes a "marceans" with the requisite despondency of a courtly suitor always "morne et pensiu" (vv. 1524, 1532; sad and downcast).[18] When Floire and his retinue arrive at the city of Baudas and lodge with another "rich bourgeois," Floire strikes his distracted amorous pose amid a detailed account of port tax. The description of his eating very little because he is thinking of love follows directly upon an explanation that those entering port must give one-sixth of the goods they carry to the emir:

218   Chapter 7

Li pors estoit a l'amirail;
maint home i a eü travail.
U soit a droit u soit a tort,
tot lor estuet doner au port
la siste part de lor avoir
et puis jurer qu'il dient voir,
et rendre toute a dam Marsile
cil qui maistres est de la vile.
Quant cel avoir orent rendu
et lor mangiers aprestés fu,
il vont laver, puis sont assis.
Et plus bel liu ont Flore mis.
A mangier ont molt ricement,
si mangierent molt l'iement.
Mais Flores molt petit manga
por s'amie dont il pensa. vv. 1439–52

(The port belonged to the emir. Many had endured hardship there. Right or wrong, at the port, they had to pay one-sixth of the value of their cargo, then swear they had reported truthfully, and give it all to Marsile, governor of the city. Once they had handed over their goods and their meal was ready, they washed up and sat down. Floire was placed in the seat of honor. They ate plentifully and happily. But Floire ate little, on account of his beloved, who occupied his thoughts.)

However "pensis" and lovelorn he may be at these moments, Floire repeatedly transacts business. He pays his hosts for information they provide about Blancheflor's transport, giving one hostess a golden *coupe* (vv. 1325–30), paying another host with a mantle and silver goblet (vv. 1473–74), and giving the *notonnier* 100 sols (v. 1547). Different from the questing Lancelot, whose exchanges with unnamed *demoiselles* in the Arthurian landscape form part of a gift economy—in payment for information the women provide about the queen's capture, Lancelot puts himself in their "service"—Floire pays in gold, silver, and items of luxury dress for information about Blancheflor. His success as a courtly suitor depends not on chivalric prowess but on advancing his quest through commercial transactions that will secure a beloved lady who is herself assessed in terms of costly silk and luxury goods:

Cil l'acaterent maintenant,
car molt ert bele par sanlant,
.xxx. mars d'or et .xx. d'argent
et .xx. pailes de Bonivent,
et .xx. mantiaus vairs osterins,
et .xx. bliaus indes porprins
et une ciere coupe d'or. vv. 435–41

(She was so beautiful they [eastern traders] bought her immediately for thirty marks of gold and twenty of silver, twenty silks from Benevent, twenty fur-lined coats of costly oriental silk, twenty tunics of indigo silk, and a costly golden goblet.)[19]

Yet while striking the pose of a "rich homme" and thus playing the role of all the wealthy merchants he deals with on his eastern journey, Floire also wages an interior battle with Amors, in the style of Chrétien's *Lancelot*:

Amors respont: "J'oi grant folie!
Raler? Et ci lairas t'amie?
Dont ne venis tu por li querre?
Sans li veus aler en ta terre!
Dont ne te membre de l'autrier,
Que del graffe de ton graffier
Por li ocirre te vausis,
Et or penses de ton païs!"
. . .
Itel bataille en lui avoit;
Amors forment le destraignoit. vv. 1619–26, 1643–44

(Love answers, "This is madness I hear! Return home and leave your beloved here? The one you came to rescue? And you want to go home without her? Have you forgotten the other day when you were about to kill yourself with the point of your stylus on her account? And now you're thinking of your homeland?" . . . This battle raged within him as he suffered Love's great torment.)

As this western-style love is played out in an eastern frame, it enters a marketplace of barter and trade effortlessly. Here, raw treasure and costly goods function as currency in courtly service, and courtly "largesse" no longer retains its feudal meaning or status. To gain access to Blancheflor, Floire must play a series of elaborate chess games with the *portier*, returning the opponent's winnings (*le gaaing*, v. 2222b) at the end of each game, thus enriching him with substantial amounts of gold and silver (v. 2153). But the crucial exchange, which gives Floire access to the captive ladylove, combines mercantile and feudal practices as the hero deploys the richly decorated Trojan goblet to secure courtly service from his eastern rival. Having first withheld the luxurious goblet from the *portier*'s winnings in the games of chess, Floire later insists on *giving* the valued object to his opponent in a gesture of putative friendship that will procure the rival's homage and his aid in finding Blancheflor:

Et dist: "Pas ne la vos vendrai,
mais par amor le vos donrai,
por çou qu'il m'ert gerredonés

se mon besoing ja mais veés."
Cil prent la coupe et puis li jure
k'en lui servir metra sa cure. vv. 2233–38

(Floire said, "I will not sell it to you; I will give it to you in friendship, provided that the favor will be returned to me if you ever see me in need." He [the *portier*] took the goblet and swore that he would be in Floire's service.)

In fact, the courtly Floire has used generosity here in a questionably uncourtly fashion: to trick and trap his covetous rival, extracting the vassal's aid not for military service but in the service of love.

As a lover spanning cultural modes of eastern trade and feudal service, Floire also crosses almost imperceptibly between Christian and pagan worlds. During one of Floire's early laments at Blancheflor's tomb, we are reminded fleetingly that this committed courtly lover, whose remorse throws him into a textbook faint, does so with a non-Christian religious affiliation:

Quant Flores ot qu'ele estoit morte,
molt durement se desconforte,
la color pert, li cuers li ment,
tos pamés ciet el pavement.
La crestiienne s'esbahi,
de la paor jeta un cri. vv. 691–96

(When Floire learned she was dead, he was overcome with grief. He lost all color, his heart faltered, and he fell into a faint. Shocked, the Christian woman cried out in fear.)

Casual reference in this passage to Blancheflor's mother as a Christian woman reminds us bluntly that the lamenting lover collapsed before her is by contrast a Muslim. Starkly different from the *Estoire*'s portrait of King Mordrain, whose love is associated with pagan idolatry, this tale depicts a western courtly lover who is also decidedly pagan.[20]

Love in the Eastern World

And what of Blancheflor? She seems, at first, the epitome of commodification. Baldly reduced to the marketable values of luxury goods and traded literally to slave merchants in Andalusia, this heroine is later sold for seven times her weight in gold (v. 2718) to an Egyptian emir who holds young women captive in an enchanted, opulent garden paradise. The very mechanisms of trade and travel that make of Floire a richly hybrid courtly hero seem only to plunge Blancheflor deeper into the role of the abducted and bartered woman. Blancheflor's worth as a marketable commodity is recorded most starkly in a single line telling how the Romans' possession of the Trojan *coupe* becomes the merchants" possession of a courtly lady:

Puis *l'*orent tot li ancissour
qui de Rome furent signor
dusqu'a Cesar, a cui *l'*embla
uns leres, qui *la* l'aporta
u li marceant *l'*acaterent
et por Blanceflor *le* donerent.
Çou *l'en donent par droit marcié*,
et il s'en font joiant et lié,
k'a double cuident gaaignier. vv. 507–15 (my emphasis)

(Then it belonged to all the former rulers of Rome until Caesar, from whom a thief stole it and transported it to the site where merchants bought it before exchanging it for Blancheflor. *They traded it for her* and were delighted, since they thought they could get double their money.)

Indeed, as the tale shifts eastward, the natural world of courtly encounter, figured initially in the idyllic garden of love at King Felix's Andalusian court, seems to be perverted by a kind of eastern extravagance used to entrap already commodified women. In Babiloine, we find a seductive and ostentatious array of eastern fauna and flora—exotic birds, trees, and spices (vv. 1995–2004, 2021–32)—augmented by the magic of precious metals and priceless gems, all of which contribute to the courtly prison holding the emir's harem captive. The river traversing the garden paradise overflows with a stupendous display of wealth in precious stones: sapphires and chalcedony, amethyst and sardonyx, rubies, bloodstone, and quartz crystals, topaz and enamels (vv. 2013–18).[21] Even more importantly however, a fabricated metallic bird sings magically when the wind blows, recalling the sculpted golden bird on the Trojan *coupe* that figured Helen's rapt (vv. 498–502, 1995–99, my emphasis).[22]

In this setting of eastern excess, there grows a seemingly courtly "arbre d'amors," flush with red flowers, like the ones used to conceal Floire, the stereotypically courtly flower, on the final leg of his journey to Blancheflor. But this tree of love too has been enchanted and bewitched; it is used to test the virginity of the emir's female entourage and to select one beauty for crowning, violation, and eventual death. Again, natural, botanical rhythms are manipulated almost mechanically, in this instance by a desirous emir plotting a woman's demise:

Aprés les fait totes passer
desous l'arbre por acerter
la quel d'eles cel an ara,
cele sor cui la flors carra.
Li arbres est de tel manière;
sor cui karra la flors premiere
eneslepas iert coronee
et dame du païs clamee;
il li noçoie a grant honor
et si l'aime comme s'oissor
desi a l'an, que jou ai dit;
adont le viole et ocit;
et se il a o soi pucele
que il miex aime et soit plus bele,
sor li fait par encantement
la flor caïr a son talent. vv. 2077–92

(Then he makes them all walk under the tree to determine which one he will have that year; the one on whom the flower falls. The tree is such that the first one to have a flower fall on her will be immediately crowned and proclaimed lady of the realm. He marries her with great pomp and loves her as a wife for a year, as I have said, then kills her brutally. And if the emir has in his entourage a beautiful maiden whom he prefers over the others, he uses magic to make the flower fall on her.)

And yet, the act of selecting "la plus bele floire" from a garden paradise, made here to seem unnatural and grotesque, does not characterize the pagan emir alone. The enchanted "love tree" growing in the eastern *locus amoenus* is replayed in the more metaphorical courtly tree that has been growing in Floire's heart throughout his journey. Planted by Amors, the graft that has taken hold and flourished inside Floire emits a pleasant odor that will lead this courtly lover to pick the delicious fruit of love, as the emir annually had picked "la plus bele floire" from his garden or as Paris plucked Helen from Troy. Interestingly, this flowering root of love's desire planted in Floire's heart smells not of western but distinctively eastern perfumes: incense, zedoary, cloves, and galanga:

Amors li a livré entente,
el cuer il a planté une ente
qui en tous tans flourie estoit
et tant doucement li flairoit
que encens ne boins citouaus

ne giroffles ne garingaus.
Et cele odour rien ne prisoit,
toute autre joie en oublioit:
le fruit de cele ente atendoit,
mais li termes molt lons estoit,
çou li ert vis, du fruit cueillir:
quant Blancheflor verra gesir
jouste soi et le baisera,
le fruit de l'ente cuellera. vv. 377–90

(Love gave him the desire by planting a graft in his heart, which flowered constantly and smelled as sweet as incense, the beneficial zedoary, cloves or galanga. But Floire did not appreciate this perfume. He ignored all pleasures, waiting for the fruit of the graft. It seemed a long way off that he would pick the fruit. As soon as he saw Blancheflor lying next to him, kissing him, he would be harvesting the fruit from the root.)

In both the eastern and western versions of male desire staged here, the natural, botanical register, whether accompanied by luxurious pagan opulence or not, reduces women to objets of desire waiting to be plucked.

The Hybrid Blancheflor

And yet Blancheflor herself, who stands tellingly astride the cultures of east and west as a contact zone between natural and mercantile worlds, as we have seen, will later deploy luxury goods from the world of trade to alter her status as a fruit ripe for picking. If this early narrative moment represents the heroine in the natural register of courtly coupling as a ripe fruit, she appears before us more often in the course of this tale in a register of eastern opulence: as a precious gem. Indeed, during the scene of Floire's lament at Blancheflor's tomb, a brief accounting of the courtly lady's standard features—she has a "cler visage," is "bele et sage" and "de parage"—is capped by reference to her being a "precïeuse jeme" (vv. 725–30). The abducted Helen too is figured on the Trojan *coupe* as "a most beautiful woman, a gemstone compared to all others" (vv. 482–83). But Blancheflor's association with the spoils of luxury trade runs far deeper than a symbolic indication of her beauty. The tomb representing this courtly heroine during her false death is encrusted with "stones possessing special qualities, capable of making miracles happen," precious gems that appear before us in a crescendo of bejeweled excess as the narrator enumerates "hyacinths, sapphires, chalcedony, emeralds, sardonyx, pearls, corals, chrysolites, diamonds, and amethysts, precious beryls and phyllades, bloodstone, topaz, and agates" (vv. 653–60). If Floire and Blancheflor both carry a strong botanical resonance in their names, she is a flower of a different kind.[23]

This distinctive feature of the tale's heroine has gone largely unnoticed by critics, who have tended to emphasize the striking physical similarity of the teenage couple. To be sure, during the voyage to Babiloine, innkeepers repeatedly recognize Floire as the very "image" of Blancheflor since both appear despondent and lovelorn (vv. 1295–1304, 1465–68, 1535–38), much as their perfectly matched *images* as "smiling" lovers mirror one another on Blancheflor's tomb (vv. 579–88).[24] And yet, if these young lovers resemble one another physically and in courtly and amorous demeanor, Floire's extraordinary beauty is compared only to natural phenomena and plants: cheeks red as the rising sun (vv. 2859–60), skin white as the lily (v. 2864), hands white as snow (v. 2865). Blancheflor by contrast emerges as a material treasure trove of incomparable wealth. Making only passing reference to the botanical (vv. 2903–4), her portrait relies most heavily on comparison to precious metals, jewels, and furs, as we saw in Chapter 6. With a "forehead whiter than ermine" (vv. 2876), "gray eyes that sparkle like gems" (vv. 2879–80), "fine skin clearer than glass" (vv. 2885–86), "small, closely set teeth, whiter than fine silver" (vv. 2895–96), she is pulled tangibly away from the natural world of courtly gardens that more fully informs her "pagan" male counterpart toward a world of eastern splendor. As we follow this courtly couple's movements across the globe, their paradoxical positioning as lovers partaking of dual cultures simultaneously only increases. The Muslim courtly hero is best characterized by association with the natural setting of western courtly encounter, while his Christian ladylove becomes recognized through her eastern opulence.

Although Nature has a definite hand in fashioning this lady's beauty—her well-formed mouth is prettier than any ever made by Nature (vv. 2889–90)—Blancheflor's overall appearance impresses the viewer repeatedly with its artificial, handmade fabrication. She bears "a well-formed body as if fashioned by hand ... and fine nostrils, as if formed by hand" (Le cors a tel et si bien fait / que s'on l'eüst as mains portrait.... Et les narines ot bien faites, / com si fuissent as mains portraites, vv. 2905–6, 2887–88), recalling the extravagant golden images of lovers holding metal flowers on her own lavish tomb and the bejeweled images of Helen and Paris painted on the costly golden *coupe*. But different from the exquisite goblet that tells of Helen's abduction and the fall of Troy, and different too from the lavish tomb that memorializes a putatively lost love, Blancheflor's gemlike perfection as a courtly lady is not frozen or fixed. She is, rather, moved to significant action during her journey eastward.

Indeed, it is in Babiloine that this heroine, earlier transported from Spain to Egypt as a mercantile commodity and subsequently returned to Andalusia by Floire on the model of a Trojan kidnapping, comes into her own. A freed slave, she convinces the Egyptian emir, described here as more powerful than any Roman emperor, to spare the life of her enslaved friend, Gloris, and to curtail his annual beheading of consorts. Once returned to Floire's "païs" in Andalusia, it is Blancheflor and the love she inspires, we are told, that causes the conversion of Floire and the entire Muslim kingdom in Andalusia:

Por Blanceflor, la soie amie,
mena puis crestiiene vie. vv. 3303–4

(On account of Blancheflor his ladylove, he led a Christian life from that time on.)

Blancheflor's role in these two transformations—one cultural, the other religious—seems in one sense simply to reiterate the actions of a western patriarch crusading against barbaric behavior and the Islamic faith. But she is not a western patriarch, nor even a typical courtly lady. Indeed, the conversions she effects significantly recast the more polarized relations between western Christian and eastern Islamic cultures that this text systematically disrupts at every turn. Whereas the conversion of King Mordrain and his followers depends, according to the narrative of the *Estoire*, on his rejection of love and on destruction of the lavishly dressed idolatrous lady/statue that inspires it, the new king of Andalusia and his followers convert to Christianity *because* of love and the gemlike beauty who advocates it.[25] The Christianity Blancheflor promotes in Muslim Spain is thus inextricably tied to an opulent and extravagant practice of courtly love that western Church officials and moralists would loudly decry, as we have seen in Chapter 4. Blancheflor, as a Christian queen in the Islamic west, retains visibly the gemlike splendor of eastern luxury goods that characterizes all three versions of the love story in this tale: from the golden lovers on the bejeweled Muslim tomb to the lovers painted on the golden, gem-encrusted Trojan *coupe* to Blancheflor's own body wrought metaphorically of ermine and jewels. The nexus of those love stories set materially in precious metals, gemstones, and costly adornments reveals, even more clearly than other tales I have discussed, the extent to which courtly love's reliance on luxury garments is in fact a reliance on material splendor generated in Saracen lands.

Golden Spurs

The conversion that Blancheflor sparks differs further from crusading efforts recorded in Old French epic or chronicle accounts because it requires no invading army and involves no violent attack. It is marked instead by a sartorial change, which significantly recasts the emblematic function of chivalric armor used by crusading knights in foreign lands. Indeed, Blancheflor records her love for Floire, a love that prompts the conversion of this pagan knight, in an item of clothing that is also a love token, as she dresses the hybrid hero of this tale simultaneously in western chivalric garb and eastern splendor. One manuscript version of *Floire et Blancheflor* adds a ten-line segment to the scene of reconciliation in Babiloine where the emir stereotypically gives Floire "s'amie" and makes him a knight.[26] In this version, the emir provides Floire with a lavish, gold-handled sword and an extraordinarily beautiful fur-lined mantle made specifically of "dras d'outremer" and embroidered with costly gold threads. But Blancheflor adds to this chivalric ensemble of eastern wealth and luxury a single item of dress that encapsulates the contact zone she represents between east and west. She gives Floire a set of golden spurs, not unlike those that the historical St. Bernard discouraged French "courtiers" from wearing because they signaled material extravagance and effeminacy. Whereas Bernard scorned the chivalric display and excessive adornment of crusading knights, complaining, "You adorn your bits and spurs with gold and silver and precious stones" (Evergates, 99; Leclercq, 216),[27] the account of conversion given in *Floire et Blancheflor* refutes the clerical stance, marking its cross-cultural hero with just such a westernization of eastern "excess."[28] This is one medieval interpretation of the tale based on an ending found in one manuscript. But it provides a significant option for understanding the complex relations between courtly lovers and systems of exchange in the courtly world.

Blancheflor's contribution to her lover/knight's courtly attire resonates materially with the golden stirrups donned by Floire earlier in the tale, at the moment of his departure for Babiloine:

Li estrier valent un castel,
d'or fin sont ovré a noiel. vv. 1195–96

(The stirrups, made of fine gold and decorated with enamel, were worth a castle.)[29]

We are told in this account that the "covreture" of Floire's saddle would be envied by a king (vv. 1187–90), his horse's beautiful bit is visibly "very costly" (v. 1197), and decorative gemstones adorning his mount's trappings are "worth a treasure" (v. 1200). The significance of Floire's stirrups too lies in their impressive material value: they are worth a castle. In stark contrast, however, the golden spurs that Blancheflor offers her lover knight, still laden with connotations of eastern luxury, are at the same time "spurs of love." As the Old French *or* echoes with *amor*, it also rhymes with the heroine's own name, Blancheflor:

Uns eperons d'or et d'amor
Li chauça bele Blancheflor.

(Spurs of gold and love did Blancheflor put on his feet; Pelan ed., vv. 2881–82.)

Thus does eastern gold merge with western love in a single material object that differs substantially from Fortune's devastatingly foreign and estranged golden house, which lovers are advised to avoid in the clerical discourse of the *Roman de la Rose* (see Chapter 1). This set of spurs, conferred as a love token by the stereotypically beautiful courtly lady, will bring foreignness home to the western court, making eastern opulence an integral part of the chivalric armor worn by knights in love.

In conferring these golden spurs of love, the hybrid heroine, Blancheflor, a courtly beauty who has lived in an eastern harem, a French noblewoman whose mother was kidnapped and traded as *gaainz* in an Andalusian court, a western Christian who has been traded, bought, and sold into captivity, reveals the opulence of courtly luxury attire to be more than decorative foreign excess. The golden spurs of love she offers could not readily be cast off as St. Bernard suggests for the effeminately decorative spurs of other knights. Rather, the golden spurs that this courtly heroine uses to dress her still-pagan yet courtly lover at the palace of an Egyptian emir reveals eastern opulence as integral to western love, not just as an oppositional "other" against which to define the courtly couple, but as a crucial icon of courtly love itself. The Egyptian gold of these spurs has been cast in an amorous mold. This gold, associated in some western clerical minds with Saracen opulence and "the trinkets of women," here marks an appropriately easternized yet still courtly love. The gesture lends new definition to the concept of feudal *largesse*, staging as it does the *largesse* not of a lord or knight but of a lady in love. Here the lady's *largesse* sets the joint cultural institutions of love and chivalry firmly in the golden opulence of eastern lands.

This version of *Floire et Blancheflor* provides an important glimpse of possible alternative configurations for the relation between women and men, love and luxury clothes within the courtly love story. As Blancheflor "dresses" her lover/knight with the golden spurs of love, she is no longer the bartered and exchanged treasure we saw earlier in the tale but a desiring subject who confers treasure, in the form of dress, on her male partner. Her gesture of "arming" a knight in golden spurs differs significantly from Enide's role in dressing the valiant Erec from head to toe in preparation for the sparrow hawk contest in *Erec et Enide* (vv. 709–26). That more traditional arming of Erec in hauberk and ventail, helmet, sword, shield, and lance prepares the courtly hero to triumph in combat and win the beautiful maiden as a most prized possession.

Blancheflor's gift of golden love spurs, by contrast, locates her at a complex intersection of a number of possible subject positions that significantly disrupt the stereotypically gendered roles of knight and lady. If she plays a female Pygmalion to Floire's Galatea, her symbolic gift also enacts, to an important degree, the *largesse* of a western feudal lord securing vasselage from an underling. And yet in the context of this tale, Blancheflor's donation of golden spurs casts her more specifically as a Saracen Pygmalion, or an eastern feudal lord more on the model of the Egyptian emir who generously outfits Floire in knightly garb, or the King of Constantinople in *Cligés*, whose lavish gifts will help make his son a knight at Arthur's court. And her partner, Floire, who converts to Christianity for love, begins to resemble the Saracen princess. Indeed, if the spurs she offers mark her lover visibly as a knight, their golden extravagance also suggests the trapping of an eastern pagan or even, in Saint Bernard's terms, a woman. He is all dolled up in pagan attire but still a Christian and a knight. The courtly lady has converted him to Christianity through love, marking both transformations with the sartorial opulence of the pagan east.

In a sense, Blancheflor's offer of golden spurs takes us back to the point at which we began, with the demoisele d'Escalot's silk sleeve, another item of costly dress imported from lands far to the east of western Europe and deployed by the courtly heroine to redefine the standard terms of the courtly love contract. Whereas the demoisele d'Escalot uses an article of her own clothing to alter Lancelot's chivalric costume and thus rewrite the love plot, Blancheflor here takes an icon of knighthood itself—the rider's spurs—and recasts their role in the service of love. Blancheflor's contribution of this item of luxury attire to her knight's chivalric regalia, which effectively "dresses him up for love," reminds us too of the assistants to Lanval's lady, who dress that knight in silks and rich fabrics in preparation for a life beyond battle, an amorous relation in an alternative court setting where women and luxury goods set the terms of love (see Chapter 5). The decorative gold that Blancheflor adds to Floire's costume recalls as well the "chains and buttons," the fancy trimmings, along with the silk blouse embroidered with many colored threads, that adorn the garments of the anonymous, inscribed trobairitz in "Ab greu cossir" (see Chapter 2). This lady's plea is to be free to dress herself up for love, but that freedom from marital, legal, and social restraint relies necessarily, as does the sartorial independence of the ladies in Lanval's alternative amorous court setting, on the use of luxury goods imported from the east. So too do the very items of fancy dress that drive the Jealous Husband to distraction bear the marks of eastern opulence: "Jewels, golden buttons and buckles, gowns and furs" (vv. 9227–29). The rich and powerful Oiseuse, too, crowned by a chaplet of gold embroidery (v. 554), surrounded by trees imported from Saracen lands, stands at the edge of an "earthly paradise" and ushers the lover into the garden of amorous courtly delights (vv. 590, 634). She sets the terms of the love contract, of leisure and pleasure, much like many working women in the *chanson de toile* who sew their way into alternative love scenarios, whether initiated through sartorial love tokens or enacted on ornately embroidered imported silk coverlets.

By reading through clothes in these various love scenarios, we can begin to see how clerical resistance to the lavish excess of courtly love, exemplified most cogently in Reason's tirade against Fortune's gown, with which we began, is in many ways a resistance to what is perceived to be the opulence of the "foreign east" (see Chapter 6). From this perspective, a range of clerical attacks on the material excesses of courtly love generally can be understood as a resistance not only to the ostentatious and vainglorious display of wealth but also to the highly disruptive effect that those eastern luxury goods can potentially bring to fragile western hierarchies of desire, social rank, and gender identity. Indeed, in dressing up its subjects, courtly love substantially undoes and shakes up a number of key cultural paradigms on which medieval amorous attachment has been thought to rely.

Coda:
Marie de Champagne and the Matière *of Courtly Love*

In closing, I would like to return to France, to the county of Champagne, which has been considered traditionally the literary center of courtly love, and more specifically to the prologue of one of the most highly discussed courtly romances in the French tradition, the inaugural tale of love between Lancelot and Guenevere: *Le Chevalier de la charrete*. The prologue to this tale of star-crossed lovers seems at first to have nothing to do with clothes. It features an influential female literary patron, not a dolled-up courtly beauty. The relationship staged in the prologue's opening line is between Marie, the historical countess of Champagne, Eleanor of Aquitaine's eldest child, and a famed twelfth-century clerical author at Marie's court, Chrétien de Troyes.[1] The countess wants him to compose a story, or so he claims: "Puis que ma dame de Chanpaigne / vialt que romans a feire anpraigne / je l'anprendrai molt volentiers" (vv. 1–3; Since my lady of Champagne wants me to begin a tale in the vernacular, I will do so willingly).[2]

Scholars have tended to focus on the issue of literary patronage in the prologue, wondering what Marie might have contributed to the tale or how she is ultimately displaced from the scene of narration, what she might have "wanted" in a love story, or how much she shaped the narrative that follows.[3] Most important, we know that Marie de Champagne's alleged role as coauthor of the *Charrete* pales significantly as the romance progresses. By line 6131, Chrétien claims to have joined forces with a second clerical writer, Godefroi de Leigni, whose participation displaces Marie entirely from the process of composition. This lady's desire and donation, posed here as irresolvable enigmas, are ultimately occluded by a literary relationship between two men.[4]

But what would happen if we read this complex prologue through the lens of clothing? More specifically, what if we attempted to read Marie's story through the demoisele d'Escalot's sleeve, with which we began?[5] To be sure, Marie wears no sleeve in the *Charrete*'s prologue. Indeed, we hear nothing of her courtly clothes. And yet Chrétien does dress her metaphorically in silks and jewels when staging the crucial issue of his lady's worth:

Par foi, je ne sui mie cil
qui vuelle losangier sa dame;
dirai je: "Tant com une jame
vaut de pailes et de sardines,
vaut la contesse de reïnes?"
Naie voir; je n'en dirai rien. vv. 14–19

(In truth, I am not one to praise his lady. Would I say, "Just as a precious gem is worth so much silk cloth and chalcedony, thus is the countess worth so many queens?" Certainly not. I would say nothing of the kind.)[6]

This playful praise of the countess as worth any number of queens attests in the most basic sense to material wealth and status, which would give her the leverage and influence important for a patron. Scholars have long noted that the highly equivocal praise of Marie de Champagne in the *Charrete*'s prologue may contain, at least in part, an indirect critique of the bombastic accolades lavished on an actual queen, Beatrice of Bourgogne, empress of Germany and Frederick Barbarossa's wife,[7] by Chrétien's contemporary at Marie's court, Gautier d'Arras. Gautier opens his romance *Ille et Galeron* with an extended portrait of Beatrice's incomparable status not only as a "dame" to whom Gautier pledges service and subservience (v. 131, "Servir le voel si com jo sai") but also as an unrivaled empress (vv. 92–93, "Rome est et ert tous jors nonper: / si est et ert l'empererris" (Rome is and always will be without equal; so too the empress). She displays exemplary comportment, knowledge, prowess, goodness, and especially *largesse* (vv. 29–32, 108).[8] Like Marie, she is a "bele geme" of such great worth, we are told, that the value of other women pales by comparison (vv. 79–83). But the *Charrete*'s allusion to *pailes et sardines* does more than simply invoke generous giving. Here costly imported goods that make the liberality of courtly conduct possible are brought to bear directly on the literary conventions of amorous storytelling.

It is well known that the prologue to Chrétien's version of the Lancelot and Guenevere story recounts another kind of love story, a mock amorous alliance between a putatively beneficent lady, "ma dame de Champagne," and a clerical author who strikes the pose of a perfect courtly suitor. Like the dutiful lover of troubadour lyric, Chrétien lavishes hyberbolic praise on the courtly lady he pledges to serve (vv. 3–5), presaging Lancelot's own pledge to Guenevere later in the tale to be entirely at her command, "suens entiers" (vv. 4, 5656).[9] Throughout the prologue, Chrétien prostrates himself rhetorically before his seemingly empowered lady/lord much as the devoted but speechless Lancelot later genuflects literally at Queen Guenevere's bedside, as if before a valued and valuable relic (vv. 4651–53). As Chrétien deftly segues between this amorous courtly register and the topos of literary patronage, *la dame de Champagne* is said to *give* not her body but, in some highly uncertain sense, the makings of a book:

Del chevalier de la charrete
comance Crestïens son livre;
matiere et san li *done et livre*
la contesse, et il s'antremet
de panser, que gueres n'i met
fors sa painne et s'antancïon. vv. 24–29; my emphasis

(Chrétien begins his book about the Knight of the Cart; the countess *gives and bestows* upon him the "matiere et san," and he begins the task, giving it little more than his hard work and diligent attention.)[10]

If Marie gives this book not only in the role of beneficent patron but also in her symbolic function as the courtly ladylove, we might consider her gift in relation to the material sleeve that the demoisele d'Escalot *gives* Lancelot.[11] That is, we might reread the prologue's most contested lines— "matiere et san li done et livre / la contesse" (vv. 26–27), in which Marie is said to *give* the author/narrator/suitor, in some highly uncertain way, the material of a love story, in relation to the other material mentioned here: the *pailes et sardines* used to assess Marie's worth. To be sure, the *pailes*, of which this countess/queen is said to be worth so many, resonate fully with the numerous scenes of lovemaking in both lyric and romance that take place atop such luxurious silk coverlets imported from Constantinople, Thessaly, Damascus, or Baghdad, or behind equally "foreign" cortines.[12] *Sardines*, similarly, recalls repeated evocations of the courtly ladylove's beauty in terms of gemstones originating in distant lands, as we have seen. Indeed, as the beloved lady/patron, Marie is first cast in this prologue in the traditional springtime register of love's flowering: "the lady who surpasses all others living, much as the west wind (warm wind) surpasses those that blow in April or May" (vv. 10–13; Que ce est la dame qui passe / totes celes qui sont vivanz, / si con li funs passe les vanz / qui vante en mai ou en avril). But that conventional assessment soon segues seamlessly into the more starkly material portrait of her worth in *pailes* and *sardines*.[13] As this cool breeze of the traditional western courtly locus amoenus meets with silks and gems imported from the east, the *Charrete*'s prologue situates the conventions of courtly love poetry, based on the exordium to spring, squarely within a broader frame of eastern luxury trade.

But what of courtly dress as an index of social status? Reading through clothes in Chrétien's difficult prologue reiterates the power of the courtly love story to imagine and stage the movement of women in love across social ranks, recalling as it does so the episode of the demoisele d'Escalot's sleeve or the Jealous Husband's account of his wife's dressing up. Through a deft rhetorical sleight of hand in the *Charrete*'s prologue, Chrétien transforms the countess Marie into a queen before our very eyes. Just as a precious gem is literally equal in worth to a given number of silk fabrics and minor gems like chalcedony, he contends, so too does this countess, bearing the value of the highest ranking jewel, even surpass in worth any number of queens. To be sure, the expected hierarchy of queen to countess is inverted here to flatter the patron and court her favor; and the *Charrete*'s transformation of Marie from countess to queen does not result from the literal donning of lavish garments. Rather, it issues from the rhetorical virtuosity of a deft narrator posed as a supplicant lover. As "dame" is made to rhyme with "jame" in this prologue, Marie is positioned symbolically as equivalent in status to a fictive but ultimately all-powerful literary queen: Guenevere, the courtly *dame* par excellence.

Furthermore, luxury goods hold a special meaning in relation to Marie as a historical countess of Champagne, whose substantial material wealth would have derived in part from imported goods, brought to France from eastern lands through the fairs fostered by her husband, count Henri le Liberal, in the county of Champagne.[14] Fairs held in the towns of Troyes, Provins, Bar-sur-Aube, and Lagny developed in the course of the twelfth century from local agricultural markets into international commercial centers, in large part because of policies established by the counts of the region like Marie's husband to provide housing and safe conduct (*conduit*) for merchants coming from Italy and other parts of Europe.[15] The city of Troyes more specifically, where the historical Marie lived and held court, was a highly prosperous commercial center that traded domestically produced wool, linen cloth, and wine to Italian merchants in contact with the east at least from the time of the Third Crusade (1189–92).[16] The literal worth of foreign silks and gems, derived from trade with distant lands to the east, could potentially cause such a countess to become as influential as the fictive Arthurian queen, Guenevere.[17]

And what of gender assignment and configurations of desire? They too are troubled by the prologue's rhetorical acrobatics, which make it unclear who controls the inception, development and composition of this love story, a man or a woman. Chrétien's lavishly deferential claims about Marie's ostensible contribution to the tale of Lancelot and Guenevere—that he takes up the task because she wants him to (v. 1), that he follows her "commandemanz," adding little more than his talent and effort (vv. 22–23, 27–29)— are systematically undercut by assertions of his own masterful control: that *he* will undertake the project of writing this *romans* and that *he*, Chrétien, here begins his book (v. 25).[18] And yet, Chrétien's rhetorical skill also fashions Marie as an empowered, authorial version of himself. In speaking for his absent patron, Chrétien puts himself, to a significant degree, in her place. If he composes the tale that she is supposed to have created, then in fabricating the courtly love story he is, in an important sense, playing her part, taking her place in the sense of taking it over. If so, the male cleric emerges before our eyes, through his own playful description, cross-dressed as a female author. In place of the age-old definition of courtly romance as a tale articulated between "un clerc et une dame qui l'écoute," we have a doubly hybrid countess/clerk and lady/suitor who produces this particular inflection of the love story. Is he/she then a woman dressed as an author or a clerk wearing the silks and gems often forbidden to his class and station? Chrétien's sly claim—that Marie is composing the story that he himself also creates—asserts, at the outset of this formative account of literary courtliness, the important volatility of subject positions in courtly amorous encounter.

The *Charrete*'s portrait of Marie differs perhaps most significantly from the depiction of the demoisele d'Escalot in *La Mort Artu* because Marie does not actively deploy the *pailes* and *sardines* mentioned in the prologue as a means of expressing her wish and will. And yet, in addition to asking what this lady wants or contributes to the courtly love story, we might ponder the further question of *who* gives the gift of this inaugural tale of love. Is it a man or a woman? A countess or a queen? An empowered subject or an object of desire? A beloved whose value comes from indigenous natural beauty or a benefactor whose worth derives from imported material wealth? In terms of the playful logic of the prologue, there is no simple answer to these ever-proliferating questions. To choose any one dyadic option or its opposite would not adequately represent the complex dynamics of desire, gendered subjectivity, or geographic hybridity characteristic of much courtly encounter.

Rather, the prologue to the *Chevalier de la charrete* locates the courtly love story elsewhere, amid a rich terrain of border crossings that can feature a hybrid lady/clerk who holds influence and power in the literary courtly world equal to that of a symbolic queen. His/her subjectivity, located geographically in the European west, derives, to an important degree, from visual markers of eastern opulence. But that courtly identity also spreads across a spectrum of gendered subject positions, which hold the potential to redefine established categories of masculine and feminine as they also disrupt the artificially imposed east/west divide.

To read the prologue in this way is not to efface the historical Marie or to lose women from sight. On the contrary, to read Marie de Champagne at the nexus of historical and literary modes, as an influential patron *and* a symbolic queen, as a cleric *and* a lady, opens new possibilities for acknowledging the complexity of the categories of women and men respectively in courtly love scenarios. Reading through clothes in the *Charrete*'s prologue, even if the clothes in question are no more than a fleeting metaphorical comparison with *pailes et sardines*, helps us to see how this brief prologue joins a number of other courtly texts in staging the phenomenon of courtly love as a site where genders are not fixed or certain, where highly codified relations of desire do not necessarily conform to established heteronormative paradigms, where female protagonists positioned in love scenarios can evade or slide across presumed divisions of social rank, and where western elite identity depends for its very definition on eastern opulence.

This reading does not tell us everything we need to know about the prologue or the *Charrete* or about courtly love. But it does point the way toward new questions we might ask. If luxury clothes in the courtly world often function in conventional ways to fetishize female bodies, to guarantee aristocratic identity, to distinguish male- and female-sexed bodies and thereby regulate gender, and to display the wealth of European court culture, they also do more. Reading through clothes in the manner I have explored here reveals that luxury attire and lavish goods represented in courtly literary scenarios, whether in the form of an ornate gown or a simple silk cloth, whether in the demoisele d'Escalot's tangible material sleeve or Marie de Champagne's metaphorically precious *pailes et sardines*, can create sartorial bodies that move unexpectedly beyond the confines of both cloth and flesh.

Notes

Introduction. The Damsel's Sleeve: Reading Through Clothes in Courtly Love

1. Odile Blanc provides a concise account of the historiography of clothing from classic works by Quicherat (*Histoire du costume en France depuis les temps les plus reculés jusqu'à la fin du xviii siècle* [Paris, Hachette, 1877]), Violet-le-Duc, and Enlart to more recent studies by Barthes and Lemoine-Luccioni. See "Historiographie du vêtement: Un bilan," in *Le Vêtement: Histoire, archaeologie, et symbolique vestimentaires au moyen âge*, ed. Michel Pastoureau (Paris: Léopard d'Or, 1989), 7–33. This collection of essays discusses a wide range of topics, as do Françoise Piponnier and Perrine Mane in *Se Vêtir au Moyen Age* (Paris: Société Nouvelle Adam Biro, 1995), trans. Caroline Beamish as *Dress in the Middle Ages* (New Haven, Conn.: Yale University Press, 1997). See also Margaret Scott, *History of Dress: Late Gothic Europe; 1400–1500* (London: Mills and Boon, 1980); and Mary Houston, *Medieval Costume in England and France: 13th, 14th and 15th Centuries* (London: Adam and Charles Black, 1950); Daniel Roche details clothes and textile production in the ancien régime in *La Culture des apparences* (Paris: Fayard, 1989), trans. Jean Birrell as *The Culture of Clothing: Dress and Fashion in the Ancien Regime*, (Cambridge: Cambridge University Press, 1994). For art historical evidence, see Joan Evans, *Dress in Medieval France* (Oxford: Clarendon Press, 1952); for clothing in literary texts, Eunice Rathbone Goddard, *Women's Costume in French Texts of the Eleventh and Twelfth Centuries* (Baltimore: Johns Hopkins University Press, 1927). Germain Demay studies the representation of medieval dress on seals in *Le Costume au Moyen Age d'après les sceaux* (Paris: Librairie de D. Dumoulin, 1880). A thorough analysis of sumptuary legislation through the Elizabethan period is provided by Alan Hunt in *Governance of the Consuming Passions: A History of Sumptuary Law* (New York: St. Martin's Press, 1996); and for Italy, Diane Owen Hughes, "Sumptuary Law and Social Relations in Renaissance Italy," in *Disputes and Settlements: Law and Human Relations in the West*, ed. John Bossy (Cambridge: Cambridge University Press, 1983) and her "Regulating Women's Fashion," in *A History of Women in the West*, vol. 2, *Silences of the Middle Ages*, ed. Christiane Klapisch-Zuber (Cambridge, Mass.: Belknap Press of Harvard University Press, 1992), 136–58; and James A. Brundage, "Sumptuary Laws and Prostitution in Medieval Italy," *Journal of Medieval History* 13 (1987): 343–55. Details of dress and fashion are examined in D. Menjot, ed., *Les Soins de la beauté du Moyen Age au début des temps modernes* (Nice: Faculté des Lettres et Sciences Humaines, 1987) and in Georges Vigarello, *Concepts of Cleanliness: Changing Attitudes in France Since the Middle Ages*, trans. Jean Birrell (Cambridge: Cambridge University Press, 1988). On underwear, Elizabeth Ewing, *Dress and Undress: A History of Women's Underwear* (New York: Drama Book Specialists, 1978)

and C. Willett Cunnington and Phyllis Cunnington, *The History of Underclothes* (London: Faber and Faber, 1981). More generally, Annette B. Weiner and Jane Schneider, *Cloth and Human Experience* (Washington, D.C.: Smithsonian Institution Press, 1989).

2. Perrine Mane, "L'Emergence du vêtement de travail à travers l'iconographie médiévale," in Pastoureau, *Le Vêtement*, 93–122; Michel Beaulieu, "Le Costume: Miroir des mentalités de la France (1350–1500)," in *Le Vêtement*, 255–76; and Pipponier and Mane, *Se Vêtir au Moyen Age*.

3. Michel Pastoureau, *Figures et couleurs: Etudes sur la symbolique et la sensibilité médiévales* (Paris: Léopard d'Or, 1986), and *Traité d'héraldique*, 3rd ed. (Paris: Picard, 1997), 250–53.

4. Dyan Elliott, "Dress as Mediator Between Inner and Outer Self: The Pious Matron of the High and Later Middle Ages," *Mediaeval Studies* 53 (1991): 279–308.

5. *Dress in the Middle Ages*, 6–7.

6. See Joachim Bumke, *Courtly Culture: Literature and Society in the High Middle Ages*, trans. Thomas Dunlap (Berkeley: University of California Press, 1991); Georges Duby, "The Transformation of the Aristocracy: France at the Beginning of the Thirteenth Century," in *The Chivalrous Society*, trans. Cynthia Postan (Berkeley: University of California Press, 1977); and Gabrielle Spiegel, *Romancing the Past: The Rise of Vernacular Prose Historiography in Thirteenth-Century France* (Berkeley: University of California Press, 1993), 21–22. On the lavish monarchal dress of literary figures, see Sara Sturm Maddox and Donald Maddox, "Description in Medieval Narrative: Vestimentary Coherence in Chrétien's *Erec et Enide*," *Medioevo Romanzo* 9 (1984): 51–64.

7. François Rigolot, "Valeur figurative du vêtement dans le *Tristan* de Béroul," *Cahiers de civilisation médévale* 10, 3–4 (1967): 447–53; Susan Crane, "Clothing and Gender Definition: Joan of Arc," *Journal of Medieval and Early Modern Studies* 26, 2 (Spring 1996): 297–320; Susan Schibanoff, "True Lies: Transvestism and Idolatry in the Trial of Joan of Arc," in *Fresh Verdicts on Joan of Arc*, ed. Bonnie Wheeler and Charles T. Wood (New York: Garland, 1996), 31–60; Valerie Hotchkiss, *Clothes Make the Man: Female Cross Dressing in Medieval Europe* (New York: Garland, 1996). On cross-dressing and gender identity in the *Roman de Silence*, see Roberta L. Krueger, "Women Readers and the Politics of Gender in the *Roman de Silence*," in her *Women Readers*, 118–24; Peggy McCracken, "The Boy Who Was a Girl: Reading Gender in the *Roman de Silence*," *Romanic Review* 85, 4 (1994): 517–46; Simon Gaunt, "The Significance of Silence," *Paragraph* 13, 2 (1990): 202–16; Regina Psaki, ed., "*Le Roman de Silence*," *Arthuriana* 7, 2 (1997). James A. Schultz, "Bodies That Don't Matter: Heterosexuality Before Heterosexuality in Gottfried's *Tristan*," in *Constructing Medieval Sexuality*, ed. Karma Lochrie, Peggy McCracken, and James A. Schultz (Minneapolis: University of Minnesota Press, 1997), 91–110; Claire Sponsler, "Narrating the Social Order: Medieval Clothing Laws," *Clio* 21, 3 (1992): 265–83; and, more recently, "Fashioned Subjectivity and the Regulation of Difference," in her *Drama and Resistance: Bodies, Goods, and Theatricality in Late Medieval England* (Minneapolis: University of Minnesota Press, 1997), 1–23.

8. Roberta L. Krueger, "'Nouvelles choses': Social Instability and the Problem of Fashion in the *Livre du Chevalier de la Tour Landry*, the *Ménagier de Paris*, and

Christine de Pizan's *Livre des Trois Vertus*," in *Medieval Conduct*, ed. Kathleen Ashley and Robert L. A. Clark (Minneapolis: University of Minnesota Press, 2001), 49–85.

9. Nancy A. Jones, "The Uses of Embroidery in the Romances of Jean Renart: History, Gender, Textuality," in *Jean Renart and the Art of Romance: Essays on Guillaume de Dole*, ed. Nancy Vine Durling (Gainesville: University Press of Florida, 1997), 13–44; Caroline Jewers, "Fabric and Fabrication: Lyric and Narrative in Jean Renart's *Roman de la Rose*," *Speculum* 71, 4 (1996): 907–24.

10. E. Jane Burns, "Ladies Don't Wear *Braies*: Underwear and Outerwear in the French *Prose Lancelot*," in the *Lancelot-Grail Cycle: Text and Transformations*, ed. William W. Kibler (Austin: University of Texas Press, 1994), 152–74.

11. Susan Crane, "Talking Garments," in *The Performance of Self: Ritual, Clothing and Identity During the Hundred Years War* (Philadelphia: University of Pennsylvania Press, 2002), 10–38. For a recent study of fabrics as central to the making and unmaking of subjects in Renaissance Europe, see Ann Jones and Peter Stallybrass, *Renaissance Clothing and the Materials of Memory* (Cambridge: Cambridge University Press, 2000). See also Kathy Krause, "The Material Erotic: The Clothed and Unclothed Female Body in the *Roman de la violette*," in *Material Culture and Cultural Materialisms in the Middle Ages and Renaissance*, ed. Curtis Perry (Turnhout: Brepols, 2001), 17–40.

12. *La Mort le roi Artu*, ed. Jean Frappier (Paris: Champion, 1964). For an English translation see Norris J. Lacy, *The Death of Arthur* in *Lancelot-Grail: The Old French Arthurian Vulgate and Post-Vulgate in Translation*, vol. 4 (New York: Garland, 1995).

13. The *demoisele* states elsewhere that the sleeve was made of silk, "une manche de soie que ge li donai par amors" (27).

14. Gauvain explains the terms of this contract most succinctly in the *Mort le roi Artu* when he offers to prove his worth and win the love of the demoisele d'Escalot by fighting against Lancelot according to the traditions of *cortoisie*: "Damoisele, or fetes tant par *cortoisie* et por l'amour de moi que ge puisse prouver encontre lui que ge vaill mieuz as armes que il ne fet; et se ge le puis conquerre as armes, lessiez le et me prenez" (25; Damsel, in the name of courtliness and for love of me, allow me to prove that I am better in combat than he is; and if I can vanquish him in combat, leave him behind and take me instead).

15. "Son douz ami presente par amours une manche, / et li cuens la reçoit, ens u tournoi se lance... Mout le fait bien Garsiles, qui prohece a et force; / pour amour a la bele s'esvertue et efforce," vv. 149–50, 161–62. Michel Zink, *Les Chansons de toile* (Paris: Champion, 1977), 119–20.

16. "Quant Lancelos entent ceste requeste, si l'en pesa moult; et nequedant il ne li ose contredire, puis qu'il li avoit creanté ... Mes toutevoies, si come il dit, se metra il en aventure por son creant tenir, car autrement seroit il desloiax, se il ne fesoit a la damoisele ce qu'il li avoit en couvenant" (10; When Lancelot heard her request, it grieved him heavily; and yet he did not dare deny her wish because of his [former] promise... Rather, as he explained, he undertook the adventure in order to keep his word; failing to carry out his promise to the lady would be disloyal). Lancelot fears Guenevere's rebuke: "Et neporquant il fu moult dolenz de cest otroi, car il set bien, se la reïne le set, ele l'en savra maugré si grant a son escient qu'il ne trouvera jamés pes envers li" (10; Nonetheless, he was dismayed by this gift, because

he was well aware that if the queen knew of it, she would so hold it against him that he would never have a moment's peace with her).

17. Later, he is the "chevalier a la manche qui avoit le tornoiement veincu" (21; the knight with the sleeve who won the tournament); and Gauvain remarks to the demoisele d'Escalot herself, "il est li plus preudom que ge veïsse puis que ge me parti de Kamaalot. Mes ge ne sei qui il est, ne comment il a non. . . avoit desus son hiaume une manche ne sei a dame ou a damoisele" (22; He's the most valiant knight I've seen since I left Camelot. I don't know who he is or what his name is. . . but he has on his helmet a sleeve belonging either to a lady or damsel).

18. The same is true of the scene in which Guenevere dresses Lancelot in the *Prose Lancelot*. See Burns, "Which Queen? Guinevere's Transvestism in the French *Prose Lancelot*," in *Lancelot and Guinevere: A Casebook*, ed. Lori J. Walters (New York: Garland, 1996), 260.

19. Although she is the daughter of a "riche vavasor" (8) and her two brothers have been knighted by King Arthur, Lancelot's higher standing puts him out of range as a potential mate. Thus does one of the *demoisele*'s brothers advise that she lower her sights (metez vostre cuer plus bas), since she cannot expect to "pick the fruit of such a tall tree" (42).

20. In the case of the Bele Ydoine, from father to lover.

21. Jean Renart, *Galeran de Bretagne*, ed. Lucien Foulet (Paris: Champion, 1925).

22. Chrétien de Troyes, *Le Chevalier de la charrete*, ed. Mario Roques (Paris: Champion, 1970), vv. 1460–69. We learn elsewhere in *Galeran de Bretagne* that Fresne made the sleeve and decorated it in silk thread, vv. 3159–61, 3215–26.

23. "Onques ne vi a home autretant fere d'armes comme il fist [Lancelot] a l'assemblee de Wincestre, ne onques manche a dame ne a damoisele ne fu mieuz emploiee ne tant regardee comme la vostre fu" (40; I have never seen a man fight so well as this man [Lancelot] did at the Winchester tournament. I have never seen a lady or young lady's sleeve used more effectively or watched more intently than yours was).

24. See especially the English painter John William Waterhouse's (1849–1917) *Lady of Shalott*, as well as paintings with the same title by Arthur Hughes and William Holman Hunt. Pre-Raphaelite interpretations of this Arthurian material derived largely from Tennyson's poem "Lady of Shalott" and Malory's *Morte d'Arthur*. See *The Arthurian Encyclopedia*, ed. Norris J. Lacy (New York: Garland, 1986), 545–46, and Debra Mancoff, *The Arthurian Revivial in Victorian Art* (New York: Garland, 1990) and *The Pre-Raphaelites* (London: Tate Gallery, 1984).

25. In the *demoisele*'s account of the incident, she confronts Lancelot, not only as a helpless victim asking to be saved, but as a master addressing a servant, delivering her message in person so he will not mistake her meaning: "por ce que nus messages ne doit estre si bien creüz de la besoigne son seigneur comme li sires meïsmes, vos di ge le mien besoing qui tant est granz" (67; Since no messenger in the service of his lord should be believed as well as the lord himself, I myself will tell you my need, which is great).

26. Chrétien de Troyes, *Cligés*, ed. Alexandre Micha (Paris: Champion, 1957), vv. 990–93. On the *trobairitz*, see Matilda Tomaryn Bruckner, "Na Castelloza, Trobairitz, and Troubadour Lyric," *Romance Notes* 25, 3 (1985): 239–53. Castelloza

both reiterates and challenges the convention when she says, "I know this is a fitting thing for me, / though everybody says it isn't proper / for a lady to plead her case with a knight," Matilda Tomaryn Bruckner, Laurie Shepard, and Sarah White, *Songs of the Women Troubadours* (New York: Garland, 1995), 19; vv. 17–19, and elsewhere directly affirms the appropriateness of ladies declaring their love: "So when it happens that a lady / loves, she ought to court / the knight if she sees / prowess and knightly worth in him (17; vv. 50–53).

27. *Le Roman de la poire*, ed. Christiane Marchello-Nizia (Paris: SATF, 1985), vv. 2493–95. The *Prose Lancelot* provides a humorous example of the lady being "too forward," in actually seducing the knight physically, to which the befuddled Lancelot responds, "Avoi, damoisele, certes bien avés tote honte perdue, kar onques mes n'oï parler de dame ne de damoisele qui volsist prendre chevalier par force" (ed. Alexandre Micha, [Geneva: Droz, 1978–83], 1: 323; Truly, lady, you have abandoned all shame. I have never heard of a lady or young lady who tried to take a knight by force). See Burns, "Ladies Don't Wear Braies," 166–68.

28. *Andreas Capellanus on Love*, ed. and trans. P. G. Walsh (London: Duckworth, 1982), 269. Parry more accurately gives "sleeves" instead of "gauntlets." Andreas Capellanus, *The Art of Courtly Love*, ed. John J. Parry (New York: Columbia University Press, 1990), 176.

29. "Mais or vous weil dire et apenre / Quex choses la fame puet penre / De son ami, sans vilonie." *Li Livre d'amours de Drouart la Vache*, ed. Robert Bossuat (Paris: Champion, 1926), 184.

30. "De douneier e de parler / e de lur beaus aveirs doner / esteit tute la druërie / Par amur en lur cumpainie." *Les Lais de Marie de France*, ed. Jean Rychner (Paris: Champion, 1973), v. 578.

31. *Erec et Enide*, ed. Mario Roques (Paris: Champion, 1976), vv. 2356–66.

32. Jean Renart, *Le Roman de la Rose ou de Guillaume de Dole*, ed. Félix Lecoy (Paris: Champion, 1962). Helen Solterer reads the *ceinture* as a sign of the man's defloration in "At the Bottom of the Mirage, a Woman's Body: *Le Roman de la rose* of Jean Renart" in *Feminist Approaches to the Body in Medieval Literature*, ed. Linda Lomperis and Sarah Stanbury (Philadelphia: University of Pennsylvania Press, 1993), 213–33. As Roberta Krueger reminds us aptly, this "spunky heroine" is ultimately displaced by the verbal tour de force of a capricious male cleric and appropriated to the project of male lineage. *Women Readers*, 153–54.

33. "Et si port Lancelos sor son hiaume .I. penonchel que ele li envoie a une langete de soie vermeille.... Et si li envoie la roine le frêmal de son col et .I. pigne moult riche don't tout li dent sont plain de ses cavex et la chainture don't ele estoit chainte et l'aumousniere." Micha, 8: 408.

34. "Et la roine mande Lancelot qui il ... port l'escu que il porta a la daraine assamblee, mais qu'il i ait une bende blanche de bellic." Micha, 8: 408.

35. The knight's banner typically bears heraldic insignia as on Guillaume de Dole's helmet, which displays a pennant showing the king's arms (v. 2603).

36. As Leautez explains to the Amant in *Le Roman de la poire*, "Par le don de son cuevrechief / que quant bohordas t'envoia; / par ce don son amor t'otroia" (vv. 2472–74; with the gift of her scarf, which she sends you when you joust, she grants her love to you).

37. As Andreas Capellanus notes succinctly, "All lovers are bound to keep their love hidden." Walsh, 271.

38. They can thus achieve through fabric and clothes what other heroines might effect through "bodytalk," a doubled discourse that can resist while it also underwrites prevailing configurations of femininity or femaleness. E. Jane Burns, *Bodytalk: When Women Speak in Old French Literature* (Philadelphia: University of Pennsylvania Press, 1993).

39. My project here is distinct from Anne Hollander's concept of "seeing through clothes," which argues that our visual perception of bodies wearing clothing is often structured by previous depictions in art. *Seeing Through Clothes* (New York: Penguin, 1978).

40. Elisabeth Grosz, *Volatile Bodies: Toward a Corporeal Feminism* (Bloomington: Indiana University Press, 1994), 18, 23.

41. Judith Butler, *Bodies That Matter: On the Discursive Limits of "Sex"* (New York: Routledge, 1993), 30. The psychoanalytic perspective on courtly love confirms the absence of any actual, prior, historical, or biological object of male desire. Lacan explains in the *Ethics of Psychoanalysis* (New York: Routledge, 1992) that the "feminine object is emptied of all real substance" 149), and in *Encore* he shows that the place of the "lady-thing" is originally empty, a void around which male desire is structured through indirection and postponement. *Le Séminaire de Jacques Lacan, Livre XX: Encore* (Paris: Seuil, 1975), 65. For an overview, see Slavoj Žižek, *Metastases of Enjoyment* (London: Verso, 1994), 89–112.

42. When Jules David Prown, for example, lists "adornment" among the range of objects that fall within the compass of material culture, he categorizes jewelry, clothing, hair styles, cosmetics, and tattooing all as "alternations of the body." "Mind in Matter: An Introduction to Material Culture Theory and Method," in *Material Life in America, 1600–1860*, ed. Robert Blair St. George (Boston: Northeastern University Press, 1988), 19.

43. Terence S. Turner, studying the Kayapro tribe of the southern borders of the Amazon forest, shows how body paint functions as a kind of dress and how hair occupies social space beyond the body while remaining integral to it. "The Social Skin," in *Reading the Social Body*, ed. Catherine B. Burroughs and Jeffrey David Ehrenreich (Iowa City: University of Iowa Press, 1993), 15–39.

44. Marjorie Garber, *Vested Interests: Cross-Dressing and Cultural Anxiety* (New York: Routledge, 1992), 374. She quotes Roland Barthes quoting Hegel: "As for the human body, Hegel has already suggested that it was in a relation of signification with clothing: as pure sentience, the body cannot signify; clothing guarantees the passage from sentience to meaning." Barthes, *The Fashion System*, trans. Matthew Ward and Donald Howard (New York: Hill and Wang, 1983), 258.

45. Grant McCracken, "Clothing as Language: An Object Lesson in the Study of the Expressive Properties of Material Culture," in *Material Anthropology*, ed. Barrie Reynolds and Margaret A. Stott (Lanham, Md.: University Press of America, 1987), 103–28. See also Prown, "Mind in Matter," 17–37 and Peter Corrigan, "Interpreted, Circulating, Interpreting: The Three Dimensions of the Clothing Object," in *The Socialness of Things: Essays on the Socio-Semiotics of Objects*, ed. Stephen Harold

Riggins (Berlin: Mouton de Gruyter, 1994), 435. One advantage of studying literary representations of material artifacts is that, while actual clothing rarely survives over time, literary texts preserve descriptions of that clothing and set it within a cultural, if highly fictive, context.

46. Jane Schneider, "The Anthropology of Cloth," *Annual Review of Anthropology* 16 (1987): 409–48. The earliest social scientists to write on the subject of clothes, Thorstein Veblen (*Theory of the Leisure Class* [New York: Macmillan, 1899] and Georg Simmel ("Fashion," 1904, reprint in *American Journal of Sociology* 62 [1957]: 541–58), argued, conversely, that what is worn and displayed publicly reinforces boundaries of class and status. For a contemporary sociologist's view of fashion, see Fred Davis, *Fashion, Culture, and Identity* (Chicago: University of Chicago Press, 1992).

47. Introduction to *Clothing and Difference: Embodied Identities in Colonial and Post-Colonial Africa*, ed. Hildi Hendrickson (Durham, N.C.: Duke University Press, 1996), 2, 6. Hilda Kuper shows similarly how in colonial southeast Africa, clothing functions as an instrument of both hegemonic western influence and indigenous attempts to resist its influence. "Costume and Identity," *Comparative Studies in Society and History* 15, 3 (1973): 348–67.

48. As Toril Moi notes, femininity for Beauvoir was part of patriarchal ideology, which included rules for dress: "'Precisely because the concept of femininity is artificially shaped by custom and fashion,' Beauvoir writes, 'it is imposed on each woman from without ... the individual is still not free to do as she pleases in shaping the concept of femininity.'" See *Simone de Beauvoir: The Making of an Intellectual Woman* (Cambridge; Basil Blackwell, 1994), 191–92; and Jane Gaines, Introduction to *Fabrications: Costume and the Female Body*, ed. Jane Gaines and Charlotte Herzog (New York: Routledge, 1990), 3–8. Gaines notes Carol Ascher as an important exception to this rule. Ascher argued early on that clothing could give women a sense of potency to act in the world in "Narcissism and Women's Clothing," *Socialist Review* 11, 3 (1981): 77, 81.

49. Elizabeth Wilson, *Adorned in Dreams: Fashion and Modernity* (Berkeley: University of California Press, 1987), 245–46; and her "All the Rage," in *Fabrications*, ed. Gaines and Herzog. For a similar argument about shoes, see Anne Brydon, "Sensible Shoes," in *Consuming Fashion: Adorning the Transnational Body*, ed. Anne Brydon and Sandra Niessen (Oxford: Berg, 1998), 1–22.

50. Angela McRobbie, "Settling Accounts with Subcultures," *Screen Education* 34 (1980): 37–49; reprint in *Culture, Ideology, and Social Process: A Reader*, ed. Tony Bennett et al. (London: Open University Press, 1981), 43; and earlier, "Working Class Girls and the Culture of Femininity," in *Women Take Issue*, ed. Women's Studies Group (London: Hutchinson, 1978), 104.

51. Laurel Thatcher Ulrich, "Cloth, Clothing, and Early American Social History," *Dress* 18 (1991): 40.

52. See Igor Kopytoff's argument that objects are created culturally and cognitively and thus move in and out of being "mere commodities." "The Cultural Biography of Things: Commoditization as Process," in *The Social Life of Things: Commodities in Cultural Perspective*, ed. Arjun Appaduri (Cambridge: Cambridge

University Press, 1986). Grant McCracken describes clothing similarly as an instrument of attempted domination and an armory of resistance and protest in "Clothing as Language,"109.

53. I cannot thus agree with John Baldwin's recent assertion that the mass of material detail in the works of romance authors Jean Renart and Gerbert de Montreuil "serves as resplendent décor, with little bearing on the central narratives of the romances." *Aristocratic Life in Medieval France: The Romances of Jean Renart and Gerbert de Montreuil* (Baltimore: Johns Hopkins University Press, 2000), 193.

54. Roberta Gilchrist, *Gender and Material Culture: The Archaeology of Religious Women* (London: Routledge, 1994), 15.

55. Anthony Giddens, *The Constitution of Society* (Cambridge: Polity Press, 1984), 25.

56. For further comment on the question of agency in courtly love, see E. Jane Burns, "Courtly Love: Who Needs It? Recent Feminist Work in the Medieval French Tradition," *Signs* 27, 1 (Fall 2001): 23–57.

Chapter 1. Fortune's Gown: Material Extravagance and the Opulence of Love

1. Guillaume de Lorris and Jean de Meun, *Le Roman de la Rose*, ed. Félix Lecoy (Paris: Champion, 1970), vol. 1, vv. 4029–4569, especially vv. 4565–69, 4123, 4145, 4192, 4203, 4318–22.

2. See, for example, vv. 4560–69: "Je veill bien qu'il aillent ensanble / et face quant qu'il doivent fere / come courtais et debonere; / mes de la fole amor se gardent / donc les queurs esprennent et ardent, / et soit l'amor sanz couvoitise, / qui les faus queurs de prendre atise. / Bone amor doit de fin queur nestre: / don n'en doivent pas estre mestre / ne quel font corporel soulaz" (I do want them to get together and do what they must in a courtly and respectable manner. But let them beware of a crazy love that inflames hearts and makes them burn. Let their love be free of this covetousness, which incites false hearts to possession. Love should not be mastered by gifts any more than by bodily pleasures). The sentiment is reiterated by the figure of Ami in vv. 7975–92.

3. Reason cites Andreas's *De Amore* almost word for word in some places, most notably vv. 3025–29 concerning the lover's suffering. Her philosophical view of love generally is highly at odds with courtly romance, although it corresponds to Andreas's rejection of love in Book 3 of the *De Amore*. See George Economou, "The Two Venuses and Courtly Love," in *In Pursuit of Perfection: Courtly Love in Medieval Literature*, ed. Joan M. Ferrante and George Economou (Port Washington, N.Y.: Kennikat Press, 1975), 29–30.

4. *Andreas Capellanus on Love*, ed. and trans. P. G. Walsh (London: Duckworth, 1982), 293.

5. The desire to possess wealth expresses itself even more precisely as a male lover's desire for sexual attack and the violation of women as "valiant men assail" Lady Riches physically, as Reason explains (vv. 5191–95).

6. See also vv. 5217–18.

7. This description of Fortune's house in vv. 5891–6088 is a translation of Alain de Lille's *Anticlaudianus*, ed. Robert Bossuat (Paris: J. Vrin, 1955), VII, 405–VIII, 14. Fortune's dress, as it appears in vv. 6089–6134, derives from VIII, 45–57, in the *Anticlaudianus*.

8. Strubel claims that Peccune in this context does not represent "Richesse" but "l'argent concret." Guillaume de Lorris and Jean de Meun, *Le Roman de la Rose*, ed. and trans. Armand Strubel (Paris: Librairie Générale Française, 1992), 301. It is, however, important for our purposes that this allusion to material wealth is allegorized in the most courtly terms, as a lady or queen who extracts service from tormented and sleepless men languishing in her service.

9. *Despoillier* in Old French means to undress or remove garments. A. J. Greimas, *Dictionnaire de l'Ancien français*, 182–83.

10. Terence S. Turner, "The Social Skin," in *Reading the Social Body*, ed. Catherine B. Burroughs and Jeffrey David Ehrenreich (Iowa City: University of Iowa Press, 1993), 15–39.

11. *L'Art d'amours*, ed. Bruno Roy (Leiden: E.J. Brill, 1974), 251. This treatise represents one of five medieval adaptation/translations of Ovid's *Ars amatoria* undertaken by Maistre Elie, Jakes d'Amiens, Guirart, and two anonymous authors, one of whom pens the *Clef d'amors*. All but the *Art d'amours* mentioned above eliminate Ovid's third book, which gives women strategies for waging the battle of love, and each contains a version of Ovid's *Remedia amoris*. See Bruno Roy, Introduction, where he also argues that Jean de Meun was familiar with this version of the *Art d'amours* (58).

12. For the period 1190–1230 as documented in literary texts of Jean Renart and Gerbert de Montreuil, see John Baldwin, *Aristocratic Life in Medieval France: The Romance of Jean Renart and Gerbert de Montreuil* (Baltimore: Johns Hopkins University Press, 2000).

13. Reto Bezzola, *Les Origines et la formation de la littérature courtoise en Occident (500–1200)* (Paris: Champion, 1960), 2: 544.

14. *La Mort le roi Artu*, ed. Jean Frappier (Paris: Champion, 1964), 57.

15. This ornate courtly setting also contains a visual record of Lancelot's famed love affair with Guenevere. Even that account contributes tellingly to the adornment of this lavish court, since Lancelot painted the story of his love for the queen on its walls in "paintures" and "ymages" (59, 61) that create the court's lush decoration while also narrating a tale of adulterous love.

16. Albert Lecoy de la Marche, *La Chaire française au Moyen Age* (Paris: Librairie Renouard, 1886), 482.

17. *Erec et Enide*, ed. Mario Roques (Paris: Champion, 1976).

18. *The Exempla, or Illustrative Stories from the Sermones Vulgares of Jacques de Vitry*, ed. Thomas Frederick Crane (London: D. Nutt, 1890; reprint. New York: Burt Franklin, 1971), 84.

19. Crane, *Exempla*, xxviii. Jacques de Vitry's reaction to this plunder of garments echoes Saladin's message: "I entered the church and saw with my own eyes how brief and vain is the uncertain glory of the world" (xxviii).

20. Béroul, *Le Roman de Tristan*, ed. Ernest Muret (Paris: Champion, 1962), vv. 3721–27, 3730.

21. Jean Renart, *Le Roman de la Rose ou de Guillaume de Dole*, ed. Félix Lecoy (Paris: Champion, 1962).

22. Indeed, Guillaume's generous distribution of luxury dress has forged tangible bonds between the court and the mercantile world beyond it, as Boidin's further conversation with Conrad attests: "'Einsi sera par tens delivres / de son avoir, s'il ne se garde,' / fet l'empereres. 'N'aiez garde, / sire, qu'il en avra assez: / mout est as borjois bel et sez / quant il vient emprunter le lor, / qu'il lor done et fet grant honor'" (vv. 1880–86; "If he's not careful he'll soon be out of money," the emperor said. "Don't worry, sir, he'll have plenty. The townspeople welcome his borrowing from them, since he gives them presents and honors them"); and as one host remarks earlier, "I am certain he will be richly repaid some day for that squirrel-lined cloak and those sables dark as mulberries" (vv. 1856–59). Matilda Bruckner has shown how *Guillaume de Dole*'s variation on *Partenopeu de Blois* suggests "competition not only between nobles and non-nobles, but between the upper and lower nobility as well." "Romancing History and Rewriting the Game of Fiction: Jean Renart's *Rose* Through the Looking Glass of *Partenopeu de Blois*," in *The World and Its Rival: Essays on Literary Imagination in Honor of Per Nykrog*, ed. Kathryn Karczewska and Tom Conley (Amsterdam: Rodopi, 1999), 93–117.

23. Jean de Joinville, *La Vie de Saint Louis*, ed. Jacques Monfrin (Paris: Classiques Garnier, 1995), 18.

24. Pierre Kraemer, *Le Luxe et les lois somptuaires au moyen âge* (Paris: Ernest Sagot, 1920), 42. Kraemer draws heavily and directly, though without citation, on an earlier thesis by Etienne Giraudias, *Etude historique sur les lois somptuaires* (Poitiers: Société Française d'Imprimerie et de Librairie, 1910), esp. 49–61. For detailed analyses of sumptuary legislation through the Elizabethan era, see Alan Hunt, *Governance of the Consuming Passions: A History of Sumptuary Law* (New York: St. Martin's Press, 1996), and H. Baudrillart, *Histoire du luxe privé et public: Le moyen âge et la renaissance*, vol. 3 (Paris: Hachette, 1881).

25. Gabrielle Spiegel, *Romancing the Past: The Rise of Vernacular Prose Historiography in Thirteenth-Century France* (Berkeley: University of California Press, 1993), 21–22; Jean Flori and Theodore Evergates have argued for the importance of distinguishing nobility from knighthood as early as the twelfth century. Knighthood was not a class but a corporation of professional soldiers from many different social ranks, according to Flori: "Seigneurie, noblesse, et chevalerie dans les *lais* de Marie de France." *Romania* 108, 2–3 (1987): 202. Evergates shows further how the category of "knights" included "nobles, nonnoble allodial proprietors, and impecunious men of all social backgrounds." "Nobles and Knights in Twelfth-Century France" in *Cultures of Power: Lordship, Status, and Process in Twelfth-Century Europe*, ed. Thomas N. Bisson (Philadelphia: University of Pennsylvania Press, 1995), 17. He continues, "If the landed elite was permeable, it was primarily by marriage at the noncastellan level" (35), as the prosperous families of allodial knights intermarried with noncastellan nobles whose resources and lifestyle brought them increasingly closer to the rising, landed knights. Gabrielle Spiegel explains how, in the aftermath of the Battle of Bouvines, which changed feudalism and the high ideals of courtly ideology by proclaiming the independence of the Capetian kings from the three estates,

vernacular historiography becomes, by the thirteenth century, a royal historiography that depicts Philip Augustus and the royal court thriving in contrast to a waning aristocracy (13). Influential barons and prelates at Philip Augustus's court were supplanted by a service aristocracy composed of lesser knights (17, 18). Although Philip Augustus's army included some bannered knights and lesser knights, most of its members were non-knightly fighters on horseback, the lowest ranks of nobility and commoners. This signaled the end of military engagement as distinctly noble (20). On the difference between knightly and noble status in Marie de France, see Glyn S. Burgess, "Chivalry and Prowess in the *Lais* of Marie de France," *French Studies* 37, 2 (1983): 129–42. For an analysis of Chrétien's romances as sending two messages to lords and lesser knights, whose ranks were slowly moving together by the end of the twelfth century, one that prepares nobles to accept the increased monarchal influence and control under Philip Augustus and another that ensures lower knights a place in the courtly world, see Judith Kellogg, "Economic and Social Tensions Reflected in the Romances of Chrétien de Troyes," *Romance Philology* 39, 1 (1985): 1–21.

26. Etienne Boileau, *Le Livre des métiers et corporations de la ville de Paris, XIIIe siècle* (Paris: Imprimerie Nationale, 1879).

27. Giraudius, *Les Lois somptuaires*, 55–56.

28. Georges Duby, "The Transformation of the Aristocracy: France at the Beginning of the Thirteenth Century," in *The Chivalrous Society*, trans. Cynthia Postan (Berkeley: University of California Press, 1977), 184.

29. Kraemer, *Le Luxe*, 45.

30. Gilles d'Orléans, cited in A. Lecoy de la Marche, "les premiers ne naissent pas rois; ils naissent nus et pauvres, bien qu'ils soient fils de monarque ou de princes" (128).

31. This attitude has changed radically by the fifteenth century, when chronicles begin to insist overtly that royal vestments do not necessarily reflect the royalty of their wearer, that clothes constitute a code of ambiguous and arbitrary signs. See Christiane Marchello-Nizia, "Codes Vestimentaires et langage amoureux au 15e siècle," *Europe: Revue littéraire mensuelle* (October 1983): 36–42.

32. Diane Owen Hughes, "Sumptuary Law and Social Relations in Renaissance Italy," in *Disputes and Settlements: Law and Human Relations in the West*, ed. John Bossy (Cambridge: Cambridge University Press, 1983) and James A. Brundage, "Sumptuary Laws and Prostitution in Medieval Italy," *Journal of Medieval History* 13 (1987): 343–55.

33. Claire Sponsler has shown how English clothing laws (1337–1603), thought previously to be motivated by economic (protectionist) interests and moral concerns (controlling excess), are instead driven by a desire to create a social order that distinguishes one class from another, regulating the appropriateness of dress for each status group, especially the middle strata between noble and common. "Narrating the Social Order: Medieval Clothing Laws," *Clio* 21, 3 (1992): 265–83 and, more recently, "Fashioned Subjectivity and the Regulation of Difference," in *Drama and Resistance: Bodies, Goods, and Theatricality in Late Medieval England* (Minneapolis: University of Minnesota Press, 1997), 1–23.

34. Guillaume le Breton, *Gesta Philippi augusti*, in *Recueil des Histoires de France*, vol. 17, 16 ff. Quoted in Baudrillart, *Histoire du luxe privé et public*, 3: 167; my translation here and following,.

35. "Il est ordené que nus ne dux, ne cuens, ne prélaz, ne bers, ne autres, soit clers soit lais, ne puisse faire ne avoir en un anz plus de iiij paires de robes vaires." H. Duplès-Agier, ed., *Ordonnance somptuaire inédite de Philippe le Hardi* (Paris: J. B. Du Moulin, 1853), 6.

36. "Nul Bourgois, ne bourgoise, ne portera vair, ne gris, ne Ermines, & se delivreront de ceux que ils ont, de Paques prochaines en un an. Il ne porteront, ne pourront porter Or, ne pierres precieuses, ne couronnes d'Or, ne d'Argent.... Nuls Escuirs n'aura que deux paires de robes.... Garcons n'auront qu'une paire de robe l'an." M. De Laurière, ed., *Ordonnances des rois de France de la troisième race*, 1 (Paris: Imprimerie Royale, 1723), 1: 541.

37. "Li Duc, li Comte, li Baron de six mille livres de terre, ou de plus, pourront faire quatre robes par an, & non plus, & les femmes autant.... Tous prelats auront tant seulement deux paires de robes par an.... Tous Chevaliers n'auront que deux paires de robes tant seulement.... Chevaliers, qui aura trois mille livres de terre, ou plus, ou li Bannerets pourra avoir trois paires de robes par an, & non plus.... Nelle Damoiselle, si elle n'est. Chastellaine, ou Dame de deux milles livres de terre, n'aura qu'une paire de robe par an." De Laurière, *Ordonnances*, 542.

38. Spiegel, *Romancing the Past*, esp. 11–54.

39. See Sally Musseter, "The Education of Enide," *Romanic Review* 73, 2 (1982): 151–52. For a reading of Enide as a perfect harmonization of natural beauty and courtly clothing, see Sara Sturm-Maddox and Donald Maddox, "Description in Medieval Narrative: Vestimentary Coherence in Chrétien's *Erec et Enide*," *Medioevo Romanzo* 9 (1984): 51–64.

40. This garment, conferred along with a prayer that Erec and Enide conceive an heir, was given to Enide by Guenevere who obtained it by *engin* through the emperor Gassa. But initially the garment had been embroidered by Morgan as a "riche vestement" for her "ami" (vv. 2357–76).

41. "Je croyais être la reine ici, et j'en vois des centaines!" Jules Quicherat, *Histoire du costume en France* (Paris: Hachette, 1877), 205.

42. See especially Lecoy de la Marche, *La Chaire française* and Michel Zink, *La Prédication en langue romane avant 1300* (Paris: Champion, 1982).

43. Jacques de Vitry, *Exempla*, 55, 185. This admonition echoes Reason's more general claim in the *Roman de la Rose* that riches do not enrich the man who locks them up as treasure: "Si ne fet pas richece riche / celui qui en tresor la fiche" (Lecoy, vv. 4945–46). See also the assertion that love of fortune is not profitable, "Por ce n'est preuz l'amour de li" (v. 5323).

44. Zink, *La Prédication*, 376.

45. See Marcia Colish, "Cosmetic Theology: The Transformation of a Stoic Theme," *Assays* 1 (1981): 3–14; and her *The Stoic Tradition from Antiquity to the Early Middle Ages*, vol. 2, *Stoicism in Christian Latin Thought* (Leiden: E.J. Brill, 1985); R. Howard Bloch, *Medieval Misogyny and the Invention of Western Romantic Love* (Chicago: University of Chicago Press, 1991), 39–47.

46. Vitry, *Exempla*, 114, 252. Maurice de Sully tells a similar story about his own

mother, recounting that when she visited him bedecked in the finery of a noblewoman he refused to acknowledge her saying, "My mother is a poor woman who wears only a dress of rough sackcloth," Lecoy de la Marche, *La Chaire française*, 43; my translation.

47. Carla Casagrande, "The Protected Woman," in *A History of Women in the West*, vol. 2, *Silences of the Middle Ages*, ed. Christiane Klapisch-Zuber (Cambridge, Mass.: Belknap Press of Harvard University Press, 1992), 94.

48. Tertullian, "The Apparel of Women," in *Disciplinary, Moral, and Ascetical Works*, trans. Rudolph Arbesmann, Sister Emily Joseph Daly, and Edwin A. Quain. (New York: Fathers of the Church, 1959), 148.

49. Maurice Maloux, *Dictionnaire des proverbes, sentences, et maximes* (Paris: Larousse, 1980), 192, cited in *Three Medieval Views of Women*, trans. and ed. Gloria K. Fiero, Wendy Pfeffer, and Mathé Allain (New Haven, Conn.: Yale University Press, 1989), 103.

50. See also p. 167, where rustic women put all their expectations in fine clothing: "but noble women of wisdom reject elegant garments unaccompanied by the adornment of honest manners."

51. See especially Erich Köhler, "Observations historiques et sociologiques sur la poésie des troubadours," *Cahiers de civilisation médiévale* 7 (1964): 27–51; Georges Duby, *Le Mâle Moyen Age* (Paris: Flammarion, 1988), 70–79; and the critique of these positions by Sarah Kay, "The Contradictions of Courtly Love and the Origins of Courtly Poetry: The Evidence of the *Lauzengiers*," *Journal of Medieval and Early Modern Studies* 26 (1996): 209–53.

52. The moral in this instance, "On ne congnoit pas les gens aux drappiaux" (258; One does not know people by their clothes), recurs throughout this treatise. See, for example, the comment under "des ornemens des abis" regarding women who "are looked at and desired because of the beautiful clothes they wear" (237–38; my translation).

53. Ed. Robert Bossuat (Paris: Champion, 1926).

54. This treatise details levels of rank and status, adding a section to Andreas's text that concerns counts and countesses, dukes and duchesses. Drouart promises to distinguish for his readers individuals who are of low lineage (v. 3828) from those who are noble (vavasors and barons) and most noble (counts and dukes) (vv. 3832 ff).

55. See page 34, above.

56. See Peter Allen, *The Art of Love: Amatory Fiction from Ovid to the* Romance of the Rose (Philadelphia: University of Pennsylvania Press, 1992), 87.

57. James Brundage explains that in thirteenth-century Paris "supervision of the city's prostitutes and enforcement of the regulations concerning their behavior was entrusted to a royal official, the *roi des ribauds*, who had counterparts in many other French towns and cities." *Law, Sex, and Christian Society in Medieval Europe* (Chicago: University of Chicago Press, 1987), 468. See also Anne Terroine, "Le Roi des ribauds de l'Hôtel du roi et les prostituées parisiennes," *Revue historique de droit français et étranger* 4th ser., 56 (1978): 253–67. Brundage adds that canonists of the period thought that prostitutes should be distinguished by their style of dress. Indeed, many items of clothing prohibited to prostitutes—such as jewelry, elaborate

headdresses, costly fabrics—were in fact the mark of courtly life and status. Ruth Karas explains similarly how English sumptuary legislation in the thirteenth and fourteenth centuries regulated class along with social behavior, prohibiting prostitutes and servants together from wearing the furred hoods and furred capes of "reputable ladies." *Common Women: Prostitution and Sexuality in Medieval England* (Oxford: Oxford University Press, 1996), 21–22.

58. The Old French "floretes" can mean inferior silk cloth as well as small flowers; A. J. Greimas, *Dictionnaire de l'ancien français*, 289.

59. *Le Ménagier de Paris*, ed. George E. Brereton and Janet M. Ferrier (Oxford: Clarendon Press, 1981), 22.

60. The *Ordene de Chevalerie* applies the trope to the pagan king Saladin when Hue de Tarbie refuses initially to teach this king the secrets of knighthood because:

Grand folie entreprendroie,
Se un fumier de dras de soie
voloie vestir et couvrir,
Qu'il ne peust jamais puir. vv. 87–90

(I would be acting very foolishly, if I tried to dress up a dunghill by covering it with silk cloth so that it would no longer stink.)

Le Roman des eles by Raoul de Hodenc and L'Ordene de chevalerie, ed. Keith Busby (Amsterdam: John Benjamins, 1983).

61. "quae cum immunditiis pulchritudo?" Tertulliano, *L'Eleganza delle donne* (Florence: Nardini Editore, 1986), 102.

62. The Husband's speech, which is related to the diatribes of Andreas's Book 3, derives in large part from the antifeminist and antimarriage discourses of John of Salisbury (*Policraticus*), Walter Map (the *Dissuasio Valerii*), and Juvenal (Satire 6 against marriage). See Lecoy's notes to vv. 8531–8802.

63. Fiero et al., *Three Medieval Views of Women*, 86–104.

64. For other examples, see Alcuin Blamires, *Women Defamed and Defended: An Anthology of Edited Texts* (Oxford: Clarendon Press, 1992), and his *Case for Women in Medieval Culture* (Oxford: Clarendon Press, 1997).

65. I have provided a more literal translation than the rhymed couplets of the text by Fiero et al. offer.

Chapter 2. Amorous Attire: Dressing Up for Love

1. *Songs of the Women Troubadours*, ed. and trans. Matilda Tomaryn Bruckner, Laurie Shepard, and Sarah White (New York: Garland, 1995), no. 29, vv. 1–11. I am grateful to both Sarah White and Matilda Bruckner for bringing this poem to my attention before their edition was published. In subsequent citations of verse, as here, references are to line numbers.

2. Bruckner et al., *Songs*, xlii. These dates have been established by William D. Paden, who remarks the absence of extant examples of poems by women troubadours during what have been termed the first and second generations of troubadour

composition (from 1100 to 1170) and during the last generation (to 1300). *The Voice of the Trobairitz: Perspectives on the Women Troubadours* (Philadelphia: University of Pennsylvania Press, 1989), 14. However, in periods 3 (1180–1220) and 4 (1220–1260), as Paden defines them, there are relatively more trobairitz than troubadours composing songs (25).

3. For a detailed discussion of the ways in which the songs of the Provençal trobairitz play off against standard male troubadour lyric, see Bruckner's comments in her introduction to *Songs*, xi–xxxii, xl; and Simon Gaunt's explanation of how the trobairitz effectively disrupt the homosocial discourse of the troubadour *canso* in his *Troubadours and Irony* (Cambridge: Cambridge University Press, 1989), 158 ff., against Sarah Kay, who argues for a more thorough assimilation of female subjectivity into the male gender system, especially in the dialogue poems. *Subjectivity in Troubadour Poetry* (Cambridge: Cambridge University Press, 1990), 102.

4. This is the "ric ome" debate. See Bruckner, *Songs*, xxi–xxii. The trobairitz speak from a wide range of subject positions, embracing sometimes the stereotypical role of the haughty and proud *domna* often evoked in troubadour lyric while playing out, at others, the role of the troubadour's ideal lady who consents to pledge her heart to him (xix–xxi).

5. Nancy Jones has shown cogently how paying attention to the embroidery subplot in feminocentric romances will help refocus our thinking about material culture, textuality, and the courtly world. See "The Uses of Embroidery in the Romances of Jean Renart: Gender, History, Textuality" in *Jean Renart and the Art of Romance: Essays on Guillaume de Dole*, ed. Nancy Vine Durling (Gainesville: University Press of Florida, 1996), 13–44.

6. The most lavish descriptions of elegant courtly clothes appear in romance texts. Lyric mentions luxurious attire much less often. Recent interest in the thirteenth-century *Roman de la Rose ou de Guillaume de Dole* has produced a number of insightful essays that address the role of clothing and clothwork in this key romance. See Durling, *Jean Renart*. For a nongendered reading of clothing as a trope for writing and the lining of garments specifically as an image of narrative *doublure* in Jean Renart's *Guillaume de Dole*, see Caroline Jewers, "Fabric and Fabrication: Lyric and Narrative in Jean Renart's *Roman de la Rose*," *Speculum* 71, 4 (1996): 907–24.

7. See, for example, Bernart de Ventadorn, "mervilhas ai, car desse / lo cor de dezirer no.m fon" (I am amazed that my heart does not break from desire), *The Songs of Bernart de Ventadorn*, ed. Stephen G. Nichols, Jr. (Chapel Hill: University of North Carolina Press, 1962), no.43, 8–9, or Giraut de Bornelh, "Soven sospir e soplei et azor" (How often I sigh and implore and adore) in *Anthology of the Provençal Troubadours*, 2nd ed., ed. R. T. Hill and Thomas G. Bergin (New Haven, Conn.: Yale University Press, 1973), 1: no. 45, 12. Of course, the irony could be read against the female singer herself, whose overly dramatic performance might appear ridiculous to some readers. But even in this instance, an ironizing stance opens the possibility for challenging and reconsidering the most basic tenets of courtly love, as Simon Gaunt has shown for the lyrics of certain troubadours (*Troubadours and Irony*). The inscribed woman's voice in this *sirventesca* spurs us to rethink courtly love not only in terms of loving and singing but also in relation to materiality and dress in communities of women.

8. See especially Frederick Goldin, *The Mirror of Narcissus and the Courtly Love Lyric* (Ithaca, N.Y.: Cornell University Press, 1967).

9. The image of Narcissus's fountain provides a highly ambiguous and problematic touchstone for renderings of courtly love from the Provençal troubadours and the Old French tale of Narcissus to the thirteenth-century *Roman de la Rose* where its competing functions are perhaps most clearly displayed. Whereas in Guillaume de Lorris's section of the poem the fountain facilitates love, presenting the lover with the irresistible image of the beloved, Jean de Meun defines the fountain as perilous and destructive. See David Hult, *Self-fulfilling Prophecies: Readership and Authority in the First Roman de la Rose* (Cambridge: Cambridge University Press, 1986).

10. On sumptuary laws see Chapter 1, n. 24 above.

11. Bruckner et al. note, following Angelica Rieger, *Trobairitz: Der Beitrag der Frau in der altokzitanischen höfischen Lyrik; Edition des Gesamtkorpus* (Tübingen: Niemeyer, 1991), 698–703, that this poem protests sumptuary legislation that restricted lavish dress, recalling laws associated with the northern French royal household and the mendicant orders that supported and were supported by the French crusading army in Occitania in the first decades of the thirteenth century. The law in question here may have been enacted while King James I of Aragon was away from court, possibly during his military campaign in Mallorca in 1230. See Bruckner et al., *Songs*, 181–82.

12. Chrétien de Troyes, *Cligés*, ed. Alexandre Micha (Paris: Champion, 1957), vv. 567–761, 865–82.

13. Gaston Paris, "Lancelot du Lac, II: Conte de la charrette," *Romania* 12 (1883): 459–534. David Hult has shown that the term *courtly love* actually first appeared without definition or elaboration in 1881, in the first segment of Paris's two-part article. See "Gaston Paris and the Invention of Courtly Love," in *Medievalism and the Modernist Temper*, ed. R. Howard Bloch and Stephen G. Nichols, Jr. (Baltimore: Johns Hopkins University Press, 1996), 192–224.

14. Goldin's formative study, *The Myth of Narcissus and the Courtly Love Lyric*, argued that the courtly lady, who stands "motionless and emotionless" amid the swirl of the troubadour's protracted lament in the Occitan *canso*, functioned primarily as a mirror reflecting an idealized image of the troubadour himself, what the poet/lover "wants to become, what he can never be" (74). Joan Ferrante extended the paradigm to a broader range of courtly genres, showing how the varied ladies of both lyric and romance offered projections of the male suitor's self-image, whether through an idealized or a more self-critical and mocking portrait. *Woman as Image in Medieval Literature: From the Twelfth Century to Dante* (New York: Columbia University Press, 1975); "Male Fantasy and Female Reality in Courtly Literature," *Women's Studies* 11 (1984): 67–97; and "The Conflict of Lyric Conventions and Romance Form," in *In Pursuit of Perfection: Courtly Love and Medieval Literature*, ed. Joan M. Ferrante and George Economou (Port Washington, N.Y.: Kennikat Press, l975), 135–78. My own analysis of the politics of desire in the early troubadour *canso* argued further that every facet of the Lady contributed to a myth of female sexual identity generated from a misreading of the feminine in terms of the masculine, revealing that there was in fact a "man behind the lady." "The Man Behind the Lady in Troubadour Lyric," *Romance Notes* 25, 3 (1985): 254–70.

15. Hult, "Gaston Paris."

16. Zumthor's premise that courtly love lyrics were self-referential poems of desire, not expressions of carnal or erotic pleasure, in which the lady's role was precisely to be absent ("Le Grand Chant courtois," in *Essai de poétique médiévale* [Paris: Seuil: 1972], 189–243), recurs in Laura Kendrick's reading of the elaborate and playful word games of troubadour lyric that make love and the ladylove into thematic foils for serious linguistic sparring between men: "For Guillaume IX and his facetious troubadour followers, the stakes in the game of love were not the sexual favors of living ladies.... The player's goal was not to win the lady, but to win the game, to conquer the masculine opponent(s)." *The Game of Love: Troubadour Wordplay* (Berkeley: University of California Press, 1988), 184. The troubadour *canso* thus becomes, above all, a competitive linguistic performance, as Simon Gaunt's avowedly feminist analysis has also shown. The troubadour, while professing love of the lady, can demonstrate his virtuosic control over language and thereby his superiority over other poets. Gaunt, *Gender and Genre in Medieval French Literature* (Cambridge: Cambridge University Press, 1995), 140–47.

17. For Köhler, troubadour poets aspired, through love of the *domna*, to be elevated to the social position of her husband, which would confer noble status if not actual noble rank upon what Köhler calls "marginal men," poor, landless knights of the lower nobility. "Observations historiques et sociologiques sur la poésie des troubadours," *Cahiers de civilisation médiévale* 7 (1964): 27–51. Thus the ceaseless battle staged between the jealous husband and the aspiring troubadour over possession of the beautiful *domna* has less to do with eroticism, passion, or desire than with class struggle between the disenfranchised squirine and the established nobility. "Les Troubadours et la jalousie," in *Mélanges de langue et de littérature du Moyen Age et de la Renaissance offerts à Jean Frappier*, vol. 1 (Geneva: Droz, 1970). On courtly literature more generally see his *L'Aventure chevaleresque: Idéal et réalité dans le roman courtois*, trans. Elaine Kaufholz (Paris: Gallimard, 1974).

18. Duby characterized the ideology of courtly love as a literary strategy used to mediate and reconcile social tensions arising between men competing for status in the feudal courts of the twelfth century. In northern France, he argues, the *juvenes*, or younger sons of established noble families, who were not allowed to marry or inherit property because of the restrictions of primogeniture, migrated to feudal courts where they vied for favor and advancement into the ranks of the aristocracy. To succeed, they had to learn subservience, restraint, and humility before their male lords. These were precisely the virtues promulgated by service to the lady in courtly literature. *Le Mâle Moyen Age*, 70–79, esp. p. 76, where he explains that courtly love is not a feminine invention but a man's game, a joust of sexual combat, which men will always win. And earlier, John Benton contended that "Courtesy was created by men for their own satisfaction, and it emphasized a woman's role as object, sexual or otherwise. "Clio and Venus: An Historical View of Medieval Love," in *The Meaning of Courtly Love*, ed. F. X. Newman (Albany: SUNY Press, 1968), 35. Duby elaborates further in *Medieval Marriage: Two Models from Twelfth-Century France* (Baltimore: Johns Hopkins University Press, 1978), 13–14. But see Sarah Kay's critique of both Köhler and Duby in "The Contradictions of Courtly Love and the

Origins of Courtly Poetry: The Evidence of the *Lauzengiers*," *Journal for Medieval and Early Modern Studies* 26 (1996): 211, 219–25; Linda Paterson on the social status of the troubadour poets in *The World of the Troubadours* (Cambridge: Cambridge University Press, 1993); and Theodore Evergates on primogeniture, "Nobles and Knights in Twelfth-century France," in *Cultures of Power: Lordship, Status, and Process in Twelfth-Century Europe*, ed. Thomas N. Bisson (Philadelphia: University of Pennsylvania Press, 1995), 11–35.

19. R. Howard Bloch reads courtly love as a means of countering and curtailing's women's increasing ability to own land and inherit property in southern France, a means of marginalizing women from economic relations that had pertained historically to men. Courtly love was "a reaction on the part of a marriage-minded nobility against increasing economic power of women ... the invention of Western romantic love represented, above all, a usurpating reappropriation of woman at the moment she became capable of appropriating what had traditionally constituted masculine modes of wealth." *Medieval Misogyny and the Invention of Western Romantic Love* (Chicago: University of Chicago Press, 1991), 196.

20. Jean-Charles Huchet has explained that the *domna*, who functions as a textualized object of masculine desire and a metaphor for the enigma of femininity, becomes ultimately a cipher for male poetic practice. Functioning as "La Femme" in the Lacanian sense of the irrecuperable lost object, the *domna* stands as the unattainable "other" of male desire, that which the lover can never reach and poetic discourse cannot represent. *L'Amour discourtois: la "fin'amor" chez les premiers troubadours* (Toulouse: Privat, 1987), 13, 35; "La Dame et le troubadour: Fin'amor et mystique chez Bernard de Ventadorn," *Littérature* 47 (October 1982): 13. For similar readings of romance see Huchet, *Le Roman médiéval* (Paris: Presses Universitaires de France, 1984); Charles Méla, *La Reine et le Graal: La "conjointure" dans les romans du Graal, de Chrétien de Troyes au "Livre de Lancelot"* (Paris: Seuil, 1984); and Henri Rey-Flaud, *La Névrose courtoise* (Paris: Navarin, 1983).

21. For an overview of these arguments current to the 1960s, see Douglas Kelly, "Courtly Love in Perspective: The Hierarchy of Love in Andreas Capellanus," *Traditio* 24 (1968): 119–48; Roger Boase, *The Origin and Meaning of Courtly Love: A Critical Study of European Scholarship* (Manchester: Manchester University Press, 1977); and further, Henry Ansgar Kelly, "The Varieties of Love in Medieval Literature according to Gaston Paris," *Romance Philology* 40 (1987): 301–27. Key studies in the French tradition include Jean Frappier, *Amour courtois et table ronde* (Geneva: Droz, 1973); and Moshé Lazar, *Amour courtois et "fin'amors" dans la littérature du xiie siècle* (Paris: Klincksieck, 1964).

22. See Julia Kristeva's *Histoire d'amour*, trans. Leon S. Roudiez as *Tales of Love* (New York: Columbia University Press, 1987), 296.

23. Christiane Marchello-Nizia, "Amour courtois, société masculine, et figures du pouvoir," *Annales E.S.C.* 36 (1981): 969–82.

24. Kathryn Gravdal, *Ravishing Maidens: Writing Rape in Medieval French Literature and Law* (Philadelphia: University of Pennsylvania Press, 1991); and "Chrétien de Troyes, Gratian, and the Medieval Romance of Sexual Violence," *Signs* 17, 3 (1992): 558–85. See also her "Metaphor, Metonymy, and the Medieval Women Trobairitz," *Romanic Review* 83, 4 (1992): 411–26.

25. Roberta Krueger, *Women Readers and the Ideology of Gender in Old French Verse Romance* (Cambridge: Cambridge University Press, 1993), 3. See also her earlier essay "Love, Honor, and the Exchange of Women in *Yvain*: Some Remarks on the Female Reader," *Romance Notes* 25, 3 (1985): 302–17; and in the same vein her argument in *Women Readers* on three romances: *Ipomedon, Le Chevalier à l'épée,* and *La Vengeance Radiguel* (99).

26. Peter Allen, *The Art of Love: Amatory Fiction from Ovid to the Romance of the Rose* (Philadelphia: University of Pennsylvania Press, 1992) 64, and, more generally, 74. Allen reads Andreas as teaching amatory fiction, the art of making love poetry, rather than the art of making love, such that "women in the *De amore* represent both the danger and frustrations of masculine lust" (64). Even in epic texts, tropes of courtly love can be deployed in the service of feudal expansion, as Sharon Kinoshita has shown in "The Politics of Courtly Love: *La Prise d'Orange* and the Conversion of the Saracen Queen," *Romanic Review* 86, 2 (1995): 265–87. In some instances, courtly love legitimates the male protagonist's repudiation of his first wife and remarriage to a second. See Sharon Kinoshita, "Two for the Price of One: Courtly Love and Serial Polygamy in the *Lais* of Marie de France," *Arthuriana* 8, 2 (1998): 33–55. Vernacular fictions in the French Middle Ages stage women in a wide range of affective interactions, many of which fall beyond the limits of strictly courtly amorous encounters. The relationship between mothers and sons is examined by Matilda Bruckner in "Rewriting Chrétien's *Conte du Graal*—Mothers and Sons, Questions, Contradictions, Connections," in *The Medieval Opus: Imagination, Rewriting, and Transmission in the French Tradition*, ed. Douglas Kelly (Amsterdam: Rodopi, 1996), 213–44. Bonds with children and family are assessed by James A. Schultz in *The Knowledge of Childhood in the German Middle Ages, 1100–1350* (Philadelphia: University of Pennsylvania Press, 1995). Adulterous relations with political and dynastic repercussions are analyzed by Peggy McCracken in *The Romance of Adultery: Queenship and Sexual Transgression in Old French Literature* (Philadelphia: University of Pennsylvania Press, 1998).

27. Kay, "Contradictions of Courtly Love." The *lausengier*, in this reading, enables the articulation of contradictory positions on sex and marriage represented by the lay and clerical interests at court. See also her "Courts, Clerks, and Courtly Love," in *The Cambridge Companion to Medieval Romance*, ed. Roberta L. Krueger (Cambridge: Cambridge University Press, 2000), 81–96.

28. Kay, *Subjectivity in Troubadour Poetry*, 97–98. Indeed, Kay's reading of the *domna* as a third or hybrid gender has revealed how this lady parades as a subject only when cross-dressed as a lord, although never actually shedding the fetishized body that maintains her lowered status as an object of male fantasy and desire. Her thesis aptly plays out Lacan's basic premise that courtly love articulates the absence of sexual relations with women. See *Le Séminaire, Livre XX: Encore* (Paris: Seuil, 1975), 65; or Kristeva's contention that courtly lyric has no referent, no object: "The lady is seldom defined and, slipping away between restrained presence and absence, she is simply an imaginary addressee, the pretext for the [male poet's] incantation" (*Tales of Love*, 287).

29. Gaunt, *Gender and Genre*, 102.

30. Hult, "Gaston Paris," 211, 214–15. Hult sees in the academic codification of

courtly love a concerted attempt by French medievalists to make philology, textual criticism, and literary analysis more "scientific" and objective, thus masculinizing the very discipline of medieval studies (204–5).

31. William E. Burgwinkle argues that at least one troubadour poet memorialized an "ambivalent, polymorphous, and bisexual poet for hire." *Love for Sale: Materialist Readings of the Troubadour Razo Corpus* (New York: Garland, 1997), 257; and Gerald Bond characterizes an emergent "loving subject" in Romanesque France as "neither stable, uniform, nor coherent." *The Loving Subject: Desire, Eloquence, and Power in Romanesque France* (Philadelphia: University of Pennsylvania Press, 1995), 41. For other examples see Joan Cadden, *Meanings of Sexual Difference in the Middle Ages: Medicine, Science, and Culture* (Cambridge: Cambridge University Press, 1993); Linda Lomperis and Sarah Stanbury, eds., *Feminist Approaches to the Body in Medieval Literature* (Philadelphia: University of Pennsylvania Press, 1993); Sarah Kay and Miri Rubin, eds., *Framing Medieval Bodies* (Manchester: Manchester University Press, 1994); Clare Lees, ed. *Medieval Masculinities: Regarding Men in the Middle Ages* (Minneapolis: University of Minnesota Press, 1994); Vern L. Bullough and James A. Brundage, eds., *Handbook of Medieval Sexuality* (New York: Garland, 1996); Karma Lochrie, Peggy McCracken, and James A. Schultz, eds., *Constructing Medieval Sexuality* (Minneapolis: University of Minnesota Press, 1997); Karen J. Taylor, ed., *Gender Transgressions: Crossing the Normative Barrier in Old French Literature* (New York; Garland, 1998); Glenn Burger and Steven F. Krueger, eds., *Queering the Middle Ages* (Minneapolis: University of Minnesota Press, 2001).

32. Krueger, *Women Readers and the Ideology of Gender*, 64, 66. The original argument appeared in "Desire, Meaning, and the Female Reader in *Le Chevalier de la Charrete*," in *The Passing of Arthur: New Essays in Arthurian Tradition*, ed. Christopher Baswell and William Sharpe (New York: Garland, l988): 31–51.

33. E. Jane Burns, *Bodytalk: When Women Speak in Old French Literature* (Philadelphia: University of Pennsylvania Press, 1993), 109–13.

34. Helen Solterer, *The Master and Minerva: Disputing Women in French Medieval Culture* (Berkeley: University of California Press, 1995).

35. Matilda Bruckner, "Fictions of the Female Voice: The Women Troubadours," *Speculum* 67, 4 (1992): 865–91; "Debatable Fictions: The *Tensos* of the Trobairitz," in *Literary Aspects of Courtly Culture: Selected Papers from the Seventh Triennial Congress of the International Courtly Literature Society*, ed. Donald Maddox and Sara Sturm-Maddox (Cambridge: D.S. Brewer, 1994), 19–28.

36. Laurie A. Finke, *Feminist Theory: Women's Writing* (Ithaca, N.Y.: Cornell University Press, 1992).

37. Marilyn Desmond and Pamela Sheingorn, "Queering Ovidian Myth: Bestiality and Desire in Christine de Pizan's *Epistre Othea*," in Burger and Krueger, *Queering the Middle Ages*, 3–27.

38. Roberta Krueger, "Transforming Maidens: Single Women's Stories in Marie de France's *Lais* and Later French Courtly Narratives," in *Singlewomen in the European Past, 1250–1800*, ed. Judith M. Bennett and Amy M. Froide (Philadelphia: University of Pennsylvania Press, 1999).

39. Jacqueline Murray, "Twice Marginal and Twice Invisible: Lesbians in the Middle Ages," in Bullough and Brundage, *Handbook*, 191–222.

40. Karma Lochrie, "Mystical Acts, Queer Tendencies," in Lochrie et al., *Constructing Medieval Sexuality*, 185–86.

41. Barbara Newman, *From Virile Woman to WomanChrist: Studies in Medieval Religion and Literature* (Philadelphia: University of Pennsylvania Press, 1995), 137–67.

42. This crucial point has been misunderstood by some commentators of *Bodytalk* who fail to grasp how female characters might speak dialogically in "monologically constructed texts." My point in *Bodytalk* and here is that the construction of female characters by a male author or actor does not preclude the possibility of a disruptive tension between what those characters are designed to portray and how they might serve *at the same time* to undermine or subvert the author's portrayal of them.

43. *Arnaut Daniel, Canzoni*, ed. Gianluigi Toja (Florence: G.C. Sansoni, 1960) no. 12, 31–32. See also Ventadorn, *Songs*, ed. Nichols, no. 27, 41–45; no. 44, 59–60; and a host of other examples provided in Moshé Lazar, *Amour courtois et "fin'amors,"* 122–34.

44. For a more detailed discussion of this process, see *Bodytalk*, 109–13. I argue that female protagonists, however fetishized by excessive courtly garb, can be seen effectively to resist such objectification through their speech. Especially cogent examples of the phenomenon in the twelfth century are provided by Enide, Iseut, and Philomena.

45. Although Queen Guenevere actually takes charge of dressing Enide, she does so according to Erec's careful directives, following his earlier insistence that Enide not be given fine clothing by her cousin before her arrival at court. For further discussion of Enide's status as the adored courtly beauty, see *Bodytalk*, 167–69, and esp. notes 19–25. There is also, however, a way in which the act of Guenevere dressing Enide constitutes a significant act of women dressing for and with each other.

46. The line detailing how Enide's beauty functions specifically as a mirror contains an ambiguity of reference that, if translated literally, could allow for the possibility that a woman too might see herself reflected in this courtly beauty. "Qui fu fete por esgarder, / qu'an se poïst an li mirer" (440–41) reads literally "she was made to be gazed upon, for *one* could see *oneself* reflected in her as in a mirror." And in fact the actual scene of dressing Enide, although carefully orchestrated by Erec in accordance with the courtly custom of fetishizing ladies, is executed, as we have seen, by a woman, Queen Guenevere.

47. The meaning of these lines is debatable. They may mean that this female speaker has chosen to cover her unadorned garments under the one luxury item not so thoroughly restricted: a fur cloak; or, alternatively, that she wishes to substitute for her previous decorative dress the coarse cloak of pilgrims. See Bruckner et al., *Songs*, 181; Rieger, *Trobairitz*, 697.

48. *Le Roman de la Rose ou de Guillaume de Dole*, ed. Félix Lecoy (Paris: Champion, 1962). Within the walls of the courtly garden in Guillaume de Lorris's *Roman de la Rose*, for example, Oisuese wears "un chapel de roses tout frois" (553), as do Deduit (829–30) and the God of Love (895–96). Leesce, who resembles a new rose (840), wears a "chapel d'orfrois" (857). Guillaume de Lorris and Jean de Meun, *Le Roman de la Rose*, ed. Félix Lecoy (Paris: Champion, 1965).

49. Although this analysis will focus on women's attire, much remains to be said about male clothing in the courtly world. For some preliminary thoughts, see E. Jane Burns, "Refashioning Courtly Love: Lancelot as Lady's Man or Ladyman?" in Lochrie et al., *Constructing Medieval Sexuality*, 111–134.

50. Elizabeth Grosz, *Volatile Bodies: Toward a Corporeal Feminism* (Bloomington: Indiana University Press, 1994), 18. Grosz offers a theoretical means for reconceptualizing the individual body within the social sphere that differs markedly from the term *social body* used to connote participation in a whole social fabric, such as English society of the nineteenth century. See Mary Poovey, *Making a Social Body: British Cultural Formation, 1830–1864* (Chicago: University of Chicago Press, 1995), 7–8; or medieval notions of the *body politic*, as in Ernst Kantorowicz, *The King's Two Bodies: A Study of Medieval Political Theology* (Princeton N.J.: Princeton University Press, 1957).

51. Nor does she perceive in herself the social virtues of courtliness that the male poet of the *canso* so often attributes to his ladylove, thus dressing her metaphorically in the cultural fabric of courtliness. Indeed, the Contessa de Dia provides another alternative to being dressed in courtly virtues in "A chantar," where she describes her beauty, lineage, rank, and her true heart as both including and exceeding her bodily self. (I owe this insight to Matilda Bruckner.)

52. See esp. Tilde Sankovitch, "Lombarda's Reluctant Mirror: Speculum of Another Poet," in Paden, *Voice of the Trobairitz*, 183–93.

53. They comment as well on how they have been led by convention and available rhetorical tropes to construct themselves especially in terms of the troubadour's rejection. See Bruckner's introduction to *Songs of the Women Troubadours*.

54. Ruth Verity Sharman, *The Cansos and Sirventes of the Troubadour Giraut de Borneil: A Critical Edition* (Cambridge: Cambridge University Press, 1989), "Iois et chanz," no. 46, 104–14; translation from Simon Gaunt, *The Troubadours and Irony*, 151. See Gaunt's discussion of this poem and the work of Giraut de Borneil generally.

55. The text thus offers an interesting twist on the standard depiction of women primping for admiring lovers provided by texts such as the Ovidian-derived *Art d'amours*, which states, "Souveraine chose qui peut aidier la femme, avec sa joliveté, . . . [elle] doit estre garnie d'un bon miroir ou elle se mire souvent," Bruno Roy, ed., *L'Art d'amours: Traduction et commentaire de "l'Ars amatoria" d'Ovide* (Leiden: E.J. Brill, 1974), 239.

56. Oiseuse has been read alternately as a figure for Luxuria, Ovidian idleness, narcissistic lethargy or as an icon for leisurely practice of courtly love and its requisite beauty. For summary accounts of these critical positions, see Carlos Alvar, "Oiseuse, Venus, Luxure: Trois dames et un miroir" *Romania* 106 (1985): 108–17; and Gregory M. Sadlek, "Interpreting Guillaume de Lorris's Oiseuse: Geoffrey Chaucer as Witness," *South Central Review* 10 (1993): 21–37. Thomas Aquinas first defines *luxuria* as "excess in venereal pleasures" and divides it subsequently into six kinds of vice, all of which, with the exception of copulation between men and women, are considered "against nature." Mark Jordan, "Homosexuality, Luxuria, and Textual Abuse," in Lochrie et al., *Constructing Medieval Sexuality*, 24–39.

57. The association of idleness with women gazing at themselves in the mirror is found, for example, in the Middle French proverb "Dame qui moult se mire, peu

file," in *Three Medieval Views of Women*, trans. and ed. Gloria K. Fiero, Wendy Pfeffer, and Mathé Allain (New Haven, Conn.: Yale University Press, 1989), 104; from Maurice Maloux, *Dictionnaire des proverbes, sentences, et maximes* (Paris: Larousse, 1980), 201. The distinction implied here between a subject who actively works cloth and an object of desire who wears it does not hold in the case of Oiseuse. Although Oiseuse does not spin her own cloth, she does fashion a self from items of clothing, thus serving to distinguish, in one way at least, the immobile, statuesque beauty of Pygmalion's creation from the courtly lady who looks more actively into a mirror that reflects her work.

58. Krueger, "Transforming Maidens."

59. Dahlberg translates alternatively, "But, of course, if she is to be admired above others, she has to be well-dressed." Guillaume de Lorris and Jean de Meun, *The Romance of the Rose*, trans. Charles Dahlberg (Princeton: Princeton University Press, 1983), 233. But Strubel gives "Mais il faut d'abord qu'elle se soit bien regardée dans son miroir pour savoir si elle est bien arrangée," 719.

60. "She should go visiting, to weddings, processions, games, feasts, and dances, for in such places the god and goddess of love hold school and sing mass to their disciples."

61. Even if the self-image generated by the inscribed female voice in lyric and romance does not differ significantly from the standard topoi of female beauty typically invoked by troubadour poets and romance authors, the rhetorical and semantic effect of those topoi change substantially when female protagonists utter them. This is the phenomenon I have termed *bodytalk* in romance texts (*Bodytalk*, xiii–xvi, 1–7). Bruckner has explained the power of an analogous process in the lyrics of the trobairitz in "Fictions of the Female Voice." To be sure, my reading differs starkly from Christine de Pisan's critique of La Vieille as giving pernicious advice to young women much as she condemns the Jealous Husband and Genius for defaming women. See Kevin Brownlee, "Discourses of the Self: Christine de Pizan and the *Romance of the Rose*, in *Rethinking the* Romance of the Rose*: Text, Image, Reception*, ed. Kevin Brownlee and Sylvia Huot (Philadelphia: University of Pennsylvania Press, 1992), 253; and from the traditional reading of La Vieille as an embodiment of Jean de Meun's misogyny. Edmond Faral, "*Le Roman de la Rose* et la pensée française du XIIIe siècle," *Revue des deux mondes* 35 (1926), esp. 439. But Sarah Kay, "Women's Body of Knowledge: Epistemology and Misogyny in the *Romance of the Rose*," in Kay and Rubin, *Framing Medieval Bodies*, reveals another possible reading of La Vieille, who, while mouthing Ovid's *Ars amatoria* 3 (addressed to women), also reverses misogynist topoi and turns antifeminist diatribe back against its authors. Unlike any other speaker in the *Rose*, La Vieille identifies herself as a woman and vaunts her authority in a speech worthy of a university *mestre*, advocating, all the while, women's right to sexual pleasure (218).

62. Kay, "Women's Body," 217.

63. "Quar, quant plus a l'ostel repose, / mains est de toutes genz veüe / et sa biauté maine conneüe, / mains couvoitiee et mains requise" (vv. 13488–91).

64. Iris Marion Young, "Women Recovering Our Clothes," in *Throwing like a Girl and Other Essays in Philosophy and Social Theory* (Bloomington: Indiana University Press, 1990), 183.

65. A thorough treatment of the topos is provided by Bloch in *Medieval Misogyny*, 37–63.

66. As Bruno Roy explains in his introduction (13), this section of the Latin text is most commonly omitted by medieval translators.

67. *Andreas Capellanus on Love*, ed. and trans. P. G. Walsh (London: Duckworth, 1982), 38–39.

68. My emphasis, following Luce Irigaray in *Ethique de la différence sexuelle* (Paris: Minuit, 1984).

69. For a discussion of how the concept of the exchange of women in romance is complicated in the gift economies figured in many *chansons de geste*, see Sarah Kay, *The Chansons de geste in the Age of Romance: Political Fictions* (Oxford: Clarendon Press, 1995), esp. 25–48, 200–231.

70. Simone de Beauvoir explained this cogently in 1949, as Toril Moi notes: "Perceived as part of patriarchal ideology 'femininity' becomes an external set of rules for how to dress, behave etc.: 'Precisely because the concept of femininity is artificially shaped by custom and fashion,' Beauvoir writes, 'it is imposed on each woman from without.... The individual is still not free to do as she pleases in shaping the concept of femininity.'" See *Simone de Beauvoir: The Making of an Intellectual Woman* (Cambridge: Blackwell, 1994), 191–92. And further: "What Beauvoir is against then is any particular activity as the desire to *produce essences*, to attribute intrinsic meanings and values to activities or persons; for her, the most execrable aspect of patriarchal ideology remains its persistent harping on the theme of 'eternal femininity'" (194).

71. Butler, *Gender Trouble: Feminism and the Subversion of Identity* (New York: Routledge, 1990), 31.

72. Chrétien de Troyes, *Yvain*, ed. Mario Roques (Paris: Champion, 1971), vv. 5219–5331.

73. Gautier d'Arras, *Ille et Galeron*, ed. Yves Lefèvre (Paris: Champion, 1988).

74. Marina Warner, trans., *The Trial of Joan of Arc* (Evesham: Arthur James, 1996), 46.

75. *Le Bien des fames*, in Fiero et al., *Three Medieval Views of Women*.

76. Heldris de Cornouaïlle, *Le Roman de Silence*, ed. Lewis Thorpe (Cambridge: Heffer, 1972).

77. See Jones, "Embroidery," 25–27.

78. See Burns, *Bodytalk*, 115–50.

Chapter 3. Love's Stitches Undone: Women's Work in the chanson de toile

1. *Ille et Galeron*, ed. Yves Lefevre (Paris: Champion, 1988). At times, in courtly love treatises the ladylove herself is charged with holding the suitor captive in her nets, as the thirteenth-century *Art d'amours* attests: "Puis que la femme a son amy prins aux laz, pour plus longuement amour continuer, elle doit garder que son amy ne ayme un autre" (Bruno Roy, ed., *L'Art d'amours: Traduction et commentaire de "l'Ars amatoria" d'Ovide* [Leiden: E.J. Brill, 1974], 267).

2. In Pierre Bec's classification, women's songs include compositions of the Provençal *trobairitz* (women troubadours)—both the *canso* in which they alone

speak and the *tenso* or debate poems in which women's voices alternate with men's—and Old French songs that feature female speakers: *chanson d'ami* and *chanson de mal mariée*. The definition of women's songs is also sometimes extended to include lyric pieces in which the female protagonist, different from the silent lady of the Occitan *canso*, actually speaks: the Occitan *pastorela* and *alba*, for example, and their northern counterparts, the Old French *pastourelle* and *aube*. See Bec, *La Lyrique française au Moyen Age (XIIe–XIIIe siècles)* (Poitiers: Picard, 1977), 1: 57–136; and his "Trobairitz et *chansons de femme*: Contribution à la connaissance du lyrisme féminin au Moyen Age," *Cahiers de civilisation médiévale* 22, 3 (1979): 235–62.

3. Unless otherwise noted, texts of the *chansons de toile* are from Michel Zink, ed., *Les Chansons de toile* (Paris: Champion, 1977). Translations are mine. The corpus of songs is generally dated between 1228 and 1250 (Zink, 23).

4. Paul Zumthor, *Essai de poétique médiévale* (Paris: Seuil, 1972), 212–17, esp. 215: "On pourrait se demander si en effet le sémantisme *aimer* (référé au sujet de la chanson) n'est pas simplement inclus dans celui de *chanter*."

5. The *chansons de toile* that allude to women sewing, spinning, or embroidering include *Bele Yolanz en ses chambres seoit, Bele Yolanz en chambre koie, Quant Vient en mai* (Erembors), *Bele Amelot soule an chambre feloit, An chambre a or se siet la bele Beatris, Fille et la mere se sieent a l'orfrois, Siet soi bele Aye as piez sa male maistre,* and *Bele Aiglentine en roial chamberine*. In addition, the narrative context for *Siet soi biele Euriaus, seule est enclose* describes her working cloth, although the song itself does not indicate it. Songs that stage an unhappy marriage (*chansons de mal mariée*), whether present or future, narrated from the woman's point of view, include *Oriolanz en haut solier, En un vergier, Bele Yolanz en chambre koie, Bele Ydoine se siet desous la verde olive, Bele Amelot soule an chambre feloit, An chambre a or se siet la Bele Beatris, Au Novel Tans pascour que florist l'aube espine, Bele Argentine,* and *Bele Emmelos es prés desouz l'arbroie*.

Only three songs in the twenty-two-song corpus generally designated as *chansons de toile* do not exhibit the otherwise prevalent feature of women's work: *Bele Ysabiauz,* a lament staged wholly from the male lover's point of view, although it contains a scenario of the *mal mariée*; *Or vienent Pasques les beles en avril,* actually a *reverdie* classed as a *chanson de toile* because its refrain cites Aigline and Guis as mutually satisfied lovers; and *Lou Samedi a soir fat la semaine* (*Gaiete et Oriour*), marked similarly by a refrain that records sweet sleep between lovers.

6. Edmond Faral, "Les Chansons de toile ou chansons d'histoire," *Romania* 69 (1946–47): 461–62; and Pierre Jonin, "Les Types féminins dans les chansons de toile," *Romania* 91 (1970): 464.

7. "De leur heroine, les chansons anonymes disent qu'elle est belle, qu'elle est assise dans sa chambre, qu'elle est malheureuse, qu'elle est amoureuse" (Zink, 26).

8. *La Lyrique française,* 109; and Zink, 25: "L'amant ou la nouvelle viennent à la rencontre de la jeune fille assise, qui alors, si l'on ose dire, ne se lève que pour se coucher (Belle Erembourg, Belle Yolande) ou dont l'activité se borne à descendre quelques marches (Belle Doette), à aller, par un effort extrême, jusqu'à la maison de son ami (Belle Aiglentine)." Bec describes the *chansons de toile* as a genre "centré autour d'une jeune femme qui exhale sa douleur" (109).

9. Jonin, "Types féminins," "C'est donc l'amour et l'amour seul qui donne son sens à l'existence de la jeune femme" (447).

10. In the Occitan tradition, the issue is addressed directly by woman singers such as Na Castelloza: "Eu sai ben c'a mi esta gen, / si be.is dizon tuich que mout descove / que dompna prei a cavallier de se / ni que.l teigna totz temps *tan lonc pressic*, mas cel q'o ditz non sap ges ben gauzir. (I know this is a fitting thing for me, though everybody says it isn't proper for a lady to plead her case with a knight, or to make such long speeches to him; he who says this has no knowledge of true joy). In *Songs of the Women Troubadours*, ed. Matilda Tomaryn Bruckner, Laurie Shepard, and Sarah White (New York: Garland, 1995), 18–19. Bruckner considers this attention to the difficulties that result from breaking with conventional notions of conduct proper for a noblewoman to be a unique feature of Castelloza's voice in "Na Castelloza, *Trobairitz*, and Troubadour Lyric," *Romance Notes* 25, 3 (1985): 239–53. In the introduction to *Songs* (xi–xxxii, xl), Bruckner explains further how these woman's songs play off against standard male troubadour lyric, speaking both within and against established literary conventions. See also Bruckner's "Debatable Fictions: The *Tensos* of the Trobairitz," in *Literary Aspects of Courtly Culture*, ed. Donald Maddox and Sara Sturm-Maddox (Cambridge: D.S. Brewer, 1994), 19–28; along with Simon Gaunt's discussion of how the *trobairitz* effectively disrupt the homosocial discourse of the troubadour *canso* in *Troubadours and Irony* (Cambridge: Cambridge University Press, 1989), 102. At issue in particular are the dialogue or debate poems (*tensos*) staged between male and female voices. See Marianne Shapiro, "Tenson et partimen: 'La Tenson fictive,'" in *XIV Congresso internazionale di linguisticá e filologia romanza: Atti V*, ed. Alberto Várvaro, 5 vols. (Naples: Macchiaroli, 1981), 287–301, and "The Provençal Trobairitz and the Limits of Courtly Love," *Signs* 3, 2 (1978): 560–71; Angelica Rieger, "*En conselh no deu hom voler femna*: Les Dialogues mixtes dans la lyrique troubadouresque," *Perspectives médiévales* 16 (1990): 47–57; against Sarah Kay, who argues for a more thorough assimilation of female subjectivity into the male gender system in *Subjectivity in Troubadour Poetry* (Cambridge: Cambridge University Press, 1990), 96–111, esp. 102; and further, Jean-Charles Huchet, for whom the putative voices of the trobairitz remain a literary fiction deriving wholly from male psychic fantasy, in "Les Femmes troubadours et la voix critique," *Littérature* 51 (1983): 59–90. Debates concerning what constitutes a "woman's song" in the corpus of the *trobairitz* can be found in Frank M. Chambers, "*Las Trobairitz soisebudas*," in *The Voice of the Trobairitz: Perspectives on the Women Troubadours*, ed. William D. Paden (Philadelphia: University of Pennsylvania Press, 1989), 45–60; and in François Zufferey, "Toward a Delimitation of the Trobairitz Corpus," also in *The Voice of the Trobairitz*, 31–43.

11. See Zink, 183–84.

12. For the terms of the debate, see Bec's definition of woman's song as a lyric "placed in the mouth of a woman," who represents a hypothetical female composer (*La Lyrique française*, 57–62) against Edmond Faral ("Les Chansons de toile"), who had argued that the sometimes lascivious woman's songs could only have been composed and sung by men. More recently Zink has read the *chanson de toile* as a complex rhetorical cover deployed by accomplished male poets (*Les Chansons de toile*, 2, 9, 33–35). For a feminist reconsideration and analysis of these approaches, see

E. Jane Burns, Sarah Kay, Roberta Krueger, and Helen Solterer, "Feminism and the Discipline of Old French Studies: *Une Bele Disjointure*," in *Medievalism and the Modernist Temper*, ed. R. Howard Bloch and Stephen G. Nichols, Jr. (Baltimore: Johns Hopkins University Press, 1996), 238–43. For the terms of a similar debate regarding the trobairitz see Bec's distinction between "féminité génétique" and "féminité textuelle" ("Trobairitz," 235–36) and Bruckner's reassessment of these problematic distinctions, especially where she explains how the trobairitz can take up the positions of *femna, domna*, and poet simultaneously.

13. For possible meanings of a third term, *chanson a istoire*, used for women's songs in *Guillaume de Dole*, see Faral, "Les Chansons de toile," 438.

14. Faral, 455.

15. "Chansons *d'amour*, elles célèbrent, dans le mètre à chanter *armes*, les amours des autres, des amours à la troisième personne, des amours féminines, alors que le poète est un homme et, une fois, l'avoue" (Zink, 38).

16. Iris Marion Young, *Throwing like a Girl and Other Essays in Feminist Philosophy and Social Theory* (Bloomington: Indiana University Press, 1990), 150.

17. Young, *Throwing*, 150.

18. *Le Roman de la violette ou de Gerard de Nevers par Gerbert de Montreuil*, ed. Douglas Labaree Buffum (Paris: Champion, 1928).

19. *Le Lai d'Aristote d'Henri d'Andeli publié d'après tous les manuscrits*, ed. Maurice Delbouille (Paris: Belles Lettres, 1951), v. 381.

20. Maureen Boulton has shown how an ironic effect results from the insertion of both these women's songs into a romance context. In the *Lai d'Aristote* the young woman singing the *chanson de toile* appears to pine for the aging Aristotle, whom she later saddles and rides, when in fact her lament refers to her own young lover. Maureen Barry McCann Boulton, *The Song in the Story: Lyric Insertions in French Narrative Fiction, 1200–1400* (Philadelphia: University of Pennsylvania Press, 1993), 125; and Euriaus in the *Roman de la violette* appropriates a *chanson de mal mariée* to express her rejection of a villain's lecherous advances. Whereas the song rejects marriage in favor of infidelity, Euriaus uses it to declare fidelity (Boulton, *Song in the Story*, 279). Bec classifies women's songs that begin with "Bele" and the heroine's name as *chansons de toile*, even when they include the lament of a married woman. Other songs critiquing unjust husbands and loveless marriages but lacking an opening signature of something like "Bele Yolanz" are classed as *chansons de mal mariée* (*La Lyrique française*, 62, 69–90).

21. "Biaus filz, ce fu ça en arriers / que les dames et les roïnes / soloient fere lor cortines / et chanter les chançons d'istoire!" Félix Lecoy, *Le Roman de la Rose ou de Guillaume de Dole* (Paris: Champion, 1962), vv. 1148–51; "'My dear son,' she said, 'ladies and queens of days gone by were always singing spinning songs as they embroidered.'" *The Romance of the Rose, or Guillaume de Dole*, trans. Patricia Terry and Nancy Vine Durling (Philadelphia: University of Pennsylvania Press, 1993), 33.

22. For Bec's typology see *La Lyrique française*, 109–11, and for Jonin's, "Les Types féminins." Several of the songs regularly classed as *chansons de toile* do not display any of these features: *Gaiete et Oriour, Bele Ysabiauz*, and *Bele Doette* and its shorter version, *Bele Doe*. *Or vienent pasques* is a *reverdie* that resembles the *chanson de toile* only in its refrain. Although the *chansons de toile* are preserved in several

types of manuscripts, their archival distribution does not correlate with thematic differences. For a detailed account of the manuscript tradition see Zink, 20–24.

23. Bec, *La Lyrique française*, 107.

24. Zink, 3–8, 38–50. The complexity of possible relationships between lyric insertions and narrative development in *Le Roman de la Rose ou de Guillaume de Dole* in particular is treated in articles by Jones, Boulton, Zink, and Psaki in *Jean Renart and the Art of Romance*, ed. Nancy Vine Durling (Gainesville: University Press of Florida, 1997).

25. In reference to Guillaume de Dole, Sylvia Huot notes, for example, that "*Chanson de toile* offers a possible model for resolution of the narrative dilemma." *From Song to Book: The Poetics of Writing in Old French Lyric and Lyrical Narrative Poetry* (Ithaca, N.Y.: Cornell University Press, 1987), 113.

26. Zink, 40–41.

27. Although the *chansons de toile* must be understood to a significant degree in relation to lyrics of the troubadours and trouvères, the male protagonists, who appear only minimally here, bear little resemblance to the courtly *fin amant*. They are more often professional warriors, mercenary soldiers, or strangers from afar (Zink, 64). If the female protagonists, whose presence dominates these songs, resemble the *trobairitz* in their status as highborn aristocrats (Jonin, "Les Types féminins," 434), their function as historical composer-singers is often called into doubt, as we have seen. Euriaus provides a striking exception to this general rule, since she is a *bourgeoise* (Zink, 14).

28. Zink, 23. It is not necessary to conclude, however, along with Faral and Zink, that the intrusion of a male narrator's comments in the closing stanza of *Oriolanz*, for example, constitutes proof that the "poet is not a woman." Faral's fundamental reason for assuming that women could not possibly have sung these songs is moralistic: "Imagine-t-on que pareil thème ait servi aux chansons chantées par des 'dames' ou par des 'reines' devant les femmes de leur service? Imagine-t-on pareille chanson chantée par une mère devant sa fille? Quel exemple! Quelle leçon!" "Les Chansons de toile," 456, 459; Zink, 45.

29. As in the case of *Bele Aliz*, it is often the male suitor of the beloved just described who speaks the refrain: "Main se levoit Aaliz / Bien se para et vesti / soz la roche Guion. / —Cui lairai ge mes amors, / amie, s'a vos non?" vv. 532–37; see Zink, 8.

30. Boulton, *Song in the Story*, 37.

31. Hélène Cixous, *Coming to Writing and Other Essays*, trans. Deborah Jenson (Cambridge, Mass.: Harvard University Press, 1991), 78–103.

32. Cixous, *Coming to Writing*, 96–97.

33. Burns et al., "Feminism and Old French Studies," 239.

34. "Escoutés moi, franc baron / cil d'aval et cil d'amont; / plairoit vos oïr un son / d'Aucassin, un franc baron, / et de Nicholete la prous? / Tant durerent lor amors / qu'il le quist u gaut parfont." *Aucassin et Nicolette*, ed. Mario Roques (Paris: Champion, 1977), vv. 14–20, pp. 36–37.

35. The *trobairitz* often express discontent with the established conventions of courtly love and provide pointed critiques of the system, but they do not typically offer material solutions comparable to those figured in the *chanson de toile*.

36. Whereas Zink observes aptly that these examples of woman's song might be called *chansons de geste* because love is expressed here less in words (the modus operandi of troubadour and trouvère lyric) than in deeds or gestures (51–60), he grants little significance to this key difference and tends to depict the female protagonists of the *chansons de toile* reductively, as passive complainers: "C'est que ces femmes, confinées dans leur jardin, sont condamnées par leur sexe et par leur rang à la passivité et ne peuvent que se plaindre en attendant un séducteur qui tarde à les rejoindre" (64). Jonin details more accurately how these heroines are assertive in love, displaying a distinctive "hardiesse" ("Les Types féminins," 444). More recently, Nancy Jones has read allusions to Lienor's embroidery in *Le Roman de la Rose ou de Guillaume de Dole* as traditional markers of female passivity ("The Uses of Embroidery in the Romances of Jean Renart," in Terry and Durling, *Jean Renart*, 26–27), whereas Matilda Bruckner shows how a number of the lyric insertions in this text prepare for Lienor's own "vigorous movement into the narrative" at subsequent moments. "Romancing History and Rewriting the Game of Fiction," in *The World and Its Rival: Essays on Literary Imagination in Honor of Per Nykrog*, ed. Kathryn Karczewska and Tom Conley (Amsterdam: Rodopi, 1999), 105.

37. The additional issue of pregnancy, which complicates this song, will be discussed below.

38. My reading of this song differs substantially from Sarah Kay's view that *Bele Aiglentine* emblematizes, along with the other *chansons de toile* inserted into *Guillaume de Dole*, a misogynous "male-authored female voice" (*Subjectivity in Troubadour Poetry*, 197–98). Reading *Bele Aiglentine* within the wider corpus of *chansons de toile* suggests, I think, other possibilities for female subjectivity.

39. See E. Jane Burns, *Bodytalk: When Women Speak in Old French Literature* (Philadelphia: University of Pennsylvania Press, 1993), 109–13.

40. Lecoy, vv. 200–209; Terry and Durling, *Jean Renart*, 21. The song about lovely Marguerite inserted within the *Guillaume de Dole* reiterates and underwrites the paradigm of the beautiful, well-dressed lady (Lecoy, vv. 3422–30; Terry and Durling, 65), which recurs in another lyric insertion in the same romance, *Or vienent pasques les beles en avril* (vv. 15–17, and earlier vv. 9–14; p. 165). See also the independent *chanson de toile Bele Ysabiauz* (Zink, vv. 52–53, 55–57; p. 109), in stark contrast to other songs in the *chanson de toile* corpus. This song combines two lines of mutual embrace, "they embraced so tenderly that they fell together on the grass" (Si s'entrebaisent par douçour / qu'andui cheïrent en l'erbour, vv. 64–65; p. 109), with more stereotypical indications of Ysabiauz being taken into marriage, possessed by her lover, "With the Church sacrament, Gerard made his lady his wife" (vv. 75–76; p. 110; Gerars par sainte Eglise / a fait de sa dame s'oissour). And in the end, joy, love, and the lady belong to Gerard alone as the long-repeated refrain "Gerard awaits his joy/love/beloved" (Et joie atent Gerars) modulates into "Gerard has his joy/love/beloved" (Or a joie Gerars). Although we have witnessed a similar tension between amorous hierarchy and mutual exchange in songs such as *Bele Aiglentine* and *Bele Beatris*, the women's work figured in those songs, which mitigates the final icon of male dominance, is crucially absent from *Bele Ysabiauz*.

41. We even find standard lines of trouvère lyric echoed in the *chanson de toile* as in "Bele Aiglentine," when the phrase "Take off your clothes, I want to see your

comely body" (vv. 12–13; p. 161) is articulated by the heroine's mother, not her lover, and the comely body in question is in fact a pregnant body. Similarly, when the daughter admits "je ai amé" (v. 20; p. 162) her words refer to the act of having slept with her lover and thus become pregnant, in stark contrast to the trouvère, for whom the repeated lament "j'ai aimé" typically connotes unfulfilled desire.

42. For an example of this convention, see the song sung by Conrad each morning (Lecoy, vv. 3403–6; Terry and Durling, *Jean Renart*, 65).

43. A few brief references elsewhere in the corpus record the lady lover's emotional distress—rather than signaling her hope for union—specifically through articles of clothing. When Belle Doette receives news of her lover's death, she vows to keep sumptuous garments from touching her skin and wear only a bristling hair shirt (vv. 28–29; p. 90). The distress of Belle Ysabel, trapped in a loveless marriage, is emblematized by tears that moisten the edge of her cloak (vv. 2–3; p. 98). Ydoine, by contrast, performs the traditional courtly gesture of giving her lover a sleeve to display as he jousts in a tournament (vv. 149–50; p. 119).

44. See *Au Novel Tans Pascour que florist l'aube espine* (v. 3; p. 143); and the mother's comment in *Guillaume de Dole* (Lecoy, vv. 1148–50; p. 36).

45. The song is distinctive in its inclusion of a brief scene where the lady and the audience along with her observe the comely and attractive male beloved who functions as the coveted object of desire: "Count Renaud climbed the steps / with wide shoulders and narrow hips. / His hair was blond and curly. / There was no man more handsome in the land" (vv. 25–28; p. 93; Li cuens R[aynaut] en monta lo degré, / gros par espaules, greles par lo baudre, / blond ot lo poil, menu recercelé: / en nule terre n'ot si biau bacheler).

46. Burns, *Bodytalk*, 116–47.

47. An even more extreme reversal of gendered roles occurs in *Bele Ysabiauz, pucele bien aprise*, where a tale of a *mal mariée* is recounted throughout from the male lover Gerard's point of view. Zink, 107–10.

48. Line 52, in which Oriolanz says, "now you have attained/ taken possession of me" (estes vos or de moi saisiz, p. 82) reverts to a more traditional model of amorous interaction, creating the kind of tension we have seen in *Bele Aiglentine* and *Bele Beatris* between the ravished ladylove and the working beauty.

49. *Bele Doette* resembles in this regard the short lyric insertions *Bele Aye* and *Bele Doe* (both in *Guillaume de Dole*) and *Bele Euriaus* (in the *Roman de la violette*) and one exception from the longer, narrativized songs, *Lou Samedi a soir*, which stage a love lament without resolution.

50. For a different view, see Stephen G. Nichols, "Medieval Women Writers: Aiesthesis and the Powers of Marginality," *Yale French Studies* 75 (Fall 1988): 77–94.

51. The Old French *tainte* indicates a change in color, either becoming more intense or more pale. In this instance, an increase in skin coloration is indicated by the initial term *perse*, suggesting that the woman has been beaten black and blue. *Tainte* is paired elsewhere with *vermeil*. The belt used to beat women red and blue should be read in contrast to the embroidered *ceintures* that women decorate, wear, send, and receive as love tokens. See especially Lienor's belt described in *Guillaume de Dole* as "embroidered with a design of fish and birds worked in gold thread"

(Lecoy, vv. 4826–27; Terry and Durling, *Jean Renart*, 83; El estoit de fin or broudee / a poissonez et a oisiaus).

52. Although this is the only specific indication of colored fabric in the *chanson de toile*, gold brocade and embroidery used typically to decorate colored silks appear in *Fille et la mere* and *Bele Yolanz*. References to *samiz* and *pailes* denote richly colored fabrics common in Old French romance narratives of the twelfth and thirteenth centuries.

53. It is unclear in this instance who is responsible for administering the beating; no husband is mentioned here. The *male maistre* indicated in line one seems a remote possibility, since no models for women beating other women exist in this corpus, although Bele Emmelos's mother drags her off by the hair to be beaten by her father (vv. 63–66; p. 116). It is also important to note here that whereas Ydoine begins by sitting under an olive tree, she is soon locked inside a high tower. In *En un vergier*, however, the heroine is beaten in the garden (vv. 14–15; p. 86) and no indication is provided as to whether Emmelos remains "in the garden" (v. 1; p. 154), where the song begins.

54. Indeed, the "work" undertaken by the heroine in this *chanson de toile* resides in her repeated and concerted efforts to sustain her husband's abusive blows, attesting to a resolve and determination in pursuing her choice in love that is reminiscent of Amelot and Aude.

55. Nancy A. Jones, "The Daughter's Text and the Thread of Lineage in the Old French *Philomena*," in *Representing Rape in Medieval and Early Modern Literature*, ed. Elizabeth Robertson and Christine M. Rose (New York: Palgrave, 2001), 161–87.

56. Luce Irigaray, *An Ethics of Sexual Difference*, trans. Carolyn Burke and Gillian C. Gill (Ithaca, N.Y.: Cornell University Press, 1984), 5.

57. Cixous, *Coming to Writing*, 97.

Chapter 4. Robes, Armor, and Skin

1. *Robert de Blois's Floris et Liriopé*, ed. Paul Barrette (Berkeley: University of California Press, 1968).

2. See Chapter 1.

3. See also vv. 87–95 and discussion in Chapter 1.

4. Roberta L. Krueger, *Women Readers and the Ideology of Gender in Medieval French Verse Romance* (Cambridge: Cambridge University Press, 1993), 162 ff.

5. I borrow this useful term from Leslie Rabine, "A Feminist Politics of Non-Identity," *Feminist Studies* 14, 1 (1988): 11–31.

6. Denise Riley, *Am I That Name? Feminism and the Category of "Women" in History* (Minneapolis: University of Minnesota Press, 1988), 6.

7. Joan Cadden, *Meanings of Sexual Difference in the Middle Ages: Medicine, Science, and Culture* (Cambridge: Cambridge University Press, 1993), 202–12.

8. Roberta L. Krueger, "Constructing Sexual Identities in the High Middle Ages: The Didactic Poetry of Robert de Blois," *Paragraph* 13 (1990): 105–31; and for the fourteenth century, "Intergeneric Combination and the Anxiety of Gender in *Le*

Livre du Chevalier de la Tour Landry pour l'enseignement de ses filles," *L'Esprit créateur* 33, 4 (1993): 61–72.

9. Susan Crane, *Gender and Romance in Chaucer's* Canterbury Tales (Princeton, N.J.: Princeton University Press, 1994), 13.

10. Simon Gaunt, *Gender and Genre in Medieval French Literature* (Cambridge: Cambridge University Press, 1995), 286. See also Willliam E. Burgwinkle, *Love for Sale: Materialist Readings of the Troubadour Razo Corpus* (New York: Garland, 1997) and Gerald A. Bond, *The Loving Subject: Desire, Eloquence and Power in Romanesque France* (Philadelphia: University of Pennsylvania Press, 1995).

11. Peggy McCracken, "Chaste Subjects: Gender, Heroism, and Desire in the Grail Quest," in *Queering the Middle Ages*, ed. Glen Burger and Steven F. Krueger (Minneapolis: University of Minnesota Press, 2001), 123–42.

12. Susan Schibanoff, "Sodomy's Mark: Alan of Lille, Jean de Meun, and the Medieval Theory of Authorship," in Burger and Krueger, *Queering the Middle Ages*, 28–56. See also her "Mohammed, Courtly Love, and the Myth of Western Heterosexuality," *Medieval Feminist Newsletter* 16 (fall 1993): 27–32.

13. Jacqueline Murray, "Twice Marginal and Twice Invisible," in *Handbook of Medieval Sexuality*, ed. Vern L. Bullough and James A. Brundage (New York: Garland, 1996); Karma Lochrie, "Mystical Acts, Queer Tendencies," in *Constructing Medieval Sexuality*, ed. Karma Lochrie, Peggy McCracken, and James A. Schultz (Minneapolis: University of Minnesota Press, 1997), 180–200; Sahar Amer, "Lesbian Sex and the Military: From the Medieval Arabic Tradition to French Literature," in *Same Sex Love and Desire Among Women in the Middle Ages*, ed. Francesca Canadé Sautman and Pamela Sheingorn (New York: Palgrave, 2001), 180–98; Judith M. Bennett, "Lesbian-Like and the Social History of Lesbianisms," *Journal of the History of Sexuality* 9 (2000): 1–24. On the complex homosocial relations in *Sir Gauvain and the Green Knight* see David Lorenzo Boyd, "Sodomy, Misogyny, and Displacements: Occluding Queer Desire in *Sir Gawain and the Green Knight*," *Arthuriana* 8, 2 (1998): 77–113.

14. Valerie R. Hotchkiss, *Clothes Make the Man: Female Crossdressing in Medieval Europe* (New York: Garland, 1996).

15. For comedic portrayals of cross-dressing see Keith Busby, "'Plus ascemez qu'une popine': Male Cross-Dressing in Medieval French Narrative," in *Gender Transgressions: Crossing the Normative Barrier in Old French Literature*, ed. Karen J. Taylor (New York: Garland, 1998), 45–59. For an explanation of how thirteenth-century literary experiments with the possibilities of transvestism diminish significantly by the fifteenth century, see Michelle Szkilnik, "The Grammar of the Sexes in Medieval French Romance," in Taylor, *Gender Transgressions*, 61–88.

16. Peter Allen, "The Ambiguity of Silence," in *Sign, Sentence, Discourse: Language and Medieval Thought in Literature*, ed. Julian N. Wasserman and Lois Roney (Syracuse, N.Y.: Syracuse University Press, 1989), 98–112; Simon Gaunt, "The Significance of Silence," *Paragraph* 13, 2 (1990): 202–16; Michèle Perret, "Travesties et Transexuelles: Yde, Silence, Grisandole, Blanchandine," *Romance Notes* 25, 3 (1985): 328–40; Roberta L. Krueger, "Women Readers and the Politics of Gender in the *Roman de Silence*," in her *Women Readers*, 101–27; Peggy McCracken, "The Boy Who Was a Girl: Reading Gender in the *Roman de Silence*," *Romanic Review* 85, 4 (1994):

517–34, who shows specifically how this complex romance "challenges the primacy of anatomy as the location of gender identity" (532). On cross-dressing in Joan of Arc see especially Susan Crane, "Clothing and Gender Definition in Joan of Arc," *Journal of Medieval and Early Modern Studies* 26, 2 (spring 1996): 297–320; and Susan Schibanoff, "True Lies: Transvestism and Idolatry in the Trial of Joan of Arc," in *Fresh Verdicts on Joan of Arc*, ed. Bonnie Wheeler and Charles T. Wood (New York: Garland, 1996), 31–60.

17. See, for example, Andreas Capellanus, who details similar symptoms as typical of the courtly lover (*Andreas Capellanus on Love*, ed. and trans. P.G. Walsh [London: Duckworth, 1982], 99).

18. This is certainly not the only possible reading of the passage. Indeed, Floris's reference to the happiness of Lyriope's parents as a couple (vv. 1031–34) reinforces a heterosexual meaning, but the syntactical ambiguity of the foregoing lines unsettles a strictly heterosexual reading.

19. I choose these texts because ever since Gaston Paris coined the term "courtly love" in 1883, scholars have taken these early tales of Lancelot and Guenevere to be the founding narratives of courtly love in the northern French tradition, "Etudes sur les romans de la Table Ronde, Lancelot du Lac, II: *Le Conte de la charrette*," *Romania* 12 (1883): 459–534. Various permutations of courtliness are, of course, attested in a broader range of romance narratives. I have argued elsewhere that the quintessential courtly couple, Lancelot and Guenevere, function in the *Prose Lancelot* as loci of displacement, substitution, and slippage between the categories of male and female, thereby calling into question the presumed natural alignment of sex and gender in courtly romance. See E. Jane Burns, "Which Queen? Guenivere's Transvestism in the French Prose *Lancelot*," in *Lancelot and Guenevere: A Casebook*, ed. Lori J. Walters (New York: Garland Publishing, 1996), 247–65.

20. John F. Benton, "Clio and Venus: A Historical View of Medieval Love," in *The Meaning of Courtly Love*, ed. F. X. Newman (Albany: SUNY Press, 1968), 36. For a recent reprinting of the image, see Brigitte Bedos-Rezak, "The Social Implications of the Art of Chivalry: The Sigillographic Evidence (France: 1050–1250)," in *Form and Other in Medieval France: Studies in Social and Quantitative Sigillography* (Brookfield, Vt.: Ashgate, 1993), 199, fig. 12; Bedos-Rezak identifies the image as a scene of homage, 21. Earlier, Marc Bloch, *Feudal Society*, trans. L. A. Manyon vol. 1, *The Growth of Ties of Dependence* (Chicago: University of Chicago Press, 1970), pl. 4.

21. In her exhaustive analyses of medieval seals, Brigitte Bedos-Rezak mentions only two seals that depict a kneeling knight paying homage to a "lady." "Medieval Women in French Sigillographic Sources," in *Medieval Women and the Sources of Medieval History*, ed. Joel T. Rosenthal (Athens: University of Georgia Press, 1990), 152–74.

22. For more on unisex dress in twelfth- and thirteenth-century France, see E. Jane Burns, "Ladies Don't Wear *Braies*: Underwear and Outerwear in the French Prose *Lancelot*," in *The Lancelot-Grail Cycle: Texts and Transformations*, ed. William W. Kibler (Austin: University of Texas Press, 1994), 152–74.

23. I do not mean to imply that there is a difference in kind between seemingly more "real" historical bodies and the fictive bodies figured in Arthurian romance. Both kinds of bodies are cultural products, each deriving from a different

structuring ideology. Whereas the interpretation of the bodies involved in the Jealous Husband's tirade described in Chapter 1, above, for example, results from a presumption that bodies can be naturally sexed, the ideology governing the creation of gender identity in Arthurian romance, by contrast, makes no such blanket or exclusive presumption.

24. Sarah Kay, *Subjectivity in Troubadour Poetry* (Cambridge: Cambridge University Press, 1990), 86.

25. It is important to emphasize that the Provençal *domna* and courtly lady do not actually acquire the lord's power or authority but remain only fictively empowered. See E. Jane Burns and Roberta L. Krueger, Introduction to "Courtly Ideology and Woman's Place in Medieval French Literature," *Romance Notes* 25, 3 (1985): 205–19; and E. Jane Burns, "The Man Behind the Lady in Troubadour Lyric," *Romance Notes* 25, 3 (1985): 254–70.

26. The system remains, however, crucially distinct from the Old Norse culture described by Carol Clover in which "maleness and femaleness were always negotiable" (378) and gender was not coextensive with biological sex but based on "winnable and losable attributes" (379). The Old Norse sagas retained a clear hierarchy of sex difference that "at the level of the body knows only the male and at the level of social behavior, only the effeminate, or emasculate, or impotent" (387). See "Regardless of Sex: Men, Women, and Power in Early Northern Europe," *Speculum* 68, 2 (1993): 363–87. Epithets such as "effeminate" or "impotent" do not typically accompany gender crossings in French courtly romance.

27. This does not mean that considerations of sexual difference are insignificant. On the contrary, I have argued in *Bodytalk: When Women Speak in Old French Literature* (Philadelphia: University of Pennsylvania Press, 1993), as here, that it is important for feminist readers of Old French literature to take the body into account but to understand that body as necessarily a product of historical, cultural, social, and linguistic processes. For more on the importance of "sexed bodies," see Elizabeth Grosz, *Volatile Bodies: Toward a Corporeal Feminism* (Bloomington: Indiana University Press, 1994), 187–210.

28. "Et que ferai jou, qui tout ai mis en vous mon cuer et mon cors?" *Lancelot: Roman en prose du XIIIe siècle*, ed. Alexandre Micha (Geneva: Droz, 1982), 8: 483, and "Et sachiés que vous porrés bien avoir compaignie de plus riche homme que je ne sui, mais vous ne l'avrés jamais a homme qui tant vous aint" (8: 81). For additional textual references, see Reginald Hyatte, "Recoding Ideal Male Friendship as *fine amor* in the *Prose Lancelot*," *Neophilologus* 75 (1991): 505–18. Hyatte's article is insightful in mapping out the details of the role reversals involved here, though his conclusion—that Lancelot and Galehout are simply friends rather than homosexual lovers—unfortunately minimizes the richness of the textual material he presents.

29. Kevin Brownlee has shown how even Chrétien de Troyes's twelfth-century *Lancelot (Le Chevalier de la charrete)* experiments with gender inversions as "Godefroi's Lancelot plays the role of Chrétien's Guenevere. At the same time, Godefroi casts Méléagant's sister in the role of Chrétien's Lancelot, i.e., the desiring subject, the active and successful quester," "Transformations of the *Charrete*: Godefroi de Leigni Rewrites Chrétien de Troyes," *Stanford French Review* 14, 1–2 (1990): 161–78.

30. See, for example, Helen Solterer, "Figures of Female Militancy in Medieval France," *Signs* 16, 3 (1991): 522–30; and Nancy Freeman Regalado, "Allegories of Power: The Tournament of Vices and Virtues in the *Roman de Fauvel* (BN MS Fr. 146)," *Gesta* 32, 2 (1993): 135–46.

31. Peter Stallybrass, "Boundary and Transgression: Body, Text, Language," *Stanford French Review* 14, 1–2 (1990): 9.

32. See Elizabeth Spelman, *Inessential Woman: Problems of Exclusion in Feminist Thought* (Boston: Beacon Press, 1988), who shows how, in his political works, Aristotle distinguishes between three categories: men, women, and slaves, thus producing gender as a class distinction that does not derive from biological sexual difference. See esp. 37–56; and James A. Schultz, on how gender is constructed by clothing and class in Gottfried's *Tristan* such that "sex difference is not visible in the body of the object" and "sexual desire is not determined by the identity of the subject, "Bodies That Don't Matter: Heterosexuality Before Heterosexuality in Gottfried's *Tristan*," in Lochrie et al., *Constructing Medieval Sexuality*.

33. For examples from the German tradition, see Joachim Bumke, *Courtly Culture: Literature and Society in the High Middle Ages*, trans. Thomas Dunlap (Berkeley: University of California Press, 1991), 138–55.

34. Theodore Evergates, ed. and trans., *Feudal Society in Medieval France: Documents from the County of Champagne* (Philadelphia: University of Pennsylvania Press, 1993), 99: "Operitis equos sericis, et pendulos nescio quos panniculos loricis superinduitis; depingitis hastas, clypeos et sellas; frena et clacaria auro et argento gemmisque circumornatis, et cum tanta pompa pudendo furore et impudenti stupore ad mortem properatis," *Tractatus et opuscula*, vol. 3 of *Sancti Bernardi Opera*, ed. Jean Leclercq and H. M. Rochais (Rome: Editiones Cistercienses, 1963), 216. See also the military code established in 1188 by Philip Augustus and Henry II prohibiting crusaders from wearing costly fabrics, "Nobody shall wear colored cloth, gray cloth, squirrel fur, sable, or purple cloth" (Nullus vario vel grisio vel sabellinis vel escarletis utatur) (Bumke, *Courtly Culture*, 129).

35. "Vos . . . oculorum gravamen ritu femineo comam nutritis, longis ac profusis camisiis propria vobis vestigia obvolvitis, delicatas ac teneras manus amplis et circumfluentibus manicis sepelitis" (*Tractatus*, 216).

36. "Militaris sunt haec insignia, an muliebria potius ornamenta?" (*Tractatus*, 216). The subject of lavish knightly dress is still at issue in 1279 when Philip the Bold institutes his sumptuary laws. As J. Quicherat notes, the bourgeoisie was "prohibited from using luxury chariots, golden spurs, and harnesses." *Histoire du Costume en France depuis les temps les plus reculés jusqu'à la fin du XVIIIe siècle* (Paris: Hachette, 1877), 204. Bernard's comment should also be set in the long tradition of cosmetic theology, exemplified by Tertullian's writing on women's apparel and discussed by Marcia Colish, "Cosmetic Theology: The Transformation of a Stoic Theme," *Assays* 1 (1981): 3–14; and R. Howard Bloch, *Medieval Misogyny and the Invention of Western Romantic Love* (Chicago: University of Chicago Press, 1991), 39–47.

37. *The Ecclesiastical History of Oderic Vitalis*, ed. and trans. Marjorie Chibnall (Oxford: Clarendon Press, 1973), 4: 188: "Femineam mollitem petulans iuuentus amplectitur, feminisque uiri curiales in omni lasciuia summopere adulantur. Pedum articulis ubi finis est corporis colubrinarum similitudinem caudarum imponuntent,

quas velutscorpiones prar oculis suis prospiciunt. Humum quoque puluerulentam interularum et palliorum superfluo sirmate uerrunt, longis latisque manicis ad omnia facienda manus operiunt, et his superfluitatibus onusti celeriter ambulare uel aliquid utiliter operari uix possunt. Sincipite scalciati sunt, ut fures, occipatio autem prolixas nutriunt comas ut meritrices."

38. "Nam capillos a uertice in frontem discriminabant, longos crines ueluti mulieres nutriebant, et summopere comebant, prolixisque nimiumque strictis camisiis indui tunicisque gaudebant" (188).

39. Eadmer, *Historia novorum*, lib. I, *PL* 159, c. 576. Cited in H. Platelle, "Le Problème du scandale: Les nouvelles modes masculines aux XIe et XIIe siècles," *Revue Belge de philologie et d'histoire* 53, 4 (1975): 1078. See Platelle for further discussion and additional examples.

40. Pierre Kraemer, *Le Luxe et les lois somptuaires au moyen âge* (Paris: Ernest Sagot, 1920), 36, quoted from H. Baudrillart, *Histoire du luxe privé et public: Le moyen âge et la renaissance* (Paris: Hachette, 1880), 4: 640.

41. Kramer, *Le Luxe*, 37–38, quoted from Helinaudin, *Histoire littéraire de la France*, vol. 17.

42. "Crinitis nostris, qui obliti quid nati sunt, libenter se in muliebris sexus habitum transformant." William of Malmesbury, *Historia novellae* I, 4, *PL* 179, c. 1396–97, cited in Platelle, "Le Problème du scandale," 1082. Behind these injunctions to maintain two clearly defined sexes lies Paul's remark in 1 Corinthians 11: 14–15, "it is shameful for a man to have long hair, although it is glorious for a woman to do so, for hair was given to her as a kind of veil"; Platelle, 1087.

43. *Le Chevalier de la charrete*, ed. Mario Roques (Paris: Champion, 1970), vv. 44–48. For examples of a knight completely covered in the *Prose Lancelot* see Micha 1: 136, 291, 363; 2: 52.

44. In the *Prose Lancelot*, the *escu* carries special weight as the exemplary marker of a knight's identity: "Por Dieu, dites nos la verite del meillor chevalier del monde, por quoi il ne li pendra james escu al col et se il est ou mors ou vis" (1: 351). Having the "escu al col" signals Lancelot as a living, breathing, functional knight. If he is accused of adultery, we are told, Lancelot would lose his status as a knight and the right to carry a shield and wear armor, "ains iroit tos jors mes en langes et nus pies, ne james n'avroit escu a col ne arme vestue" (1: 352). Indeed, Lancelot's *escu* is venerated and fetishized as a substitute for his very being in 1: 361. For a sampling of other instances in which the knight's identity is vested in the *escu*, see 1: 361, 387. Other knights described as "bien taillies" include Hector 8: 277, Gauvain 2: 408, Segurade 8: 177, and Lancelot 1: 128.

45. It is this thorough covering that makes both literary and historical knights into what John of Salisbury called "les mains armées du roi" (the king's armed and armored hands), Jean Flori, "La Chevalerie chez Jean de Salisbury," *Revue d'histoire ecclésiastique* 77, 1–2 (1982): 35–77.

46. See also 1: 344 and further how Galehaut, riding without a helmet, receives an unexpected blow to the face, 1: 359.

47. "Et vous, fait il [Galehos], mesire Gauvain, se Diex vous doinst le santé que vous desirés, quel meschief feriés vous por avoir tous jours mais .I. si preudome?" 8: 94.

48. Burns, "Which Queen?"

49. Judith Butler, *Gender Trouble: Feminism and the Subversion of Identity* (New York and London: Routledge, 1990), 137.

50. Danielle Régnier-Bohler has shown how in Old French narrative generally men of varying social ranks must be covered to be fully socialized, whereas women are always already nude, since their identity is fundamentally sexual rather than social. "Le Corps mis à nu: Perception et valeur symbolique de la nudité dans les récits du moyen âge," *Europe: Revue littéraire mensuelle* (October 1983): 51–62.

51. See also 2: 376 and Guenevere as "desvelopee" in 1: 18.

52. See Burns, *Bodytalk*, 109–12; Alice Colby, *The Portrait in Twelfth-Century French Literature* (Geneva: Droz, 1965).

53. It is often that very beauty, revealed in female skin exposed to view, that is said to provoke knights to seize women, as in the following passage from the *Prose Lancelot*, where a "bone pucele" is "si bele de cors" that "an tout le païs n'avoit si bele ne chevalier si puissant que volentiers ne la preist por sa biauté" (4: 134, there was not a more beautiful maiden in all the country nor a more powerful knight who would not readily seize her on account of her beauty).

54. Roberta Krueger has explained how Guenevere's abduction constitutes a version of the *coutume de Logres* in "Desire, Meaning, and the Female Reader: The Problem in Chrétien's *Charrete*," in *The Passing of Arthur: New Essays in Arthurian Tradition*, ed. Christopher Baswell and William Sharpe (New York: Garland, 1988), 31–51. For other examples of noble women being "handed off" as the prize in a tournament, see Jean-Louis Pichérit, "Le Motif du tournoi dont le prix est la main d'une riche et noble héritière," *Romance Quarterly* 36, 2 (1989): 141–52, esp. 149.

55. My interest in investigating how knights and ladies are "made" in the Arthurian world was sparked by Marjorie Garber, "Spare Parts: On the Surgical Construction of Gender," in her *Vested Interests: Cross-Dressing and Cultural Anxiety* (New York: Routledge, 1992), 93–117.

56. I do not mean to suggest here that the courtly lady's skin is somehow more concrete, real, or material than the knight's armor. Rather, that while his gendered identity is created by and located in the suit of armor, hers is fabricated and read as skin.

57. Burns, *Bodytalk*, 4–7.

58. This damsel, it should be noted, is not the typical courtly lady but a temptress whose actions were designed by a third party to test the knight's resistance, as Lancelot later learns (1: 326). Yet this in no way diminishes the force of the scene in revealing what can happen when courtly ladies are not "ladies."

59. Burns, "Which Queen?"

60. Actually, Lancelot is here described as "denuded" though he retains his *chemise*, much as many female figures in Arthurian romance are said to be "nue en sa chemise." See Burns, "Ladies Don't Wear *Braies*," 163. A narrative progression similar to the one outlined in the scene with the temptress occurs on pp. 78–82, where Lancelot exchanges his armor for a mantle (vv. 2534–37) and is helpless to defend himself against the charges of the *chevalier orgueilleux*, at least until he rearms (vv. 2661 ff.) and exits the castle. The exchange of *escu* for mantle does not always prove problematic, as the scenes on pp. 63 ff. and 90 ff. attest.

61. See Matilda Tomaryn Bruckner, *Narrative Invention in Twelfth-Century French Romance* (Lexington, Ky.: French Forum, 1980).

62. See also the dame du Lac dressed like Lancelot ("la dame si fu atornee moult richement, car ele fu vestue d'un blanc samit, cote et mantel a une pene d'ermine," 7: 266 and Lancelot wearing a "robe d'un blanc samit, cote et mantel, et estoit li mantiax fourés d'ermines," 7: 259); the ailing Gauvain wearing a *demoisele*'s robes (1: 212) and the recovering Lancelot borrowing a lady's gown (6: 210). We must of course remember that the unisex robe and mantle also belong to the wardrobe of the courtly lord, such that the more an unarmored knight comes to look like a lady, the more he also resembles an empowered aristocratic man.

63. These examples of Lancelot's gender crossing provide a very different picture from the scenario of the "man in the dress" mentioned in Gregory of Tours that Nancy Partner interprets as exhibiting a "core gender identity of maleness," "No Sex, No Gender," *Speculum* 68, 2 (1993): 442.

64. Marc Bloch, *Feudal Society*, 146.

65. See the dubbing ceremony 8: 106.

66. See, for example, how Arthur takes Guenevere "by the hand" in the opening scenes of the *Charrete* (vv. 188–96) and hands her off to the armored Keu (*toz armez*), who will later fight the equally armed Méléagant for possession of the queen.

67. There is one key moment in the *Charrete* where Lancelot's status as the "perfect knight" derives precisely from his ability to cross gender boundaries without losing social status. He proves his mettle as the superhero of Arthurian romance by doing exactly what knights cannot do: remove portions of armor and perform heroic feats. In the episode of the sword bridge, for example, Lancelot uses bare hands and feet to traverse the deadly blade while wearing, it seems, no more than the otherwise degrading *chemise*: "Bien s'iert sor l'espee tenuz, / qui plus estoit tranchanz que fauz, / as mains nues et si deschauz" (vv. 3100–3102; He held tightly to the sword blade, sharper than a scythe, with his bare hands and feet); "Le sanc jus de ses plaies tert / a sa chemise tot antor" (vv. 3136–37; The blood from his wounds stained his *chemise*). Are these the hands and dress of a lady? Far from the standard of masculine prowess signaled by the fully armored and contained body of the rival Méléagant (v. 3541), Lancelot's body in this episode remains equally removed from the vulnerable body of the temptress "tote descoverte" or the compliant and possessed body of the *demoisele* in tow. Lancelot seems here to be both "naked" and adequately clothed at once, vulnerable yet empowered.

68. Eve Kosofsky Sedgwick, *Tendencies* (Durham, N.C.: Duke University Press, 1993), 8.

69. Sedgwick's project could hypothetically lead to such an end, however, as Elizabeth Weed has cogently argued: "The risk, then is that the cleavage of sexuality and gender in some queer criticism will—has already—rendered the difference of sexual difference *once again* unreadable. "The More Things Change," *differences* (summer-fall 1994): 268.

70. Albert Lecoy de la Marche, *La Chaire française au moyen âge* (Paris: Librairie Renouard, 1886), 438.

Chapter 5. From Woman's Nature to Nature's Dress

1. Tibaut, *Le Roman de la poire*, ed. Christiane Marchello-Nizia (Paris: SATF, 1985), vv. 453–56, 477–78.

2. Jean Renart, *Le Lai de l'ombre*, ed. Joseph Bédier (Paris: Firmin-Didot, 1913), vv. 919–20.

3. Chretién de Troyes, *Le Roman de Perceval ou le conte du Graal*, ed. William Roach (Paris: Champion, 1959), vv. 8176–82.

4. R. Howard Bloch, *Medieval Misogyny and the Invention of Western Romantic Love* (Chicago: University of Chicago Press, 1991), 39–47. Clothing, to be sure, plays a key role in the biblical fall recorded in Genesis. Not only do Adam and Eve cover their nakedness with fig leaves in an initial attempt to clothe the fallen body: "Then the eyes of both were opened, and they knew that they were naked; and they sewed fig leaves together and made themselves aprons" (Gen. 3: 7). God himself subsequently sews animal skins together, fashioning more substantial garments for the first couple: "And the Lord God made for Adam and for his wife garments of skins, and clothed them" (Gen. 3: 21). Although both sets of early clothing derive from natural elements, they become highly charged as markers of the fall from innocence into the knowledge of good and evil, from nature into culture. Within the founding Western system of sexual difference, then, the "fall of man" is marked by a concomitant fall into clothing.

5. Albert Lecoy de la Marche, *La Chaire française au moyen âge* (Paris: Librairie Renouard, 1886), 440.

6. Pope Innocent III, *On the Misery of Man*, in *Two Views of Man*, ed. Bernard Murchland (New York: Ungar, 1966), 58. For the Latin text, see *De Miseria condicionis humane*, ed. Robert E. Lewis (Athens: University of Georgia Press, 1978), 197. Lewis dates the text to 1195.

7. Earlier, Tertullian had cited luxury adornments as appropriate trappings for "a woman who was condemned and is dead, arrayed as if to lend splendor to her funeral." Female imitators of a properly penitent Eve, hoping to be restored to life again, Tertullian explains, should not be tempted by those fineries that the original Eve did not have or know when she lived in God, fineries such as wool, silk, dye, embroidery, weaving, gleaming pearls, sparkling rubies, gold, and mirrors, with their "lying image." "The Apparel of Women," in *Disciplinary, Moral, and Ascetical Works*, trans. Rudolph Arbesmann, Sister Emily Joseph Daly, and Edwin A Quain. (New York: Fathers of the Church, 1959), 118.

8. *La Queste del Saint Graal*, ed. Albert Pauphilet (Paris: Champion, 1980), 105, 180; and the corroborating view in Book 3 of Andreas Capellanus's The *Art of Courtly Love* that courtly lovers do "the devil's service," rather than God's or the lady's since, according to scripture, the devil is the creator of love and sexual indulgence (*luxuria*). *Andreas Capellanus on Love*, ed. P. G. Walsh (London: Duckworth, 1982), 299. For Guenevere, *Lancelot: roman en prose du XIIIe siècle*, ed. Alexandre Micha (Paris: Champion, 1978), 1: 7, 47, 57, where Guenevere appears both as a love serpent who beguiles the unsuspecting Lancelot and as the stunningly beautiful "dame des dames" of inestimable value. In comparison to many romance heroines,

Guenevere's lavish dress is actually described infrequently, although she maintains, along with Queen Iseut, the reputation as the most beautiful of courtly ladies. See Christiane Marchello-Nizia, "Amour courtois, société masculine, et figures du pouvoir," *Annales E.S.C.* 36 (1981): 969–82.

9. Guillaume's depiction of Nature as a key figure in Love's Garden contrasts sharply in most manuscript versions with Jean de Meun's more extensive treatment of Nature as an advocate of procreation rather than love. See especially Genius's distinction between the true paradise of the Park of Heaven and the vain delights of the Garden of Deduit in Lecoy, vv. 20305–20566, and George Economou, *The Goddess Natura in Medieval Literature* (Cambridge, Mass.: Harvard University Press, 1972). A late thirteenth-century rewriting of the *Rose* by the cleric Gui de Mori omits the contrast between the two gardens, returning Genius to his earlier form in Alain de Lille's *De Planctu Naturae* and significantly reducing Nature's role. Here love is grounded in divinity apprehended through rational intellect, not natural sexual drives. See Sylvia Huot, "Authors, Scribes and Remanieurs," in *Rethinking the* Romance of the Rose, ed. Kevin Brownlee and Sylvia Huot (Philadelphia: University of Pennsylvania Press, 1992), 206–11.

10. In this detail too his portrait differs from that of Deduit, whose body (*cors*) is mentioned specifically.

11. See Chapter 1, above.

12. Sarah Kay provides another view in her reading of Jean de Meun's Nature as sensual, embodied, and highly learned at the same time, thus offering an alternative to Alain de Lille's Nature, who identifies with Reason against flesh and the feminine. See her "Women's Body of Knowledge: Epistemology and Misogyny in the *Romance of the Rose*," in *Framing Medieval Bodies*, ed. Sarah Kay and Miri Rubin (Manchester: Manchester University Press, 1994), 211–35.

13. Alain de Lille, *Plaint of Nature*, trans. James J. Sheridan (Toronto: Pontifical Institute of Mediaeval Studies, 1980), 98. This version of Nature, along with Alain's depiction of her in his *Anticlaudianus*, serves as the primary model for Jean de Meun's vision of Nature. Significantly, however, Jean refuses to describe Nature in his account, since she is God's perfect creation (vv. 16135–218). Not even Pygmalion could create her, we are told.

14. Nature is here unclothed so that she will go like a harlot to a brothel, causing injury and insult to her modesty (142). The seasons of winter and spring, by contrast, are said in Alain's text to acquire garments of flowers or to weave garments for trees with their foliage (111), and "Spring, like a fuller with renewed strength, mending the meadow's cloak, set the mantles of flowers afire with the glow of purple" (113). But the conflation of garments with natural substances does not apply to Nature herself. Indeed, what the poet has seen in Nature's torn garment, without fully realizing it, is the fall of man (Economou, *Goddess Natura*, 77).

15. Alexandre Leupin has read Nature's censure of sodomy and insistence on reproduction as a complex celebration of hermaphroditic or sodomitic writing, as Alain's text actively undermines Nature's project. *Barbarolexis: Medieval Writing and Sexuality*, trans. Kate M. Cooper (Cambridge, Mass.: Harvard University Press, 1989), 59–78.

16. Bruno Roy, ed., *L'Art d'amours: Traduction et commentaire de "l'Ars amatoria" d'Ovide* (Leiden: E.J. Brill, 1974), 247, 243.

17. *Le Roman de la Rose ou de Guillaume de Dole*, ed. Félix Lecoy (Paris: Champion, 1962), vv. 4717–27.

18. Roberta Krueger explains how the narrator's depiction of Lienor's "natural" beauty in this scene of unveiling constitutes a "highly self-conscious moment of narrative mystification." *Women Readers and the Ideology of Gender in Old French Verse Romance* (Cambridge: Cambridge University Press, 1993), 151–52, as opposed to previous readings by Henri Rey-Flaud, *La Névrose courtoise* (Paris: Navarin, 1983), 104; Michel Zink, *Roman rose ou rose rouge: Le Roman de la Rose ou de Guillaume de Dole* (Paris: Nizet, 1979), 107–8; and Marc-René Jung, "L'Empéreur Conrad chanteur de poésie lyrique," *Romania* 101 (1980): 35–50, all of whom understand Lienor's disrobing to reveal her true "nature." For extended comments on Lienor as part of an elaborate intertextual tour de force, see Regina Psaki, "Jean Renart's Expanded Text: Lienor and the Lyrics of *Guillaume de Dole*, in *Jean Renart and the Art of Romance: Essays on Guillaume de Dole*, ed. Nancy Vine Durling (Gainesville: University Press of Florida, 1997), 122–42; and Norris J. Lacy, "Amer par oïr dire: *Guillaume de Dole* and the Drama of Language," *French Review* 54, 6 (1981): 779–87. For an analysis of how Lienor herself deploys clothing in the form of a decorative belt to stage a mock rape of the seneschal who has wrongly accused her, see Helen Solterer, "At the Bottom of the Mirage: The *Roman de la rose* of Jean Renart," in *Feminist Approaches to the Body*, ed. Linda Lomperis and Sarah Stanbury (Philadelphia: University of Pennsylvania Press, 1993), 213–33; against Roger Dragonetti's comments on this helmeted beauty as a nonwoman in *Le Mirage des sources: L'Art du faux dans le roman médiéval* (Paris: Seuil, 1987), 189.

19. Claude Luttrell explains how specific aspects of Nature in Arthurian romance derive from twelfth-century Latin poets in "The Figure of Nature in Chrétien de Troyes," *Nottingham Medieval Studies* 17 (1973): 3–16.

20. See also indications of Nature's failed handiwork because the task of creating such beauty requires skilled workmanship possible only by God, documented in Alice Colby's account of the portraits of Fenice, Soredamor, Laudine, and Philomena (the latter is made by both God and Nature), *The Portrait in Twelfth-Century French Literature* (Geneva: Droz, 1965).

21. For a fuller discussion of the issue and a response provided by Old French vernacular literature see E. Jane Burns, "A Taste of Knowledge: Genesis and Generation in the *Jeu d'Adam*," in *Bodytalk: When Women Speak in Old French Literature* (Philadelphia: University of Pennsylvania Press, 1993), 71–106.

22. Chrétien de Troyes, *Cligés*, ed. Alexandre Micha (Paris: Champion, 1957).

23. See the discussion of Riches's arrows in Chapter 1, above.

24. See pp. 152–57.

25. Many critics have noted how this *lai* offers an inversion of and an alternative to the world of Arthurian romance, pulling the hero away from Arthur's court to an "other realm." See especially Laurence Harf-Lancner, *Les Fées au Moyen Age: Morgane et Mélusine* (Paris: Champion, 1984), and W. T. H. Jackson, "The Arthuricity of Marie de France," *Romanic Review* 70 (1979): 1–18. Thelma Fenster's analysis shows further how this other world underscores the ability of supernatural women to remedy human ills at court and "demonstrates the complementary indispensability of the woman's realm." *Arthurian Women: A Casebook*, ed. Thelma Fenster (New York: Garland, 1995), xli. It is important to note, however, that Lanval's

ladylove is never called a "fée" in this text. She is a *pucele* of extraordinary beauty (v. 93), a *meschine* (v. 131) who engages in a traditional pact of love service with Lanval (v. 127), becoming his courtly *amie* (v. 158 ff.). She is the *dame* of the *puceles* in her entourage (v. 493) and she presides over a court more wealthy than Arthur's. Her supernatural powers are not insignificant—she can come to Lanval any time of the day or night and no one else will be able to see or hear her—but these powers are mentioned only once in a few brief lines (vv. 167–70). For most of the tale, she appears and behaves more as a lady or in fact more as a knight than a fairy. We should also keep in mind the description of Lienor in Jean Renart's *Guillaume de Dole*, who "seemed a miracle or a beautiful enchantment" (vv. 4620–21). The text thus indicates her extraordinary beauty by comparing her to a fairy: "une mervelle tote droite, / la plus bele et la plus adroite. / Ne sai se c'est ou fee ou fame" (Lecoy, vv. 4687–89). In *Aucassin et Nicolette*, ed. Mario Roques (Paris: Champion, 1977), 23, shepherds mistake the heroine for a "fée": "et une pucele vint ci, li plus bele riens du monde, si que nos quidames que ce fust une fee." Indeed in these examples, as in the *Lanval*, the assignation "fairy" is used primarily to connote extraordinary beauty.

26. For a survey of critical readings of this *lai*, see Fenster, *Arthurian Women*, lxii, notes 49–53, On the significance of these textiles as imported from Eastern lands see Chapter 6, below.

27. When Lanval does later exhibit recognizable signs of lovesick distress, they are in response to his having reneged on his promise to the lady rather than an expression of being rejected by the ladylove (vv. 407–14).

28. Walsh, p. 81, "omni curialitate muniri."

29. See vv. 25, 39, 66, 77.

30. Henceforth, Lanval, described earlier as wearing a simple mantle (v. 49), is found by his men to be "bien vestu" (v. 202), much as the *puceles* who attired him appear "vestues richement" (v. 57).

31. A relatively contemporary example is provided by Iseut's dressing her lover Tristan in the disguise of a leper in the *Roman de Tristan*; see Burns, *Bodytalk*, 203–40.

32. Sharon Kinoshita has aptly assessed the "feminism" of this *lai* as residing in Lanval's rejection of feudal and chivalric values. "Cherchez la femme: Feminist Criticism and Marie de France's *Lai de Lanval*," *Romance Notes* 34, 3 (1994): 363–73.

33. Kathy Krause reads this lady in contrast to Euriaus in *Le Roman de la violette*, clothed materially as a fée and rhetorically as a virgin martyr. "The Material Erotic: The Clothed and Unclothed Female Body in the *Roman de la violette*," in *Material Culture and Cultural Materialisms in the Middle Ages and Renaissance*, ed. Curtis Perry (Turnhout: Brepols, 2001), 17–34.

34. At a later moment, the *demoisele* calls Lanval specifically her *vassal* (vv. 615–16).

35. See Burns, *Bodytalk*, 4–7.

36. But her clothes do not fully cover a body beneath any more than do those of her attendants, who are said to be both *vestues* and *nues*: "De cendal purpre sunt vestues / Tut senglement a lur chars nues" (vv. 475–76). The lady herself remains

here, as in the opening scene, *descoverte*, her ribs peeking through the laces of her garments: "Ele iert vestue en itel guise / De chainse blanc e de chemise / Que tuit li costé li pareient, / Ki de deus parz lacié esteient" (vv. 559–62).

37. Jeanne Wathelet-Willem explains that this destructive and depraved version of Guenevere, one of the few negative portrayals of women in Marie de France, results in part from Celtic antecedents noted by Jean Marx and Ernst Hoepffner, which Marie negotiates without embracing fully. "Le Personnage de Guenievre chez Marie de France," *Marche Romane* 13, 4 (1963): 119–31.

Chapter 6. Saracen Silk: Dolls, Idols, and Courtly Ladies

1. *Le Saint Graal*, ed. Eugène Hucher (Le Mans: Monnoyer, 1875), 2: 318; *L'Estoire del Saint Graal*, ed. Jean-Paul Ponceau, (Paris: Champion, 1997), 1: 172–73. For an English translation, see *The History of the Holy Grail*, in *Lancelot-Grail: The Old French Arthurian Vulgate and Post-Vulgate in Translation*, trans. Carol Chase (New York: Garland, 1993), 1: 52–53.

2. Literally, "the outfit she was wearing and the wood inside it." To be sure, the reference to burning the ladylove effectively recasts the Ovidian trope of a burning, uncontrollable passion, which figures in medieval love treatises such as *L'Art d'amours*: "Qui femme alume a trop a alumer!" (*L'Art d'amours: Traduction et commentaire de "l'Ars amatoria" d'Ovide*, ed. Bruno Roy [Leiden: E.J. Brill, 1974], 173, 230). For another reading of Mordrain's passion in the *Estoire*, see C. Van Coolput, "La Poupée d'Evalach," in *Continuations: Essays in Medieval French Literature and Language*, ed. Norris J. Lacy and Gloria Torrini-Roblin (Birmingham, Ala.: Summa, 1989). She sees the incident as a veiled reference to incest.

3. The *Estoire* explains that Saracens are so named because they came originally from the city of Sarras, their official site of worship (Ponceau, 42). Although Sarras is often referred to as a city, Mordrain is king of the "royaume de Sarras," situated vaguely in Egyptian lands. In the *Queste del Saint Graal*, Sarras is "vers les parties de Jherusalem" (Pauphilet, 84) and "es parties de Babiloine" (i.e., Cairo; Pauphilet, 279).

4. Guillaume de Lorris and Jean de Meun, *Le Roman de la Rose*, ed. Félix Lecoy (Paris: Champion, 1965).

5. Jean Favier explains how both merchants and pilgrims nourished western Europe with silk imports from Constantinople, "the new Rome," and its extensions in Egypt and Syria. *De l'Or et des épices: Naissance de l'homme d'affaires au Moyen Age* (Paris: Fayard, 1987), 18. Katharine Reynolds Brown details how semiprecious stones came to Europe with the crusaders and inspired contemporary gem cutting so that by the end of the thirteenth century, Paris lapidaries had their own guild. "Gems and Jewelry," in Joseph Strayer, *Encyclopedia of the Middle Ages* (New York: Scribner, 1982–89), 380. See Joachim Bumke for the German tradition: *Courtly Culture: Literature and Society in the High Middle Ages*, trans. Thomas Dunlap (Berkeley: University of California Press, 1991), 133–34. Bumke notes that in German literature, the oriental provenance of silk was attributed to Arabia, Persia, Syria, Morocco, Libya, and various cities: Alexandria, Baghdad, Nineveh, and Almería in Spain and

Greece (133). For the French tradition, see Germain Demay, *Le Costume au Moyen Age d'après les sceaux* (Paris: Librairie de D. Dumoulin, 1880).

6. Chrétien de Troyes, *Le Conte du Graal*, ed. William Roach (Paris: Champion, 1959); *Les Lais de Marie de France*, ed. Jean Rychner (Paris: Champion, 1973).

7. See Eunice Rathbone Goddard on "costly high priced materials which were frequently imported from the Orient." *Women's Costume in French Texts of the Eleventh and Twelfth Centuries* (Baltimore: Johns Hopkins University Press, 1927), 45. Eastern silks were not limited to women. A "dïapre noble qui fu fez a Costantinoble" signals the distinguished status of the courtly hero Erec, along with imported "chauces de paile" and a "mantel hermin." *Erec et Enide*, ed. Mario Roques (Paris: Champion, 1976), vv. 97–99, 95.

8. See most specifically the *romans d'antiquité*. I do not wish to support Alexander Denomy's theory in *The Heresy of Courtly Love* that courtly love was an Arabic heresy (New York: Macmillan, 1947) and in his "Concerning the Accessibility of Arabic Influences to the Earliest Provençal Troubadours," *Mediaeval Studies* 15 (1953): 147–58, which only polarizes the relation between Christian and Saracen. I want to suggest a more productive relationship between east and west evidenced by cultural contact recorded in fictional representations of luxury clothing and adornment. Reading through clothes does indicate, however, the need to revisit carefully the long-discarded issue of "Arabic origins," in light of recent work by Samir Amin, Edward Said, Thomas Glick, María Rosa Menocal, Janet Abu-Lughod, Robert Bartlett, and others. For a cogent argument in favor of rethinking the Arabic dimensions of Old French literature, see Sahar Amer, *Esopé au féminin: Marie de France et la politique de l'interculturalité* (Amsterdam: Rodopi, 1999), esp. 1–27. Michael McCormick explains that even with regard to medieval Byzantium, scholarly interests would best be served by understanding not only the "Byzantine influence" on the "west" or the diffusion eastward of Latin European culture but also the substantial relations between medieval Byzantium and the Muslim world. "Byzantium and Modern Medieval Studies," in *The Past and Future of Medieval Studies*, ed. John Van Engen (Notre Dame, Ind.: University of Notre Dame Press, 1994), 62–63.

9. Jacoby, 459–60; Michel Patroureau, *La Vie quotidienne en France et en Angleterre (XIIe–XIIIe siècles)* (Paris: Hachette, 1976), 93–94. Maurice Lombard, *Les Textiles dans le monde musulman 7e–12e siècles* (Paris: Mouton, 1978), 90.

10. Silk clothing also plays an important role in Old French epic texts but they are beyond the scope of this study.

11. Jean Frappier, "La Peinture de la vie et des héros antiques dans la littérature française du XIIe et du XIIIe siècle," in his *Histoire, mythes, et symbols: Etudes de littérature française* (Geneva: Droz, 1976), 21–54.

12. *Aucassin et Nicolette*, ed. Mario Roques (Paris: Champion, 1977). See Sarah Kay on the political and ethical irony generated by the subversive status and positioning of the Saracen princess in Old French *chansons de geste*, "The Problem of Women: Price or Gift?" *The* Chansons de geste *in the Age of Romance: Political Fictions* (Oxford: Clarendon Press, 1995), 25–48.

13. Interestingly, she wears a domestic "chemise de blanc lin" (12) with no imported silks.

14. *La Prise d'Orange*, ed. Claude Régnier (Paris: Klincksieck, 1977), vv. 666, 683. See Jacqueline de Weever, *Sheba's Daughters: Whitening and Demonizing the Saracen Woman in Medieval French Epic* (New York: Garland, 1998), 14–18. On Nicolette, see María Rosa Menocal, "Signs of the Times: Self, Other, and History in *Aucassin et Nicolette*," *Romanic Review* 80 (1989): 506. Steven Krueger argues that examples of racial conversion are relatively rare such that "Jews and Saracens, thought of as both religiously and racially different and as possessing bodies somehow other than Christian bodies, are often depicted as strongly resistant to conversion." "Conversion and Medieval Sexual, Religious, and Racial Categories," in *Constructing Medieval Sexuality*, ed. Karma Lochrie, Peggy McCracken, and James A. Schultz (Minneapolis: University of Minnesota Press, 1997), 165. The Saracen princess complicates this paradigm.

15. Jean Flori has shown the confluence of depictions of "Saracens" in the rhetoric of Old French epic and crusading sermons, where they were imagined as agents of the Antichrist representing the converse of Christian, chivalric, and courtly values. "Mourir pour la croisade," *L'Histoire* 109 (March 1988): 13. His view is based on what Pierre Jonin describes as "une conception du musulman ennemi héréditaire ostiné dans le mal" in "Le Climat de croisade des chansons de geste," *Cahiers de civilisation médiévale* 3 (1964): 288. The west was haunted, Paul Bancourt argues, by a hallucinatory fear of an infidel world composed as a negative mirror image of Christian feudalism. *Les Musulmans dans les chansons de geste du cycle du roi* (Aix-en-Provence: Université de Provence, 1982), 2: 1005. See also Michelle Houdeville, "Une arme étrange dans la *Chanson de Roland*," in *De l'Etranger à l'étrange ou la conjointure de la merveille* (Aix-en-Provence: CUERMA, 1988), 249–52. It is following this same logic that Micheline de Combarieu describes the heroine of the *Prise de Cordes*, Nubie, as a figure who "n'est musulmane que de nom; en fait, elle est déjà toute chrétienne et 'française'; sa condition de sarrasine ne sert qu'à rendre plus éclatante la supériorité des français (chrétiens) sur les sarrasins (musulmans)." "Un personnage épique: La Jeune musulmane," in *Mélanges de langue et de littérature françaises du Moyen Age offerts à Pierre Jonin*, *Sénéfiance* 7 (Aix-en-Provence: CUERMA, 1979): 184.

16. Kay, *The* Chansons de geste, 25–48.

17. In certain instances, the generally lush aura of rich clothing and elegant trappings in courtly tales has been attributed to Celtic or classical antecedents. Such cultural resonances can, however, coexist with simultaneous evocations of the luxurious east in narratives that often record the nexus of many cultural strains. For two examples, see Bernard Guidot, "Pouvoirs et séductions, pouvoir de séduction dans les *lais* de Marie de France," *Romanische Forschungen* 102, 4 (1990): 429; and Micheline de Combarieu, "Les Objets dans les lais de Marie de France," *Marche Romane* 30, 3–4 (1980): 38–39.

18. "S'ot un chapel d'orfrois tot nuef," ed. Lecoy, v. 855.

19. Although the God of Love himself wears a garment sewn from flowers rather than silk (vv. 876–77), it too bears the widest range of colors, complementing the horticultural violet and periwinkle and the black, white and yellow blooms with blue hues of "ynde" and "perse" used typically as dyes for imported cloth (vv. 887–92). Nature's dress in the *Roman de la Rose* contains "maintes colors diverses"

(v. 64), indeed, "one hundred kinds of colors" among which white and "perse" alone are specified (vv. 62–64).

20. More specifically, the two bows used by the God of Love to shoot his amorous golden arrows into unsuspecting lovers do not follow a European model but are made, we are told, "in the Turkish fashion" (vv. 907–9).

21. David Jacoby, "Silk in Western Byzantium Before the Fourth Crusade," in *Trade, Commodities, and Shipping in the Medieval Mediterranean* (Brookfield, Vt.: Variorum, 1997), 461. A. J. Greimas gives "Riche draps d'or ou de soie, généralement rayé," *Dictionnaire de l'ancien français* (Paris: Larousse, 1969).

22. Jacques Le Goff, *La Civilisation de l'occident médiévale* (Paris: Arthaud, 1967), 190.

23. It is even used at times to refer to Roman ruins, according to Greimas, *Dictionnaire de l'ancien français*. Lecoy glosses it as "originaire d'Orient" in his edition.

24. R. Bezzola, *Les Origines et la formation de la littérature courtoise en Occident (500–1200)* (Paris: Champion, 1960), 2: 547, my translation. When this allegorical representation of "generous giving," wearing silk tagged as "porpres sarazinesche," joins hands with her courtly partner—a knight who champions the cause of love at tournaments (vv. 1181–84)—her "lignage Alixandre" bonds physically with the locally esteemed chivalric line of King Arthur:

Largeice la vaillant, la sage,
tint un chevalier dou lignage
le bon roi Artu de Bretaigne;
ce fu cil qui porta l'enseigne
de valor et le gonfanon:
encor est il de tel renon
que l'en conte de li les contes. vv. 1173–79

(Largesse, valiant and wise, took the hand of a knight descended from the good king Arthur of Britain who carried the banner and standard of valor. He is of such renown that they still tell stories of him before both kings and counts.)

25. See Lombard, *Textiles*, 79–104. The dual resonance of Alexander's name recurs indirectly in Guillaume de Lorris's characterization of the very site of courtly lovemaking that Largesse inhabits in the *Roman de la Rose*. The trees growing in Love's garden are said in different manuscript versions to have been imported by the garden's founder, Deduit, from "la terre Alexandrins" and "la terre aus Saradins." Lecoy gives the first reading (v. 590), Langlois the second.

26. Anna Muthesias, *Byzantine Silk Weaving: A.D. 400 to A.D. 1200* (Vienna: Verlag Fassbaender, 1997), 145; Muthesias, "The Impact of the Mediterranean Silk Trade on Western Europe Before 1200 A.D.," in *Textiles in Trade: Proceedings of the Second Biennial Symposium of the Textile Society of America* (Washington, D.C.: Textile Society of America, 1990), 126–35; and her "Byzantine Silk Industry: Lopez and Beyond," *Journal of Medieval History* 19 (1993): 1–67.

27. Muthesias, *Byzantine Silk Weaving*, 145.

28. Jacoby, "Silk," 482–93.

29. Robert Lopez, "The Trade of Medieval Europe: The South," in *The Cambridge Economic History*, ed. M. Postan and E. E. Rich (Cambridge: Cambridge University Press, 1952), 2: 331; Jacoby, "The Migration of Merchants and Craftsmen: A Mediterranean Perspective," in *Trade, Commodities*, 538–46; Elisabeth Crowfoot, Frances Pritchard, and Kay Staniland, *Textiles and Clothing* (London: HMSO, 1992), 130. Italy produced silk cloth from the thirteenth century in Lucca and Bologna, following the introduction of sericulture into Muslim Sicily in the later eleventh or early twelfth century. Previously, Arabs had introduced silk production into Spain, recorded as early as the ninth century in Almería (John Munro, "Silk," in Strayer, *Encyclopedia of the Middle Ages*, 295; Lombard, *Textiles*, 96).

30. Henri Dubois, "Le Commerce et les foires au temps de Philippe Auguste," in *La France de Philippe Auguste: Le Temps des mutations*, ed. Robert-Henri Bautier (Paris: CNRS, 1982), 689–709.

31. By the thirteenth century, commerce was further guaranteed by a system of contracts and legal protection known as *gardes*. Robert-Henri Bautier, *Sur l'Histoire économique de la France médiévale* (Brookfield, Vt.: Varorium, 1991), 145, 116–17.

32. Elizabeth Chapin, *Les Villes des foires de Champagne: Des origines au début du XIVe siècle* (Paris: Champion, 1937), 105.

33. Janet Snyder, "Clothing as Communication: A Study of Clothing and Textiles in Northern French Early Gothic Sculpture" (Ph.D. dissertation, Columbia University, 1996), 506.

34. J. Morize, "Aigues Mortes au 13e siècle," *Annales du Midi* 26 (1914): 342.

35. Lombard, *Textiles*, 94. In the mid-twelfth century Lotharingian merchants are reported to have arrived in London carrying luxury goods that included gold and silver wares, precious stones, and "silk cloth from Constantinople" (Bumke, *Courtly Culture*, 579).

36. Robert S. Lopez, "Silk Industry in the Byzantine Empire," in *Byzantium and the World Around It: Economic and Institutional Relations* (London: Variorum Reprints, 1978), 40.

37. Robert S. Lopez, "Les Influences orientales et l'éveil économique de l'Occident," in *Byzantium and the World Around It*, 608.

38. See also vv. 443–46, 478–79.

39. The distant "lovers" in the *Conte du Graal* similarly come together visually and most tangibly, if still indirectly, by means of a valuable sword composed of precious metal from Arabia and Greece and a gold brocade from Venice: "Li pons de l'espee estoit d'or, / Del meillor d'Arrabe ou de Grisce, / Li fuerres d'orfrois de Venisce. / Si richement appareillie / L'a li sire au vallet [Perceval] baillie" (vv. 3162–66). When the Fisher King confers this sword on Perceval, his attendant explains that Blanchefleur sent it to a special quester (vv. 3144–53). In this instance, the sword itself is "richement pare," like many courtly ladies we have seen.

40. For a discussion of furs in medieval romance generally, see Reginald Abbott, "What Becomes a Legend Most? Fur in Medieval Romance," *Dress* 21 (1994): 4–16.

41. The Greek city of Thessaloniki was the second most important commercial center in the twelfth century, frequented by merchants from the Byzantine Empire, Italy, Spain, and France who traded principally in cloth. Thebes was also a

center of silk production until sacked by the Normans in 1147 (Angeliki E. Laiou, "Trade, Byzantine," in Strayer, *Encyclopedia of the Middle Ages*, 102).

42. The distinction is made by Michel de Certeau in *The Practice of Everyday Life* (Berkeley: University of California Press, 1984), 117, where he opposes an empty street (defined as a "place") to a street full of moving vehicles and people (a "space"). In this view a "place" (*lieu*) is "the order (of whatever kind) in accord with which elements are distributed in relationships of co-existence"; the elements of "place" are situated in a proper and distinct location and imply stability. "A space exists when one takes into consideration vectors of direction, velocities, and time variables. Thus space is composed of intersections of mobile elements. It is in a sense actuated by the ensemble of movements deployed within it."

43. Michelle Szkilnik, *L'Archipel du Graal: Etude de L'Estoire del Saint Graal* (Geneva: Droz, 1991), 15.

44. Hucher, *Le Saint Graal*, 47. Michelle Warren, *History on the Edge: Excalibur and the Borders of Britain, 1100–1300* (Minneapolis: University of Minnesota Press, 2000), 183.

45. John Ganim has shown in another context how medieval distinctions between western and nonwestern were highly uncertain, enabling medieval Europe to be characterized at times as both domestic and foreign. "Native Studies: Orientalism and Medievalism," in *The Postcolonial Middle Ages*, ed. Jeffrey Jerome Cohen (New York: St. Martin's Press, 2000), 125, 131.

46. Glenn Burger, "Cilician Armenian Métissage and Hetoum's *La Fleur des Histoires de la Terre d'Orient*," in Cohen, *The Postcolonial Middle Ages*, 79–80. Cilician Armenia, by contrast, had a diverse population ruled by a native Christian elite not completely Frankicized.

47. Robert Bartlett, *The Making of Europe: Conquest, Colonization and Cultural Change, 950–1350* (Princeton, N.J.: Princeton University Press, 1993), 24–31; and documentary evidence provided by Theodore Evergates, ed. and trans., *Feudal Society in Medieval France: Documents from the County of Champagne* (Philadelphia: University of Pennsylvania Press, 1993), esp. 108–15. See also William McNeill, *Venice: The Hinge of Europe, 1081–1797* (Chicago: University of Chicago Press, 1974), 1–45.

48. M. Chazzaud, "Inventaire et comptes de la succession d'Eudes, comte de Nevers," *Mémoires SNAF* 32 (1871): 190.

49. On the orientalism of medieval scholarship, see, for example, Samir Amin, *Eurocentrism* (New York: Monthly Review Press, 1989), 26–27, 60.

50. Edward Said, *Orientalism* (New York: Random House, 1994), 71–72. For recent commentary on Said's book, see Kathleen Biddick's discussion of orientalism and medievalism, esp. her note 1, "Coming Out of Exile: Dante on the Orient Express," in Cohen, *The Postcolonial Middle Ages*, 35–52; and Kathleen Davis's claim that Said's medieval orientalism remains purely textual, derived from European literary representations "untainted by experiential intercourse with the east," "Time Behind the Veil: The Media, the Middle Ages, and Orientalism Now," in Cohen, *Postcolonial Middle Ages*, 105–22. See also Richard W. Bulliet, "Orientalism and Medieval Islamic Studies," in Van Engen, *Past and Future*. Jane Schneider provides an account of "Orientalism in a wider context" in her edited volume, *Italy's "Southern Question": Orientalism in One Country* (Oxford: Berg, 1998), 4–8.

51. Robert C. J. Young, *Colonial Desire: Hybridity in Theory, Culture, and Race* (New York: Routledge, 1995), 85.

52. The lady's male counterpart similarly bears naturally lovely features prized for their material value when Cligés's seductive visage recalls a "rose novele" (v. 2737) and his hair shimmers like gold (v. 2736).

53. María Rosa Menocal, *The Arabic Role in Medieval Literary History* (Philadelphia: University of Pennsylvania Press, 1987), 40.

54. Evergates, *Feudal Society*, 99–100.

55. An example of a positive valuation of the term foreign is found in Marie de France's *Yonec*, which provides a Celtic and domestic version of the paradigm. Here the wondrous and exotic qualities of the chivalric lover are registered in his foreign homeland, in particular in a city made entirely of silver:

Asez pres ot une cité.
De mur fu close tut entur;
N'i ot meson, sale ne tur
Ki ne parust tute d'argent;
Mut sunt riche li mandement. vv. 360–64

The sumptuous wealth of the heroine's husband, who bears the typical courtly epithet of a "riche hume" (v. 23), cannot compare with the extravagant luxury of the lover's foreign city, although this knight remains more courtly than any other (v. 520).

56. *Tertullian: Disciplinary, Moral and Ascetical Works*, trans. Rudolph Arbesmann et al. (New York: Fathers of the Church, 1959), 125.

57. At the end of the *Queste*, however, the Grail returns to the east, marking the failure of western knights generally to merit it. Michelle Szkilnik documents the complex movement from east to west in the *Estoire* in *L'Archipel du Graal*, 13–34, explaining that whereas the *Queste* paints a more somber picture of chivalric moral failing that necessitates the Grail's eventual return to Sarras and to God, the *Estoire* tips the balance to favor the west (18).

58. Jean Ebersolt, *Constantinople byzantine et les voyageurs du Levant* (London: Pindar Press, 1985), 32–33.

59. Robert de Clari, *La Conquête de Constantinople*, ed. Phillipe Lauer (Paris: Champion, 1924), sec. 81, pp. 80–81, cited in Donald A. Queller and Thomas F. Madden, *The Fourth Crusade: The Conquest of Constantinople*, 2nd ed. (Philadelphia: University of Pennsylvania Press, 1997), 198.

60. Geoffrey de Villehardouin, *La Conquête de Constantinople*, ed. M. Natalis de Wailly (Paris: Firmin-Didot, 1882), 146.

61. The emperor too is "si richement vestu que par noient demandast on home plus richement vestu" (Villehardouin, 106).

62. *Ille et Galeron*, ed. Yves Lefèvre (Paris: Champion, 1988).

63. *The Capture of Constantinople*, ed. and trans. Alfred J. Andrea (Philadelphia: University of Pennsylvania Press, 1997).

64. Jeffrey Jerome Cohen has analyzed other hybrid bodies in the Middle Ages as related to monstrousness, "both alluringly strange and discomfortingly familiar." See his *Of Giants: Sex, Monsters, and the Middle Ages* (Minneapolis: University of

Minnesota Press, 1999) and "Monsters, Hybrids, and Borderlands: The Bodies of Gerald of Wales," in *Postcolonial Middle Ages*, 85–104.

65. Gloria Anzaldúa, *Borderlands/La Frontera: The New Mestiza* (San Francisco: Aunt Lute Books, 1987), 3–5.

66. The issues are outlined cogently by Caren Kaplan in *Questions of Travel: Postmodern Discourses of Displacement* (Durham, N.C.: Duke University Press, 1996), 1–26.

67. Kaplan, *Questions*, 145. These concerns receive detailed treatment in Inderpal Grewal, *Home and Harem: Nation, Gender, Empire, and the Cultures of Travel* (Durham, N.C.: Duke University Press, 1996), 1–20.

Chapter 7. Golden Spurs: Love in the Eastern World of Floire et Blancheflor

1. In a number of Old French texts, the name Babiloine is used to indicate Cairo, presumably because of the Roman fortress called Babylon located on the outskirts of Cairo. Patricia Grieve explains that the eastern emir is located alternately in Alexandria, Cairo, or Babylon (see her Appendix B) but she also indicates that the geography of the French aristocratic version of *Floire et Blancheflor* is often more fanciful than real. *"Floire et Blancheflor" and the European Romance* (Cambridge: Cambridge University Press, 1997), 135, 137. See in this regard William Calin, "Flower Imagery in *Floire et Blancheflor*," *French Studies* 18 (1964): 103–11. Robert Bossuat contrasts the fanciful and imprecise geography of eastern lands in this tale with the very detailed and accurate renderings of geographic settings on the pilgrimage route to Compostela in "*Floire et Blancheflor* et le chemin de Compostelle," *Bolletino del Centro di Studi Filologici et Linguistici Siciliani* 6 (1962): 263–73.

2. This intriguing and complex, if brief, narrative has raised a number of critical issues for readers of French romance. Most notably, Roberta L. Krueger shows how it stages women as storytellers only to displace them significantly from the center of narration in *Women Readers and the Ideology of Gender in Old French Verse Romance* (Cambridge: Cambridge University Press, 1993), 4–11. Stylistic analyses are provided by Matilda T. Bruckner, "Repetition and Variation in Twelfth-Century French Romance," in *The Expansion and Transformation of Courtly Literature*, ed. Nathaniel B. Smith and Joseph T. Snow (Athens: University of Georgia Press, 1980), 95–114 and Peter Haidu, "Narrative Structure in *Floire et Blancheflor*: A Comparison with Two Romances of Chrétien de Troyes," *Romance Notes* 14 (1972–73): 383–86. On religious conversion, see Patricia Grieve. On archetypal imagery, William W. Kibler, "Archetypal Imagery in *Floire et Blancheflor*," *Romance Quarterly* 35 (1988): 11–20. More recently, Matilda Tomaryn Bruckner has demonstrated the extent to which nondisjunctive oppositions are in fact characteristic of many Old French romances in *Shaping Romance: Interpretation, Truth, and Closure in Twelfth-Century French Fictions* (Philadelphia: University of Pennsylvania Press, 1993).

3. See, for example, the discussion of King Mordrain's conversion in the *Estoire del Saint Graal* in Chapter 6.

4. *Le Conte de Floire et Blancheflor*, ed. Jean-Luc Leclanche (Paris: Champion, 1980), whose edition follows ms A (Paris: B.N. fr. 375), one of three mss forming

the "aristocratic version," dated around 1150. For an account of differences between these texts and the thirteenth-century popular versions, see Du Méril's edition, *Floire et Blancheflor: Poèmes du XIIIe siècle* (Paris: P. Jannet, 1856; reprint Nendeln, Liechtenstein: Kraus, 1970); and Roberta L. Krueger, "*Floire et Blancheflor's* Literary Subtext: The *version aristocratique*," *Romance Notes* 24 (1983–84): 65–70. For a detailed description of the numerous European versions of this tale, see Grieve, "*Floire et Blancheflor*," 15–50. On the German version, see T. R. Jackson, "Religion and Love in *Flore et Blanscheflur*," *Oxford German Studies* 4 (1969): 12–25.

5. Maurice Lombard, *Les Textiles dans le monde musulman, 7e–12e siècles*, Etudes d'économie médiévale 3 (Paris: Mouton, 1978), 90, 96.

6. As such, it lacks the A1 function and its further narrative ramifications analyzed by Bruckner in *Narrative Invention and Twelfth-Century Romance: The Convention of Hospitality* (Lexington, Ky.: French Forum, 1980).

7. Although the emir's chamberlain who makes this observation is mistaken—the entwined lovers he views are in fact Blancheflor and Floire—his assertion that two women are bound together by the "greatest love ever" suggests the possibility that courtly love might indeed include both same-sex and heterosexual liaisons.

8. This is the view of at least one critic of the thirteenth-century *Cleomadés*, by Adenet le Roi, and *Meliacin*, by Girart d'Amiens, who shows how both texts are based on a specific antecedent from the *Thousand and One Nights*, the story of the magic horse. See Antoinette Saly, "Les Mille et une Nuits au XIIIe siècle: Conte oriental et matière de Bretagne," *Travaux de littérature* 3 (1990): 18. Gédéon Huet concedes that we have no such equivalent tale for *Floire et Blancheflor*; its Arabic source remains hypothetical. "Encore *Floire et Blancheflor*," *Romania* 35 (1906): 100.

9. Myrrha Lot-Borodine, *Le Roman idyllique au moyen âge* (Paris: A. Picard, 1913).

10. Leclanche indicates that the romance derives from the Arabic tale of Neema and Noam from the *Thousand and One Nights* (12), while containing elements from the *Roman de Thèbes* and *Roman d'Enéas* and *Roman d'Alexandre, Apollonius de Tyr, Le Siège de Troie, Partenopeu de Blois*, and the biblical accounts of Genesis and the Apocalypse (11–12). Others arguing for Arabic origins include Gaston Paris, *Les Contes orientaux dans la littérature française* (Paris: A. Franck, 1875); reprint from *Revue politique et littéraire* 15 (1870): 1010–17; Gédéon Huet, "Sur l'origine de *Floire et Blancheflor*," *Romania* 28 (1899): 348–59, and his "Encore *Floire et Blancheflor*," 95–100; Réné Basset, "Les Sources arabes de *Floire et Blancheflor*," *Revue des traditions populaires* 22 (1907): 241–45, against Joachim Henry Reinhold's argument for the influence of the *romans antiques* in "Quelques remarques sur les sources de *Floire et Blancheflor*," *Revue de philologie française* 19 (1905): 153–75 and Du Méril's earlier insistence on Byzantine sources in his edition. Robert Bossuat makes a case for the *Pilgrim's Guide* as a source in his "*Floire et Blancheflor*." For general background, Lot-Borodine, *Roman idyllique*, 9–74.

11. Caren Kaplan, "'Getting to Know You': Travel, Gender, and the Politics of Representation in *Anna and the King of Siam* and *The King and I*," in *Late Imperial Culture*, ed. Román de la Campa et al. (London: Verso, 1995), 38; Inderpal Grewal,

Home and Harem: Nation, Gender, Empire, and Cultures of Travel (Durham, N.C.: Duke University Press, 1996), 5. On Saracens as generic non-Christians, see Michael Frassetto, "The Image of the Saracen as Heretic in the Sermons of Ademar of Chabannes"; and for a wider range of medieval views on Saracens, Jo Anne Hoeppner Moran Cruz, "Popular Attitudes Toward Islam in Medieval Europe," both in *Western Views of Islam in Medieval and Early Modern Europe: Perception of Other*, ed. David R. Blanks and Michael Frassetto (New York: St. Martin's Press, 1999), 97–117 and 83–96 respectively.

12. Caren Kaplan, *Questions of Travel: Postmodern Discourses of Displacement* (Durham, N.C.: Duke University Press, 1996), 2.

13. Introduction of the Trojan *coupe* creates important intertextual resonances with the Old French *romans d'antiquité*, which, earlier in the twelfth century, had set up and complicated the east-west dichotomy in other ways. Those textual resonances are beyond the scope of this study.

14. Thus is Floire in some sense another Enéas, and his function within the gender hierarchy of Old French romance bears further scrutiny in terms of recent analyses that show how the hero's relation to territory in the *Enéas* reinscribes male homosocial bonds and imagines erotic relations between men, against the grain of the heterosexual love story. See Vincent A. Lankewish, "Assault from Behind: Sodomy, Foreign Invasion, and Masculine Identity in the *Roman d'Enéas*," in *Text and Territory: Geographical Imagination in the European Middle Ages*, ed. Sylvia Tomasch and Sealy Gilles (Philadelphia: University of Pennsylvania Press, 1998), 207–44; and earlier Simon Gaunt, "Gender and Sexuality: From Epic to Romance in the *Roman d'Enéas*," *Romanic Review* 83 (1992): 1–27; and Susan Crane, *Gender and Romance in Chaucer's Canterbury Tales* (Princeton, N.J.: Princeton University Press, 1994).

15. King Felix too has formerly "led away" Blancheflor's pregnant mother into captivity (v. 104).

16. See Chapter 3 above.

17. Lombard, *Textiles*, 99. See note given in Leclanche's translation that the text's reference to "Naples" (v. 121) means Niebla, which in the twelfth century was the capital of a Muslim kingdom.

18. When Floire himself explains that he has come on this eastern journey "to buy and sell," he also invokes the standard courtly descriptor of the distraught lover to indicate his doubled amorous and mercantile quest, stating, "jou sui pensis / de mon marcié" (vv. 1659–60; I'm dreaming/dreamy about my business). The series of "rich bourgeois" who facilitate Floire's journey by providing food, lodging, and advice often comment on his distracted state, noting that Floire eats and sleeps little (vv. 1451–52, 1487). One of his hostesses calls attention to the paradox of this "lovesick merchant," insisting that he is not a merchant but "a nobleman in search of something else": "Par mon cief, n'est pas marceans, / gentix hom est, el va querans" (vv. 1287–88).

19. As Floire's host Daires observes, this merchant selling cloth also has "another kind of business" (travail d'autre marcié) as a quester trafficking in love: "Molt me sanle que çou soit gas / que vos dras vendés a detail; / d'autre marcié avés travail" (vv. 1722–24; I don't believe you're here to sell cloth, but for another kind of business).

20. This Byzantine tale of star-crossed lovers challenges pat assumptions about courtly and uncourtly behaviors by expanding the geographical and cultural parameters of both western and eastern worlds in a number of instances. It is the emir in Babloine who makes the courtly lover Floire into a knight (v. 3120) and that same emir who displays the stereotypically courtly attribute of jealousy in love: "Griement le point la jalousie. / Tex est amors et tex sa teke" (vv. 2644–45; Jealousy attacked him severely; thus is love, and that's its mark). The son of a king in Muslim Spain, Floire is named after a Christian holiday, "Paske Flourie," and linked by birth to the Christian ladylove Blancheflor: both were conceived the same night and born the same day (v. 163). Even the *engin* devised by the wily *portier* to secure Floire's ladylove straddles the divide between courtly and commercial worlds. This money-driven Muslim invents a plan that perfectly suits his courtly/lover lord, whose name Flor rhymes in its generic meaning with *amor* (vv. 2387–88, 2401–2). Drawing on a botanical subterfuge rather than on the gaming and bartering that is his wont, this eastern "lige" enables the pagan merchant Floire to become an actual flower for love, in a bold literalization of courtly metaphor. This flower, imbued with *grant vertu*, we are told, remains distinctly different from all others "in that country," "Tel flor n'a nule en cest païs" (v. 2379). The merchant/lover turned flower dresses accordingly in a "bliaut vermel"—as opposed to the *reubre porprine* he later wears (v. 2869)—to help him blend with the flowers concealing him in a basket carried openly into the emir's palace (vv. 2295–98). As the merchant Floire disappears into a miniature version of the garden of love's delights, the competitive gatekeeper of the emir's harem deploys flowers to promote western-style amorous coupling, at the risk of losing his life.

21. The fountain that springs from a meadow falls into channels made of silver and crystal (vv. 2041–44).

22. On magic put to the service of courtly love in the fabrication of Blancheflor's tomb earlier in the tale where the golden images of two young lovers, Floire and Blancheflor, move together by *ingremance*, hugging and kissing in the perfect embrace (vv. 597–600), see Jocelyn Price, "*Floire et Blancheflor*: Magic and the Mechanics of Love," *Reading Medieval Studies* 8 (1982): 12–33 and Helen Cooper, "Magic That Does Not Work," *Medievalia et Humanistica* n.s. 7 (1976): 131–46.

23. My reading here and following disagrees with Phillip McCaffrey's contention that this tale thoroughly erases cultural difference, making the female, Christian Blancheflor look identical to the male, pagan Floire: "Sexual Identity in *Floire et Blancheflor* and *Ami et Amile*," in *Gender Transgressions: Crossing the Normative Barrier in Old French Literature*, ed. Karen J. Taylor (New York: Garland, 1998), 129–51.

24. Their physical description later in the tale presents Floire with blond hair, a white forehead, delicate brown eyebrows, large eyes, red cheeks, thin thighs, a large chest, ample arms, and white skin (vv. 2848–64); and Blancheflor with blond hair, brown eyebrows, smiling gray eyes, clear skin, well-formed nose and mouth, plump reddish lips, small teeth, white skin, thin thighs and a low waist, and thin white hands with long fingers (vv. 2875–2910).

25. As Patricia Grieve notes, the emir's garden paradise offers an inverted version of the Garden of Eden, since "here, the sexuality associated with the Garden,

the fall of Adam and Eve, leads to conversion" the spiritual redemption "of the lovers, so it is a kind of reversal of the Fall" ("*Floire et Blancheflor*," 136.)

26. "Floires velt fere chevalier. / Des meilleurs conroiz que il ot / li conroia au mielz qu'il pot. / Onques Prians, li rois de Troie, / Ne fu adobez a tel joie" (vv. 2877–81). This segment appears in ms B (B.N. fr. 1447). Margaret Pelan, *Floire et Blancheflor*, 2nd ed. (Paris: Les Belles Lettres, 1956).

27. See Chapter 4 above.

28. The gesture also provides, retrospectively, a kind of literary antidote to royal admonitions against luxury dress that will appear in thirteenth-century sumptuary legislation like Philip the Bold's royal ordinance of 1279, which limits the use of golden spurs to nobles alone: "et ne porteront li borgois dès or en avant ne lorains ne esperons dorez" (From now on, bourgeois will not wear golden bits or spurs). See Chapter 1.

29. The hero of *Erec et Enide*, also sumptuously clad in courtly garments fashioned from luxurious eastern cloth, has golden spurs that complete his noble attire:

Sor un destrier estoit montez,
afublez d'un mantel hermin;
galopant vient tot le chemin;
s'ot cote d'un dïapre noble
qui fu fez an Costantinoble;
chauces de paile avoit chauciees,
molt bien fetes et bien tailliees;
Et fu es estriés afichiez,
uns esperons a or chauciez. vv. 94–102

(He had mounted a charger, dressed in an ermine-trimmed cloak, an elegant tunic of brocaded silk from Constantinople, and silk leggings that were finely formed and cut. As he galloped along the road, he was firmly fixed in the stirrups, wearing gold spurs).

Coda: Marie de Champagne and the Matière of Courtly Love

1. Rita Lejeune, "Role littéraire d'Aliénor d'Aquitaine et de sa famille," *Cultura Neolatina* 14 (1954): 1–57; June Hall McCash, "Marie de Champagne and Eleanor of Aquitaine: A Relationship Reexamined," *Speculum* 54, 4 (1979): 698–711; and her "Marie de Champagne's 'cuer d'ome et cors de fame': Aspects of Feminism and Misogyny in the Twelfth Century," in *The Spirit of the Court*, ed. Glyn S. Burgess and Robert A. Taylor (Cambridge: D.S. Brewer, 1985), 234–45, John F. Benton challenges the close association between Marie de Champagne and Chrétien de Troyes in his "The Court of Champagne as a Literary Center," *Speculum* 36 (1961): 551–91.

2. Chrétien de Troyes, *Le Chevalier de la charrete*, ed. Mario Roques (Paris: Champion, 1970).

3. Gaston Paris, "Lancelot du Lac—II: *Le Conte de la Charrete*," *Romania* 12 (1883): 516–34; William Nitze, "Sens et matière dans les oeuvres de Chrétien de Troyes," *Romania* 44 (1915–17): 14–36; Jean Frappier, "Le Prologue du *Chevalier de la charrete*," *Romania* 93 (1972): 337–77. Some critics have distinguished hypothetically

between "Marie's story" as a tale of *fin'amor* or adulterous passion and Chrétien's contribution in the form of an adventure story, although the prologue itself does not stipulate this division. See Maurice Accarie, "Guenievre et son chevalier de la charrette: L'Orgasme des anges," in *Et c'est la fin pourquoi nous sommes ensemble*, ed. Jean-Claude Aubailly et al. (Paris: Champion, 1993), 1: 45; Tony Hunt, "Chrétien's Prologues Reconsidered," in *Medieval Studies in Honor of Douglas Kelly*, ed. Keith Busby and Norris J. Lacy (Amsterdam: Rodopi, 1994), 161. On the complex relation between structures of patronage and erotic paradigms in troubadour lyric, see Laurie A. Finke, *Feminist Theory, Women's Writing* (Ithaca, N.Y.: Cornell University Press, 1992), 33–57; and on patronage generally, June Hall McCash, ed., *The Cultural Patronage of Medieval Women* (Athens: University of Georgia Press, 1996). Critics who have emphasized the playful cultivation of ambiguous meaning throughout the *Charrete* include Norris J. Lacy, *The Craft of Chrétien de Troyes: An Essay on Narrative Art* (Leiden: E.J. Brill, 1980), 54–60, 88–93; and Matilda T. Bruckner, "An Interpreter's Dilemma: Why Are There So Many Interpretations of Chrétien's *Lancelot*, *Romance Philology* 40, 2 (1986): 159–80. On ambiguity in the prologue in particular, see Bruckner, "*Le Chevalier de la charrete (Lancelot)*," in *The Romances of Chrétien de Troyes: A Symposium*, ed. Douglas Kelly (Lexington, Ky.: French Forum, 1985), 132–81. Wendy Knepper offers a reading of the prologue in terms of competing wills: Marie's versus Chrétien's, in her "Theme and Thesis in the *Chevalier de la charrete*, *Arthuriana* 6, 2 (1996): 54–68.

4. See Roberta L. Krueger on Marie's enigmatic desire and displacement from the tale, in her *Women Readers and the Ideology of Gender in Old French Verse Romance* (Cambridge: Cambridge University Press, 1993), 51–55. Further comments on the crucial relationship between the "author/narrator" of the prologue and his supposed continuator, Godefroi de Leigni, are provided by David F. Hult, "Author/Narrator/Speaker: The Voice of Authority in Chrétien's *Charrete*," in *Discourses of Authority in Medieval and Renaissance Literature*, ed. Kevin Brownlee and Walter Stephens (Hanover, N.H.: University Press of New England, 1989), 76–96; and Simon Gaunt, *Gender and Genre in Medieval French Literature* (Cambridge: Cambridge University Press, 1995), 100–102.

5. See Introduction above.

6. The prologue appears in only three manuscripts. Roques's edition, which I follow here, based on the Guiot manuscript (B.N. fr. 794, C), B.N. fr. 12560 (T), and Escurial, M III. 21 (E). See Jean Rychner, "Le Prologue du *Chevalier de la charrete*," *Vox Romanica* 26, 1 (1967): 1–23. The Guiot manuscript contains "pailes," meaning rich and costly silk cloth; the other two manuscripts give "pelles," meaning pearls. Both readings make sense: "pelles" as a jewel falling at the midpoint of a hierarchical list moving from *jame* (a most precious gem, or diamond) to pearls, and then to the shell-like chalcedony (*sardoine*); and *pailes* as a highly valued commodity and key indicator of courtly opulence and identity, a generic term for the expensive and coveted imported silk used to make courtly clothes, bed quilts, curtains, decorative tents, and wall hangings. The issue of Lancelot's worth, as evaluated by Guenevere, forms an important part of the narrative that follows. See Matilda Tomaryn Bruckner, *Shaping Romance: Interpretation, Truth, and Closure in Twelfth-Century French Fictions* (Philadelphia: University of Pennsylvania Press, 1993), 83, 104.

7. Anthime Fourrier, *Le Courant réaliste dans le roman courtois en France au Moyen-Age* (Paris: A.G. Nizet, 1960), 1: 206–7.

8. See also "tos li avoirs a lui s'adrece / et ele en paist sa grant largece" (vv. 53–54; she directed all her goods to him and she nurtured him with her great generosity).

9. Bruckner, "*Le Chevalier de la charrete*," 138; and *Shaping Romance*, 241 n. 31.

10. For a brief summary of Gaston Paris's reading of "matiere et san" as "le sujet du roman" and its "esprit" and, following him, Foerster, Nitze, Cohen, Roques, and Frappier, see Jean Frappier's rebuttal of Rychner in "Le Prologue," 344. Subsequently see Marie Louise Ollier, "The Author in the Text: The Prologues of Chrétien de Troyes," *Yale French Studies* (1974): 26–41, who reads "matière" as a source that engenders a "sens" with the participation of both author and reader; and Douglas Kelly, who details Chrétien's inherited *matière*, in "La Specialité dans l'invention des topiques," in *L'Archaeologie du signe*, ed. Lucie Brind'Amour and Eugene Vance (Toronto: Pontifical Institute of Mediaeval Studies, 1983), 102–3.

11. See Jean Rychner's reading of "matiere et sens" in terms of "doner san de," meaning "to inspire someone to do something" and "doner matiere de" meaning "donner l'occasion de." Thus does Marie in Rychner's view provide the "occasion" (*le lieu*) and the "inspiration" (*le talent*) to compose a story: "Le Prologue," and "Le Prologue du *Chevalier de la charrete* et l'interprétation du roman," in *Mélanges offerts à Rita Lejeune* (Gembloux: Duculot, 1969), 2: (1969): 1121–35. Tony Hunt follows Rychner, translating the problematic lines as "Chrestien begins his tale of the knight of the cart. The countess inspires him and prompts him to do it, and he puts his mind to it and simply applies his effort and his understanding." "Tradition and Originality in the Prologues of Chrestien de Troyes," *Forum for Modern Language Studies* 8 (1972): 328.

12. As key components of courtly dress, both *pailes* and *pelles* from the "Oriant" are worked (*ovré*) as they become part of costly luxury garments. Pearls sewn onto cloth to embellish it are "ouvree," much as *pailes* are embroidered and worked in gold thread by women.

13. Even Karl Uitti's alternative reading of these lines as "much as the wind that blows in April or May surpasses the morning fog" retains the traditional courtly allusion to springtime: "Autant en emporte *li funs:* Remarques sur le prologue du *Chevalier de la charrete* de Chrétien de Troyes," *Romania* 105 (1984): 270–94.

14. See Chapter 6 above.

15. By the thirteenth century, commerce was further guaranteed by a system of contracts and legal protection known as *gardes*. See Robert-Henri Bautier, *Sur l'histoire économique de la France médiévale* (Brookfield, Vt.: Variorum, 1991), 116–17, 145. Certainly, the celebrated fairs of Champagne provide an important material context for the cryptic allusion to *matière* in the *Charrete*'s prologue. Even the cart used by Chrétien to stage the arduous testing of Lancelot as the "world's best knight" who must humble himself by riding in a vehicle used typically to transport criminals and prisoners holds specific commercial significance in Champagne's history. It was either by cart or pack animals that merchants transported their wares to and from the fairs of Champagne along with traders who moved goods among the four key commercial towns. See Elizabeth Chapin, *Les Villes des foires de*

Champagne: Des Origines au début du XIVe siècle (Paris: Champion, 1937), 106; and Bautier, *Histoire,* 169. The prominence accorded to the cart itself in this love story might then record a significant irruption of the mercantile concerns of Champagne into the literary world of courtly romance.

16. Henri Dubois, "Le Commerce," 696–703.

17. Judith Kellogg has argued more generally that Chrétien's romances contain evidence of marketplace values superimposed on the feudal legacy of *largesse.* See her *Medieval Artistry and Exchange: Economic Institutions, Society, and Literary Form in Old French Narrative* (New York: Peter Lang, 1989). Drawing on Hugh of St. Victor's valorization of commerce as one of the seven mechanical arts, Eugene Vance argues that courtly erotic discourse in Chrétien's romances provides a vernacularization of *grammatica* in a culture where commerce was on the rise. *From Topic to Tale* (Minneapolis: University of Minnesota Press, 1987), 72–77. Peter Haidu argues that material objects in Chrétien's *Yvain* often carry symbolic value far beyond their material worth, thus creating the possibility for ironic distancing and commentary. *Lion Queue-Coupée* (Geneva: Droz, 1972), 23–24. Love itself is often rendered in starkly material terms in the *Charrete,* based on the *don réciproque,* as Charles Méla explains in his edition and translation of *Le Chevalier de la charrete* (Paris: Livre de Poche, "Lettres Gothiques," 1992), 12. Chrétien's own love poems, exemplifying the northern French (*trouvere*) version of the lyric lover's lament, complain repeatedly of serving the ladylove without sufficient payment. Here, the courtly lady emerges as a ruthless entrepreneur who alone derives profit from the lover's attempts to adore, serve, and praise her. See Maria Luisa Meneghetti, "Marie et Leonor, Lancelot et Amadis; Historie et fiction dans la poésie romanesque," in *Lancelot-Lanzelet: Hier et Aujourd'hui,* ed. Danielle Buschinger (Griefswald: Reineke-Verlag, 1995), 277.

18. These equivocal claims have caused some critics to read Chrétien's assertions about Marie's authorship as highly ironic. See J. Janssens, "Le Prologue du *Chevalier de la charrete*: Une Clef pour l'interprétation du roman?" in *Bien dire et bien aprandre: Bulletin du Centre d'études médiévales et dialectales de Lille III* 4 (1986): 29–57; Hunt, "Chrétien's Prologues Reconsidered," 160–65.

Bibliography

Primary Sources

Alain de Lille. *Anticlaudianus*. Ed. Robert Bossuat. Paris: J. Vrin, 1955.
———. *Plaint of Nature*. Ed. and trans. James J. Sheridan. Toronto: Pontifical Institute of Mediaeval Studies, 1980.
Andreas Capellanus. *Andreas Capellanus on Love*. Ed. and trans. P. G. Walsh. London: Duckworth, 1982.
Anthology of the Provençal Troubadours. Ed. R. T. Hill and Thomas Bergin. 2nd ed., rev. 2 vols. New Haven, Conn.: Yale University Press, 1973.
Arnaut Daniel. *Canzoni*. Ed. Gianluigi Toja. Florence: G. C. Sansoni, 1960.
L'Art d'amours (The Art of Love). Trans. Lawrence B. Blonquist. New York: Garland, 1987.
L'Art d'amours: Traduction et commentaire de "l'Ars amatoria" d'Ovide. Ed. Bruno Roy. Leiden: E.J. Brill, 1974.
Aucassin et Nicolette: Chantefable du XIIIe siècle. Ed. Mario Roques. Paris: Champion, 1977.
Bernard of Clairvaux. *Tractatus et opuscula*. Vol. 3 of *Sancti Bernardi Opera*. Ed. Jean Leclercq and H. M. Rochais. Rome: Editiones Cistercienses, 1963.
Bernart de Ventadorn. *Songs*. Ed. Stephen G. Nichols, Jr. Chapel Hill: University of North Carolina Press, 1962.
Béroul. *Le Roman de Tristan*. Ed. Ernest Muret. Paris: Champion, 1962.
———. *The Romance of Tristan*. Ed. and trans. Norris J. Lacy. New York: Garland, 1989.
Bodel, Jean. *La Chanson des Saisnes*. Ed. Annette Brasseur. Geneva: Droz, 1989.
Boileau, Etienne. *Le Livre des métiers et corporations de la ville de Paris, XIIIe siècle*. Paris: Imprimerie Nationale, 1879.
Les Chansons de toile. Ed. Michel Zink. Paris: Champion, 1977.
Chazzaud, M. "Inventaire et comptes de la succession d'Eudes, comte de Nevers." *Mémoires SNAF* 32 (1871): 164–206.
Chrétien de Troyes. *Le Chevalier de la charrete*. Ed. Mario Roques. Paris: Champion, 1970.
———. *The Complete Romances of Chrétien de Troyes*. Trans. David Staines. Bloomington: Indiana University Press, 1990.
———. *Cligés*. Ed. Alexandre Micha. Paris: Champion, 1957.
———. *Erec et Enide*. Ed. Mario Roques. Paris: Champion, 1976.
———. *Le Roman de Perceval ou le conte du Graal*. Ed. William Roach. Paris: Champion, 1959.
———. *Philomena*. Ed. C. De Boer. Paris: Paul Guethner, 1909.

———. *Yvain ou le chevalier au lion*. Ed. Mario Roques. Paris: Champion, 1971.
Le Conte de Floire et Blancheflor. Ed. Jean-Luc Leclanche. Paris: Champion, 1980.
The Death of Arthur. Trans. Norris J. Lacy. In vol. 4 of *Lancelot-Grail: The Old French Arthurian Vulgate and Post-Vulgate in Translation*. New York: Garland, 1995.
Drouart la Vache. *Li Livre d'amours de Drouart la Vache*. Ed. Robert Bossuat. Paris: Champion, 1926.
Eadmer. *Eadmeri Historia Novorum in Anglia, et opuscula duo de vita Sancti Anselmi et quibusdam miraculis ejus*. Ed. Martin Rule. London: Longman, 1884.
L'Estoire del Saint Graal. Ed. Jean-Paul Ponceau. 2 vols. Paris: Champion, 1997.
Floire et Blancheflor. Ed. Margaret Pelan. Paris: Les Belles Lettres, 1937; 2nd ed., 1956.
Floire et Blancheflor, poème du XIIIe siècle. Ed. Edélestand du Méril. Paris: P. Jannet, 1856. Reprint Nendehn, Liechtenstein: Kraus, 1967.
Gautier d'Arras. *Ille et Galeron*. Ed. Yves Lefèvre. Paris: Champion, 1988.
Giraut de Borneil. *The Cansos and Sirventes of the Troubadour Giraut de Borneil: A Critical Edition*. Ed. Ruth Verity Sharman. Cambridge: Cambridge University Press, 1989.
Greimas, A. J. *Dictionnaire de l'ancien français*. Paris: Larousse, 1969.
Guillaume de Lorris and Jean de Meun. *Le Roman de la Rose*. Ed. Félix Lecoy. 3 vols. Paris: Champion, 1965–66, 1970.
———. *Le Roman de la Rose*. Ed. and trans. Armand Strubel. Paris: Librairie Générale Française, 1992.
———. *The Romance of the Rose*. Trans. Charles Dahlberg. 3rd ed. Princeton, N.J.: Princeton University Press, 1995.
Gunther of Pairis. *The Capture of Constantinople: The "Hystoria Constantinopolitana" of Gunther of Pairis*. Ed. and trans. Alfred J. Andrea. Philadelphia: University of Pennsylvania Press, 1997.
Heldris de Cornuäille. *Le Roman de Silence*. Ed. Lewis Thorpe. Cambridge: Heffer, 1972.
The History of the Holy Grail. Trans. Carol Chase. In vol. 1 of *Lancelot-Grail: The Old French Arthurian Vulgate and Post-Vulgate in Translation*. Ed. Norris J. Lacy. New York: Garland, 1993.
Innocent III, Pope (Lotario dei Segni). *De Miseria condicionis humane*. Ed. Robert E. Lewis. Athens: University of Georgia Press, 1978.
———. "On the Misery of Man." In *Two Views of Man: Pope Innocent III, On the Misery of Man; Giannozzo Manetti, On the Dignity of Man*. Trans. Bernard Murchland. New York: Ungar, 1966.
Jacques de Vitry. *The Exempla, or Illustrative Stories from the Sermones Vulgares of Jacques de Vitry*. Ed. Thomas Frederick Crane. London: D. Nutt, 1890. Reprint New York: Burt Franklin, 1971.
Jean de Joinville. *La Vie de Saint Louis*. Ed. Jacques Monfrin. Paris: Classiques Garnier, 1995.
Le Lai d'Aristote d'Henri d'Andeli publié d'après tous les manuscrits. Ed. Maurice Delbouille. Paris: Les Belles Lettres, 1951.
Lancelot: Roman en prose du XIIIe siècle. 9 vols. Ed. Alexandre Micha. Geneva: Droz, 1978–83.

Maloux, Maurice. *Dictionnaire des proverbes, sentences, et maximes.* Paris: Larousse, 1980.
Marie de France. *Les Lais de Marie de France.* Ed. Jean Rychner. Paris: Champion, 1973.
———. *The Lais of Marie de France.* Trans. Glyn Burgess and Keith Busby. London: Penguin, 1986.
Le Ménagier de Paris. Ed. George E. Brereton and Janet M. Ferrier. Oxford: Clarendon Press, 1981.
La Mort le roi Artu. Ed. Jean Frappier. Paris: Champion, 1964.
Orderic Vitalis. *Ecclesiastical History of Orderic Vitalis.* Ed. and trans. Marjorie Chibnall. 6 vols. Oxford: Clarendon Press, 1973.
Ordonnance somptuaire inédite de Philippe le Hardi. Ed. H. Duplès-Agier. Paris: J. B. Du Moulin, 1853.
Ordonnances des rois de France de la troisième race. Vol. 1. Ed. M. De Laurière. Paris: Imprimerie Royale, 1723.
La Prise d'Orange: Chanson de geste de la fin du XIIe siècle. Ed. Claude Régnier. Paris: Klincksieck, 1977.
La Queste del Saint Graal. Ed. Albert Pauphilet. Paris: Champion, 1980.
Renart, Jean. *Galeran de Bretagne.* Ed. Lucien Foulet. Paris: Champion, 1925.
———. *Le Lai de l'ombre.* Ed. Joseph Bédier. Paris: Firmin-Didot, 1913.
———. *Le Roman de la Rose ou de Guillaume de Dole.* Ed. Félix Lecoy. Paris: Champion, 1962.
Robert de Blois's Floris et Liriopé. Ed. Paul Barrette. Berkeley: University of California Press, 1968.
Robert de Clari. *La Conquête de Constantinople.* Ed. Philippe Lauer. Paris: Champion, 1924.
Romance of the Rose, or Guillaume de Dole. Trans. Patricia Terry and Nancy Vine Durling. Philadelphia: University of Pennsylvania Press, 1993.
Le Roman de la violette ou de Gerard de Nevers par Gerbert de Montreuil. Ed. Douglas Labaree Buffum. Paris: Champion, 1928.
Le Roman des eles by Raoul Hodenc and l'Ordene de chevalerie. Ed. Keith Busby. Amsterdam: John Benjamins, 1983.
Le Saint Graal. Ed. Eugene Hucher. Le Mans: Monnoyer, 1875.
Songs of the Women Troubadours. Ed. and trans. Matilda Tomaryn Bruckner, Laurie Shepard, and Sarah White. New York: Garland, 1995.
Tertullian. "The Apparel of Women." In *Disciplinary, Moral, and Ascetical Works.* Trans. Rudolph Arbesmann, Sister Emily Joseph Daly, and Edwin A. Quain. New York: Fathers of the Church, 1959.
———. *L'Eleganza delle donne.* Florence: Nardini Editore, 1986.
Three Medieval Views of Women. Trans. and ed. Gloria K. Fiero, Wendy Pfeffer, and Mathé Allain. New Haven, Conn.: Yale University Press, 1989.
Tibaut. *Le Roman de la poire.* Ed. Christiane Marcello-Nizia. Paris: SATF, 1985.
Villehardouin, Geoffroi de. *La Conquête de Constantinople.* Ed. M. Natalis de Wailly. Paris: Firmin-Didot, 1882.
William of Malmesbury. *Historia novellae* I, 4. PL 179, c. 1396–97.

Secondary Sources

Abbott, Reginald. "What Becomes a Legend Most? Fur in the Medieval Romance." *Dress* 21 (1994): 4–16.

Accarie, Maurice. "Courtoisie et amour courtois dans le *Guillaume de Dole.*" *Razo* 3 (1982): 7–16.

———. "Guenievre et son chevalier de la charrette: L'Orgasme des anges." In *Et c'est la fin pourquoi nous sommes ensemble*, vol. 1, ed. Jean-Claude Aubailly et al. Paris: Champion, 1993.

Allen, Peter. "The Ambiguity of Silence." In *Sign, Sentence, Discourse: Language and Medieval Thought in Literature*, ed. Julian N. Wasserman and Lois Roney. Syracuse, N.Y.: Syracuse University Press, 1989. 98–112.

———. *The Art of Love: Amatory Fiction from Ovid to the Romance of the Rose*. Philadelphia: University of Pennsylvania Press, 1992.

Alvar, Carlos. "Oiseuse, Venus, Luxure: Trois dames et un miroir." *Romania* 106 (1985): 108–17.

Amer, Sahar. *Esopé au féminin: Marie de France et la politique de l'interculturalité*. Atlanta: Rodopi 1999.

———. "Lesbian Sex and the Military: From the Arabic Tradition to French Literature." In *Same-Sex Desire Among Women*, ed. Francesca Sautman and Pamela Sheingorn. New York: Palgrave, 2001. 180–98.

Amin, Samir. *Eurocentrism*. New York: Monthly Review Press, 1989.

Anzaldúa, Gloria. *Borderlands/La Frontera: The New Mestiza*. San Francisco: Aunt Lute Books, 1987.

Ascher, Carol. "Narcissism and Women's Clothing." *Socialist Review* 11, 3 (1981): 75–86.

Ashley, Kathleen and Robert L. A. Clark, eds. *Medieval Conduct*. Minneapolis: University of Minnesota Press, 2001.

Baldwin, John. *Aristocratic Life in Medieval France: The Romances of Jean Renart and Gerbert de Montreuil*. Baltimore: Johns Hopkins University Press, 2000.

Bancourt, Paul. *Les Musulmans dans les chansons de geste du cycle du roi*. Vol. 2. Aix-en-Provence: Université de Provence, 1982.

Barthes, Roland. *The Fashion System*. Trans. Matthew Ward and Donald Howard. New York: Hill and Wang, 1983.

Bartlett, Robert. *The Making of Europe: Conquest, Colonization, and Cultural Change, 950–1350*. Princeton, N.J.: Princeton University Press, 1993.

Baudrillart, H. *Histoire du luxe privé et public: le moyen âge et la renaissance depuis l'antiquité jusqu'à nos jours*. Vols. 3, 4. Paris: Hachette, 1880, 1881.

Bautier, Robert-Henri. *Sur l'histoire économique de la France médiévale*. Brookfield, Vt.: Variorum, 1991.

Beaulieu, Michel. "Le Costume: Miroir des mentalités de la France (1350–1500)." In *Le Vêtement*, ed. Pastoureau. 255–76.

Bec, Pierre. *La Lyrique française au Moyen Age (XIIe–XIIIe siècles)*. Vol. 1, *Etudes*. Poitiers: Picard, 1977.

———. "Trobairitz et *chansons de femme*: Contribution à la connaissance du lyrisme féminin au Moyen Age." *Cahiers de civilisation médiévale* 22, 3 (1979): 235–62.

Bedos-Rezak, Brigitte. "Medieval Women in French Sigillographic Sources." In *Medieval Women and the Sources of Medieval History*, ed. Joel T. Rosenthal. Athens: University of Georgia Press, 1990. 152–74.

———. "The Social Implications of the Art of Chivalry: The Sigillographic Evidence (France: 1050–1250)." In *Form and Other in Medieval France: Studies in Social and Quantitative Sigillography*. Brookfield, Vt.: Ashgate, 1993.

Bennett, Judith M. "'Lesbian-like' and the Social History of Medieval Lesbianisms." *Journal of the History of Sexuality* 9 (2000): 1–24.

Benton, John F. "Clio and Venus: An Historical View of Medieval Love." In *The Meaning of Courtly Love*, ed. F. X. Newman.

———. "The Court of Champagne as a Literary Center." *Speculum* 36 (1961): 551–91.

Bezzola, Reto R. *Les Origines et la formation de la littérature courtoise en Occident (500–1200)*. 3 vols. Paris: Champion, 1944–63.

Biddick, Kathleen. "Coming Out of Exile: Dante on the Orient Express." In *The Postcolonial Middle Ages*, ed. Cohen. 35–52.

Blamires, Alcuin. *The Case for Women in Medieval Culture*. Oxford: Clarendon Press, 1997.

———. *Women Defamed and Defended: An Anthology of Edited Texts*. Oxford: Clarendon Press, 1992.

Blanc, Odile. "Vêtement féminin, vêtement masculin à la fin du Moyen Age." In *Le Vêtement*, 243–51.

Blanks, David R. and Michael Frassetto, eds. *Western Views of Islam in Medieval and Early Modern Europe: Perception of Other*. New York: St. Martin's Press, 1999.

Bloch, Marc. *Feudal Society*. Vol. 1, *The Growth of Ties of Dependence*. Trans. L. A. Manyon. Chicago: University of Chicago Press, 1970.

Bloch, R. Howard. *Medieval Misogyny and the Invention of Western Romantic Love*. Chicago: University of Chicago Press, 1991.

Bloch, R. Howard and Stephen G. Nichols, Jr., eds. *Medievalism and the Modernist Temper*. Baltimore: Johns Hopkins University Press, 1996.

Boase, Roger. *The Origin and Meaning of Courtly Love: A Critical Study of European Scholarship*. Manchester: Manchester University Press, 1977.

Bond, Gerald A. *The Loving Subject: Desire, Eloquence, and Power in Romanesque France*. Philadelphia: University of Pennsylvania Press, 1995.

Bossuat, Robert. "*Floire et Blancheflor* et le chemin de Compostelle." *Bolletino del Centro di Studi Filologici et Linguistici Siciliani* 6 (1962): 263–73.

Boulton, Maureen. *The Song in the Story: Lyric Insertions in French Narrative Fiction, 1200–1400*. Philadelphia: University of Pennsylvania Press, 1993.

Bourgain, Pascale. "Alienor d'Aquitaine et Marie de Champagne mises en cause par André le Chapelain." *Cahiers de civilisation médiévale* 29 (1986): 29–36.

Boyd, David Lorenzo. "Sodomy, Misogyny, and Displacements: Occluding Queer Desire in *Sir Gawain and the Green Knight*." *Arthuriana* 8, 2 (1998): 77–113.

Brand, Charles M. *Byzantium Confronts the West, 1180–1204*. Cambridge, Mass.: Harvard University Press, 1968.

Brown, Katharine Reynolds. "Gems and Jewelry." In *Encyclopedia of the Middle Ages*, ed. Joseph Strayer. New York: Scribner, 1982–1989.

Brownlee, Kevin. "Discourses of the Self: Christine de Pizan and the *Romance of the*

Rose." In *Rethinking the Romance of the Rose: Text, Image, Reception*, ed. Kevin Brownlee and Sylvia Huot. Philadelphia: University of Pennsylvania Press, 1992.

———. "Transformations of the *Charrete*: Godefroi de Leigni Rewrites Chrétien de Troyes." *Stanford French Review* 14, 1–2 (1990): 161–78.

Bruckner, Matilda Tomaryn. "Debatable Fictions: The *Tensos* of the Trobairitz." In *Literary Aspects of Courtly Culture: Selected Papers from the Seventh Triennial Congress of the International Courtly Literature Society*, ed. Donald Maddox and Sara Sturm-Maddox. Cambridge: D.S. Brewer, 1994. 19–28.

———. "Fictions of the Female Voice: The Women Troubadours." *Speculum* 67, 4 (1992): 865–91.

———. "An Interpreter's Dilemma: Why Are There So Many Interpretations of Chrétien's *Lancelot*?" *Romance Philology* 40, 2 (1986): 159–80.

———. "Na Castelloza, *Trobairitz*, and Troubadour Lyric." *Romance Notes* 25, 3 (1985): 239–53.

———. *Narrative Invention in Twelfth-Century French Romance*. Lexington, Ky.: French Forum, 1980.

———. "Repetition and Variation in Twelfth-Century French Romance." In *The Expansion and Transformation of Courtly Literature*, ed. Nathaniel B. Smith and Joseph T. Snow. Athens: University of Georgia Press, 1980.

———. "Rewriting Chrétien's *Conte du Graal*—Mothers and Sons, Questions, Contradictions, Connections." In *The Medieval Opus: Imagination, Rewriting and Transmission in the French Tradition*, ed. Douglas Kelly. Amsterdam: Rodopi, 1996.

———. "Romancing History and Rewriting the Game of Fiction: Jean Renart's *Rose* Through the Looking Glass of *Partenopeu de Blois*." In *The World and Its Rival: Essays on Literary Imagination in Honor of Per Nykrog*, ed. Kathryn Karczewska and Tom Conley. Amsterdam: Rodopi, 1999. 93–117.

———. *Shaping Romance: Interpretation, Truth, and Closure in Twelfth-Century French Fictions*. Philadelphia: University of Pennsylvania Press, 1993.

Brundage, James. *Law, Sex, and Christian Society in Medieval Europe*. Chicago: University of Chicago Press, 1987.

———. "Sumptuary Laws and Prostitution in Late Medieval Italy." *Journal of Medieval History* 13 (1987): 343–55.

Brydon, Anne. "Sensible Shoes." In *Consuming Fashion: Adorning the Transnational Body*, ed. Anne Brydon and Sandra Niessen. Oxford: Berg, 1998. 1–22.

Bulliet, Richard W. "Orientalism and Medieval Islamic Studies." In *The Past and Future of Medieval Studies*, ed. John Van Engen. Notre Dame, Ind.: University of Notre Dame Press, 1994. 94–104.

Bullough, Vern L. and James A. Brundage, eds. *Handbook of Medieval Sexuality*. New York: Garland, 1996.

Bumke, Joachim. *Courtly Culture: Literature and Society in the High Middle Ages*. Trans. Thomas Dunlap. Berkeley: University of California Press, 1991.

Burger, Glenn. "Cilician Armenian Métissage and Hetoum's *La Fleur des histoires de la terre d'orient*." In *The Postcolonial Middle Ages*, ed. Cohen.

Burger, Glenn and Steven F. Krueger, eds. *Queering the Middle Ages*. Minneapolis: University of Minnesota Press, 2001.

Burgess, Glyn S. "Chivalry and Prowess in the *Lais* of Marie de France." *French Studies* 37, 2 (1983): 129–42.
Burgwinkle, William E. *Love for Sale: Materialist Readings of the Troubadour Razo Corpus*. New York: Garland, 1997.
Burns, E. Jane. *Bodytalk: When Women Speak in Old French Literature*. Philadelphia: University of Pennsylvania Press, 1993.
———. "Knowing Women: Female Orifices in Old French Farce and Fabliau." *Exemplaria* 4, 1 (Spring 1992): 81–104.
———. "Courtly Love: Who Needs It? Recent Feminist Work in the Medieval French Tradition." *Signs* 27, 1 (2001): 23–57.
———. "Ladies Don't Wear *Braies*: Underwear and Outerwear in the French *Prose Lancelot*." In *The Lancelot-Grail Cycle: Texts and Transformations*, ed. William W. Kibler. Austin: University of Texas Press, 1994. 152–74.
———. "The Man Behind the Lady in Troubadour Lyric." *Romance Notes* 25, 3 (1985): 254–70.
———. "Refashioning Courtly Love: Lancelot as Lady's Man or Ladyman?" In *Constructing Medieval Sexuality*, ed. Lochrie et al. 111–34.
———. "Which Queen? Guenivere's Transvestism in the French *Prose Lancelot*." In *Lancelot and Guenivere: A Casebook*, ed. Lori J. Walters. New York: Garland, 1996. 247–65.
Burns, E. Jane, and Roberta L. Krueger. Introduction to "Courtly Ideology and Woman's Place in Medieval French Literature." *Romance Notes* 25, 3 (1985): 205–19.
Burns, E. Jane, Sarah Kay, Roberta Krueger, and Helen Solterer. "Feminism and the Discipline of Old French Studies: *Une Bele Disjointure*." In *Medievalism and the Modernist Temper*, ed. Bloch and Nichols. 225–66.
Busby, Keith. "'Plus acesmez qu'une popine': Male Cross-Dressing in Medieval French Narrative." In *Gender Transgressions*, ed. Taylor. 45–59.
Butler, Judith. *Bodies That Matter: On the Discursive Limits of "Sex"*. New York: Routledge, 1993.
———. *Gender Trouble: Feminism and the Subversion of Identity*. New York: Routledge, 1990.
Cadden, Joan. *Meanings of Sexual Difference in the Middle Ages: Medicine, Science, and Culture*. Cambridge: Cambridge University Press, 1993.
Calin, William. "Flower Imagery in *Floire et Blancheflor*." *French Studies* 18 (1964): 103–11.
Casagrande, Carla. "The Protected Woman." In *A History of Women in the West*, vol. 2, *Silences of the Middle Ages*, ed. Christiane Klapisch-Zuber. Cambridge, Mass.: Belknap Press of Harvard University Press, 1992.
Certeau, Michel de. *The Practice of Everyday Life*. Trans. Steven F. Rendall. Berkeley: University of California Press, 1984.
Chambers, Frank M. "Las Trobairitz soisebudas." In *The Voice of the Trobairitz*, ed. Paden. 45–60.
Chapin, Elizabeth. *Les Villes des foires de Champagne: Des Origines au début du XIVe siècle*. Paris: Champion, 1937.
Ciggaar, Krijnie. "Encore une fois Chrétien de Troyes et la 'matière byzantine': La

Révolution des femmes au palais de Constantinople." *Cahiers de civilisation médiévale* 38 (1995): 267-74.
Cixous, Hélène. *Coming to Writing and Other Essays*. Trans. Deborah Jenson. Cambridge, Mass. : Harvard University Press, 1991.
Clover, Carol. "Regardless of Sex: Men, Women, and Power in Early Northern Europe." *Speculum* 68, 2 (1993): 363-87.
Cohen, Jeffrey Jerome. *Of Giants: Sex, Monsters, and the Middle Ages*. Minneapolis: University of Minnesota Press, 1999.
―――. "Monsters, Hybrids, and Borderlands: The Bodies of Gerald of Wales." In *The Postcolonial Middle Ages*, ed. Cohen.
―――, ed. *The Postcolonial Middle Ages*. New York: St. Martin's Press, 2000.
Colby, Alice. *The Portrait in Twelfth-Century French Literature*. Geneva: Droz, 1965.
Colish, Marcia. "Cosmetic Theology: The Transformation of a Stoic Theme." *Assays* 1 (1981): 3-14.
―――. *The Stoic Tradition from Antiquity to the Early Middle Ages*. Vol. 2, *Stoicism in Christian Latin Thought*. Leiden: E.J. Brill, 1985.
Combarieu, Micheline de. "Les Objets dans les lais de Marie de France." *Marche Romane* 30, 3-4 (1980): 38-39.
―――. "Un personage épique: La Jeune musulmane." In *Mélanges de langue et de littérature françaises du Moyen Age offerts à Pierre Jonin*. Sénéfiance 7. Aix-en-Provence: CUERMA, 1979.
Coolput, C. van. "La Poupée d'Evalach." In *Continuations: Essays in Medieval French Literature and Language*, ed. Norris J. Lacy and Gloria Torrini-Roblin. Birmingham, Ala.: Summa, 1989.
Cooper, Helen. "Magic That Does Not Work." *Medievalia et Humanistica* n.s. 7 (1976): 131-46.
Corrigan, Peter. "Interpreted, Circulating, Interpreting: The Three Dimensions of the Clothing Object." In *The Socialness of Things: Essays on the Socio-Semiotics of Objects*, ed. Stephen Harold Riggins. Berlin: Mouton de Gruyter, 1994.
Crane, Susan. "Clothing and Gender Definition in Joan of Arc." *Journal of Medieval and Early Modern Studies* 26, 2 (Spring 1996): 297-320.
―――. *Gender and Romance in Chaucer's Canterbury Tales*. Princeton, N.J.: Princeton University Press, 1994.
―――. *The Performance of Self: Ritual, Clothing, and Identity During the Hundred Years War*. Philadelphia: University of Pennsylvania Press, 2002.
Crowfoot, Elisabeth, Frances Pritchard, and Kay Staniland. *Textiles and Clothing*. London: HMSO, 1992.
Crozet, R. "Sur un détail vestimentaire féminin du XIIe siècle." *Cahiers de civilisation médiévale* 4 (1961): 55-56.
Cruz, Jo Ann Hoeppner Moran. "Popular Attitudes Toward Islam in Medieval Europe." In *Western Views of Islam*, ed. Blanks and Frasetto. 55-82.
Cunnington, C. Willett and Phyllis Cunnington. *The History of Underclothes*. London: Faber and Faber, 1981.
Davis, Fred. *Fashion, Culture, and Identity*. Chicago: University of Chicago Press, 1992.
Davis, Kathleen. "Time Behind the Veil: The Media, the Middle Ages and Orientalism Now." In *The Postcolonial Middle Ages*, ed. Cohen. 105-22.

Demay, Germain. *Le Costume au Moyen Age d'après les sceaux*. Paris: Librairie de D. Dumoulin, 1880.
Denomy, Alexander. "Concerning the Accessibility of Arabic Influences to the Earliest Provençal Troubadours. *Mediaeval Studies* 15 (1953): 147–58.
———. *The Heresy of Courtly Love*. New York: Macmillan, 1947.
Desmond, Marilyn and Pamela Sheingorn. "Queering Ovidian Myth: Bestiality and Desire in Christine de Pizan's *Epistre Othea*. In *Queering the Middle Ages*, ed. Burger and Krueger. 3–27.
Dragonetti, Roger. *Le Mirage des sources: L'Art du faux dans le roman médiéval*. Paris: Seuil, 1987.
Dubois, Henri. "Le Commerce et les foires au temps de Philippe Auguste." In *La France de Philippe Auguste: Le Temps des mutations*, ed. Robert-Henri Bautier. Paris: CNRS, 1982. 689–709.
Duby, Georges. *Le Mâle Moyen Age*. Paris: Flammarion, 1988.
———. *Medieval Marriage: Two Models from Twelfth-Century France*. Trans. Elborg Forster. Baltimore: Johns Hopkins University Press, 1978.
———. "The Transformation of the Aristocracy: France at the Beginning of the Thirteenth Century." In *The Chivalrous Society*, trans. Cynthia Postan. Berkeley: University of California Press, 1977.
Durling, Nancy Vine, ed. *Jean Renart and the Art of Romance*. Gainesville: University Press of Florida, 1997.
Ebersolt, Jean. *Constantinople byzantine et les voyageurs du Levant*. London: Pindar Press, 1986.
Economou, George. *The Goddess Natura in Medieval Literature*. Cambridge, Mass.: Harvard University Press, 1972.
———. "The Two Venuses and Courtly Love." In *In Pursuit of Perfection: Courtly Love in Medieval Literature*, ed. Joan M. Ferrante and George Economou. Port Washington, N.Y.: Kennikat Press, 1975. 29–35.
Elliott, Dyan. "Dress as Mediator Between Inner and Outer Self: The Pious Matron of the High and Later Middle Ages." *Mediaeval Studies* 53 (1991): 279–308.
———. *Fallen Bodies: Pollution, Sexuality, and Demonology in the Middle Ages*. Philadelphia: University of Pennsylvania Press, 1999.
Evans, Joan. *Dress in Medieval France*. Oxford: Clarendon Press, 1952.
Evergates, Theodore, ed. *Aristocratic Women in Medieval France*. Philadelphia: University of Pennsylvania Press, 1999.
———. "The Feudal Imaginary of Georges Duby." *Journal of Medieval and Early Modern Studies* 27, 3 (1997): 641–60.
———, ed. and trans. *Feudal Society in Medieval France: Documents from the County of Champagne*. Philadelphia: University of Pennsylvania Press, 1993.
———. *Feudal Society in the Bailliage of Troyes Under the Counts of Champagne, 1152–1284*. Baltimore: Johns Hopkins University Press, 1975.
———. "Louis VII and the Counts of Champagne." In *The Second Crusade and the Cistercians*, ed. Michael Gervers. New York: St. Martin's Press, 1992. 109–17.
———. "Nobles and Knights in Twelfth-Century France." In *Cultures of Power: Lordship, Status, and Process in Twelfth-Century Europe*, ed. Thomas N. Bisson. Philadelphia: University of Pennsylvania Press, 1995. 11–35.

Ewing, Elizabeth. *Dress and Undress: A History of Women's Underwear.* New York: Drama Book Specialists, 1978.
Faral, Edmond. "Les Chansons de toile ou chansons d'histoire." *Romania* 69 (1946–47): 433–62.
———. "*Le Roman de la Rose* et la pensée française du XIIIe siècle." *Revue des deux mondes* 35 (1926): 433–62.
Favier, Jean. *De l'Or et des épices: Naissance de l'homme d'affaires au moyen âge.* Paris: Fayard, 1987.
Fenster, Thelma, ed. *Arthurian Women: A Casebook.* New York: Garland, 1995.
Ferrante, Joan M. "The Conflict of Lyric Conventions and Romance Form." In *In Pursuit of Perfection: Courtly Love and Medieval Literature,* ed. Joan M. Ferrante and George Economou. Port Washington, N.Y.: Kennikat Press, 1975. 135–78.
———. "Male Fantasy and Female Reality in Courtly Literature." *Women's Studies* 11 (1984): 67–97.
———. *Woman as Image in Medieval Literature: From the Twelfth Century to Dante.* New York: Columbia University Press, 1975.
Finke, Laurie A. *Feminist Theory, Women's Writing.* Ithaca, N.Y.: Cornell University Press, 1992.
———. "Sexuality in Medieval French Literature: Separés, on est ensemble." In *Handbook of Medieval Sexuality,* ed. Bullough and Brundage. 345–68.
Fisher, Sheila and Janet E. Halley. "The Lady Vanishes: The Problem of Women's Absence in Late Medieval and Renaissance Texts." In *Seeking the Woman in Late Medieval and Renaissance Writing: Essays in Feminist Contextual Criticism,* ed. Sheila Fisher and Janet E. Halley. Knoxville: University of Tennessee Press, 1989.
Flori, Jean. "La Chevalerie chez Jean de Salisbury." *Revue d'histoire ecclésiastique* 77, 1–2 (1982): 35–77.
———. "Mourir pour la croisade." *L'Histoire* 109 (March 1988): 8–19.
———. "Seigneurie, noblesse, et chevalerie dans les *lais* de Marie de France." *Romania* 108, 2–3 (1987): 183–206.
Fourrier, Anthime. *Le Courant réaliste dans le roman courtois en France au Moyen Age.* Paris: A.G. Nizet, 1960.
Fradenburg, Louise and Carla Freccero, eds. *Premodern Sexualities.* New York: Routledge, 1996.
Frappier, Jean. *Amour courtois et table ronde.* Geneva: Droz, 1973.
———. "La Peinture de la vie et des héros antiques dans la littérature française du XIIe et du XIIIe siècle." In *Histoire, mythes, et symboles: Etudes de littérature française.* Geneva: Droz, 1976. 21–54.
———. "Le Prologue du *Chevalier de la charrette.*" *Romania* 93 (1972): 337–77.
———. "Vues sur les conceptions courtoises dans les littératures d'oc et d'oil au XIIe siècle." *Cahiers de civilisation médiévale* 2 (1959): 15–56.
Frassetto, Michael. "The Image of the Saracen as Heretic in the Sermons of Ademar of Chabannes." In *Western Views of Islam,* ed. Blanks and Frassetto. 83–96.
Gaines, Jane and Charlotte Herzog, eds. *Fabrications: Costume and the Female Body.* New York: Routledge, 1990.

Ganim, John. "Native Studies: Orientalism and Medievalism." In *The Postcolonial Middle Ages*, ed. Cohen. 123–34.
Garber, Marjorie. *Vested Interests: Cross-Dressing and Cultural Anxiety*. New York: Routledge, 1992.
Gaunt, Simon. "Bel Acueil and the Improper Allegory of the *Romance of the Rose*." In *New Medieval Literatures*, vol. 2, ed. Rita Copeland, David Lawton, and Wendy Scase. Oxford: Clarendon Press, 1998. 65–93.
———. *Gender and Genre in Medieval French Literature*. Cambridge: Cambridge University Press, 1995.
———. "Gender and Sexuality: From Epic to Romance in the *Roman d'Enéas*." *Romanic Review* 83 (1992): 1–27.
———. "Marginal Men, Marcabru, and Orthodoxy: The Early Troubadours and Adultery." *Medium Aevum* 59 (1990): 55–72.
———. "The Significance of Silence." *Paragraph* 13, 2 (1990): 202–16.
———. "Straight Minds/'Queer' Wishes in Old French Hagiography: La Vie de Sainte Euphrosine." *Gay and Lesbian Quarterly* 1, 4 (1995): 439–57.
———. *Troubadours and Irony*. Cambridge: Cambridge University Press, 1989.
Giddens, Anthony. *The Constitution of Society*. Cambridge: Polity Press, 1984.
———. *The Transformation of Intimacy: Sexuality, Love, and Eroticism in Modern Societies*. Cambridge: Polity Press, 1994.
Gilchrist, Roberta. *Gender and Material Culture: The Archaeology of Religious Women*. London: Routledge, 1994.
Giraudias, Etienne. *Etude historique sur les lois somptuaires*. Poitiers: Société française d'imprimerie et de librairie, 1910.
Goddard, Eunice Rathbone. *Women's Costume in French Texts of the Eleventh and Twelfth Centuries*. Baltimore: Johns Hopkins University Press, 1927.
Goldin, Frederick. *The Mirror of Narcissus and the Courtly Love Lyric*. Ithaca, N.Y.: Cornell University Press, 1967.
Gravdal, Kathryn. "Chrétien de Troyes, Gratian, and the Medieval Romance of Sexual Violence." *Signs* 17, 3 (Spring 1992): 558–85.
———. "Metaphor, Metonymy, and the Medieval Women Trobairitz." *Romanic Review* 83, 4 (1992): 411–26.
———. *Ravishing Maidens: Writing Rape in Medieval French Literature and Law*. Philadelphia: University of Pennsylvania Press, 1991.
Grewal, Inderpal. *Home and Harem: Nation, Gender, Empire and the Cultures of Travel*. Durham, N.C.: Duke University Press, 1996.
Grieve, Patricia. *"Floire et Blancheflor" and the European Romance*. Cambridge: Cambridge University Press, 1997.
Grosz, Elizabeth. *Volatile Bodies: Toward a Corporeal Feminism*. Bloomington: Indiana University Press, 1994.
Guidot, Bernard. "Pouvoirs et séductions, pouvoir de séduction dans les *lais* de Marie de France." *Romanische Forschungen* 102, 4 (1990): 425–33.
Haidu, Peter. *Lion Queue-Coupée*. Geneva: Droz, 1972.
———. "Narrative Structure in *Floire et Blancheflor*: A Comparison with Two Romances of Chrétien de Troyes." *Romance Notes* 14 (1972–73): 383–86.

Harf-Lancner, Laurence. *Les Fées au Moyen Age: Morgane et Mélusine.* Paris: Champion, 1984.
Hendrickson, Hildi. Introduction to *Clothing and Difference: Embodied Identities in Colonial and Post-Colonial Africa,* ed. Hendrickson. Durham, N.C.: Duke University Press, 1996.
Hollander, Anne. *Seeing Through Clothes.* New York: Penguin, 1978.
Hotchkiss, Valerie R. *Clothes Make the Man: Female Cross Dressing in Medieval Europe.* New York: Garland, 1996.
Houdeville, Michelle. "Une Arme étrange dans la *Chanson de Roland*: En hommage à Marguerite Rossi et Paul Bancourt." In *De l'Etranger à l'étrange ou la conjointure de la merveille.* Aix-en-Provence: Université de Provence, 1988.
Houston, Mary. *Medieval Costume in England and France: The 13th, 14th, and 15th Centuries.* London: Adam and Charles Black, 1950.
Huchet, Jean-Charles. *L'Amour discourtois: La "Fin'Amor" chez les premiers troubadours.* Toulouse: Privat, 1987.
———. "La Dame et le troubadour: Fin'amor et mystique chez Bernard de Ventadorn." *Littérature* 47 (October 1982): 12–30.
———. "Les Femmes troubadours et la voix critique." *Littérature* 51 (1983): 59–90.
Huet, Gédéon. "Encore *Floire et Blancheflor.*" *Romania* 35 (1906): 95–100.
———. "Sur l'origine de *Floire et Blancheflor.*" *Romania* 28 (1899): 348–59.
Hughes, Diane Owen. "Regulating Women's Fashion." In *A History of Women in the West.* Vol. 2, *Silences of the Middle Ages,* ed. Christiane Klapisch-Zuber. Cambridge, Mass.: Belknap Press of Harvard University Press, 1992, 136–58.
———. "Sumptuary Law and Social Relations in Renaissance Italy." In *Disputes and Settlements: Law and Human Relations in the West,* ed. John Bossy. Cambridge: Cambridge University Press, 1983.
Hult, David F. "Author/Narrator/Speaker: The Voice of Authority in Chretien's *Charrete.*" In *Discourses of Authority in Medieval and Renaissance Literature,* ed. Kevin Brownlee and Walter Stephens. Hanover, N.H.: University Press of New England, 1989. 76–96.
———. "Gaston Paris and the Invention of Courtly Love." In *Medievalism and the Modernist Temper,* ed. Bloch and Nichols. 192–224.
———. *Self-Fulfilling Prophecies: Readership and Authority in the First* Roman de la Rose. Cambridge: Cambridge University Press, 1986.
Hunt, Alan. *Governance of the Consuming Passions: A History of Sumptuary Law.* New York: St. Martin's Press, 1996.
Hunt, Tony. "Chrétien's Prologues Reconsidered." In *Medieval Studies in Honor of Douglas Kelly,* ed. Keith Busby and Norris J. Lacy. Amsterdam: Rodopi, 1994.
———. "Irony and the Rise of Courtly Romance." *German Life and Letters* 35 (1981): 98–104.
———. "Tradition and Originality in the Prologues of Chrestien de Troyes." *Forum for Modern Language Studies* 8 (1972): 320–44.
Huot, Sylvia. "Authors, Scribes, and Remanieurs." In *Rethinking the Romance of the Rose: Text, Image, Reception,* ed. Kevin Brownlee and Sylvia Huot. Philadelphia: University of Pennsylvania Press, 1992.

———. *From Song to Book: The Poetics of Writing in Old French Lyric and Lyrical Narrative Poetry*. Ithaca, N.Y.: Cornell University Press, 1987.

Hyatte, Reginald. "Recoding Ideal Male Friendship as *fine amor* in the Prose *Lancelot*." *Neophilologus* 75 (1991): 505–18.

Irigaray, Luce. *An Ethics of Sexual Difference*. Trans. Carolyn Burke and Gillian C. Gill. Ithaca, N.Y.: Cornell University Press, 1984.

———. *Ethique de la différence sexuelle*. Paris, Minuit, 1984.

———. "When the Goods Get Together." In *This Sex Which Is Not One*, trans. Catherine Porter. Ithaca, N.Y.: Cornell University Press, 1985.

Jackson, T. R. "Religion and Love in *Flore et Blancheflur*." *Oxford German Studies* 4 (1969): 12–25.

Jackson, W. T. H. "The Arthuricity of Marie de France." *Romanic Review* 70 (1979): 1–18.

Jacoby, David. "The Migration of Merchants and Craftsmen: A Mediterranean Perspective." In Jacoby, *Trade, Commodities, and Shipping in the Medieval Mediterranean*. Brookfield, Vt. : Variorium, 1997. 538–46.

———. *Recherches sur la Méditerranée orientale du XIIe au XVe siècle: Peuples, sociétés, économies*. London: Variorum, 1979.

———. "Silk in Western Byzantium Before the Fourth Crusade." In Jacoby, *Trade, Commodities*, 452–500.

Jaeger, Stephen. *The Origins of Courtliness: Civilizing Trends and the Formation of Courtly Ideals, 939–1210*. Philadelphia: University of Pennsylvania Press, 1985.

Janssens, J. "Un Fin Amant et l'ironie romanesque." *Arthurian Literature* 8 (1989): 29–78.

———. "Le Prologue du *Chevalier de la charrete*: une clef pour l'interprétation du roman?" *Bien dire et bien aprande: Bulletin du Centre d'études médiévales et dialectales de Lille III* 4 (1986): 29–57.

Jewers, Caroline. "Fabric and Fabrication: Lyric and Narrative in Jean Renart's *Roman de la Rose*." *Speculum* 71, 4 (1996): 907–24.

Jones, Ann Rosalind and Peter Stallybrass. *Renaissance Clothing and the Materials of Memory*. Cambridge: Cambridge University Press, 2000.

Jones, Nancy A. "The Daughter's Text and the Thread of Lineage in the Old French *Philomena*." In *Representing Rape: Sexual Violence in Medieval and Early Modern Europe*, ed. Elizabeth Robertson and Christine Rose. New York: Palgrave, 2001. 161–87.

———. "The Uses of Embroidery in the Romances of Jean Renart: Gender, History, Textuality." In *Jean Renart and the Art of Romance*, ed. Durling. 13–44.

Jonin, Pierre. "Le Climat de croisade des chansons de geste." *Cahiers de civilisation médiévale* 3 (1964): 279–88.

———. "Les Types féminins dans les chansons de toile." *Romania* 91 (1970): 433–66.

Jordan, Mark. "Homosexuality, Luxuria, and Textual Abuse." In *Constructing Medieval Sexuality*, ed. Lochrie et al. 24–39.

Jung, Marc-René. "L'Empéreur Conrad chanteur de poésie lyrique." *Romania* 101 (1980): 35–50.

Kantorowicz, Ernst. *The King's Two Bodies: A Study of Medieval Political Theology*. Princeton, N.J.: Princeton University Press, 1957.

Kaplan, Caren. "'Getting to Know You': Travel, Gender, and the Politics of Representation in *Anna and the King of Siam* and *The King and I.*" In *Late Imperial Culture*, ed. Román de la Campa, E. Ann Kaplan, and Michael Sprinker. London: Verso, 1995.

———. *Questions of Travel: Postmodern Discourses of Displacement.* Durham, N.C.: Duke University Press, 1996.

Karras, Ruth Mazo. *Common Women: Prostitution and Sexuality in Medieval England.* Oxford: Oxford University Press, 1996.

Kay, Sarah. *The Chansons de geste in the Age of Romance: Political Fictions.* Oxford: Clarendon Press, 1995.

———. "The Contradictions of Courtly Love and the Origins of Courtly Poetry: The Evidence of the *Lauzengiers.*" *Journal of Medieval and Early Modern Studies* 26 (1996): 209–53.

———. "Courts, Clerks and Courtly Love." In *Cambridge Companion*, ed. Krueger. 81–96.

———. *Subjectivity in Troubadour Poetry.* Cambridge: Cambridge University Press, 1990.

———. "Women's Body of Knowledge: Epistemology and Misogyny in the *Romance of the Rose.*" In *Framing Medieval Bodies*, ed. Sarah Kay and Miri Rubin. Manchester: Manchester University Press, 1994. 211–25.

Kellogg, Judith. "Economic and Social Tensions Reflected in the Romance of Chrétien de Troyes." *Romance Philology* 39, 1 (1985): 1–21.

———. *Medieval Artistry and Exchange: Economic Institutions, Society, and Literary Form in Old French Narrative.* New York: Peter Lang, 1989.

Kelly, Douglas. "Courtly Love in Perspective: The Hierarchy of Love in Andreas Capellanus." *Traditio* 24 (1968): 119–48.

———. "La Spécialité dans l'invention des topiques." In *L'Archaeologie du signe*, ed. Lucie Brind'Amour and Eugene Vance. Toronto: Pontifical Institute of Mediaeval Studies, 1983. 101–25.

Kelly, Henry Ansgar. "The Varieties of Love in Medieval Literature According to Gaston Paris." *Romance Philology* 40 (1987): 301–27.

Kendrick, Laura. *The Game of Love: Troubadour Wordplay.* Berkeley: University of California Press, 1988.

Kibler, William W. "Archetypal Imagery in *Floire et Blancheflor.*" *Romance Quarterly* 35 (1988): 11–20.

Kinoshita, Sharon. "Cherchez la femme: Feminist Criticism and Marie de France's *Lai de Lanval.*" *Romance Notes* 34, 3 (1994): 363–73.

———. "The Politics of Courtly Love: *La Prise d'Orange* and the Conversion of the Saracen Queen." *Romanic Review* 86, 2 (Autumn 1995): 265–87.

———. "Two for the Price of One: Courtly Love and Serial Polygamy in the *Lais* of Marie de France." *Arthuriana* 8, 2 (Summer 1998): 33–55.

Knepper, Wendy. "Theme and Thesis in the *Chevalier de la charrete.*" *Arthuriana* 6, 2 (1996): 54–68.

Köhler, Erich. *L'Aventure chevaleresque: Idéal et réalité dans le roman courtois.* Trans. Elaine Kaufholz. Paris: Gallimard, 1974.

———. "Observations historiques et sociologiques sur la poésie des troubadours." *Cahiers de civilisation médiévale* 7 (1964): 27–51.

———. "Les Troubadours et la jalousie." In *Mélanges de langue et de littérature du Moyen Age et de la Renaissance offerts à Jean Frappier*, vol. 1. Geneva: Droz, 1970.

Kopytoff, Igor. "The Cultural Biography of Things: Commoditization as Process." In *The Social Life of Things: Commodities in Cultural Perspective*, ed. Arjun Appadurai. Cambridge: Cambridge University Press, 1986.

Kraemer, Pierre. *Le Luxe et les lois somptuaires au Moyen Age*. Paris: Ernest Sagot, 1920.

Krause, Kathy. "Material Erotic: The Clothed and Unclothed Female Body in the *Roman de la violette*." In *Material Culture and Cultural Materialisms in the Midde Ages and Renaissance*, ed. Curtis Perry. Turnhout: Brepols, 2001. 17–34.

Kristeva, Julia. *Histoires d'amour*. Trans. Leon S. Roudiez as *Tales of Love*. New York: Columbia University Press, 1987.

Krueger, Roberta. "Constructing Sexual Identities in the High Middle Ages: The Didactic Poetry of Robert de Blois." *Paragraph* 13 (1990): 105–31.

———. "Desire, Meaning, and the Female Reader in *Le Chevalier de la charrete*." In *The Passing of Arthur: New Essays in Arthurian Tradition*, ed. Christopher Baswell and William Sharpe. New York: Garland, 1988. 31–51.

———. "*Floire et Blancheflor*'s Literary Subtext: The *version aristocratique*." *Romance Notes* 24 (1983–84): 65–70.

———. "Intergeneric Combination and the Anxiety of Gender in *Le Livre du Chevalier de la Tour Landry pour l'enseignement de ses filles*." *L'Esprit créateur* 33, 4 (1993): 61–72.

———. "Love, Honor, and the Exchange of Women in *Yvain*: Some Remarks on the Female Reader." *Romance Notes* 25, 3 (1985): 302–17.

———. "'Nouvelles choses': Social Instability and the Problem of Fashion in the *Livre du Chevalier de la Tour Landry*, the *Ménagier de Paris*, and Christine de Pizan's *Livre des Trois Vertus*." In *Medieval Conduct*, ed. Ashley and Clark. 49–85.

———. "Transforming Maidens: Single Women's Stories in Marie de France's *Lais* and Later French Courtly Narratives." In *Singlewomen in the European Past, 1250–1800*, ed. Judith M. Bennett and Amy M. Froide. Philadelphia: University of Pennsylvania Press, 1999.

———. *Women Readers and the Ideology of Gender in Old French Verse Romance*. Cambridge: Cambridge University Press, 1993.

———, ed. *The Cambridge Companion to Medieval Romance*. Cambridge: Cambridge University Press, 2000.

Krueger, Steven. "Conversion and Medieval Sexual, Religious, and Racial Categories." In *Constructing Medieval Sexuality*, ed. Lochrie et al. 158–79.

Kuper, Hilda. "Costume and Identity." *Comparative Studies in Society and History* 15, 3 (1973): 348–67.

Lacan, Jacques. *The Ethics of Psychoanalysis*. New York: Routledge, 1992.

———. *Le Séminaire de Jacques Lacan. Livre XX, Encore*. Paris: Seuil, 1975.

Lacy, Norris J. "Amer par oïr dire: *Guillaume de Dole* and the Drama of Language." *French Review* 54, 6 (1981): 779–87.

———, ed. *The Arthurian Encyclopedia*. New York: Garland, 1986.

———. *The Craft of Chrétien de Troyes: An Essay on Narrative Art*. Leiden: E.J. Brill, 1980.

———. *Lancelot-Grail: The Old French Arthurian Vulgate and Post-Vulgate in Translation*. 4 vols. New York: Garland, 1995.

Laiou, Angeliki E. "Trade, Byzantine." In *Encyclopedia of the Middle Ages*, ed. Joseph Strayer. New York: Scribner, 1982–1989. 103.

Lankewish, Vincent A. "Assault from Behind: Sodomy, Foreign Invasion, and Masculine Identity in the *Roman d'Enéas*." In *Text and Territory: Geographical Imagination in the European Middle Ages*, ed. Sylvia Tomasch and Sealy Gilles. Philadelphia: University of Pennsylvania Press, 1998.

Lazar, Moshé. *Amour courtois et "fin'amors" dans la littérature du XIIe siècle*. Paris: Klincksieck, 1964.

Lecoy de la Marche, Albert. *La Chaire française au Moyen Age*. Paris: Librairie Renouard, 1886.

Lees, Clare, ed. *Medieval Masculinities: Regarding Men in the Middle Ages*. Minneapolis: University of Minnesota Press, 1994.

Le Goff, Jacques. *La Civilisation de l'occident médiévale*. Paris: Arthaud, 1967.

Lejeune, Rita. "La Femme dans les littérature française et occitane du XIe au XIIIe siècle." *Cahiers de civilisation médiévale* 20 (1977): 201–8.

———. "Le Rôle littéraire d'Aliénor d'Aquitaine et de sa famille." *Cultura neolatina* 14 (1954): 1–57.

Lemoine-Luccioni, Eugénie. *La Robe: Essai psychanalytique sur le vêtement*. Paris: Seuil, 1983.

Léonard, Monique. "Le Dit de la femme." In *Ecrire pour dire: Etude sur le dit médiéval*, ed. Bernard Ribémont. Paris: Klincksieck, 1990.

Leupin, Alexandre. *Barbarolexis: Medieval Writing and Sexuality*. Trans. Kate M. Cooper. Cambridge, Mass.: Harvard University Press, 1989.

Lochrie, Karma. "Mystical Acts, Queer Tendencies." In *Constructing Medieval Sexuality*, ed. Lochrie et al. 180–200.

Lochrie, Karma, Peggy McCracken, and James A. Schultz, eds. *Constructing Medieval Sexuality*. Minneapolis: University of Minnesota Press, 1997.

Lombard, Maurice. *Les Textiles dans le monde musulman, 7e–12e siècles*. Etudes d'économie médiévale 3. Paris: Mouton, 1978.

Lopez, Robert S. "Les Influences orientales et l'éveil économique de l'Occident." In *Byzantium and the World Around It: Economic and Institutional Relations*. London: Variorum, 1978. 594–662.

———. "Silk Industry in the Byzantine Empire." In *Byzantium and the World Around It: Economic and Institutional Relations*. London: Variorum, 1978.

———. "The Trade of Medieval Europe: The South." In *The Cambridge Economic History*. Vol. 2, *Trade and Industry in the Middle Ages*, ed. M. Postan and E. E. Rich. Cambridge: Cambridge University Press, 1952.

Lot-Borodine, Myrrha. *La Femme et l'amour au XIIe siècle d'après les poèmes de Chrétien de Troyes*. Paris: Picard, 1909.

———. *Le Roman idyllique au moyen âge*. Paris: Picard, 1913.

Luttrell, Claude. "The Figure of Nature in Chrétien de Troyes." *Nottingham Medieval Studies* 17 (1973): 3–16.
Mancoff, Debra. *The Arthurian Revival in Victorian Art.* New York: Garland, 1990.
Mane, Perrine. "Emergence du vêtement de travail à travers l'iconographie médiévale." In *Le Vêtement,* ed. Pastoureau. 93–122.
Marchello-Nizia, Christiane. "Amour courtois, société masculine, et figures du pouvoir." *Annales E.S.C.* 36 (1981): 969–82.
——. "Codes vestimentaires et langage amoureux au 15e siècle." *Europe: Revue littéraire mensuelle* (October 1983): 36–42.
Marx, Jean, and Ernst Hoepffner. "Le Personnage de Guenivere chez Marie de France." *Marche Romane* 13 (1963): 119–31.
McCaffrey, Phillip. "Sexual Identity in *Floire et Blancheflor* and *Ami et amile.*" In *Gender Transgressions,* ed. Taylor. 129–51.
McCash, June Hall, ed. *Cultural Patronage of Medieval Women.* Athens: University of Georgia Press, 1996.
——. "Marie de Champagne and Aliénor d'Aquitaine: A Relationship Reexamined." *Speculum* 54, 4 (1979): 698–711.
——. "Marie de Champagne's 'cuer d'ome et cors de fame': Aspects of Feminism and Misogyny in the Twelfth Century." In *The Spirit of the Court,* ed. Glyn S. Burgess and Robert A. Taylor. Cambridge: D.S. Brewer, 1985. 234–45.
McCormick, Michael. "Byzantium and Modern Medieval Studies." In *The Past and Future of Medieval Studies,* ed. John Van Engen. Notre Dame, Ind.: University of Notre Dame Press, 1994. 58–72.
McCracken, Grant. "Clothing as Language: An Object Lesson in the Study of the Expressive Properties of Material Culture." In *Material Anthropology: Contemporary Approaches to Material Culture,* ed. Barrie Reynolds and Margaret A. Stott. Lanham, Md.: University Press of America, 1987. 103–28.
McCracken, Peggy. "The Boy Who Was a Girl: Reading Gender in the *Roman de Silence.*" *Romanic Review* 85, 4 (1994): 515–34.
——. "Chaste Subjects: Gender, Heroism, and Desire in the Grail Quest." In *Queering the Middle Ages,* ed. Burger and Krueger. 123–42.
——. *The Romance of Adultery: Queenship and Sexual Transgression in Old French Literature.* Philadelphia: University of Pennsylvania Press, 1998.
McNeill, William. *Venice: The Hinge of Europe, 1081–1797.* Chicago: University of Chicago Press, 1974.
McRobbie, Angela. "Settling Accounts with Subcultures." *Screen Education* 34 (1980): 37–49. Reprint in *Culture, Ideology, and Social Process: A Reader,* ed. Tony Bennett et al. London: Open University, 1981.
——. "Working Class Girls and the Culture of Femininity." In *Women Take Issue,* ed. Women's Studies Group. London: Hutchinson, 1978.
Méla, Charles. *La Reine et le Graal: La "conjointure" dans les romans du Graal de Chrétien de Troyes au Livre de Lancelot.* Paris: Seuil, 1984.
Meneghetti, Maria Luisa. "Marie et Leonor. Lancelot et Amadis: Histoire et fiction dans la poésie romanesque." In *Lancelot-Lanzelet: Hier et Aujourd'hui,* ed. Danielle Buschinger. Greifswald: Reineke-Verlag, 1995. 275–83.

Menocal, María Rosa. *The Arabic Role in Medieval Literary History.* Philadelphia: University of Pennsylvania Press, 1987.

———. "Signs of the Times: Self, Other, and History in *Aucassin et Nicolette.*" *Romanic Review* 80 (1989): 497–511.

Moi, Toril. *Simone de Beauvoir: The Making of an Intellectual Woman.* Cambridge: Blackwell, 1994.

Morize, J. "Aigues Mortes au 13e siècle." *Annales du Midi* 26 (1914): 313–48.

Munro, John H. "Silk." In *Encyclopedia of the Middle Ages*, ed. Joseph Strayer. New York: Scribner, 1982–89.

Murray, Jacqueline. "Twice Marginal and Twice Invisible: Lesbians in the Middle Ages." In *Handbook of Medieval Sexuality*, ed. Bullough and Brundage.

Musseter, Sally. "The Education of Enide." *Romanic Review* 73 (1982): 151–52.

Muthesias, Anna. "The Byzantine Silk Industry: Lopez and Beyond." *Journal of Medieval History* 19 (1993): 1–67.

———. *Byzantine Silk Weaving: A.D. 400 to A.D. 1200.* Vienna: Verlag Fassbaender, 1997.

———. "The Impact of the Mediterranean Silk Trade on Western Europe Before 1200 A.D." In *Textiles in Trade: Proceedings of the Second Biennial Symposium of the Textile Society of America.* Washington, D.C.: Textile Society of America, 1990. 126–35.

Newman, Barbara. *From Virile Woman to WomanChrist: Studies in Medieval Religion and Literature.* Philadelphia: University of Pennsylvania Press, 1995.

Newman, F. X., ed. *The Meaning of Courtly Love.* Albany: SUNY Press, 1968.

Nichols, Stephen G. "Medieval Women Writers: Aiesthesis and the Powers of Marginality." *Yale French Studies* 75 (Fall 1988): 77–94.

Nitze, William. "Sens et matière dans les oeuvres de Chrétien de Troyes." *Romania* 44 (1915–17): 14–36.

Noonan, John. "Power to Choose." *Viator* 4 (1973): 420–34.

Oldenziel, Ruth. "Objections: Technology, Culture, and Gender." In *Learning from Things: Method and Theory of Material Culture*, ed. David W. Kingery. Washington, D.C.: Smithsonian Institution Press, 1996.

Ollier, Marie Louise. "The Author in the Text: The Prologues of Chrétien de Troyes." *Yale French Studies* 51 (1974): 26–41.

———. "Sumptuary Law and Social Relations in Renaissance Italy." In *Disputes and Settlements: Law and Human Relations in the West*, ed. John Bossy Cambridge: Cambridge University Press, 1983.

Paden, William D., ed. *The Voice of the Trobairitz: Perspectives on the Women Troubadours.* Philadelphia: University of Pennsylvania Press, 1989.

Paris, Gaston. *Les Contes orientaux dans la littérature française du moyen âge.* Paris: A. Franck, 1875. Reprint from *Revue politique et littéraire* 15 (1870): 1010–17.

———. "Etudes sur les romans de la Table Ronde: Lancelot du Lac." *Romania* 10 (1881): 465–96.

———. "Etudes sur les romans de la Table Ronde, Lancelot du Lac. II: *Le Conte de la charrette.*" *Romania* 12 (1883): 459–534.

Partner, Nancy. "No Sex, No Gender." *Speculum* 68, 2 (1993): 419–43.

Pastoureau, Michel. *Figures et couleurs: Etudes sur la symbolique et la sensibilité médiévales.* Paris: Léopard d'Or, 1986.
———. *Traité d'héraldique.* 3rd ed. Paris: Picard, 1997.
———, ed. *Le Vêtement: Histoire, archaeologie, et symbolique vestimentaires au Moyen Age.* Paris: Léopard d'Or, 1989.
———. *La Vie quotidienne en France et en Angleterre (XII–XIIIe siècles).* Paris: Hachette, 1976.
Paterson, Linda M. *The World of the Troubadours: Medieval Occitan Society, c. 1100– c. 1300.* Cambridge: Cambridge University Press, 1993.
Perret, Michèle. "Travesties et transexuelles: Yde, Silence, Grislandole, Blanchandine." *Romance Notes* 25, 3 (1985): 328–40.
Pichérit, Jean-Louis. "Le Motif du tournoi dont le prix est la main d'une riche et noble héritière." *Romance Quarterly* 36, 2 (1989): 141–52.
Piponnier, Françoise. "Etoffes de ville." In *La Ville et la cour*, ed. Daniela Romagnoli. Paris: Fayard, 1995.
———. "Une révolution dans le costume masculin au 14e siècle." In *Le Vêtement*, ed. Pastoureau. 225–42.
Piponnier, Françoise and Perrine Mane. *Se Vetir au Moyen Age.* Paris: Société nouvelle Adam Biro, 1995. Trans. Caroline Beamish as *Dress in the Middle Ages.* New Haven, Conn.: Yale University Press, 1997.
Platelle, H. "Le Problème du scandale: Les Nouvelles modes masculines aux XIe et XIIe siècles." *Revue Belge de philologie et d'histoire* 53, 4 (1975): 1071–96.
Poovey, Mary. *Making a Social Body: British Cultural Formation, 1830–1864.* Chicago: University of Chicago Press, 1995.
Price, Jocelyn. "*Floire et Blancheflor*: The Magic and Mechanics of Love." *Reading Medieval Studies* 8 (1982): 12–33.
Prown, Jules David. "Mind in Matter: An Introduction to Material Culture Theory and Method." In *Material Life in America, 1600–1860*, ed. Robert Blair St. George. Boston: Northeastern University Press, 1988.
Psaki, Regina. "Jean Renart's Expanded Text: Lienor and the Lyrics of *Guillaume de Dole*." In *Jean Renart and the Art of Romance*, ed. Durling.
———, ed. "*Le Roman de Silence.*" *Arthuriana* 7, 2 (1997).
Queller, Donald A. and Thomas F. Madden. *The Fourth Crusade: The Conquest of Constantinople.* 2nd ed. Philadelphia: University of Pennsylvania Press, 1997.
Quicherat, Jules. *Histoire du costume en France depuis les temps les plus reculés jusqu'à la fin du XVIIIe siècle.* Paris: Hachette, 1877.
Ragland, Ellie. "Psychoanalysis and Courtly Love." *Arthuriana* 5, 1 (1995): 1–20.
Rasmussen, Ann Marie. "Medieval German Romance." In *The Cambridge Companion*, ed. Krueger. 183–202.
———. *Mothers and Daughters in Medieval German Literature.* Syracuse, N.Y.: Syracuse University Press, 1977.
Regalado, Nancy Freeman. "Allegories of Power: The Tournament of Vices and Virtues in the *Roman de Fauvel* (BN MS Fr. 146)." *Gesta* 32, 2 (1993): 135–46.
Régnier-Bohler, Danielle. "Le Corps mis à nu: Perception et valeur symbolique de la

nudité dans les récits du moyen âge." *Europe: Revue littéraire mensuelle* 654 (October 1983): 51–62.

Reinhold, Joachim Henry. "Quelques remarques sur les sources de *Floire et Blancheflor*." *Revue de philologie française* 19 (1905): 153–75.

Reisinger, Deborah. "The Other and the Same: The Ambiguous Role of the Saracen in *La Chanson de Roland*." *Romance Languages Annual* 9 (1997): 94–97.

Rey-Flaud, Henri. *La Névrose courtoise*. Paris: Navarin, 1983.

Rieger, Angelica. "*En conselh no deu hom voler femna*: Les Dialogues mixtes dans la lyrique troubadouresque." *Perspectives médiévales* 16 (1990): 47–57.

———. *Trobairitz: Der Beitrag der Frau in der altokzitanischen höfischen Lyrik*. Tübingen: Niemeyer, 1991.

Rigolot, François. "Valeur figurative du vêtement dans le *Tristan* de Béroul." *Cahiers de civilisation médiévale* 10, 3–4 (1967): 447–53.

Riley, Denise. *Am I That Name? Feminism and the Category of "Women" in History*. Minneapolis: University of Minnesota Press, 1988.

Roche, Daniel. *The Culture of Clothing: Dress and Fashion in the "Ancien Regime"*. Trans. Jean Birrell. Cambridge: Cambridge University Press, 1994.

Rychner, Jean. "Le Prologue du *Chevalier de la charrette*." *Vox Romanica* 26, 1 (1967): 1–23.

———. "Le Prologue du *Chevalier de la charrette* et l'interprétation du roman." In *Mélanges offerts à Rita Lejeune*. Vol. 2. Gembloux: J. Duculot, 1969. 1121–35.

Sadlek, Gregory M. "Interpreting Guillaume de Lorris's Oiseuse: Geoffrey Chaucer as Witness." *South Central Review* 10 (1993): 21–37.

Said, Edward. *Orientalism*. New York: Random House, 1994.

Saly, Antoinette. "Les 'Mille et Une Nuits' au XIIIe siècle: Conte oriental et matière de Bretagne." *Travaux de littérature* 3 (1990): 15–24.

Sankovitch, Tilde. "Lombarda's Reluctant Mirror: Speculum of Another Poet." In *Voice of the Trobairitz*, ed. Paden. 183–93.

Sargent, Barbara Nelson. "A Medieval Commentary of Andreas Capellanus." *Romania* 94 (1973): 528–41.

Schibanoff, Susan. "Mohammed, Courtly Love, and the Myth of Western Heterosexuality." *Medieval Feminist Newsletter* 16 (Fall 1993): 27–32.

———. "Sodomy's Mark: Alan of Lille, Jean de Meun, and the Medieval Theory of Authorship." In *Queering the Middle Ages*, ed. Burger and Krueger. 28–56.

———. "True Lies: Transvestism and Idolatry in the Trial of Joan of Arc." In *Fresh Verdicts on Joan of Arc*, ed. Bonnie Wheeler and Charles T. Wood. New York: Garland, 1996. 31–60.

Schneider, Jane. "The Anthropology of Cloth." *Annual Review of Anthropology* 16 (1987): 409–48.

———, ed. *Italy's "Southern Question": Orientalism in One Country*. Oxford: Berg, 1998.

Schultz, James A. "Bodies That Don't Matter: Heterosexuality Before Heterosexuality in Gottfried's *Tristan*." In *Constructing Medieval Sexuality*, ed. Lochrie et al. 91–110.

———. *The Knowledge of Childhood in the German Middle Ages, 1100–1350*. Philadelphia: University of Pennsylvania Press, 1995.

Schulze-Busacker, Elisabeth. *Proverbes et expressions proverbiales dans la littérature narrative du Moyen Age français.* Paris: Champion, 1985.
Scott, Margaret. *History of Dress Series: Late Gothic Europe, 1400–1500.* London: Mills and Boon, 1980.
Sedgwick, Eve Kosofsky. *Tendencies.* Durham, N.C.: Duke University Press, 1993.
Serper, Arie. "Les Sarrasins en France et à Paris: Xe Congrès International de la Société Rencesvals pour l'Etude des Epopées Romanes." In *Au carrefour des routes d'Europe: La Chanson de geste*, ed. François Suard. 2 vols. Aix-en-Provence: CUERMA, 1987.
———. "The Troubadour's Vassalage: An Axiology of Courtly Love." In *Rewards and Punishments in the Arthurian Romances and Lyric Poetry of Medieval France*, ed. Peter V. Davies and Angus J. Kennedy. Cambridge: D.S. Brewer, 1987.
Shapiro, Marianne. "The Provençal Trobairitz and the Limits of Courtly Love." *Signs* 3, 2 (1978): 560–71.
———. "Tenson et partimen: 'La Tenson fictive'." In *XIV Congresso internazionale di linguisticá e filologia romanza: Atti*, ed. Alberto Várvaro. 5 vols. Naples: Macchiaroli, 1981.
Simmel, Georg. "Fashion." 1904. Reprint in *American Journal of Sociology* 62 (1957): 541–58.
Snyder, Janet Ellen. "Clothing as Communication: A Study of Clothing and Textiles in Northern French Early Gothic Sculpture." PhD dissertation, Columbia University, 1996.
Solterer, Helen. "At the Bottom of the Mirage, a Woman's Body: *Le Roman de la rose* of Jean Renart." In *Feminist Approaches to the Body*, ed. Linda Lomperis and Sarah Stanbury. Philadelphia : University of Pennsylvania Press, 1993. 213–33.
———. "Figures of Female Militancy in Medieval France." *Signs* 16, 3 (1991): 522–49.
———. *The Master and Minerva: Disputing Women in French Medieval Culture.* Berkeley: University of California Press, 1995.
Spelman, Elizabeth. *Inessential Woman: Problems of Exclusion in Feminist Thought.* Boston: Beacon Press, 1988.
Spiegel, Gabrielle. *Romancing the Past: The Rise of Vernacular Prose Historiography in Thirteenth-Century France.* Berkeley: University of California Press, 1993.
Sponsler, Claire. "Fashioned Subjectivity and the Regulation of Difference." *Drama and Resistance: Bodies, Goods, and Theatricality in Late Medieval England.* Minneapolis: University of Minnesota Press, 1997.
———. "Narrating the Social Order: Medieval Clothing Laws." *Clio* 21, 3 (1992): 265–83.
Stallybrass, Peter. "Boundary and Transgression: Body, Text, Language." In *Boundaries and Transgressions in Medieval Culture*, ed. Marina S. Brownlee and Stephen G. Nichols. *Stanford French Review* 14, 1–2 (1990): 9–23.
Szkilnik, Michelle. *L'Archipel du Graal: Etude sur l'Estoire del Saint Graal.* Geneva: Droz, 1991.
———. "The Grammar of the Sexes in Medieval French Romance." In *Gender Transgressions*, ed. Taylor. 61–88.
Sturm-Maddox, Sara and Donald Maddox. "Description in Medieval Narrative:

Vestimentary Coherence in Chrétien's *Erec et Enide*." *Medioevo Romanzo* 9 (1984): 51–64.
Tate Gallery. *The Pre-Raphaelites*. London: Tate Gallery, 1984.
Taylor, Karen J., ed. *Gender Transgressions: Crossing the Normative Barrier in Old French Literature*. New York: Garland, 1998.
Terroine, Anne. "Le Roi des ribauds de l'Hôtel du roi et les prostituées parisiennes." *Revue historique de droit français et étranger* 4th ser. 56 (1978): 253–67.
Tissier, André. "Le Rôle du costume dans les farces médiévales." *Fifteenth Century Studies* 13 (1988): 371–86.
Turner, Terence S. "The Social Skin." In *Reading the Social Body*, ed. Catherine B. Burroughs and Jeffrey David Ehrenreich. Iowa City: University of Iowa Press, 1993. 15–39.
Uitti, Karl. "Autant en emporte *li funs*: Remarques sur le prologue du *Chevalier de la charrete* de Chrétien de Troyes." *Romania* 105 (1984): 270–94.
Ulrich, Laurel Thatcher. "Cloth, Clothing, and Early American Social History." *Dress* 18 (1991): 39–48.
Ulysse, Robert. *Les Signes d'infamie au Moyen Age*. Paris, 1891.
Vance, Eugene. "Chrétien's *Yvain* and the Ideologies of Change and Exchange." *Yale French Studies* 70 (1986): 42–62.
———. *From Topic to Tale: Logic and Narrativity in the Middle Ages*. Minneapolis: University of Minnesota Press, 1987.
Vigarello, Georges. *Concepts of Cleanliness: Changing Attitudes in France Since the Middle Ages*. Trans. Jean Birrell. Cambridge: Cambridge University Press, 1988.
Warren, Michelle. *History on the Edge: Excalibur and the Borders of Britain, 1100–1300*. Minneapolis: University of Minnesota Press, 2000.
Wathelet-Willem, Jeanne. "Le Personnage de Guenievre chez Marie de France." *Marche Romane* 13, 4 (1963): 119–31.
Weed, Elizabeth. "The More Things Change." *differences* 6 (1994): 249–73.
Weever, Jacqueline de. *Sheba's Daughters: Whitening and Demonizing the Saracen Woman in Medieval French Epic*. New York: Garland, 1998.
Weiner, Annette B. and Jane Schneider. *Cloth and Human Experience*. Washington, D.C. : Smithsonian Institution Press, 1989.
Wilson, Elizabeth. *Adorned in Dreams: Fashion and Modernity*. Berkeley: University of California Press, 1985.
———. "All the Rage." In *Fabrications: Costume and the Female Body*, ed. Jane Gaines and Charlotte Herzog. New York: Routledge, 1990.
Wollen, Peter. "Fashion/Orientalism/The Body." *New Formations* 1 (Spring 1987): 5–34.
Wood, Christopher. *The Pre-Raphaelites*. London: Tate Gallery, 1984.
Young, Iris Marion. *Throwing Like a Girl and Other Essays in Philosophy and Social Theory*. Bloomington: Indiana University Press, 1990.
Young, Robert C. J. *Colonial Desire: Hybridity in Theory, Culture, and Race*. New York: Routledge, 1995.
Zink, Michel. *La Prédication en langue romane avant 1300*. Paris: Champion, 1982.
———. *Roman rose ou rose rouge: Le Roman de la Rose ou de Guillaume de Dole*. Paris: Nizet, 1979.

Žižek, Slavoj. *Metastases of Enjoyment*. London: Verso, 1994.
Zufferey, François. "Toward a Delimitation of the Trobairitz Corpus." In *The Voice of the Trobairitz*, ed. Paden. 31–43.
Zumthor, Paul. "Le Grand Chant courtois." In *Essai de poétique médiévale*. Paris: Seuil, 1972.

Index

Abuse, women in *chansons de toile* and, 112–16
Adam and Eve, 149–52, 163
Adultery, 255 n.26
Alain de Lille, 245 n.7. See also *Plaint of Nature*
Alamanda, 76
Allen, Peter, 66
Andreas Capellanus, *De Amore (The Art of Courtly Love)*, 7, 8, 10, 19, 25, 41, 43–44, 124–25, 156, 170, 244 n.3. See also Love treatises
Anzaldúa, Gloria, 209
Armor, 226, 272 n.44; of cloth, 170, 172, 175; and gender, 131, 132, 135–36, 138, 141–42
Arnaut Daniel, 69
Arnaut, Bernart, 74
Arrow of love, 164–66, 282 n.20
Ars amatoria, 25, 80–81, 83. See also Love treatises
Art d'amours, 42, 156, 157, 166, 260 n.1, 279 n.2
Arthurian court, 26–27
Aucassin et Nicolette, 99, 186, 277–78 n.25
Audefroi le Batard, 93

Baldwin, John, 244 n.53
Barthes, Roland, 242 n.44
Bartlett, Robert, 196
Basc, P., 60, 75, 77
Beauty. See Courtly lady
Beauvoir, Simone de, 14, 243 n.48, 260 n.70
Bec, Pierre, 92, 260–61 n.2
Bedchamber, 40, 107
Bele Aelis, 39, 97
Bele Aiglentine, 90–91, 97, 98–99, 101–2, 109, 112
Bele Amelot, 96, 104–5, 112
Bele Argentine, 110–11, 113
Bele Aye, 92, 106, 114–15, 266 n.49
Bele Beatris, 101, 102–3, 112
Bele Doe, 266 n.49
Bele Doette, 111, 113, 266 n.43

Bele Emmelos, 114, 115–16, 267 n.53
Bele Euriaus, 266 n.49
Bele Ydoine, 4, 6, 109, 113–14, 266 n.43, 267 n.53
Bele Yolanz en chambre koie, 90, 96, 100–101, 103–4, 109, 112, 113, 117
Bele Yolanz en ses chambres seoit, 91, 98, 106
Bele Ysabel, 110, 112, 266 n.43
Benjamin of Toledo, 205–6
Benton, John, 130–31, 132
Bernard, St., 38–39, 133–34, 202, 226
Bernart de Ventadorn, 8, 61, 69, 97
Bien des fames, 86
Bliaut. See *Robe*
Bloch, Howard, 66, 150
Bloch, Marc, 130–31, 132
Body: as artful, 156–64; sartorial, 12–13, 22–26, 34, 41, 53–55, 65, 73–74, 82–83, 128–30, 166–67, 198, 236; as social construct, 12–13, 73–74, 78–79, 84–85, 122, 142, 145, 269–70 n.23, 270 n.27
Bodytalk. See Burns, E. Jane
Bossuat, Robert, 286 n.1
Boulton, Maureen, 97
Brownlee, Kevin, 270 n.29
Bruckner, Matilda, 68
Bumke, Joachim, 279–80 n.5
Burger, Glenn, 195–96
Burns, E. Jane, 252 n.14, 269 n.22, 277 n.21; and bodytalk, 68, 107, 173, 257 nn.42, 44, 259 n.61, 260 n.78, 270 n.27
Butler, Judith, 12, 86, 137

Cadden, Joan, 122
Castelloza, Na, 8, 240–41 n.26, 262 n.10
Certeau, Michel de, 284 n.42
Champagne: and fairs, 190–91, 234–35, 292 n.15; families of, 196; as literary center, 231
Chanson de Guillaume, 186
Chansons de geste, 260 n.69, 265 n.36
Chansons de mal mariée, 261 n.5, 263 n.20
Chansons de toile: and authorship, 38; and

criticism, 92–94; defined, 90, 93, 96–97, 260–61 n.2, 263–64 n.22; and female desire, 91, 100–103, 105, 109, 115; and gaze, 106–7; list of, 261 n.5; and mutual love, 103–5, 108, 110–11, 215–16, 229; and physical abuse, 112–16; protagonists of, 264 n.27; and sewing, 90–91, 94, 100; and space, 110–11; and subjectivity, 101–2; and themes, 95–96; and tournaments, 4; and women's work, 108–11; and voice, 93, 97–99

Chapelet. *See* Garland

Chemise: in *Cligés*, 63–65; in *Charrete*, 274 n.67. See also *Robe*

Chevalier de la charrete: and authorship, 231–36; Gauvain, 143; and gender roles, 136–37; Guenevere, 6, 137–38, 215, 232–33, 273 n.54; as homosocial, 66–67; and knights, 135–36; Lancelot, 6, 68, 135–37, 140–41, 215, 232–33, 292–93 n.15; Méléagant, 135–36, 143, 213

Chivalry, 5

Chrétien de Troyes: and authorship, 231–36; and commerce, 293 n.17; and Marie de France, 290–91 n.3. See also *Cligés*; *Erec et Enide*; *Perceval ou le conte du Graal*

Christine de Pisan, 68, 259 n.61

Cixous, Hélène, 97, 118

Class, social: border crossings, 5, 13, 23–25, 29–30, 41; and knights, 246–47 n.25; and upward mobility for men, 43; and upward mobility for women, 43–44, 45, 49, 53, 83

Clement of Alexandria, 150

Cleomadés, 287 n.8

Clerical discourses: and clothing as superficial, 38; and condemnation of courtly love, 19; and condemnation of material excess, 24, 37–41, 53–54, 201–2; and the east 201–2; and effeminacy, 133–35, 204; and the fall, 150–51, and gender boundaries, 146–47; and women and clothing, 38–39, 52–53, 61–62

Cligés: Alixandre, 63–64, 89, 164–67, 193–94; Cligés, 198; and clothwork, 63–65; Guenevere, 63–64; Love, 164; Love's arrow, 164–66; Soredamor, 8, 63–64, 87, 89, 167, 198, 200–201, 209

Clothing: as a class marker, 238 n.6; 247 nn.31, 33; and cultural anthropology, 13, 242 n.42; as currency, 25–26, 27–28, 30, 38, 43, 85, 106–7; and deception, 81, 83; and feminist theory, 14, 16; as love token, 64, 100–101, 106–7; and physical abuse, 114; and pleasure, 83; and sexual encounter, 45; and social status, 31–37, 46; as superficial cover, 24, 38–39, 48–49, 50–51, 52–53, 69–70, 106, 121

Clothwork, 63–65, 86–87, 94. See also Embroidery

Cohen, Jeffrey Jerome, 285–86 n.64

Comtessa de Dia, 76, 258 n.51

Constantine, 207–8

Constantinople, 183, 185, 188, 191–92, 193, 205–7

Contenance des fames, 53–54

Coronation: of Erec, 35; of King Arthur, 31–32; of Lienor, 161

Corrigan, Peter, 15

Courtesy manuals, gender roles and, 122

Courtly lady: as absent, 253 n.16; and beauty, 10, 75, 78, 85, 106, 124–25, 137, 158–59, 161–62, 163, 172, 174, 186, 275–76 n.8; as borderland, 209; as civilizing, 151–52; in criticism, 254 n.21; as mirror, 252 n.14; as third gender, 131–32, 255 n.28; and skin, 137–38

Courtly love: between men, 66–67; and criticism, 59–60, 65–67, 252 n.13; and economics, 254 n.19; feminist rereadings, 67–69; and feudal expansion, 255 n.26; tradition, 1; and *trobairitz*, 264 n.28

Coverlet, 94, 169, 192, 193, 215–16, 229

Crane, Susan, 123

Cross-dressing, 123, 125–30, 132, 140, 141–42, 146, 167. See also Transvestism

Crusades: Fourth, 187, 188, 206, 207; and relics, 204–5, 207; Second, 188, 205; Third, 234

Cycle du Roi, 187

Cyprian, 52

Desire, female: in *chansons de toile*, 100–101, 102–5, 108–9, 115–16; and the *Charrete*, 68; and *demoiselle* d'Escalot, 4, 6–7, 10, 240 n.25; and eastern luxury goods, 10–11; in *Floire et Blancheflor*, 228; and Fresne, 8–11; and Ganor, 89–90; and Jealous Husband, 47, and La Vielle, 81–82, 259 n.61; and Marie de France, 291 n.4; and Narcissus, 63; in *Prose Lancelot*, 139–40, 241 n.27; public expression of, 9–10; and

Soredamor, 65; in *trobairitz*, 76, 240–41 n.26. See also Narcissism
Desmond, Marilyn, 68
Dress: male, 258 n.49; as marker of social status, 1, 3; as transgressing gender boundaries, 3; unisex, 122, 140–41, 166–67
Dressing up: women dressing each other, 161–62, 257 n.45; women dressing men, 5, 7, 9, 170, 226, 228–29, 278 n.31; women dressing themselves, 71–72
Drouart la Vache, 42–44, 116, 249 n.54. See also Love treatises
Duby, Georges, 66

Eadamer, 134
East-west: border crossings, 11, 13, 212, 236, 284 n.45, 288 n.13, 289 n.20; and courtly lady, 186–87; and Grail, 285 n.57; in relational dynamic, 197, 280 n.8; and trade, 189, 190–91, 210; and transfer of luxury goods, 183, 189, 209. See also Crusades
Edrisi, 205
Eliduc, 8
Embroidery, 8–9, 251 n.5, 263 n.21, 265 n.36
En un vergier, 109, 113
Erec et Enide: Enide and clothes, 35–36, 70–71, 82, 161–63, 182, 186, 257 nn.45, 46; Enide and *largesse*, 36; Erec and coronation, 35; Erec and *largesse*, 35–36; Guenevere, 82, 161, 162, 248 n.40, 257 n.45; Morgan, 248 n.40; and quilt, 193; and sparrow hawk contest, 174, 228; and spurs, 290 n. 28; wedding of, 27
Estoire del Saint Graal: Galahad, 181; and geography; and idolatry, 182; Josephus, 181–82, 206; Matagran, 187–88, 206–7; Mordrain, 187–88, 195, 207–9, 213, 225; Mordrain's doll, 181–84, 198, 200, 202, 205; and relics, 204–5
Etienne de Bourbon, 37, 52

Fabric, subjectivity and, 239 n.9
Fall, biblical, 149–52
Faral, Edmond, 93
Fetish: and armor, 272 n.44; and dress, 257 n.46; and female body, 69, 77, 87, 173; and hair, 64–65; and hands, 106; and sleeve, 6, 9
Fille et la mere, 92, 96, 104, 267 n.52
Finke, Laurie, 68

Floire et Blancheflor: Amors, 222; and Arabic origins, 287 n.8, 10; Blancheflor, 213, 214, 219, and beauty, 224, 200–201, as commodity, 220, as courtly lady, 225, 227, as desiring subject, 228, as a gem, 198, 223–25; and conversion, 211, 225, 226, 228; and courtly quest, 211–12, 214–15, 216; and cultural integration, 226–29; emir, 221–22; and geography, 211–12, 286 n.1; Floire, and beauty, 224, and lovesickness, 217–19, 224, as non-Christian, 211, 220; as trader, 216–20, 288 n.18; and garden, 216, 221–23; Gloris, 213, 225; and *largesse*, 227–28; and love between men, 288 n.14; and narrator, 286 n.2; and orientalism, 214; and sartorial change, 226–29; and spurs, 226–29; and trade, 212, 214–15; and traditional romance, 211–12, 213–14; versions of, 286–87 n.4
Floris et Lyriope: and cross-dressing, 125–30; and dung, 49–50; Floris, 124–27; and gender identity, 127–30; Lyriope, 124–25; Narcissus, 121, 127–28, 130; and unisex dress, 122
Flowers, 153–55, 221–23, 250 n.58. See also Garland
Frappier, Jean, 185
Fresne, 191–92

Galeran de Bretagne, Fresne, 6, 8–9
Ganim, John, 284 n.45
Garber, Marjorie, 12
Garden. See *Floire et Blancheflor*
Garden of Eden, 151, 289–90 n.25
Garland: of flowers, 54, 72, 83, 160, 162, 163; golden, 186
Gaunt, Simon, 66, 123
Gautier d'Arras, 232. See also *Ille et Galeron*
Gaze: male, 10, 79, 94–95, 106, 107, 117; women gazing at themselves, 74–75, 79, 80–84, 86
Gender: as ambiguous, 131, 213, 271 n.32; as crossed, 5–6, 7, 140–44, 170–71, 177, 266 n.47, 270–71 nn. 27–29, 274 n.67; as flexible, 67, 97–100, 129–30, 143, 235–36, 256 n.31; on a sartorial continuum, 146–48, 152, 168, 178; as subverted, 11, 24–25, 38, 41, 86, 122
Geoffrey of Monmouth, 189
Gerbert de Montreuil. See *Roman de la violette*

Giddens, Anthony, 16
Gift giving: and affection, 8; men to women, 48; women to men, 8–9, 100–101. See also *Largesse*
Gilchrist, Roberta, 16
Gilles d'Orléans, 37, 147
Giraut de Bornelh, 76, 77
Godefroi de Leigni, 231
Golden, Frederick, 66
Gravdal, Kathryn, 66
Grosz, Elizabeth, 12, 73, 78
Guibert de Tournai, 37, 39
Guigemar, 192
Gui de Mori, 276 n.9

Hair, 63–65, 78, 135, 159–60, 162, 199–200
Hands, 144–45
Helmet, 4–5, 9, 143, 241 n.35; of hair, 159–60
Hendrickson, Hildi, 13
Henri d'Andeli. See *Lai d'Aristote*
Henri le Liberal, 234
Homage, 144–46
Huchet, Jean-Charles, 66
Hult, David, 67, 252 n.13
Humbert de Romans, 37
Hystoire de Julius Caesar, 185
Hystoria Constantinopolitana, 207–8

Idleness, 258–59 n.57
Ille et Galeron: Beatrice, 232; Galeron, 86, 89; Ganor, 88–90; Goddess of Love, 90; Ille, 207; and sewing, 86, 88–90
Innocent III, 28, 40, 52, 151, 187
Irigaray, Luce, 117

Jacques de Vitry, 27, 37, 38–39, 245 n.19
Jean de Meun. See *Roman de la Rose*
Jerome, 150
Joan of Arc, 86, 268–69 n.16
Joan of Navarre, 37
John of Salisbury, 250 n.62
Joinville, 187, 188
Jones, Nancy, 116–17, 251 n.5
Jonin, Pierre, 93
Journal of Nicholas de Braye, 32
Juvenal, 53, 83

Kay, Sarah, 66, 81, 131, 186, 259 n.61, 276 n.12
Kendrick, Laura, 253 n.16
King Philip III, 33
Kinoshita, Sharon, 278 n.32

Knights: and appearance, 156, 272 n.45; and clerical critique, 133; and dubbing with clothes, 142–43; and gender swapping, 136–37, 147–48; and Round Table, 147–48; and social status, 31, 246–47 n.25; women as, 173–75
Köhler, Erich, 66
Krause, Kathy, 278 n.33
Kristeva, Julia, 66
Krueger, Roberta, 66, 67–68, 79, 122, 286 n.2, 291 n.4

Lai d'Aristote, 93, 96, 99, 263 n.20
Lai de l'Ombre, 149
Lai de Lanval: and courtly economy, 167–68; and gender identity, 168; Guenevere, 171–72, 176–77, 279 n.37; King Arthur, 168–69, 171, 173, 176; Lanval, 169–78, 229; and *largesse*, 168–71; *pucele*, 167, 169, 171–74, 178, 183; and the supernatural, 277–78 n.25
Largesse: and Chrétien de Troyes, 293 n.17; and class, 29; in *Cligés*, 193; in cloth, 25, 168–71, 194, 197, 227–28, 232, 246 n.22, 282 n.24; and court, 26–27, 28; in *Erec et Enide*, 35–37; as foolish, 42–43; in Lanval, 168–69; as useless, 219
Lacan, Jacques, 242 n.41
Lauzengier, 66
Le Goff, Jacques, 188
Leupin, Alexandre, 276 n.15
Lesbianism, 68, 123, 213, 287 n.7
Livre des métiers, 31
Lochrie, Karma, 68
Lombard, Maurice, 191, 217
Lombarda, 74–75
Lopez, Robert, 190
Lou Samedi a soir, 266 n.49
Love as avarice, 19
Love treatises, 8, 19, 25, 26, 41–44, 81–82, 156
Lovesickness, 7, 21, 61, 88–89, 108, 116, 124–25, 132, 164, 212, 217–19, 224, 245 n.8, 278 n.27
Luxuria, 168, 258 n.56

Magic, 289 n.22
Makeup, 39–41, 52, 54, 77, 81, 156
Marchello-Nizia, Christiane, 66
Marie de Champagne, 8, 10; as co-author of the *Charrete*, 231, 235; as courtly lady, 232–33, 234; and gender roles, 235; as literary patron, 231, 233; and trade, 234–35

Marie de France: and Chrétien de Troyes, 290–91 n.3; and desire, 291 n.4. See also *Eliduc*; *Fresne*; *Guigemar*; *Lanval*; *Yonuc*
Material culture, 1, 13, 15–16
Matière, 231, 292 nn.10–11, 292–93 n.15
Maurice de Sully, 37, 39–40, 248–49 n.46
McCaffrey, Phillip, 289 n.23
McCracken, Peggy, 123
McRobbie, Angela, 14
Medical texts, and gender, 122, 133
Meliacin, 287 n.8
Menocal, María, 201
Mirror: and desire, 74–75; and subjectivity, 71, 79–80, 84, 85, 252 n.14, 259–60 n.57. See also Gaze
Mort le roi Artu: demoisele d'Escalot, 3–8, 239 n.14, 240 nn.17, 19; demoisele d'Escalot's sleeve, 4–6, 10, 14, 16, 228, 232, 234, 239 n.13, 240 n.23; her death, 7; Gauvain, 5–6, 239 n.14, 239–40 n.16; Guenevere, 4, 6, 7, 240 n.17; King Arthur, 5, 27; Lancelot, 4–8, 239 n.14, 239–40 n.16, 240 n.19; Morgan, 27; opulence, 27
Mother/daughter relationship, 90, 92, 96, 103–5, 110, 117, 265–66 n.41
Mother/son relationship, 255 n.26
Mouth, 144–46
Mystics, female, 68–69

Nakedness: 39, 70, 76, 144, 273 n.60, 274 n.67, 275 n.4, 276 n.14, 278–79 n.36; as debased 21–22
Narcissism, 61–62. See also Mirror
Narcissus, 63, 74–75, 78, 85, 121, 127–28, 130, 252, n.9; in scholarship, 69
Nature: and beauty, 156–64, 165; and dress, 70–71, 155, 157; women's nature as debased, 48–50, 52–53. See also *Roman de la Rose*
Newman, Barbara, 68–69

Odon de Deuil, 205
Ordene de Chevalerie, 250 n.60
Orientalism, 194–97, 214, 264 n.28
Oriolanz, 108–9, 112
Ovid. See *Ars amatoria*

Paris, Gaston, 65, 67, 269 n.19, 292 n.10
Patronage, 290–91 n.3
Paul, 150

Perceval ou le conte du Graal: Blanchefleur, 157–59, 182–83, 219; Fisher King's Grail castle, 205; Guenevere, 150; Perceval, 158
Peter the Venerable, 201
Philip the Fair, 33, 37
Philomena, 86, 107, 116, 200
Pierre de Limoges, 39
Plaint of Nature, 155, 276 nn. 9, 13
Pregnancy, 112, 265 n.37, 265–66 n.41
Pride, 50, 121
Prose Lancelot: and cross-dressing, 141–42; dame du Lac, 142–43; duc de Clarence, 141–42; Galehaut, 132, 143, 145; Gauvain, 136–37, 145; Guenevere, 9, 14, 145, 151, 269 n.19; Griffin, 143; Hector, 141; and knights, 135, 136–37; Lancelot, 9, 132, 137, 138–40, 144–45, 269 n.19; male friendship, 270 n.28; Malehaut, 144; and transvestism, 137
Prostitutes, and dress, 249–50 n.57
Provençal lyric, 60–61, 68
Pygmalion, 70, 71, 87, 181

Quant vient en mai, 106, 107
Queste del Saint Graal, 151, 181, 204

Reading through clothes, 12–13, 15, 85–87, 164, 182, 184, 210
Robe, 126, 127, 166–67
Robert de Clari, 188, 206
Robert de Blois, 52, 68,122, 128. See also *Floris et Liriope*
Roman de la poire, 8, 9, 14, 149
Roman de la Rose ou de Guillaume de Dole: Boidin, 29; and *chansons de toile*, 265 n.40; Conrad, 29; and criticism on clothing, 251 n.6; and garlands, 72; Guillaume and *largesse*, 29–30, 246 n.22; Lienor, 159–61, 198, 209, 277 n.18; Nature, 276 n.9; and sewing, 86, 96, 265 n.36; and voice, 93
Roman de la Rose, by Jean de Meun: Ami, 203–4, 206, 244 n.2; Beauty, 198, 200; Bel Accueil, 80; (Lady) Fortune, as avarice, 20–21; Fortune as disrupting social categories, 23–24; Fortune's gown, 21–23, 25, 168; Fortune's house 22–23; and garlands, 72; Genius, 259 n.61; Jealous Husband, 44–51, 53, 154, 203–4, 229, 234, 259 n.61; Jealous Husband and class, 44–45; Jealous Husband and expenses, 47–48; La Vielle,

80–81; Nature, 276 nn. 9, 10, 12, 13; Pygmalion, 183–84; (Lady) Reason, 244 n.3, 248 n.43 criticism of Fortune, 19–20, 23–24, 40–41, 49, 55, 166, 202–4, 229; (Lady) Richesse, 198–200

Roman de la Rose, by Guillaume de Lorris: Alexander the Great, 189; Cortoisie, 182; Deduit, 154; God of Love, 153–54, 281–82 n.19, 20; Largesse, 187, 189, 200, 202, 282 n.25; Narcissus, 78; and Nature's dress, 152–56, 161, 166, 168, 281–82 n.19; Oiseuse, 77–80, 84, 85, 163, 182, 186, 229; Richesse, 186

Roman de Silence, 68, 86, 123, 177

Roman de Tristan: King Arthur, 28; Queen Iseut, 28–29, 278 n.31

Roman de la violette, 93, 96, 97, 263 n.20, 278 n.33

Romans d'antiquité, 185, 280 n.8, 288 n.13

Rychner, Jean, 292 n.11

Said, Edward, 197
Saracen, 187–88, 279 n.3, 281 n.15, 287–88 n.11
Saracen princess, 186–87, 228
Schibanoff, Susan, 123
Schneider, Jane, 13
Seals, medieval, 269 n.21. *See also* de Mondragon, Simon
Sedgwick, Eve, 146
Sermons. See Clerical discourses
Sewing. See Clothwork
Sheingorn, Pamela, 68
Silk: and identity, 184; and labor, 86; manufacture of, in France, 191; and men, 280 n.7; as *pailes*, 187, 197, 234, 267 n.52, 291 n.6, 292 n.12; provenance, 11, 182–83, 185, 279–80 n.5, 283 n.29, 283–84 n.41; and trade, 190–91, 212, 217, 279–80 n.5; types of, 184
Simon de Mondragon, and seal, 130–31, 132, 135, 141
Single women, 68, 79
Sirventes, 60
Sirventesca, 60–63, 72, 74
Skin: as armor, 147–48; as clothing, 137–38; and vulnerability, 136, 137–38, 141
Sleeve, 4, 6. *See also* demoisele d'Escalot; *Le Mort le roi Artu*
Snyder, Janet, 193
Solterer, Helen, 68

Space: in *chansons de toile*, 111–12; courtly, 10, 87; defined, 284 n.42; east/west, 195–97, 209–10
Spelman, Elizabeth, 271 n.32
Spiegel, Gabrielle, 24
Spurs, 226–29
Stallybrass, Peter, 133, 146
Subjectivity, female, 60, 76, 115
Sumptuary law, 24, 31–37, 71, 271 nn.34, 36, 290 n.28; and women, 32, 61. *See also* Clerical discourses
Szkilnik, Michelle, 195

Tertullian, 39–40, 52, 83, 150, 204, 271 n.36
Thousand and One Nights, 212, 287 nn.3, 10
Touch, poetics of, 63, 84–85, 87, 90, 116–17
Tournament, 4–6, 109, 273 n.54
Trade. See East-west
Transvestism, 12, 137, 238 n.7. *See also* Cross-dressing
Trobairitz: and clothing, 65, 71, 73–74, 76–77; dating, 250–51 n.2; and irony, 251 n.7; and Lombarda, 74–75; and subject position, 251 n.4; and troubadours, 60–61, 73, 258 n.53, 251 n.3; and voice, 262–63 n.12
Troubadour, 59
Turner, Terence, 25

Ulrich, Laurel Thatcher, 14
Underwear, 2
Undressing, 69, 76, 141, 173–74, 245 n.9
Uitti, Karl, 292 n.13

Vigeois, prior of, 134
Villehardouin, 206–7
Vie de Saint Louis, 30–31
Vitalis, Oderic, 134

Warren, Michelle, 195
William of Malmesbury, 135
Wilson, Elizabeth, 14
Wounds, 136, 144–45

Yonec, 285 n.55
Young, Iris Marion, 83, 84–86, 94–95, 117–18
Young, Robert, 197
Yvain, 201

Zink, Michel, 40, 52, 92–93, 97
Zumthor, Paul, 66, 91

Acknowledgments

Many hands and minds have helped fashion the pages of this book. I would like to thank everyone for their generous contributions, however great or small. Early input from Roberta L. Krueger and Nancy Jones proved especially crucial in deciding the book's scope and honing its focus. Over the years, careful comments from members of the North Carolina Research Group on Medieval and Early Modern Women helped shape specific chapters. Most recently, extended conversations with Helen Solterer and Ann Marie Rasmussen spurred me repeatedly to tailor the argument and re-write its details. For their help with individual chapters, thanks are due to Sahar Amer, Sarah Beckwith, Judith Bennett, Matilda Bruckner, Susan Crane, Theodore Evergates, Jaroslav Folda, Barbara J. Harris, Meagan Matchinske, Kristin Neuschel, James Schultz, and Gabrielle Spiegel.

I benefited greatly from thoughtful suggestions made by the two press readers, Peggy McCracken and Sharon Farmer, and from insightful comments offered by Mary D. Sheriff.

I am especially grateful to the Institute for the Arts and Humanities at the University of North Carolina, to the Reynolds Research fund, the College of Arts and Sciences, and the Johnston family, whose bequest supports distinguished professorships. Their generous contributions made this book possible. I owe a special debt to my colleagues in Women's Studies for their invaluable support.

Thanks to Jerry Singerman, who continues to deserve the title of editor extraordinaire, and to Laine E. Doggett and Jennifer Heller who provided editorial assistance above and beyond the call of duty.

Extra special thanks go to Fred Burns and to Ned.

Earlier versions of portions of this volume appeared in the following sources, and are reprinted by permission. Earlier versions of portions of Chapter 2 first appeared as "Speculum of the Courtly Lady: Women, Love and Clothes," *Journal of Medieval and Early Modern Studies* 29, 2 (1999): 253–92 (Duke University Press) and "Courtly Love, Who Needs It?" *Signs* (Fall 2002; © 2001 University of Chicago). An earlier version of Chapter 3 appeared as "Sewing like a Girl: Working Women in the *chansons de toile,*" in *Medieval Woman's Song: Cross-Cultural Approaches,* ed. Anne L. Klinck and Ann Marie Rasmussen (Philadelphia: University of Pennsylvania Press, 2002), 99–126. An earlier version of Chapter 4 appeared as "Refashioning Courtly Love: Lancelot as Ladies' Man or Lady/Man?" in *Constructing Medieval Sexuality,* ed. Karma Lochrie, Peggy McCracken, and James Schultz (Minneapolis: University of Minnesota Press, 1997), 111–34.